CONFLICT RESOLUTION THROUGH NON-VIOLENCE

VOLUME ONE

SCIENCE AND ETHICS

List of books published under Gandhian Studies and Peace Research Series

1. Gandhian Model of Development and World Peace, **R.P. Misra**
2. Conflict Resolution Through Non-Violence : Role of the Universities (In 2 Vols.), **K.D. Gangrade** and **R.P. Misra** *(eds.)*
   Vol. 1 : Science and Ethics, **K.D. Gangrade** and **R.P. Misra**
   Vol. 2 : Development without Destruction, **K.D. Gangrade** and **R.P. Misra**
3. The Social Philosophy of Mahatma Gandhi, **K.S. Bharathi**
4. Gandhian Humanism, **Mohit Chakrabarti**
5. Gandhian Holistic Economics, **Shashi Prabha Sharma**
6. Gandhian Spiritualism : A Quest for Essence of Excellence, **Mohit Chakrabarti**
7. Gandhian Perspective on Population and Development, **A.K. Sharma**
8. Thoughts of Gandhi and Vinoba : A Comparative Study, **K.S. Bharathi**
9. Economic Philosophy of Mahatma Gandhi, **Shanti Swarup Gupta**
10. Political Thought of Mahatma Gandhi (The), **K.S. Bharathi**
11. Gandhi and 21st Century, **Janardhan Pandey** *(ed.)*
12. Gandhian Philosophy of the Spinning Wheel, **Mohit Chakraborti**
13. Gandhian Satyagraha : An Analytical and Critical Approach, **Ajay Shanker Rai**
14. Gandhi and His Religion, **(Lt. Col.) P.A. Raju**
15. महात्मा गाँधी विचार वीथिका, **एस.पी. अग्रवाल**
16. Poverty of Gandhian Philosophy, **Himansu Roy**
17. Right to Equality in the Indian Constitution : A Gandhian Perspective, **Shashi Nath Saraswati**
18. Meditations on Gandhi : A Ravindra Varma Festschrift, **M.P. Mathai, M.S. John** and **Siby K. Joseph** *(eds.)*
19. Politico-Economic Ideas of Mahatma Gandhi : Their Relevance in the Present-Day, **Sukhendu Mazumdar**
20. Moral Lessons from Gandhi's Autobiography and Other Essays, **K.D. Gangrade**
21. Fire Sans Ire : A Critical Study of Gandhian Nonviolence, **Mohit Chakrabarti**
22. Gandhian Alternative (Volume 1 : Towards a Gandhian World Order), **Suresh Misra** *(ed.)*
23. Gandhian Alternative (Volume 2 : Nonviolence in Action), **Savita Singh** and **Bharati Misra** *(eds.)*
24. Gandhian Alternative (Volume 3 : Socio-Political Thoughts), **Anil Dutta Mishra** and **Sushna Yadav** *(eds.)*
25. Gandhian Alternative (Volume 4 : Economics Where People Matter), **V. K. Natraj, Kamlesh Misra** and **Neeru Kapoor** *(eds.)*
26. Gandhian Alternative (Volume 5 : Education for Human Development), **Suresh Misra** *(ed.)*
27. Gandhian Approach to Development Planning, **Ram Vinod Singh**

GANDHIAN STUDIES AND PEACE RESEARCH SERIES-2

CONFLICT RESOLUTION THROUGH NON-VIOLENCE

Role of the Universities

VOLUME ONE

SCIENCE AND ETHICS

K.D. GANGRADE
and
R.P. MISRA

CONCEPT PUBLISHING COMPANY, NEW DELHI 110059

ISBN: 81-7022-310-5 (Set)
ISBN: 81-7022-311-3 (Vol. I)

Reprinted 2007
First Published 1990

Published and Printed by
Ashok Kumar Mittal
Concept Publishing Company
A/15-16, Commercial Block, Mohan Garden
New Delhi-110 059 (INDIA)
Phones : 25351460, 25351794 *Fax* : 091-11-25357103
Email : publishing@conceptpub.com

PREFACE

OF THE fifty odd papers discussed in the national seminar on "Conflict Resolution Through Non-violence — Role of the Universities" held at the Gandhi Bhavan, Delhi University in February 1989 fourteen papers have been included in this volume. These papers cover different aspects but are interlinked by a common theme of spiritualising science and rationalising spirituality through educational processes advocated by Gandhiji. Another set of fourteen papers dealing with conflicts arising from developmental styles is being published separately (Volume Two).

The papers included in this volume stress on the need to circumscribe science by ethics and assert, that both science and spirituality seek the same truth. Spirituality begins where science ends. That is why Einstein said, 'Science without religion is lame and religion without science is blind'.

We thank all the authors for the valuable work they did and thus helped the Bhavan to contribute to the growing movement for peace and harmony in the world. We are specially grateful to Prof. D.S. Kothari, and Dr. Larry Dossey for their contributions. These papers were discussed in the Seminar but were published elsewhere earlier.

We thank our colleagues in Bhavan but for whose help and cooperation neither the Seminar nor this volume would have been possible.

Gandhi Bhavan
Delhi 110007

K.D. GANGRADE
R.P. MISRA

CONTENTS

LIST OF TABLES AND FIGURE

TABLES

FIGURE

LIST OF CONTRIBUTORS

Larry Dossey
President, The Isthonics Institute, Dallas, U.S.A.

Fr. T.K. John
Vidya Jyoti, Raj Niwas Marg, Delhi.

K.D. Gangrade
Pro-Vice-Chancellor, University of Delhi, Delhi.

D.S. Kothari
Chancellor, Jawaharlal Nehru University, Mehrauli Road, New Delhi.

Bimlendra Kumar
Department of Buddhist Studies, University of Delhi, Delhi.

R.P. Misra
Director, Gandhi Bhavan, University of Delhi, Delhi.

Indira Mylarapu
Department of Politics and Public Administration, University of Poona, Pune.

N. Radhakrishnan
Gandhigram Rural Institute, Gandhigram-624302.

G.P. Krishna Rao
Professor of Social Work, Department of Social Work, Visva Bharati, Sriniketan, West Bengal.

K. Raghavendra Rao
Yamuna Bharati, Kalyan Nagar, Dharwad, Karnataka.

Ashok R. Rattan
Department of Gandhian Studies, Panjab University, Chandigarh.

Amardeep S. Sandhu
Department of Gandhian Studies, Panjab University, Chandigarh.

Ramjee Singh
Prof. and Head, Department of Gandhian Thought, University of Bhagalpur-812007.

Mahesh Tiwary
Department of Buddhist Studies, University of Delhi, Delhi.

1

INTRODUCTION

R.P. MISRA

THE ISSUE

HUMAN SURVIVAL and development depends on world peace, on whether we can prevent nuclear war; whether we can harness modern science and technology to the betterment of human life; whether we can forestall serious natural resource and environmental damages; and whether we can develop the appropriate adjustments and institutions to share the fruits of technical change equitably enough to ward off hunger, malnutrition and conflicts, between the haves and the havenots.

The question of conflict resolution and peace has to be addressed from two complementary perspectives. One derives from a perspective of peaceful co-existence among nation States. It focuses on avoidance of war and includes strategies, processes and instrumentalities that minimize tension, augment the balance of power, attempt to reduce arms and armed forces and promote negotiated settlement of international problems. It builds on the large corpus of research on international relations, superpower rivalries, regional conflicts and security, the technological and organizational innovations that may help manage arms control negotiations and peacetime cross-national links between military and civilian groups.

The second perspective is "bottom up" and stems from a view of local conflicts among group of peoples and sub-national units that often spill over into the rest of the nation, neighbouring nations and have the potential to threaten regional and international peace. Indeed, many major conflicts have been rooted in small-scale conflicts resulting from the real or perceived ethnic, political, social and economic deprivation of one group or the other. Frequently, such local conflicts derive from the change process underway in the developing regions of Latin America, Africa and Asia, where the pace of technological change and economic development is very brisk; where the adverse impact of man on certain elements of the environment is already severe and where social injustice of the vastly unequal relations between groups and regions within and among countries has tended to get accentuated. While the seeds of many of these conflicts lie in the colonial experience, they have been exacerbated greatly in the post-colonial period by the choice of development technologies, by strategies of natural resource management, typology of institutional development and the nature of insertion of these countries in the World Order.

A deeper analysis of these two dimensions of the problem suggests considerable correlation between them. International conflicts generate their impacts on peoples everywhere often affecting their occupational structure, earning capacities, social relations and life-styles, in general. On the other hand, local conflicts, originating in some form of socio-economic injustice, often spill over into the larger world region in terms of contagious conflicts, involuntary migration, etc., and where super-power involvement occurs, they become major threats to peace. Consequently, the conflicts have to be managed at both the international and local levels.

Survey of the literature and works in progress concerned with peace and conflict resolution suggests, however, the dominance of the first perspective, i.e., avoidance of major conflicts resulting from super-power and large regional power rivalries. Little, if any, attention seems to have been devoted to local conflicts among groups of people that have considerable potential for international repercussions. Greater attention to the latter problem would require a broader approach wherein the analysis of apparent and immediate causes of conflicts in these Third World Societies is matched by a simultaneous inquiry into the conflicts inherent in the ongoing complex process of transformation — the wrenching process of formation of nation States out of highly heterogeneous ethnic and social groups, the massive dislocations associated with sweeping technological and economic changes and the processes of changes in attitudes and life styles associated with modernisation.

The approaches that do exist partially address this problem range from the liberal to the Marxist. A model that has been inadequately emphasised, but holds out considerable potential is the Gandhian Model of Conflict Resolution wherein non-violence plays a catalytic role. Gandhi's life was devoted to the perfection of non-violent technique of conflict resolution. And everything that he said and did was always informed of non-violence. He firmly believed that the lasting peace in the world was possible only through non-violence.

This powerful, but difficult to practise, method of conflict resolution is being increasingly considered as the only method to create a humane and peaceful society. Recent statements of world leaders — Gorbachev, Reagan, Rajiv Gandhi and others — corroborate this assessment. Equally corroborative are the recent writings of social scientists, scientists, politicians and public leaders in general that Gandhian approach alone can generate a movement for harmony in family, community, nation and the world.

THE FOCUS OF THE SEMINAR

The Gandhi Bhavan, University of Delhi, with the assistance of the University Grants Commission, New Delhi, organised a national seminar to discuss the issue. The theme of the seminar was 'Conflict Resolution Through Non-Violence: Role of Universities'.

The seminar discussed the causes and consequences of various types of conflicts tearing human society and polity to pieces, examined the efficacy of non-violence as a means to resolve these conflicts and deliberated on the ways our universities could help generate an environment in which non-violence becomes an accepted norm and practical means to create harmony in the world.

The aspects of the problems which got major attention of the seminar were:

1. Arms race and military conflicts and their implications for human survival and development;
2. Recent trends in conflict resolution and world peace;
3. Conflicts resulting from rapid technological changes and the inability of the society to internalise these changes without losing values essential for sustainable development and change;
4. Causes and consequences of conflicts between Nature and Man, and treatment of earth as a real estate;
5. Family, group, community and ethnic conflicts resulting from

adversary democratic processes and loss of time-honoured ethical values;

6. Non-Violence as an instrument to resolve the emergent and emerging conflicts;
7. Role of universities in promoting peace and harmony in the society.

The issue of peace is indivisible; it concerns all and demands action at all levels and through all conceivable forums. Universities are centres of knowledge generation and diffusion. They have, therefore, a great role in the issue of conflict resolution and peace. The seminar was, therefore, addressed not only to the academicians and students but also to all those past students who are functioning as social animators for a peaceful world order. Participants were thus drawn from amongst:

1. Academicians and peace researchers;
2. University students with leadership qualities;
3. Field-workers and activists involved in organising people for peaceful resolution of conflicts.

Almost every State of the country and thirty universities were represented in the seminar. Perhaps the most unique feature of the seminar was the active participation of students both in terms of number and input.

INAUGURAL CALL FOR INTROSPECTION

Inaugurating the seminar, Prof. K.S. Murthy, Vice-Chairman, UGC, traced the history of non-violence as an instrument of peace in India to pre-Buddhist times. Then he pointed out that *Ramayana* and *Mahabharata* laid the foundations of a social order based on ethics and spirituality. The emergence of two major religions — Buddhism and Jainism — which preached *Ahimsa* as the only way to salvation was a major step in this direction. To what extent these religions were in a position to save humanity, from wars and conflicts, was debatable. The search for peace, however, continues and Mahatma Gandhi may be said to be the latest among the greatmen of wisdom who not only preached truth and non-violence but also lived them.

"We are not sure whether our times are the most violent ones, we cannot, however, deny the fact that we are passing through a difficult period in human history. It is not perhaps the violence proneness which has increased. The major threat lies in the technological power which the man has now acquired — the power which can destroy the world in minutes and seconds. In this new context renewed efforts to secure peace in the world is not only desirable but also necessary".

"To what extent the universities can help in this task? The universities themselves are full of violence. Their functioning needs much to be desired. May be, they can start from introspection and gradually get more oriented to the problems of the society at large. There is vast scope. To what extent it can be converted into action, is one of the tasks, the seminar must address to". Dr. Murthy closed his address thanking the University of Delhi for inviting him to inaugurate the seminar.

Prof. K.D. Gangrade and Prof. R.P. Misra thanked Dr. Murthy and other participants of the seminar and hoped that the dialogue started at Gandhi Bhavan, University of Delhi, would contribute to the creation of an environment in which introspection by the universities would begin soon. They felt that there was lot that every section of the society had to contribute to create peace and harmony. Universities, despite their systemic weaknesses, cannot be marginalised. They have always played a catalytic role in creation and diffusion of knowledge. They have to play their role in educating the people about the emergent need to work for peace.

Prof. Yash Pal, Chairman, UGC, in his keynote address to the first plennary session of the seminar called for a scientific basis of spirituality and a spiritual and ethical basis of science. Spirituality may not necessarily have much to do with religion. Organised religions have not infrequently transgressed the spiritual and ethical principles. On the other hand, Buddha, who was the incarnation of non-violence did not accept the concept of God. It is the commitment to life and its preservation through love and compassion that matters. Fortunately all the religions teach this ethical principle.

Following Prof. Yash Pal's presentation various approaches to world peace were discussed at the seminar. It was emphasised that India always stood for peace and harmony. Non-violence and peace have constituted the core of Indian philosophy ever since the *Vedic* times. But its use for group action and socio-economic and political emancipation of the people had to await the advent of Gandhi on the Indian scene. Gandhi emphasised that man and his world were potentially non-violent, peaceful and co-operative contradicting the Darwin's Theory of Survival of the Fittest. Man appeared to be violent because the acquired *Samskaras* were violence based.

The balance of terror approach to world peace has escalated conflict and led to world wars. This model has been used not only at the international level but also at the national, regional, local and individual levels. The war and conflict psychology has gripped the humanity as a whole. The threat of war is all pervading and has taken a variety of forms. There is conflict between man and nature leading to environmental threats to all human beings; conflict between one ethnic, religious and linguistic group and the other, leading to wanton destruction of life on every street corner of the world; conflict between the rich and the poor so that both are in constant danger of annihilation and destruction, and between the urban and rural areas so that neither can grow in peace and harmony. In fact, there is conflict in each family and individual.

WORLD PEACE

Status Report

A number of papers presented a status report on pervading violence in the world visible in the form of wars, conflicts, tensions, killings, cruelty, hatred, intolerance and absence of empathy. These have resulted from a variety of forces and factors. A summary of the papers presented, discussions raised and facts given, through poster, etc., is given below:

A New World Order in the Making

There are two contradictory forces visible today. There are forces of integration resulting largely from global technologies and vast expansion of scientific as well as spiritual knowledge; we call our world, a global village. A great variety of problems are no longer local, regional and national; they are global problems. Environmental problems, problems of war and peace, problems of poverty and development and most of many others problems affect each nation and country, in fact, each individual no matter where they occur.

Mobility of the people has increased and despite passport and visa restrictions, a world citisenry is in the process of making.

Interdependence among nations and peoples has also increased, trade restrictions by individual nations notwithstanding. The communication technology has done wonders. It is no longer possible to remain insular, nor can one remain insensitive to the views and opinions of others.

Yet, at the same time, there are equally strong forces fragmenting the world into pieces. Wars and conflicts among nations are not yet rare, but what worries us today are the wars within nations. People are getting divided on class, religion, political ideology, caste, colour, place of origin and several other even unknown lines. Hundreds of innocent men, women and children die in wars in which they have never participated. These internal wars are challenging the very concept of nation States. People appear to have lost faith in the nation State as a viable institution to protect their legitimate interests.

Or may one say that the super-imposition of the concept of political state on the time honoured concept of a nation has now given way and the conflicts, that one sees within the states, are indicative of the mis-match between the two. Whatever may be the case, the fact remains that the disintegrating forces are now visible almost everywhere heralding a major change in the spatial structure of human polity.

Inequities in the Prevailing World Order

It is no longer necessary to quote statistics to prove inequities in the world today even if we look at these with nation States as the units of measurement. Figure 1.1 showing the GNP, population and natural resource endowments of major countries of the world diagrammatically dramatises this situation. If more details are needed one should see data pertaining to energy (Table 1.1). Who would believe that an average Nepali consumes only one-thousandths of commercial energy of what an average American consumes? The number of persons per physician, for example, is 370 in Israel as compared to 58,000 in Ethiopia, and infant mortality rate in Bangladesh is 133 whereas in Japan it is only six and in the USA only 11.

These inequities are partly because of inequities in the distribution of natural resources. There are countries whose known natural resources are not adequate enough to maintain high quality of life particularly when population growth is as fast as we witness today in the developing countries. But this alone does not explain the whole situation. Much of the misery in the world today does not emanate from the natural resistances. It is man-made and is the product of the inequities of world economic order.

TABLE 1.1: **Consumption of commercial sources of Energy in kg of Coal Equivalent per head in 1984**

Selected Developed Countries		*Selected Developing Countries*	
USA	9,577	China	664
Australia	6,128	Indonesia	263
USSR	5,977	India	237
UK	4,760	Bangladesh	53
Japan	3,800	Ethiopia	20
Spain	2,180	Nepal	11

Source: *UN Energy Statistics Year Book, 1985.*

The three major factors which have accentuated the problem of poverty in the Third World countries is inequitous access to natural resources, to markets for finished products, and to modern technology. More details of each of these were discussed in the seminar.

Militarisation of the World

Two aspects of militarisation constituted the main concern of the seminar: arms race among developed countries, particularly super-powers and militarisation of the Third World countries. It was pointed out, time and again, that the nuclear arsenal with the super-powers could destroy this world several times. 1987 was marked by a new high global military expenditure at $ 1.8 million a minute. Fortunately, the year also signalled a welcome change for the better in the fever of militarism. The two super-powers further enlarged their enormous stock of nuclear weapons, but for the first time agreed on a treaty to destroy part of it. There were more wars underway in the world than at any previous time in history, but also were several promising breakthroughs for peace. While there is no convincing statistical evidence as yet on a turning point in the world's arms race, the momentum for change now seems irreversible. A variety of factors re-enforce it.

> "The strain on the world economy has become as ominus as the oversupply of kill-power in nuclear stock-pile. A military joyride on credit has left mountains of debt for future generations. Rising poverty and lengthening lines of the unemployed contrast with affluence with which military programmes operate. Public pressures for restraint are more vocal and insistent. Increasingly government policies have begun to respond to these pressures."[1]

Quoting Sivard, one of the participants thus highlighted the problems facing the world and pointed out the need for strengthening peace movements in the Third World countries where defence expenditure was still considered to be a holy cow:

> "Hunger-related causes kill as many people in two days as the atomic bomb killed at Hiroshima. The USSR, which has spent an estimated $4.6 trillion (constant 1984 dollars) for military purposes since 1960, ranks 23 among 142 countries in economic-social standing. The fuel consumed by the Pentagon in a single year would run the entire US public transit system for 22 years. Military defence budgets in the Third World are about seven times as large as in 1960, but for one person in two the only water available to drink is unsafe and possibly deadly.
>
> The world's annual military budget equals the income of 2.6 billion people in 44 poorest nations. To protect Kuwaiti oil tankers in the Persian Gulf the US Navy spends an extra $365 million a year above normal operating costs, about three times as much as the US budget for research on energy conservation. On the eve of the 40th anniversary of the Universal Declaration of Human Rights, two billion people live in Third World countries where governments make frequent use of torture and other forms of violence against their own people.
>
> The world spends 2,900 times as much on national military forces as on international peace-keeping efforts. The nuclear bomb inventories of the two super-powers, already sufficient to destroy all life on earth many times over, increased in 1987 at the rate of 16 per week. More wars were being fought in 1987 than in any previous year on record; four-fifths of the deaths in those wars were civilian.

FIG. 1.1: *Income, Population, Resources: World distributions*

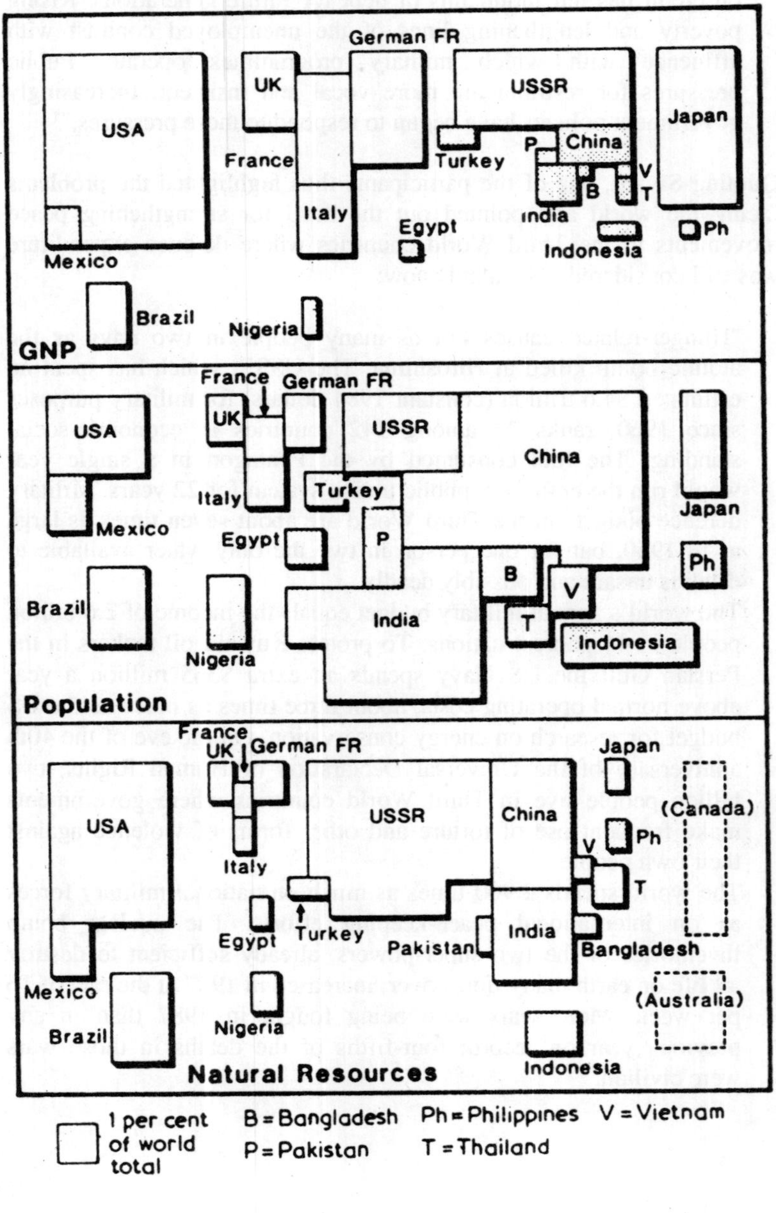

> Research on Acquired Immune Deficiency Syndrome (AIDS) is to receive $344 million from US public funds in the coming year which is about 9 per cent of the amount to be spent on Star Wars research".[2]

It was noted with distress that in most of the developing countries military expenditures were far higher than those on welfare and social services. Table 1.2 gives a bird's eye-view of Third World militarisation.

TABLE 1.2: *Military Expenditure by Income, 1984*

Groups of Country	*Number of Countries*	*Military Expenditure as proportion of GDP*	*Defence Expenditure as proportion of Central Govt. Expenditure*	*Defence Expenditure per capita (US $)*
1. Low Income	8	3.1	15.1	24
2. Low Income	4	2.0	5.6	N.A.
3. Lower Middle Income	5	6.1	15.0	72
4. Upper Middle Income	4	5.0	21.8	20.9
5. Japan	1	10.0	N.A.	87

1-2. Low Income	:	Six SAARC countries, Burma and China, GNP per capita less than $400.
3. Lower Middle Income	:	All south-east Asian countries except Malaysia, South Korea, Hong Kong, Singapore, Brunei, Japan. GNP. per capita US $400 to 1,700.
4. Upper Middle Income	:	Malaysia, S. Korea, Hong Kong and Singapore, Per capita GNP US $1,700-7,260.
5. Japan	:	Per capita GNP US $10,630.

Military spending by the newly industrialising countries of the world and the LDCs grew 13-fold between 1952 and 1983, by far surpassing the growth of super-power military outlays which doubled over the same period. Third World defence spending went up from three to 12 per cent of GDP during 1955-75. All this had a telling effect on human welfare: the growth of the economy failed to pick up due to diversion of investment funds for purchase of weapons. As more wars were fought by the Third World countries, military coups became common and internal oppressions increased.

By mid-1980s, the mounting debts slowed down military

expenditures. World leaders launched a peace offensive with the new leadership in USSR spearheading the movement. Indian Prime Minister not only supported these moves but also took initiative. The six-nation appeal for complete nuclear disarmament was a signal contribution to this change in the direction of peace.

It was noted rather painfully that the 17 million people who died in war since 1945, the overwhelming majority has been from Third World countries. But more people in these countries died of under-and malnutrition, of curable diseases and of ignorance. These tragedies could be avoided, if the militarisation was avoided. It was pointed out that just 10-12 per cent cut in military expenditure in Third World countries would be enough to cover the cost of a comprehensive social development programme including education, literacy and community medical care. Quoting Ruth Sivard, it was said that about US $ five billion would be enough to provide primary schools for 100 million children, adult-education for 700 million illiterates and community health services for 85 per cent of the villages of the Third World.

GANDHIAN WORLD ORDER

Several papers and speakers deliberated on Gandhian approach to world peace. It was repeatedly pointed out that Truth and Non-violence, the basic tennets of Gandhian ideology, were not other-worldly goals. These constituted the foundation-stone of peace and harmony and they were to be relentlessly pursued and unless our policies were tuned to these goals, we couldn't expect to have a peaceful world order.

Gandhi and World peace was the focus of several papers presented in different sessions of the seminar. It would not be possible to review them all here. A few points which emerged prominently are mentioned below.

> Gandhi laid emphasis on ethical principles of respect and love for life in its all manifestations. Sharing and sacrifice must be the corner-stones of human relations. As such he laid great emphasis on non-violence. For him *Ahimsa* (non-violence) did not mean just absence of physical injury. It was an active force of love towards all living and even non-living things.

Gandhi insisted on not only good and noble ends but also equally good and noble means. Wrong means applied to right ends would only contribute to injustice, violence, etc., said he.

Among the other aspects which got major attention of the seminar were *Satyagrah* as a means to resolve conflict. In the words of Martin Luther King, "One day we must come to see that peace is not merely a distant goal that we seek but a means by which we arrive at that goal. We must pursue peaceful ends through peaceful means. How much longer must we play at deadly war games before we heed the plaintive plea of the unnumbered dead and maimed of the past wars".

Gandhian World order considers the whole humanity to be a single community. Each individual is a centre of a series of oceanic circles each merging into the whole but retaining its identity. In this world order hierarchies give place to oceanic circles. And hence, it is the horizontal relations among the equals which will govern the social system not the hierarchic relations among few big and many smalls, the former sitting on the backs of the latter.

Gandhi conceived of human settlements to be small and rural. He thought of a system of autonomous villages linked with other villages horizontally. His village was in no way less prosperous than modern cities not only in India but even in the developed world without the stresses and strains of speed and environmental pollution. He was not against cities, but he did not want the current exploitative relationship to continue. In his scheme of things urban settlements would be generative not exploitative, they would not grow to megalopolitan dimensions as they would be more self-reliant than what they are today.

Gandhi was not against machines, nor was he against industrialisation. He was against industrialism and dehumanised machine culture. A number of papers focused on these aspects of what one may call Gandhian social order. Several participants pointed to the need for rural industrialisation which could integrate agriculture, industry and services and help people stand on their own feet. Gandhi wanted industry to be in each home and family. That is why he laid special emphasis on *Khadi* and related activities. Unless a non-exploitative economic system evolves, possibility of peace would remain a distant dream.

BRIDGING THE GREAT DIVIDES

How to bridge the gaps and bring harmony in the society? How can non-violence become an accepted medium of human behaviour? The seminar tried to examine these questions and sought answers even if tentative:

Science and Spirituality

There was considerable discussion on science and spirituality — whether the two could go together. Dr. D.S. Kothari said that both science and spirituality ultimately reached the same point provided that science was not devoid of ethics and spirituality was not devoid of rationality.

Science has, while on the one hand, served humanity solve many problems of health, nutrition and material welfare, it has also been used to destroy life. Scientific laws and discoveries have created a situation in which very survival of the earth and all living things on it are in danger. It is, however, not the fault of science. It is the result of the absence of ethical base for science and rationality.

Spirituality too has gone hay-wire not once but innumerable times; not only recently but all through human history. If religions are the fountain-head of spirituality then one wonders how millions of people have been killed or maimed in the name of religion. Most religions of the world have sought the peace of the graveyard, not the peace of a living and thriving humanity. It was not again the fault of spirituality; it was the use of spirituality for hedonistic and base purposes; for eliminating people not adhering to a particular faith; for gaining political control over others. None of the people who perpetrated such crimes were ever known for spirituality; as none of those using science against humanity are really scientists. The man who dropped atom bomb on Hiroshima was not a scientist. The bomb was made by the scientist because he was a scientist without ethics.

Man and Nature

In the Gandhian order, nature is not a resource to be exploited. Nature is living: it sustains human life. Nothing should be done which will destroy or pollute it. Gandhi was profusely quoted to prove that he was far ahead of modern environmentalists. He warned as early as 1927 that industrialism would create problems of the type we see today.

If one reads Gandhian views on industrialism in the present context of poverty, environmental destruction and paucity of resources, one can understand him and his ideas better. Earth being a living phenomenon; it has limits of re-generation and recovery. It has tolerance limits. If the interference goes beyond the tolerance limits, the earth will not be the same again.

Linguistic and Communal Conflicts

Languages should become unifying forces if seen in their proper perspectives. The three-language formula adopted in India is ideal for a multilingual nation. Sanskrit has always played a unifying role among Indian languages and hence should not be neglected. Devangari, being almost a complete script, should be adopted by other Indian languages. The linguistic conflicts emerge due to three factors:

1. politicisation of the issue,
2. fear of losing job opportunities, and
3. linguistic fanaticism.

Communalism which has acquired serious proportions in India has to be curbed through an education system, both formal and non-formal, which is built on the foundation of Gandhian ideals and respect for the values and feelings of other groups and peoples having different styles of life. Tolerance for things different should be part of the psyche. Unless the basic principle of unity in diversity is adhered to, communalism would continue to grow.

Fanaticism is the basic cause of communalism. But why do people become victims of fanaticism? It is the fear of real or imaginary dangers and loss of identity and it is the hatred propagated by vested interests. Education on right lines alone can help resolve the problem. We must re-examine the Gandhian education system and lead the world in education for peace.

Socio-economic Conflicts

Socio-economic conflicts have increased in number and range in the process of economic development. Adversary democratic structure has divided groups and communities which were once united and cohesive. The position of the weaker sections of the society has remained vulnerable.

It was argued that India must adopt a fresh approach to these conflicts drawing upon Gandhian principles. Such an approach would naturally be based on the projection of the self as preached by Gandhi and ancient Indian philosophers.

The socio-economic conflicts in tribal belt were taken up as a special case. It was suggested that one noticed four types of conflicts :

(a) at the ideational level,
(b) within the tribal communities,
(c) between different communities, and
(d) between tribal communities and the state.

Small-scale enterprises which are free from conflicts between management and labour and are within the reach of the people needed to be promoted. The concept of trusteeship, propounded by Gandhiji, should get fresh attention of all concerned. One cannot visualise a peaceful economic order without trusteeship, decentralisation, bread labour and voluntary poverty.

The inadequacy of the prevailing economic paradigms in dealing with the emerging economic conflicts was also highlighted in the seminar. It was pointed out that we could neither understand conflict, nor resolve them unless we adopted a wholistic approach encompassing material, psychic, philosophical and other aspects of human life. Some participants opined that decentralised small-scale operations which Gandhiji advocated were not only more efficient when seen in their broader contexts but also more humane. Many participants said that peace required conflict resolution processes to begin at the individual as much as at the global level.

Developmental Conflicts

The conflicts emerging from the pressure of population on natural resources and the pursuit of specific development goals and styles received good attention of the seminar.

It was argued that show piece efforts at development often proved to be misguided symbols of progress and culminated in mal-development. Lack of organic links between macro-plans and ground level needs and realities have tended to generate developmental conflicts. Micro-level approaches within broader macro-frame and focused on self-organised and managed communities were considered to be most appropriate for a country like India, and in the long-run perhaps for the whole world.

ROLE OF UNIVERSITIES

The role of the universities in ushering in an era of non-violence was discussed in three sessions. The discussions centred on two aspects of the issue: conflicts on the university campuses and university's role in creating an environment of peace and harmony in the society at large.

Conflicts within Universities

The factors that lead to conflict on the campus are many. University is part of the social system. It cannot function as an island. Many student participants pointed out that when our parliamentarians indulged in violence inside the legislatures, how could the youth be expected to behave non-violently. It was, however, pointed out by many others that universities had always given light to the society. They could not be compared to any other social institution. They had special responsibilities and they should find ways and means to play their roles effectively.

It was also forcefully argued that universities had by-and-large been given step-motherly treatment by the government, as they were often the centres of dissent. They have been starved of resources. Lack of resources, political interference, loss of autonomy and anti-intellectual wave prevailing in the country, came in the way of universities playing their due roles in the society.

Many of the internal problems of the universities emerged from the following factors:

a. Lack of academic environment resulting partly from unmotivated teachers and partly from students who were neither ready for higher education, nor interested in it.
b. Lack of suitable mechanism to resolve student problems, and grievances in time.
c. Lack of understanding and faith between students and teachers.
d. Poor facilities for teachers and students.
e. Involvement of political parties in university affairs.
f. Unhealthy interference by government agencies responsible for education.
g. Poor quality of Vice-Chancellors.
h. Inability to change the examination system to make it learning-oriented.

i. Lack of interaction with parents.
j. Degeneration of teachers' associations into goal-less trade unions.
k. Loss of university autonomy. States, like Bihar, have completely destroyed universities as centres of leaning; U.P. is following suit rather speedily.

The suggestions made to improve the situations could be grouped under the following heads:

a. *Appointment of Vice-Chancellors:* Something needs to be done to change the system so that only those who are known scholars/administrators are appointed to this prestigious post. Position of a Vice-Chancellor should be something like that of a Judge of the High Court/Supreme Court. He should be a man of stature and he be treated like that.
b. *Appointment of teachers:* The university service should be nationalised and teachers be appointed through an all-India competitive test followed by Ph.D. level training of two to three years. No teacher should be appointed in the university from which be received post-graduate education.
c. *Bar on private tuitions:* Bar on private tuitions by university and college teachers should be vigorously implemented. And the teachers who treat teaching as a side business should be disciplined.
d. *Interference from outside elements* particularly partisan politicians in the functioning of the university be stopped and student unions should start working for the improvement of the university and welfare of students. The BHU model of students union should be looked into for implementation elsewhere with suitable modification.
e. *Incentive* based on evaluation of academic achievement should be given to good teachers/researchers.
f. The universities are moving away from the society not in the ivory towers but in the cesspool of mediocrity. The change has to be brought about by the universities themselves. They must introspect, use their resources more prudently and try to improve the situation.

Role of Universities in Promoting Peace and Harmony

There are those who think that the universities in their present form can play no useful role. This was considered by the seminar to be an extreme view. That way no institution can play its role because there is no such institution which does not have its internal management problems.

Since universities are not going to be abolished, our effort should be to help them to improve themselves, rather than to discard them as irrelevant centres.

The three pillars of university education are: Teaching, Research/ Training and Extension. Only through an integrated and combined efforts of these three can the university play any useful role in society:

a. Through a vigorous and innovative teaching programme a university can promote awareness of conflicts and tensions utilising seminars, symposia, peace exhibitions, etc., as media and instruments of publicity.
b. Inclusion of peace education in the syllabi at all levels.
c. Teaching and research on constructive and sustainable man-nature relationship.
d. Educating youth on peace in day-to-day life, and in the unifying and harmonising principles of our culture, religion, history, geography, etc.

Research and training constitute the backbone of learning and scientific progress. Universities can play an important role in promoting peace and non-violence by way of conducting research on various facets of conflicts in the society including conflicts between man and nature. They can also launch training programmes for both teachers and students in peace initiatives and non-violent approach to conflict resolution. Similar programmes can be initiated for the benefit of government officials.

Orientation course for teachers of various disciplines such as history, geography, economics, etc., laying emphasis on peace research, decentralisation, disarmament, non-violent development models, social change and transformation, etc., could be organised. Peace camps and publication of books, journals, etc., on peace and related issues might also be taken up.

Extension programme bring the concepts, theories and new ideas to the door of the common man. This can involve:

a. Organisation of national integration camps,
b. Programmes to take Gandhi to schools and villages,
c. Establishment of Gandhi Study Circle in each college and school,
d. Strengthening of people's education,
e. Preparation of small books on Gandhian thought to be supplied to students at nominal price.

It was the general consensus of the group that a motivated group of persons who had abiding faith in non-violence and Gandhian concept of social justice had to act as pressure group to promote the cause of peace and harmony.

WORKING GROUP REPORT

A working group appointed for the purpose prepared a special report on the role of universities in peace studies and Gandhian philosophy. The report was approved by the seminar.

Teaching and Training

There could be three types of teaching and training programme. Each has its own merits and demerits. Universities should adopt whichever they found suitable:

a. Universities like Gandhigram, which were wholly devoted to Gandhian system of higher education, should be encouraged not to fall in the trap of other general universities and lose their bearings. They deserved all assistance from the UGC, State Governments, and private sector, so that they could start influencing other universities and educational centres. We needed more such universities so that the educational needs of the country were better served.
b. A number of general universities have started departments of Gandhian Studies and Peace Research. These departments too needed encouragement and assistance. While it was true that Gandhian studies should not be conducted in isolation and should enter all relevant disciplines, one could not also deny the

fact that the present structure of the university system did not allow such lateral entry easily. If we want any department to take up Gandhian aspects as its discipline, we see a signal lack of interest. No one is prepared to try this. It is not 'modern'. Such is the situation with all disciplines. People have very stereotyped view of Gandhiji. It is because of ignorance about this great man and his works. One of the ways this ignorance could be reduced, if not eliminated, is to start departments with appropriate faculty offering B.A., M.A., and Ph.D. in Peace Research and Gandhian Studies, etc. True, it was not the ideal way of doing things. But could we say that all other departments were working ideally? If not, we should launch such departments in the hope that some of them would come to the expectations and play their roles effectively.

c. Eleven universities had Gandhi Bhavans which were started for the specific purpose of promoting Gandhian studies, peace research, national integration, harmony between man and nature and between man and man, etc. Many of these Bhavans have lost their moorings. The work being done at Gandhi Bhavan, University of Delhi, deserves to be commended and emulated by other Bhavans in the country.

University of Delhi's Gandhi Bhavan, has successfully launched programmes of education which involve the head, heart and hand of the trainees simultaneously. If Delhi University could accomplish such a task, there was no reason why other universities having Gandhi Bhavan could not follow suit.

It was highly satisfying that Delhi University's Gandhi Bhavan was starting short-term training courses in Gandhian studies, Yoga and Naturopathy, Bee-keeping, Spinning and Weaving, Screen Printing and *Dari*-making, etc. This will be in addition to other academic activities which go on at the Bhavan on a continuous basis. All Gandhi Bhavan directors should meet under the aegis of the UGC and decide on a joint action programme on lines being done at Delhi University. The UGC should extend all necessary assistance for such endeavours. Director, Delhi University, Gandhi Bhavan, may take initiative in this regard. The UGC may by approached for financial assistance.

Research

In order to promote the ideas and the ideals that the Father of the

Nation personified, our university system might consider implementing the following:

> *Research ideas:* There have been many recent developments in the physical, social and life sciences which indicate the possibility of emergence of an intellectual revolution along the lines desired by Mahatma Gandhi in *'Hind Swaraj'*. Unfortunately, research along these new lines is taking place mostly in the West, even though the contents of the research have a distinctly Indian/Gandhian flavour. Our universities could sponsor research into these ideas in a big way. Apart from the great intellectual stimulation that this research would give, it could provide a wonderful opportunity to Indians to contribute towards fundamental and applied research of practical significance in the years to come, especially in sciences and technologies. The following sampling of research publications indicates the range of possibilities available:

Books containing new ideas pertaining to the physical sciences:

Title	**Author**
The Tao of Physics	Fritjof Capra
The Dancing Wu Li Masters	Gary Zukav
Wholeness and the Implicate Order	David Bohm
The Reflexive Universe	Arthur Young
Space, Time and Beyond	Bob Toben
The Mechanics of Enlightenment	Anthony Campbell
From Being to Becoming	Illya Prigogine
Some Thoughts on Science and Religion	D.S. Kothari
The Geometry of Meaning	Arthur Young
The Structure of Scientific Revolutions	Thomas Kuhn
Taking the Quantum Leap	Fred Alan Wolf
Vedic Mathematics	Jagadguru Swami Bharti Krishna Tirtha
Infinity and the Mind	Rudy Rucker
Godel, Escher and Bach Hoffstadter	Douglas
Order out of Chaos	Illya Prigogine
Looking Glass Universe	Peat & Briggs

Books containing new ideas pertaining to the social sciences and to social change:

Title	Author
A Guide for the Perplexed	E.F. Schumacher
The Aquarian Conspiracy	Marlyn Ferguson
Voluntary Simplicity	Duane Elgin
The Marriage of East and West	Bede Griffiths
The Human Condition	Hannah Arendt
The Hundredth Monkey	Ken Keyes
Entropy	Jeremy Rifkin
Debt Shock	Darrell Delamaide
The Turning Point	Fritj of Capra
Heading Toward Omega	Kenneth Ring
A Gandhian Theology of Liberation	Fr. Ignatius Jesudasan

Books containing new ideas pertaining to the life sciences:

Title	Author
A New Science of Life	Rupert Sheldrake
The Holographic Paradigm	Karl Pribram/Ken Wilber
The Roots of consciousness	Jeffrey Mishlove
Life At Death	Kenneth Ring
Recollections of Death	Machael Sabom
Sciences, Animals and Evolution	Catherine Roberts
Living Time	Maurice Nicoll
The New Man	Maurice Nicoll
The Psychology of Consciousness	Robert Ornstein
The Human Mystery	John Eccles
The Body Electric	Thelma Moss
Living Systems	James Miller

Book containing new ideas pertaining to technologies:

Title	Author
The One Straw Revolution	Masanobu Fukuoka
The Natural Way of Farming	Masanobu Fukuoka
Small Is Possible	George McRobie
Handbook of Homemade Power	Compiled by Mother Earth News
Forest Farming	Douglas & Hart
Soft Energy Paths	Amoury Lovins
Human Scale	Kirkpatrick Sale
Laurel's Kitchen	Robertson, Flinders & Godfrey
Diet for a Small Planet	Frances Moore Lappe

Every Gandhi Bhavan should take up research on local and regional conflicts; on poverty and unemployment and on the role of rural industries, village *Panchayats* and host of related issues. At least one village and urban community should be consistently studied and some development programmes on lines of Gandhi Bhavan, Delhi University, be started.

Efforts, should be made to enroll students for M.Phil. or Ph.D. on themes relevant to Gandhian studies.

Extension

a. *Extension Programme:* While individual colleges may not be able to sponsor research on their own, they can organise programmes to understand and debate the feasibility and desirability of the Gandhian Alternative. These could be in the form of lectures, discussions, seminars and presentations by experts in the field, especially those who have done research as given above. UGC could make a special provision for such an extension programme.

b. *Field Work:* Under the aegis of Gandhi Bhavan, NSS or similar schemes, colleges and universities can organise camps where students can experience the life-style that Gandhi had recommended. These camps must involve physical labour, community living and social interaction. In addition, they can be used to investigate the practical aspects and feasibility of the ideas being generated by research. For instance, the following three ideas can be investigated at such a camp:—

i. *Sulabh Sauchalaya*: Is this idea workable on a mass scale?
ii. *Natural Farming*: Can this provide a sound and productive alternative to modern forms of agriculture? If so, what does it demand in terms of re-structuring of our life-style?
iii. *Indigenous medicine*: Do herbs and other forms of traditional medicine offer any advantages over allopathy, especially for the rural and poor sections of society?

An investigation of such practical questions would make these camps interesting and relevant from the point of view of the search for a Gandhian Alternative.

These extension works of the Gandhi Bhavans, etc., could be seen in oceanic circle form. There should be more constructive work near the centre. Then as one goes away from the centre, teaching, training and lectures become important. Further away from the centre the use of modern communication media becomes critical. It becomes distant education programme which has not been started by any university or institution of higher education.

Concluding Remarks

The Seminar on "Conflict Resolution through Non-violence: Role of Universities" was a great success. The idea of inviting students with leadership qualities was a novel one and gave a new meaning to the ensuing discussions. At least one seminar of this scale should be held each year on a relevant theme, so that the misconceptions about Gandhi, particularly among the youth, is minimised and hopefully eliminated.

The UGC has been playing a good role in promoting Gandhian studies. Much more needed to be done. The group hopes that the UGC support will not be wanting. It thanked Mr. Hira, UGC, V-C., Pro.-V-C. and Director, Gandhi Bhavan, for organising such a seminar and making excellent arrangements for participants.

NOTES

1. Ruth Leger Sivard, (1987). *World Military and Social Expenditures, 1987-88,* Washington D.C. World Priorities, page 1.
2. *Ibid.*

2

SCIENCE AND AHIMSA*

D.S. KOTHARI

Material Progress and Moral Fervour

WHILE INAUGURATING an All India Industrial Exhibition at Ajmer in 1943 Bapna Sahib had said : "In our country, the masses are poor and illiterate. Poverty is the cause of illiteracy and unless the country is industrialised, the standard of living cannot be raised. India has, no doubt, made progress, but the progress achieved so far is insignificant in comparison to the achievements of the other countries where materialistic mentality, scientific discoveries and technical inventions have pulled them up almost to the goal of their ambition. We are far behind them in this respect, but we have seen the other side of the picture also and, *therefore, can avoid pitfalls*. The culture and civilisation of India are based on *spiritualism* and this has saved us from extinction in the gigantic world race, but no country can survive onslaughts on it and rise and maintain its position, unless there is a *harmonious blending of material progress with moral and religious fervour*. The geographical position and the climatic conditions of India are a sufficient guarantee that it will never be divorced from spiritualism." These are simple, profound words. Their relevance today is beyond question. A clear distinction is necessary between "Westernisation" — which we must avoid — and "Modernisation".

In stirring words, Nehru said:

---

* Edited version of the first Memorial Lecture in memory of Sir Siremal Bapna delivered at the University of Indore on 30th October, 1987.

> "Can we combine the progress of science and technology with this progress of the mind and spirit also? We cannot be untrue to science because that represents the basic fact of life today. Still less can we be untrue to those essential principles for which India has stood in the past throughout the ages. Let us then pursue our path to industrial progress with all our strength and vigour and, at the same time, remember that material riches without toleration and compassion and wisdom may well turn to dust and ashes."[1]

The Atomic Age and the 'Indian Way'

In the Atomic Age without *Ahimsa*, that is, compassion and wisdom, there can be no survival for mankind. In his foreword to Swami Ghanananda's book, *Sri Ramakrishna and His Unique Message* (1970), Arnold Toynbee says :

> "At this supremely dangerous moment in human history, the only way of salvation for mankind is an Indian way. In the Atomic Age, the whole of human race has a utilitarian motive for following this Indian way. No such motive could be stronger, or more respectable, in itself. The survival of the human race is at stake. Yet even the strongest and the most respectable utilitarian motive is only a secondary reason for taking Ramakrishna's, Gandhi's and Ashoka's teaching to heart and acting on it. The primary reason is that this teaching is right — and is right because it flows from a true vision of spiritual reality."[2]

In March, 1951, Einstein stated:

> "Revolution without the use of violence was the method by which Gandhi brought liberation of India. It is my firm belief that the problem of bringing peace to the world on a supernational basis will be solved only by employing Gandhi's method on a large scale."[3]

Gandhi, the greatest political genius of our time, indicated the path to be taken. He gave proof of what sacrifice man is capable of once he has discovered the right path. His work on behalf of India's liberation is the living testimony to the fact that man's will, sustained by indomitable conviction, is more powerful than material forces that seem insurmountable.

Truth and 'Ahimsa' for Practice by Groups and Communities of Nations

In the *Stride Towards Freedom* (1959), Martin Luther King declared :

> "The intellectual and moral satisfaction that I failed to gain from the utilitarianism of Bentham and Mill, the revolutionary methods of Marx and Lenin, the special contract theory of Hobbes, the 'back to nature' optimism of Rousseau and the superman philosophy of Nietzsche, I found in the non-violent resistance philosophy of Gandhi. I came to feel that this was the only morally and practically sound method open to oppressed people in their struggle for freedom".[4]

It is important to recognise that the new chapter — the new dimension — of collective action in the theory and practice of *Ahimsa* and *Satyagraha* opened by Mahatma Gandhi is closely interlinked with the Industrial-Scientific Revolution. It is an integral part of it. It could hardly have been possible earlier. Above all it needs rapid means for mass communications. And let us not forget that as yet we are only at the beginning of this great chapter in man's history.

The two supreme events of our Age are, undoubtedly, the discovery of nuclear energy and its use to make nuclear weapons, and, on the other hand, the organisation and use of collective *Ahimsa* and *Satyagraha* under Gandhi for the liberation of India. The Mahatma says :

> "We have to make truth and non-violence not matters for mere individual practice but for practice by groups and communities and nations. That at any rate in my dream. I shall live and die in trying to realise it. My faith helps me to discover new truths every day. *Ahimsa* is the attribute to the Soul, and, therefore, to be practised by everybody in all affairs of life."[5]

I spoke of Einstein's views about Gandhi's *Ahimsa* and *Satyagraha*. At a UNESCO conference Robert Oppenheimer speaking on Einstein said that if he had to think of a single word for Einstein's attitude towards human problems, he would have to pick the Sanskrit word *Ahimsa*.[6]

And if we think of Niels Bohr, no less appropriate for him would be the word *Ahimsa*. The complementarity approach which we owe principally to Bohr, and which is of the profoundest significance for modern physics, is inextricably linked with the theory and practice of *Ahimsa*.

May I, at this point, refer to a remarkable reference book, *The Gaia Atlas of Planet Management* edited by Norman Myers. It is the book "for today's caretakers of tomorrow's world". It provides a most telling and insightful account of the interdependence, for man's survival, of science and technology and *Ahimsa*. The book powerfully stimulates further thought and action. A highly instructive review by Sir Eric Ashby in the *Nature* says: "The book pricks the *conscience* of the general public."[7]

A recent issue of the *Daedalus* (Winter, 1980) is devoted entirely to the problem of technology and values. As Harvey Brooks, a leading US Professor of Technology, says :

> "There are those who, like myself, think it (technology) is absolutely essential for survival, and there are others who think in fact it is almost the opposite. . . . It seems to me that because technology opens up options, it takes a strong value system to control the choice of options, and so where technology is disastrous is where it enters a culture or a social situation with a weak value system and very little sense of collective welfare."[8]

Foremost Task of Education

Technological development in general widens at a terrific pace the already frightening gap between the rich and the poor within a country, and between the rich and the poor countries. Never before a value system firmly and effectively committed to serve the interests of the common people was more necessary than today. And the situation is desperate.

Science and technology tell us what can be done and what cannot be done, science describes the limits of the possible. But science cannot tell us what we ought to do. That decision is an ethical-moral decision. Scientific truths and moral truths are not contradictory. These are complementary. It is the exploration and practice of the complementarity of scientific and moral truths that give to life richness, dignity, beauty and happiness.

The history of man's advancement in *Ahimsa* — taken in its widest sense — is undoubtedly the most important aspect of the history of man. Yet nearly all the history we are taught in the schools the world over including our country — the land of Gandhi is the history of *himsa* (violence). As Karl Popper writes:

> "There is no history of mankind, there is only an indefinite number of histories of all kinds of aspect of human life. And one of these is the history of political power. This is elevated into the history of the world. But, this, I hold, is an offence against every decent conception of mankind. It is hardly better than to treat the history of embezzlement or of robbery or of poisoning as the history of mankind. *For the history of power politics is nothing but the history of international crime and mass murder* (including, it is true, some of the attempts to suppress them). This history is taught in schools, and some of the greatest criminals are extolled as its heroes."[9]

What educational reform could be more important and crucial than to change this situation? At least, a first step in this direction is long over due. In the atomic age what could be more unfortunate and lamentable that *Ahimsa*, the human part of human history, finds no place in today's education. What could be more important and desperately needed man's survival than the theory and practice of *Ahimsa* finding an effective place in school education.

We may recall Einstein's statement (20 November, 1950) so inspiring and so relevant in the Atomic Age :

> "The most important human endeavour is the striving for morality in our actions. Our inner balance and even our very existence depends on it. Only morality in our actions can give beauty and dignity to life.
> To make this a living force and bring it to clear consciousness is perhaps the foremost task of education.
> The foundation of morality should not be made dependent on myth nor tied to any authority lest doubt about the myth or about the legitimacy of the authority should imperil the foundation of sound judgement and action."[10]

'Ahimsa' and Open Society

The most gruesome mass murder in history was the dropping of atomic bombs on Hiroshima and Nagasaki in August 1945. That decision was not taken in the *open*, but in the utmost *secrecy*. It was not a democratic decision. No one is likely to hold that deployment of weapons or mass destruction (whether atomic, chemical or biological) would be or should be done after a public debate. But few would dissent that effective decentralisation of decision-making processes tends to discourage gross misuse and perversion of power. It is also worth remembering that though there were some top scientists, in the U.S. and outside, in the know of the development of the atomic bomb, and who were against its use on Japan, none of them lodged a public protest of any kind. And, of course, no one offered or even thought of offering *Satyagraha*. Even one utterly sincere *Satyagrahi* against the bomb, prepared to give-up everything even his life, might have influenced President Truman's conscience and the course of events. Or, it might not have. Who can tell? But the fact is there was no *Satyagraha* against the atomic bomb.

The discovery of nuclear fission (in 1938), an epochal discovery in pure science, was the achievement of persons with not the slightest idea or any intention whatsoever to use it for military purposes. There was no motivation other than to advance pure science — in this case the physics and chemistry — of interaction of neutrons with matter. And yet within barely seven years it was applied to murder hundred to thousands of innocent human beings. The history of man has been, as Bertrand Russell said, that if any folly or crime, howsoever cruel or despicable, was at all *possible*, then man would commit it. But, in the nuclear age man's folly could put an end to all civilisation — even an end to all life. The way out is to perserve with courage and faith, individually and collectively, for an open society and *ahimsa* as a way of life. The great lesson of modern science and particularly biology is that the world is closely integrated interdependent system. And, therefore, my happiness, in the long run, can only be ensured by working for the happiness of others.

Bohr in his 1950 Open Letter to the UN Secretary-General — a letter that expresses his deepest faith and hope — said: "An open world where each nation can assert itself solely by the extent to which it can contribute to the common culture and is able to help others with experience and resources must be the goal to be put above everything else. . . . The very fact that knowledge is in itself the basis for civilisation points directly to openness as the way to overcome the present crisis.

"The efforts of all supporters of international co-operation, individuals as well as nations, will be needed to create in all countries an opinion to voice, with ever-increasing clarity and strength, the demand for an open world."[11] Bohr's letter forcefully reminds us of Kant's prophetic essay (1795) on *Perpetual Peace*. It is so pertinent today.

Gandhi-Gorbachov Declaration (Delhi, 27 November, 1986)

The world is hopefully — frustratingly, agonisingly — moving towards an "Open World", that is, a world based increasingly on Science and *Ahimsa*. Any other course can lead only to mankind's total annihilation. Note that both Science and *Ahimsa* are capable inherently of unlimited advancement, of ever-increasing richness and moral-spiritual upliftment.

There can be little doubt that the Gandhi-Gorbachov Declaration is a momentous step forward. In a basic sense it is a profoundly inspiring step, a landmark, in man's continuing quest along the path of *Truth and Ahimsa* which goes back to Buddha and Mahavira, and to which Mahatma Gandhi in our own times made a contribution of the utmost significance and highest value for man's future, even his very survival.

The ten principles of the Declaration are:

1. Peaceful co-existence must become the universal norm of international relations.
2. Human like must be recognised as supreme.
3. Non-violence (*Ahimsa*) should be the basis of community life.
4. Understanding and trust must replace fear and suspicion.
5. The right of every State to political and economic independence must be recognised and respected.
6. Resources being spent on armaments must be channelled towards social and economic development.
7. Conditions must be generated for the individual's harmonious development.
8. Mankind's material and intellectual potential must be used to solve global problems.
9. The balance of terror must give way to comprehensive international security.
10. A nuclear weapon-free and non-violent world requires specific and immediate action for disarmament.

The editorial in *Science* on *Arms and the Men* emphasises the point that arms control "will be valuable only if we seek to understand and defuse the causes of war. . . . In depth psychological studies could possibly tell us that proper education can direct national pride from jingoistic competition to constructive co-operation. . . . We might even learn to understand ourselves, once it becomes clear that it is the only way that we are going to survive."[12]

'Ahimsa' and Beyond-Science

Ahimsa is not a part of science: *Ahimsa goes beyond science. And beyond-science, beyond reasons, is not anti-science or anti-reason. Ahimsa* has no meaning for matter (physics) as such, it has a meaning only for a *Conscious being*, for an "I" of self (psyche) with free-will. To ignore this simple fact can be only ruinous.

Questions, such as, *Who are we*?, *What is the purpose of life*?, lie beyond-reason. To understand and to endeavour to answer such "ultimate questions" is in the very nature of things an endless ever-expanding quest. For such a quest, reason is *absolutely necessary*, but it is not sufficient. We have to go beyond reason — of course, *never* anti-reason. The basic distinction between the two concepts of *necessary* and *sufficient* is well known in mathematics, but not often appreciated in sociology and philosophy, and it has led to untold confusion.

The case for an open-world — for a world based on *Science* and *Ahimsa* cannot be established scientifically or by *rational* arguments alone. It goes beyond science. It is a question of choice. And choice implies a value judgement. The choice here is between man's survival and universal death. And survival depends directly on the complementarity of Science and *Ahimsa*. The highest type of scientific activity is not possible without a supreme faith in science and in man. This is a moral quality. There is no inherent contradiction in the same person being an intellectual giant and a spiritual pigmy, but in real life it is most unlikely. When asked (during a serious illness) whether he was at all afraid of death, Einstein said: "I feel such a sense of solidarity with all living things that it does not matter to me where the individual begins and ends." And he said, "There is nothing in the world which I could not dispense with at a moment's notice." How close to Gandhi are the ethical convictions of Einstein! He regarded Gandhi as "the greatest man of the age".

Principle of Complementarity Basically, Spiritual Concept

It is time I say something about complementarity itself. I have used the word frequently. I must admit I have not used it consistently. The concept is not an easy one, and our understanding is still rudimentary. That makes the subject interesting, but also irritating.

In speaking of the complementarity of two aspects or view points, an important element is that the situations under which the two aspects occur are different in some essential respects. Complementarity of the two aspects implies some irreducible element of incompatibility between them. This is necessary.

The complementarity principle has emerged, in the modern context, from the study of atomic phenomena. The complementarity of the wave and particle aspects of matter is well-known. The two aspects are incompatible. An experiment which demonstrates the wave aspect would automatically exclude demonstration of the particle aspect, and *vice versa*. Why so? It arises from an interaction, inherent in the nature of thing between a system and the measuring instrument. The interaction cannot be eliminated even under ideal conditions. It cannot be reduced below a certain minimum limit, defined by the Planck's constant, for any conceivable experiment — or "thought experiment". The interaction disturbs the state of the system under observation. An experiment, which provides some information about an atomic system, inevitably destroys (in general) some other information which we had about the system from an earlier experiment on the system. We cannot accumulate information indefinitely, because of an unavoidable interaction between the system and the measuring device and the accompanying disturbance of the state of the system. This is totally different from the situation in the classical physics. If interaction between a system and the measuring device could be completely ignored, made zero — as was the assumption in classical physics — then, in principle, the measuring instrument becomes redundant. Not so in quantum mechanics! The complementarity principle is forced upon us because there can be no measurement without a certain minimum interaction; and the experimental arrangement for determining different properties of an atomic system are, in general, incompatible with one another.

In fact, if we could think of an experiment which is inherently incapable of giving us information about some obvious, characteristic property of the system, then such an experiment is likely to reveal unexpected features of the system. This in a sense is the essence of complementarity mode of thinking in physics.

Bhor had great faith in the future role in human affairs of the practical philosophy of complementarity. It can enable people to see that seemingly irreconcilable points of view need not be contradictory. These, on deeper understanding, may be found to be complementary and mutually illuminating the two opposing, contradictory aspects being parts of a 'totality', seen from different perspectives. The complementarity approach allows the possibility of accommodating widely divergent human experiences into an underlying harmony, and bringing to light new social and ethical vistas for exploration and for alleviation of human suffering. Bohr fervently hoped that one day complementarity would be an integral part of everyone's school education, and provide guidance to the problems and challenges of life. For Bohr, the complementarity approach which generated one of the greatest revolutions in natural philosophy was also of the utmost relevance for every aspect of man's life. The complementarity approach or *Syadvada* is indispensable for the pursuit of truth and *ahimsa* in all their varied aspects.

H. Yukawa, the Japanese physicist who predicted the existence of the mesons on the basis of the principle of complementarity, was asked whether young physicists in Japan found the same great difficulty in comprehending the idea of complementarity as physicists do in the West. He replied that Bohr's complementarity always appeared to them as quite evident. "You see we in Japan have not been corrupted by Aristotle (Aristotle's Logic)", he added.

It is interesting to recall that Bohr as a student attended lectures on formal logic and on the history of philosophy. He liked Spinoza's concept of the psycho-physical parallelism; but later rejected it, as parallelism is not a true expression of complementarity. He read Kierkegaard. He was much impressed by Paul Muller's Tale of Danish Student, a delightful humorous story of Hegelian dialectics. A soul-searching research scholar struggles desperately to unravel the intricacies of human thinking. How can thought arise in the mind? "And before you think it, you must have had an idea of it, otherwise how could it have occurred to you to think it? And so it goes on to infinity, and this infinity is enclosed in an instant." And while the scholar is trying to prove that thoughts cannot move, in that very process the thoughts are rapidly moving. We are involved in an inexplicable contradiction, similar, in a sense, to the celebrated Zeno's paradox on the impossibility of motion of objects.

The most significant lesson we can learn from the marvellous epoch-making developments and discoveries in atomic physics in our century is not to be misled by apparent contradiction, but try to understand the *complementarity* underlying. The great lesson we owe primarily to Niels Bohr is that we must learn to take the complementarity approach seriously not only in science but in life. And the philosophy of complementarity is essentially the philosophy of *Upanishads* and the *Gita*.

Complementarity of Matter and Mind

The profoundest, richest and most fundamental of all *complementarities* is of course and that of *matter* and *consciousness* (mind). Perhaps, Wolfgang Pauli (of the Pauli Exclusion Principle) has stated the matter most clearly and succinctly. "To us . . . the only acceptable point of view appears to be one that recognises *both* sides of reality — the quantitative and the qualitative, the physical and the psychical — as compatible with each other, and can embrace them simultaneously. . . . It would be most satisfactory of all if *phusis* and *psyche* (i.e. matter and mind) could be seen as complementary aspects of reality.[13]

We are gradually moving away from what is "one of the most firmly entrenched taboos of 20th century science" that "any mingling of knowledge with values is unlawful, forbidden". The taboo is disastrous for humanism, disastrous for theory and practice of values. To man's great good fortune science — perhaps unexpectedly — is now slowly but steadfastly moving towards a more unified world view which includes both knowledge and values as complementary and mutually reinforcing.

As we have said repeatedly, scientific truths and ethical truths are not contradictory but complementary. There can be no great advancement in science without some measure of ethics in society. In the practice of science a high level of ethical norms is absolutely essential. Equally, on the other hand, in the modern world there is not much room for the practice of ethics without science and technology.

Take questions such as: Is there consciousness or mind in animals? What about plants? Is there consciousness in a single cell? Do plants feel pain? And what about bacteria and single cells? It is apparent that these questions — essentially qualitative, *subjective* — cannot be resolved *within* the framework of objective science. They go beyond science. But if we accept the complementarity of matter and mind — and there seems to be no escape — then consciousness is ever present at all levels of existence — from minerals to man. Only the degree of manifestation is different. In a highly thoughtful article '*Life and Mind in the Universe*'[14] George Wald has considered some aspects of this problem.

It needs to be emphasised that the wave-particle complementarity lies entirely *within* the domain of objective science. It is a direct expression of the existence of the *quantum of action* (Planck's constant). The wave-particle complementarity can serve as a launching pad, as it were, to gain some insight into higher complementarities which lie beyond science. The deepest complementarity is of *matter* and *consciousness* — of *phusis* and *psyche*. It is ultimately, an expression of the *Vedantic Identity : Ataman Brahman*. This is discussed in an illuminating manner by Erwin Schroedinger in the Epilogue to his great classic, *What is Life?*[15] (1944). [Also relevant to our discussion in Henri Poincare's Essay, Dover (1963). James Lighthill the recently *recognised failure of predictability in Newtonian dynamics*.[16]

Notice that all living organisms are subject to the laws of physics and chemistry which make no distinction whatsoever whether the atoms are parts of a living body or otherwise. Equally, one cannot deny the incontrovertible direct experience that the motions of one's body are under his or her control. My body is a "machine" but "I" control its movements. Let us assume, as undisputed, the two facts of experience (a) My body is a machine, and (b) its motions are under my control: (a) is a scientific, and *objective fact of experience*, (b) is a *subjective fact of experience*. From these two *facts* what is the inference we can draw which would not be contradictory to science, that is, not violate the objectivity and autonomy of Natural Sciences? The only possible inference, as Schroedinger has stressed, is that every mind that has ever said or felt "I" is the *One* (if any) who controls the 'Motions of the atoms', controls the universe, according to the Laws of Nature.

Says Schroedinger: "Within a cultural milieu where certain conceptions (which once had or still have a wider meaning among other peoples) have been limited and specialised, it is daring to give to this conclusion the simple wording that it requires. In Christian termino-logy to say: "Hence I am God the Almighty" sounds both blesphemous and lunatic. But please disregard these connotations for the moment and consider whether the above inference is not the closest a biologist can get to proving "God and immortality at one stroke". And he continues "in itself, the insight is not new". The earliest records to my knowledge date back some 2500 years or more. From the early great *Upanishads* the recognition *Ataman-Brahaman* (the personal self equals the omnipresent, all-comprehending eternal self) was in Indian thought considered, far from being blasphemous to represent the quintessence of deepest insight into the happenings of the world. The striving of all the scholars of *Vedanta* was, after having learnt to pronounce with their lips, to really assimilate in their minds this grandest of all thoughts.[17]

Notice the stunning sweep and profundity of the argument. From two straight forward, undeniable facts of experience it leads directly to that insight or truth which irrespective of differing ideologies is, in the end, the only real foundation of all truly social and moral endeavours and activities.

Moral-Spiritual Experiments

The most significant lesson of science for ethics is that "experimentation" in ethics is as necessary for its development — its practice and philosophy — as it is in natural science. The method — par excellence — of ethical or moral "experimentation" is *Ahimsa* and *Syadvada*.

Mahatma Gandhi gave to his autobiography the title: *The Story of My Experiments with Truth*. He wrote (1926): "what I want to achieve — what I have been striving and pining to achieve these 30 years — is self-realisation, to see God face to face, to attain *Moksha* (salvation). I live and move and have my being in pursuit of this goal. . . . The 'experiments' narrated are spiritual, or rather moral, for the essence of religion is morality." And he says: "I claim for them nothing more than does a scientist. . . . I have gone through deep self-introspection, searched myself through and through, and examined and analysed every psychological situation. Yet I am far from claiming any finality or infallibility about my conclusions. One claim I do indeed make and it is this. For me they appear to be a absolutely correct, and seem for the time being to be final. . . . And so long as my acts satisfy my reason and my heart, I must firmly adhere to my original conclusions."[18]

In the concluding chapter of *The Story of My Experiments with*

Truth, Gandhiji says: "My uniform experience has convinced me that there is no other God than Truth . . . and . . . the only means for the realisation of Truth is *Ahimsa*. . . . After all, however sincere my strivings after *Ahimsa* may have been, they have still been imperfect and inadequate, as a result of all my experience, that a perfect vision of truth can only follow a complete realisation of *Ahimsa*." And he continues: "I must reduce myself to zero. So long as a man does not of his own free will put himself last among his fellow creatures, there is no salvation for him. *Ahimsa* is the farthest limit of humility."[19] Speaking on Scientific truth Einstein says: "This firm belief, a belief bounds up with deep feeling in a Superior mind that reveals itself in the world of experience represents my conception of God. In common parlance this may be described as 'pantheistic' (Spinoza)."[20]

There is a chapter with the title, *Face to Face with Ahimsa*. This refers to the first *Satyagraha* in India initiated by Gandhiji after 21 years of "preparation" in South Africa. Writes Gandhiji about his meeting, early in 1917, with the indigo cultivators at Champaran (Bihar): "It is no exaggeration, but the literal truth, to say that in this meeting with the peasants I was face to face with God. *Ahimsa* and Truth."

Says Gandhiji:

> "I began to prise non-violence only when I began to shed cowardice. . . . The path of true non-violence requires much more courage than violence."[21]

Gandhiji's "experiments" are moral-spiritual experiments. The basis of morality is self-control or self-conquest through self-suffering. And indeed declared the Mahatma in *Hind Swaraj*: Swaraj is self-control. "Liberation from the bondage of the self-constituted the only way towards a more satisfactory society", stated Einstein.

A discussion of Science and *Ahimsa* immediately brings to mind recent far-reaching studies on the biology of animal and human behaviour, including aggression. Under natural conditions, animals of the same species do not kill one another. When they fight it is a kind of ritual, a play, and the fight instinctively stops short of causing fatality. Among animals of the same species the rule is harmony not killing. *But men kill one another*. It has no parallel in Nature. (An exception are rats). *It is man's invention*. Some domesticated animals, e.g., dogs, kill one another in fight between members of the same species, but this is a result of domestication. It does not occur in the wild. In the case of man, the invention of lethal weapons, and especially the use of fire arms, rendered the natural instinctive reactions to stop the fight short of fatality too slow to be effective. Man must learn and develop more quick ways of responding to a violent situation before it goes out of control as it were. This is a task for science and technology — the task, the goal, is *ahimsa*, not *himsa*.[22] Konrad Lorenz concludes his great fascinating book *On Aggression* with the inspiring message : "I believe in the power of human reason, as I believe in the power of natural selection. I believe that this, in the not too distant future, will endow our descendants with the faculty of fulfilling the greatest and most beautiful of all commandments"[23] (1966).

The famous statement, issued in 1955, jointly by Bertrand Russell, Einstein, Yukawa and others is, if any thing, even more relevant today. The declaration of the Pugwash Movement on the occasion of the 25th Pugwash Anniversary Conference in Warsaw (August 1982), signed by amongst others, nearly a hundred Nobel-Laureates, concludes:

> "In the circumstances in which mankind now finds itself, the warning, sounded so eloquently 27 years ago in the Russel-Einstein Manifesto, takes on a new urgency. There lies before us, if we choose, continual progress in happiness, knowledge and wisdom. Shall we, instead, choose death, because we cannot forget our quarrels? We appeal, as human beings to human beings. Remember your humanity and forget the rest."[24]

There can be no better homage to the inspiring memory of persons, such as Bapna Sahib, than to endeavour to the best of our ability to work for a world based on *Ahimsa* (Wisdom) and Science (Knowledge). It is no easy road but every step counts, how so small.

NOTES

1. Jawaharlal Nehru, *India and the World*. Maulana Azad Memorial Lecture 1959 cited in Education Commission Report, 1966.
2. Arnold Toynbee, 'Forword' to Swami Ghanananda, *Sri Ramakrishna and His Unique Message*, Calcutta Vedanta Press, 1970.
3. O. Nathan and H. Norden, *Einstein On Peace* New York, Simon & Schuster, 1960, p. 584.
4. Martin Luther King, *Stride Towards Freedom: The Montgomary story*, New York: Harper Row, 1959.

5. M.K. Gandhi, Harijan, 6.1.1940.
6. Bulletin of Atomic Scientist, March 1979, p. 38.
7. Eric Ashby, Review of *Gaia Atlas of Planet Management*, New York, PAN, 1985 in *Nature*, March 21, 1985.
8. Harvey Brooks, *Daedalus*, winter 1980.
9. Karl Popper, *The Open Society and its Enemies*, Vol II, Tide of Prophecy. princeton: Princeton University Press, 1966.
10. Helen Dukas and Banesh Half Mann, *A. Einstein: The Human Side* Princeton. Princeton University Press, 1979, p. 69; also published Albert Einsten: Selections from and on Einsten: New Delhi: Indian Academy of Sciences, 1984.
11. Niels Bohr *open Letter to the UN Secretary General*, 1950.
12. Editor *Science*, "Editorial on Arms and the Men", 2 Oct., 1987.
13. W. Pauli *The Interpretation of Nature and Pschye*, "Matter and Conciousness", in C.C. Jung and W. Pauli (eds): New York, Bollingen, 1955, pp. 208-10.
14. George Wald, "Life and Mind in the Universe", *International Journal of Quantum Chemistry*, 1984.
15. Erwin Schroedinger, "Epilogue" *What is Life*, London: Cambridge University Press, 1944.
16. Henri Poincare, "Ethics and Science in Mathematical Science, in *Last Essays*, New York Dover, see also James Righthill", Failure of Predictability in Newtonian Dynamics, *Proceedings of the Royal Society London*, 1986, p. 407.
17. Erwin Schroedinger. *op. cit*.
18. M.K. Gandhi, *My Experiments with Truth*, Ahmedabad: Navajeevan, 1927, p. xiv.
19. *Ibid*.
20. Indian National Science Academy *Einsteins Contributions*, New Delhi INSA, 1984.
21. Much valuable information on prevention of cruelty — often unspeakably cruel — to animals in scientific and medical experiments is provided by *Frame News*, Eastgate House, 34, Stoney Stress, Nottingham, NGI INB (U.K.) FRAME — *The Fund for the Replacement of Animals in Medical Experiments*.
22. For more details about cruelty to animals in Scientific research see *Frame News* (Fund for the Replacement of Animals to Medical Experiments (FRAME). Eastgate House, 34, Stoney Stress, Nottingham, NGI INB (UK).
23. Konrad Z Lorenz, *On Aggression*, London: Methuen, 1966.
24. Declaration of Pugwash Movement 25th Pugwash Anniversary conference in Washaw, August 1982.

3

MEDICAL SCIENCE AND NON-VIOLENCE

LARRY DOSSEY

I BELIEVE that Gandhi's message of non-violence remains a powerful force in our world. As a scientifically trained Western physician, it is in the area of medical science that I am particularly struck with the relevance of Gandhi's vision of non-violence as a guide to understanding and action.

No one in the world today having the slightest acquaintance with the nature of medical science can doubt that it is permeated with violence. Perhaps this sounds strange to those outside the profession. The goal of physicians, after all, is to relieve people of pain and suffering and to reduce the sum total of human misery. What could be violent about this? But violence, of course, always passes for something else. It is so sinister that physicians and medical scientists are themselves generally unaware of it.

It surfaces in many ways in medicine. One of the commonest is in the language we use in medicine. This is particularly dramatic in the field of immunology which concerns itself with infectious diseases, cancer, and auto-immune problems. In this field the dominant metaphors employed are military in nature. Dr. Fred Karush, an immunologist at the University of Pennsylvania, expressed the way we think about our immune system this way:

> A foreign organism invades, perhaps camouflaged as something else. The body, if its advance warning system detects the enemy, puts up a line of defence. Antibodies attack. A lot of killing goes

on. Researchers look for magic bullets or guided missiles. The metaphors make it sound as though we each provide a battle-ground for our own internal Star Wars.[1]

It may be claimed that these are mere figures of speech and, while they may indeed sound violent, they do not really represent medical reality, which is still based on the ideals of compassion and non-violence. But this is not absolutely true. Even in the *practice* of medicine in some of the finest teaching hospitals in the United States, which are affiliated to our best medical schools, violence erupts in the most dramatic ways. Surveys have shown that as many as one-third of the admissions to critical care units in these fine institutions due to *iatrogenic* diseases. An *iatrogenic* disease is one which is caused by the physician. In practice, these are either mistakes in technique such as errors at surgery, or side-effects, or complications of treatments. And they may be so violent as to be fatal.

For many months I have conducted an unscientific informal survey of my own in which I keep track of the number of articles in the mainstream medical journals which I read, such as the *Journal of the American Medical Association, the New England Journal of Medicine, the American Journal of Medicine* and the *Archives of Internal Medicine*, which are specifically devoted to medical problems which relate directly or indirectly to complications of treatments. The results, I have found, are sobering. It is common for one-fourth of the articles to be devoted to problems caused by therapies and, in some issues, up to 50 per cent of the articles deal with the harmful side-effects of treatments.

But what of it? It can be argued that modern scientific medicine is so vastly complicated that this has to be only expected. Violence is simply unavoidable. Surely we must expect things to go wrong when our therapies are so complex. There is nothing here that deserves criticism.

For my part, I do not agree. Today violence in medicine is so common that we have become numbed to it. We have come to accept the tragic as a matter of course. Sometimes we do not even recognise it when we see it and, when confronted with violence, we call it some-thing else — as for example, "side effects" or "complications".

We simply fail to see violence in the language we employ. Let me give another example of the way our thought is gradually moulded towards a perspective of violence. Recently a beautiful book was published in the United States containing over 300 astonishing photographs taken with the electron microscope. These pictures deal mainly with the immune system, showing the various kinds of cells in action. The name of the book is *The Body Victorious* written by one of the most gifted medical photographers of all time, Lennart Nilsson. The publisher's description of this work is as follows:

> Of all the *dangers* the human body faces during a lifetime — from a broken leg while skiing to a simple papercut — the most prevalent and consistent of these hazards arise from *invaders* invisible to the naked eye. These are the bacteria, protozoa, fungi and viruses that inhabit our bodies in countless forms and numbers. And it is our own immunological system that *strikes* with *defensive force* to rid the body of these *foreign* cells. . . . This *revolutionary* photographic essay . . . depicts the architecture of blood clots, the *battles* between white blood cells and bacteria, *killer* T-cells *attacking* cancer and antibodies *struggling* to locate and repel foreign, sometimes *deadly* substances in the body, including the AIDS virus [*emphasis added*].[2]

The tendency to think in the images of violence has surfaced dramatically in recent years in cancer therapy. There is a lot of evidence suggesting that the brain and the immune system form a unitary, integrated system in which feedback loops between the two abound. It seems apparent that one's mental state enters into the overall behaviour of the immune system. For instance, it appears that there is a higher incidence of cancer in persons who cannot express emotions and those who keep things bottled up inside die more frequently of cancers of all types.[3] Moreover, once one develops cancer, its prognosis is worse if one is chronically depressed psychologically.[4] This has led many researchers to ask whether, alternatively, the course of cancer can be positively affected by the purposeful use of certain kinds of thoughts. The results are intriguing. There are today many cases on record in which the regular, disciplined use of specific types of mental images seem to be associated with an improved clinical result. In these cases, the patient is asked to think about his or her own immune system getting rid of the cancer in some way. In the most famous cases the images reported are almost always incredibly violent. For example, in one celebrated case the tumor is visualised as a piece of raw meat, and the immune cells of the body are seen as a pack of ravenous wolves who attack the meat, the cancer and rip it to shreds. In a variation on this theme, violent images from medieval antiquity are employed. Cancer is seen as an evil dragon and the immune cells as St. George riding his horse. Here the noble knight spears the dragon, the cancer, killing it.

These kinds of cases have been widely publicised. They have led many therapists to the conclusion that the way to control the immune system voluntarily is through the use of extremely aggressive, violent mental images. Patients are encouraged to manufacture their own thoughts in ways which embody this approach. The results are some-times devastating for patients. In many instances the thoughts and feelings which *naturally* arise about one's cancer are *not* hostile. Yet patients frequently begin to feel as if they are failures because they cannot come up with the "right" kind of image — a *violent* image — to use against their illness. Rating scales have even been developed in which the image is given a numerical value; the more violent and aggressive, the higher the score. That one might employ peaceful co-existence as a mental strategy, or that one might even "help" the cancer to disappear, that one might "love" it to death — these non-violent mental strategies are simply not prised in this area of medical research at this time.

II

What support can we give for alternative views — views which might be based on non-violence instead of violence? Today we can begin to make out the outlines of what in my opinion is a better way — a non-violent way — in which to think about health and illness. It is a way which is consistent with our best science. Not only this. The new ways of thinking have the decided advantage of being in harmony with some of the most ancient spiritual messages the human race has produced, many of which originated in the soil of ancient India.

My own search for an alternative approach in conceptualising medical problems began about 20 years ago when I was in a medical school, I had been introduced by a fellow medical student to the philosophy of the East through the writings of Alan Watts, the Englishman, who, along with D.T. Suzuki, was so influential in bringing the teachings of the Orient to the West. This was for me a most sobering and challenging experience. I discovered in the tenets of Buddhism and Taoism a view of the world which for the first time rang true for me. I finished my formal training — medical school, internship and residency in internal medicine — and then I ran headlong into another body of knowledge from which I had been shielded all my life. It was the information having to do with the modern world-view as it has been elaborated in modern physics, specifically in quantum mechanics and relativity theory. This new area of learning proved to be as invigorating and challenging as the spiritual views of the East.

I must say that my encounter with these precepts was in many ways shattering. I could not believe, but also could not deny, that the world worked in the ways the physicists described. Every single, commonsense assumption I had made about the world was turned upside down. Although I could not readily accept these ideas, retreat from them seemed equally impossible, for this was "science" — the *best* science at that. As the Zen Buddhists put it, it was like swallowing a red-hot iron ball — too hot to swallow, too hot to regurgitate. My ego took a significant beating. For, I considered myself a reasonably well-educated person. I had been trained at the best schools, had graduated with honours and had posed the highest certifying examinations in internal medicine. Yet I was forced to admit, quite literally, that I was an ignoramus in the most basic ways imaginable.

It may be an exaggeration to say that this realisation created within me an existential crisis. But it was something close to that. My own particular approach to a resolution was to read everything I could understand about the new world-view. At first, the more I read, the more confused my world became. My experience epitomised the warning of the great physicist Niels Bohr who said that the person who first encounters modern physics and does not come away dizzy has obviously not understood the situation. Well, I was plenty dizzy.

The realisation which gradually dawned on me can simply be put thus: Every single tenet of modern medicine — the most basic assumptions we make about the body, and the meanings we attribute to the events and processes we call life and death, and health and illness — is based upon a classical, Newtonian, traditional view of reality. Yet this view of the world has been transcended in modern physics. But medicine, for at least three hundred years, has wished to be consistent with science. Oddly, however, we find that it is not the *modern* scientific view to which we adhere to today but the old. The question from which we cannot escape is this: if we enlarge our-basic concepts in medicine to incorporate the radically new features of the world which are described in *modern* physics instead of the classical

Newtonian views, what will the results be? What will our new models of medical reality look like?

It became apparent to me that we indeed do rely on a world-view in medicine at every turn. We can do nothing without invoking a view of the world. Taken a case history from a patient, performing a physical examination, giving an injection — even the simplest act — depend upon the assumptions we make about reality. Our world-view is a powerful, invisible hand that guides all that we do. We cannot escape from it. Thus, the question is never *whether* or not we shall choose to exercise a world-view but *which* world-view we will invoke.

What, then, is the view of the world which so much influences our medical thought today? In those parts of the world which are influenced by modern science, it is the Newtonian, classical view of physical reality. It can be summarised as follows:

Time is linear.
Cause and effect are fundamental.
There are certain unbridgeable categories in nature: space and time, mass and energy, matter and the void.
All matter is made up of individual and indivisible building blocks.

The influence of this classical world-view on our decision-making and on our actions in medicine can be easily illustrated. In the United States, there are persons who understand intimately how physicians think. They are called pharmaceutical drugs salesmen. They are intrepid at activating those "hidden persuaders" which influence us to prescribe the drugs made by their companies. Thus it seemed reasonable to me that if the physician's world-view is a really influential element in our thinking, this fact should surface in the advertisements used by the drug companies. To test this idea, one day in my office I picked up three prominent medical journals and flipped through them, looking at the drug advertisements. This unscientific survey revealed the prevailing classical world-view of modern medicine very forcefully.

III

But as everyone is beginning to learn, this view of the world has been transcended by a new view of reality, the one that is given by modern physics. All the facets of Newton's world which we examined above have been superseded by views which are more broadly applicable. This does not mean that the older views have been discarded for, they are still widely used, of course. But they break down when nature is studied under certain situations. For instance, where great speeds are concerned or when gigantic distances come into play, the old views of Newton no longer apply and predictions become inaccurate.

These new views reverse, as it were, the former ones. For example:

(i) At the sub-atomic level, cause and effect are not fundamental. Individual, single sub-atomic events are said to be uncaused — i.e., they occur randomly, and can only be understood when gigantic numbers of them are considered in aggregate. Statistical, probabilistic descriptions become necessary, and one cannot speak about what single, sub-atomic events are "going to do next".

(ii) The idea of an external, linear, flowing time — a time which can be divided into an absolute past, present and future that are the same for all observers — has broken down.

(iii) The unbridgeable categories in nature are no longer considered absolute. Space and time, matter and energy, and matter and the void are now seen to be interrelated.

(iv) The idea of an external reality that is completely independent of our own existence is no longer accepted. This does not mean that the physical world has suddenly vanished with the insights of modern physics, only that certain of its features are known to be influenced by our decisions and actions.

This means that the question of the relationship between mind and matter, consciousness and the material world, is once again placed on the table as a respectable issue in science. Yet, having said that, we must acknowledge that we cannot find in modern science any consensus on this matter. There are still physicists who believe that human consciousness plays no role whatsoever in the elaboration of reality and that someday the deterministic world of Newton will once again be restored when physics undergoes further clarification. On the other end of the spectrum are those who see a central role for the mind in unfolding of, what we call, physical reality. This position is perhaps most dramatically represented in the strong interpretation of the so-called anthropic principle in which the entire universe is said to owe its existence to the cumulative acts of observers. Yet even those physicists who go this far differ about what actually constitutes an observation. Is a human mind always required? Or can a machine do as well?

The extreme divisions of modern physicists on the role of the mind places medicine in a peculiar position. Which experts shall we believe? Those who say that the mind matters! Or those who say that is is inconsequential! As we have said, we have looked to physics to guide us in understanding our medical reality. But if the messages from physics are mixed, what shall we do?

I believe we should be cautious in placing too much reliance on modern physical theory as a guide in thinking about *medical* reality. The well-known physicist, John Archibald Wheeler, expressed this same attitude in speaking of religion.

> Until we know the true constitution of the world, I think we have to depend much more on what wise men of the past have told us about the subject of religion than on anything that science shows us.[5]

This point deserves to be emphasised. In medicine we have veered away from the messages of the "wise men of the past". We have believed that only modern messages — specifically those from modern science — are worth believing. Perhaps this approach is valid when we want to know something about the behaviour of light, nuclear fission, or birth of stars. But medicine concerns itself with issues which physics, as we know it, may be poorly adapted to pursue. Until recently we have assumed that matters of life, specifically mind and consciousness, could be lumped together with all the other things physicists study. This assumption lies at the heart of the philosophy of materialism and reductionism which implies that all the phenomena, which we call mind and consciousness, thought and feeling, ultimately have a material basis and can furthermore be understood by analysing the behaviour of the most elemental constituents of the world.

This idea, however, has of late come under suspicion after enjoying almost uncritical acceptance for a hundred years in medical science. One of the most eloquent criticisms ever levelled against the radical philosophy of materialism has been made by Prof. D.S. Kothari. In his Meghnad Saha Memorial Lecture entitled "Atom and Self", which was delivered on 5th October, 1979, he provided a point of view which should be studied by anyone having any pretensions whatsoever-as a scientist, a physician, or a philosopher.[6] In this landmark paper, Prof.

Kothari states that, when it comes to matters of the mind, physics may not be up to the job of providing us with a full description.

In taking this view, Prof. Kothari joins a group of illustrious physicists who have warned us against substituting physical models for spiritual wisdom. He reminds us that when we assert a primary role for matters of the mind and spirit, we are dealing not with the domain of physics, but with an area that is "beyond physics". There is no violation of physics because these concerns occupy different levels of reality, as it were. This point of view is similar to the positions taken by other eminent physicists, including Sir Arthur Eddington and Sir James Jeans, as well as a prominent contemporary Novelist in physics, Eugene Wigner, whose words I would like to quote to illustrate this point further. Wigner says:

> . . . the most important phenomena not dealt with by our physical theories are those of life and consciousness. . . . Even if the physical theories could completely describe the motions of the atoms in our bodies, they would not give a picture of the content of our consciousness, they would not tell us whether we experience pain or pleasure, whether we are thinking of prime numbers or of our grand-daughters. This fact is, in my opinion, the most obvious but also the most convincing evidence that life and consciousness are outside the area of present-day physics.[7]

Prof. Kothari has taken up this same theme which, in my view, is one of the most crucial realisations to be made at this point in the scientific study of mankind. He has stated:

> The views about the primacy or otherwise of mind, by their very nature, are not a part of physics, not within physics. These go beyond physics. To say 'beyond physics' is not to imply anti-physics, or contradiction of physics. Not at all. Anti-physics, or anti-science, should be ruthlessly denied any place whatsoever in human thought and affairs. One must remember the distinction clear in principle, even if in practice it be difficult to apply between *anti-physics, physics* and *beyond physics.*
>
> It is of the utmost importance to grasp the fundamental distinction between 'atom' and 'self', or, what comes to the same thing, between brain and mind. Atom or brain belongs to the external, objective world of space-time and matter-energy. Self or mind

> belongs to the internal subjective world. This subjective (mental) world is not describable in terms of space-time and matter energy concepts. *Self or mind, therefore, lies outside natural science.*[8]

Unfortunately, these precautions, which belong not only to the insights of some of the most perceptive scientists of our time, as well as to the highest realisations of the world's greatest spiritual traditions, have been utterly confused in the mainstream of medical science.

This confusion provides a massive entry point for violence — violence to the human spirit, to that which makes us of a different order than an atom, a rock, a lump of clay, or even a brain. This error goes by the twin names of reductionism and materialism and it can be illustrated in numerous remarks of famous contemporary scientists, such as the following comment by a famous astronomer:

> [The brain's] working — what we sometimes call mind — are a consequence of its anatomy and physiology, and nothing more.[9]

Although this belief is dominant in medical science today, the slightest reflection, I believe, reveals the difficulties of this position. First, there is the objection to this view that comes from universal experience of all human beings, including those who hold to the view of materialism. Everyone believes, whether they admit it or not, that *their* mind at least is emphatically different from the world of matter. Second, those who espouse the doctrine to materialism must admit that this very belief belongs to the mind which seems to set the mind on a more proximal and fundamental level than the matter to which it is referring. As the American philosopher and scientist Michael Polanyi pointed out, we speak of the thoughts of Shakespeare and not the thoughts of zinc and hydrochloric acid because humans think and atoms do not.

Then there is the difficulty of claiming truth for the view of materialism. As the late French micro-biologist Jacques Monod enunciated in his influential book, *Chance and Necessity*, which has become a manifesto for materialistic scientists, there are no intrinsic goals or purposes in nature.[10] Nature is all a matter of deterministic laws acting against a background of randomness. This means that questions of "truth" or "rightness" are not contained in nature and we should not speak of them. But if this is so, then there is no reason why the materialist should try to persuade us of the truth of his own view. For, he could not possibly have arrived at these conclusions as a result of reason and a careful search for the truth of the matter, for "reason" and "truth," by his [own] claim, are completely missing in nature. He can only say that the actions of his own atoms, expressed through his own chemistry, anatomy and physiology, forces him; to say what he is saying.

I must admit that for a time I believed that one *could* find in the new physics all the guidelines for a new model of medicine which spoke to new meanings of birth and death, health and illness. Although I continue to believe that these new models of reality offer us a vast new body of data on which to construct *some* aspects of medical reality, I nonetheless must acknowledge that my enthusiasm has been tempered somewhat in this regard. We must always be careful to remember that when we are comparing atoms and selves, mind and matter, the comparisons always involve *analogies* and not *homologies*. Otherwise we fall into traps from which we cannot extricate ourselves, such as basing our spiritual notions, which are eternal and beyond science, on the shifting sands so physical theory which is not constant and eternal but dynamic.

Aside from physics, there is a vast area of data that has been neglected which deals with a more immediate source of information than the atoms themselves. It is the actual *experiences* of human beings that have been overlooked, and to which we must return, if we are to build a medicine for the future which embodies non-violence. We do not need linear accelerators or cloud chambers to gather this data: It can be found at the *macroscopic* level, and it is there for anyone to see. In my opinion it resolves beyond doubt the nagging question of whether the mind is of any importance in matters of health and illness, and it provides the outlines of a medicine of the future that is potentially as non-violent as our current mechanistic approach is violent.

There are hundreds of clinical studies which provide a completely new way of looking at the role of the mind in health and illness. In the face of this kind of information, it is not possible for us to continue in the Cartesian tradition which forces a violent denial of any true influence of the mind on the body.

It is possible today to see the outlines of a new model of scientific medicine. It is important to recognise that the new model does not discard the old. It includes it, it subsumes it. The body continues to be important — the genetic influences remain, as do the situations in which the chemical and physiological forces sometimes seem to be dominant. But these are seen as special cases whose explanatory power sometimes breaks down when attempts are made to use them as broad, comprehensive principles.

The analogies to the transitions in physics which have already occurred in this century should be obvious. As we have already mentioned, the new physics of quantum mechanics and relativity did not do away with Newton's physics. Classical physics still works well for the majority of situations. One can still put man on the moon and rockets into space using Newton's concepts. But if one wants to describe the situations which obtain at conditions involving gigantic distances or very fast speeds, other models — those offered by the new physicist — become necessary.

So it is in medicine. We have discovered the special conditions where the old models no longer apply. In general, these conditions come into play any time the mind is involved. So, in order to properly describe these new conditions, a new outlook on the mind has become necessary.

What is this new outlook to be?[11] What are its features?[12]

First and foremost, it is necessary to reserve a potency for the mind. We must acknowledge — in spite of the Cartesian legacy which maintains that such a thing is impossible — that the mind, however we may wish to define it or whatever it may prove to be, can act on matter. At the very mention of this possibility we can hear a million Western philosophers turn over in their grave, for, it has been roundly denied that something immaterial could affect something material. However, many current thinkers do not agree with this. Among those I would mention in this regard is physicist Henry Margenau, Prof. Emeritus of Physics at Yale University. In his seminal book, *The Miracle of Existence*. Margenau provides a quantum-mechanical rationale for suggesting that interactions may indeed occur between the mind and the physical world which includes the body.[13]

I realise this may seem a trivial point to philosophers of the East, most of whom cannot imagine that the mind could *not* affect the state of the physical world. But in the West we have struggled with this question for millennia. It has become part of our science to say "no" to this question of interaction. Thus it is vastly important to begin to re-think on this issue, for we shall never find a way to acknowledge the clinical data which confronts us unless this sticky point is resolved.

Another characteristic of the new model in medicine must be an expanded view of the nature of the mind. If I were to attribute a single quality to the mind which is necessary to explain what it can apparently do in medical situations, it would be the work *non-local*. This is simply a way of saying that the mind is not a thing. It cannot be regarded as something that is in a place — whether a place in space or a place in *time*.

The idea prevalent in medicine today is that the mind is local. It is in a place, the brain. It is completely derived from the brain's chemistry and it will perish with the death of the brain. This idea, however, is in deep trouble even from a conservative, classical point of view. Based on the work of researchers such as Candace B. Pert, co-discoverer of the celebrated chemicals, the endorphins, and chief of brain bio-chemistry at the National Institute of Mental Health in Bethesda, Maryland,we know today that many of the brain's chemicals such as the endorphins, as well as the receptor sites for them, are found not only in the brain but in distant sites in the body as well. These receptor sites are found in locations in the gastro-intestinal tract from the esophagus to the anus, as well as on certain types of white blood cells which are distributed throughout the body.[14] They are found wherever the blood flows. These chemicals contribute to our mental life, our moods and feelings. What, then, are we to say about the location of the mind? It seems that part of our "mental equipment" is clearly outside the brain. How can we say that the mind is located in the brain? As a result of this new information, we face the possibility that the entire body is alive with thought.

But mind which is confined to the body is still a local concept because it is mind confined to a point in space and time. In order to account for what the mind can do, we must manage to free the mind from, even, the body itself.

A modern thinker who has taken this step is anthropologist and philosopher Gregory Bateson. Based on his study of the interaction of living systems, Bateson left us with this view prior to his recent death:

> The individual mind is immanent but not only in the body. It is immanent also in pathways and passages outside the body; and there is a larger Mind of which the individual mind is only a sub-system. This larger Mind is comparable to God and is perhaps what some people mean by "God," but it is still immanent in the total inter-connected social system and planetary ecology.[15]

Today we have reason in medicine to assert the importance of the view that mind is non-local — for instance, the study of cardiologist Randy Byrd at San Francisco General Hospital referred to above.[16] These results cannot be explained through a concept of a mind that is local. Only by invoking a non-local view of the mind can we come to grips with such data. So non-local mind is not a "luxury idea" which we import into medicine as a philosophical nicety. It is a necessary step in explaining actual observations at the clinical level.

To say that the mind is non-local — that it is not confined to specific points in space or time — leads to the idea that the mind is *unbounded*. And if mind is unbounded, it is not separate from other minds. Thus non-local mind cannot fundamentally be divided into 4.5 billion minds, one for each body which exists on the Earth today. Ultimately they must be united. This is the idea, of course, of the One Mind — which Prof. Kothari has called "the great *Upanishadic* formula" — "the different individual selves on the empirical plane are One and the Same on the transcendental plane: *tat tvam asi*."

One speaks of this view with hesitation, realising that most persons in science today may take this to be a bizarre, audacious claim. Yet it is not a new idea in science. In fact, some of the greatest scientists in our century have believed in this view of the mind. One of these was physicist Erwin Schroedinger, whose wave equations underline quantum mechanics. Schroedinger, who was thoroughly informed of the central thought of the *Vedanta*, expressed his view this way:

> Mind by its very nature is a *singulare tantum*. I should say, the over-all number of minds is just one.[17]

To the views of Bateson and Schroedinger on the unitary nature of the mind can be added the opinion of Kurt Godel whom many believe to be the greatest logician of this century. In a celebrated interview with Godel just before his death, physicist Rudy Rucker asked Godel if he believed there is a single mind behind all the various appearances and activities of the world. Godel replied that he did indeed hold this view. Yes, the mind did manifest individual properties, he said, but it exists independently of these properties. Rucker further asked Godel if he believed that the mind is everywhere, as opposed to being localised in the brains of people. Godel replied: "Of course, this is the basic mystical teaching."[18]

Today in medicine we struggle with conflicting data on the nature of the mind. On the one hand, there is the overwhelming evidence that the contents of awareness — our emotions, thoughts and feelings — can be affected by manipulating our chemistry, anatomy and physio-logy. In sum, these observations have led us to say that the mind is completely material and that it is local in space and time. On the other hand, we cannot reconcile this material, local view with other sorts of observations. For instance, the material, local view of the mind, is incapable of providing any explanation whatsoever of how distant healing can occur, how intercessory prayer might work, and how sudden, radical and sweeping physiological changes in the body might come about, such as those which have been verified in several dozen cases by the Council; on Miracles at Lourdes. Neither can we explain how transmission of information might occur from the future to the present, as seems to be the case in the careful studies conducted by Prof. Robert John of Princeton's Engineering Anomalies Research Laboratory.[19] This has led to a schism on the question as to how to think about the mind. Those who insist on a material, local view of the mind suggest that these kinds of happenings must be somehow misguided at best of fraudulent at worst, while others are convinced of their validity and suggest that our concepts of reality must be expanded in order to accommodate them.

Since it is increasingly impossible to deny the empirical evidence for a non-local action of the mind, I personally believe that we are being swept forward to a new view of the self. The new view is going to resemble that which has been advanced in your own culture for millennia. It will, I feel, follow "the great *Upanishadic* formula" of the One Mind, of mind that is not based on explanations involving materiality and local space and time. Instead, this view of the mind will emphasise immateriality and non-locality in space and time.

In so doing it will bring man and God closer together; for, it will acknowledge that man's mind contains attributes which have traditionally been reserved for God himself: *omnipresence, infinity* and *eternity*. After all, this is the full meaning of non-local mind, of mind that knows no bounds in either space or time. But this is simply another way of expressing what has been recognised in many spiritual traditions for thousands of years: man contains the spark of divine; in the end, *Ataman* and *Brahman* are one.

In the West, however, this idea will continue for a while to cause great consternation. We are used to viewing man as essentially and fundamentally a fallen creature with no intrinsic, redeeming qualities whatsoever. He is by his very nature a creature who is damned, and can only be saved by an act of grace. To say that man has innate qualities that are infinite and eternal is blasphemy and heresy. It is a usurpation of God by man — which it is said, is a further proof of man's arrogant, despicable nature.

However, throughout the past 2000 years in the West a few thinkers, including some of the great mystics within the Christian tradition, have gone beyond this idea and have seen the essential unity between God and man. The medieval mystics, Jacob Boehme and Meister Eckhart, are examples. Frequently, they have been put to death for these views. Yet the views have never died within the esoteric core of Christianity, and we are seeing them surface one again — oddly, in the form of scientific thought.

IV

Against the backdrop of human history, perhaps the most violent act ever committed by humankind has been the amputation of man's spirit from his definition of himself. Unfortunately, science has played a major role in this hideous action. The effect of this dissociation has been almost a complete forgetting of who we are and what our relations to others should be. These effects have been disastrous. Not realising the divine elements of our own being, we have behaved like beasts towards each other. Believing nature to be dead, we have demonstrated no reverence for the earth and have been oblivious of the effects of pollution, deforestation, and disturbing the composition of the atmosphere. As if this were not enough, we now pose the ultimate threat to all of nature, including ourselves, through a final nuclear commentary. Since the law of all of life has been declared to be the survival of the fittest, we have felt free to use any method whatsoever against the weak to advance our own causes. And since our minds have been declared to be nothing more than an epiphenomenon of the cold, neutral actions of the atoms within the brain, we have said that there is ultimately nothing fundamental about the concepts of morality, love and caring. In sum, the result of these views has been the most unspeakable violence — all because we have forgotten *who we are*.

Surely there are reasons for optimism about this abysmal state of affairs, for we are in the process of rediscovering who we are. This dismal portrait of ourselves can no longer be justified, even by a conservative reading of the data now available dealing with the nature of the interaction of mind and body. And just as the old views of our nature provided the entry point for incalculable *violence* in human affairs perhaps the new views will provide an opportunity for the flowering of a genuinely *non-violent* approach.

One of the most remarkable qualities of great Gandhi was his mixing of spirituality and politics. Today we see, or so I believe, the same movement is beginning to take place in medicine. It is now clear that medicine without spirituality cannot be medicine at all. The reason is that the body is the sounding board of the *meanings* we take from the universe. Do we believe that the world has no meaning? Or do we believe that we belong to a grand pattern, that the world does have purposes and goals which include us in an essential way? Are we nothing but the blind play of our atoms? Or are we related in some way to the Divine? We are free to call these considerations "spiritual" or "religious" if we wish, but they are also "medical", because the answers we give to them create actual changes in our bodies, which eventually remify into health or illness. There can be no defence is totally separating these two domains through the reason that one is "physical" and the other "mental" or "spiritual." For, as we are in the process of rediscovering, the spirit leaves its tracks in the flesh.

It will require great skill to apply these insights, and we desperately need a Gandhi to tell us how to do it. We must be careful not to dilute the great effectiveness of scientific medicine, which is unparalleled in any age. But we do wish to humanise it to make it less violent, and to make it a medicine which, for the first time in the age of science, is truly fit to be applied to the living.

NOTES

1. J. Silberner, "Metaphor in Immunology," *Science News*, 18 October, 1986, 130, p. 254.
2. L. Nilsson, *The Body Victorious*, New York: Delacorte Press, 1987.
3. C.B. Thomas, "Precursors of Premature Disease and Death: The Predictive Potential of Habits and Family Attitudes." *Annals of Internal Medicine*, pp. 653-58.
4. B. Bower, "Depression and Cancer: A Fatal Link", *Science News*, 17 October, 1987, 132, p. 244.
5. J.A. Wheeler, "Communication to The Isthmus Institute", Dallas, Texas, October 1987.
6. D.S. Kothari, "Atom and Self", Meghnad Saha Memorial Lecture, in *proceedings of the Indian National Science Academy*, Part A, *Physical*

Sciences, 46, 1978, pp. 1-28.

7. E. Wigner The "Extension of the Area of Science" in R. Jahn, ed., *The Role of Consciousness in the Physical World*, Boulder: Westview Press, Inc., 1981, pp. 13-14.
8. D.S. Kothari, "Atom and Self", p. 8.
9. Carl Sagan, Quoted in *Brain/Mind Bulletin* 6:5, 16 February, 1981, p. 1.
10. J. Monod, *Chance and Necessity*, New York: Random House, 1972.
11. For details on this question see L. Dossey, *Space, Time and Medicine* Boston: New Science Library, 1982.
12. See L. Dossey, *Mind Beyond Body*, 1988.
13. H. Margenau, *The Miracle of Existence*, Boston: New Science Library, 1987.
14. C.B. Pert, "The Wisdom of the Receptors: Neuropeptides, the Emotions, and Bodymind", *Advances*, 3, pp. 8-16.
15. G.B. Bateson, *Steps to an Ecology of Mind*, San Francisco, Chandler Press, 1972, p. 467.
16. Randy Byrd, in "Cardiologist Studies Effect of Prayer on Patients", *Brain/Mind Bulletin*, p. 1.
17. E. Schroedinger, *What is Life*? and *Mind and Matter*, London: Cambridge University Press, 1959, p. 145.
18. R. Rucker, *Infinity and the Mind*, New York: Bantam, 1983, pp. 177-83.
19. R. Jahn and B. Dunne, *Margins of Reality*, New York: Harcourt Brace Jovanovich, 1987.

4

SCIENTIFIC TEMPER AND SPIRITUAL VALUES: Quest for Spirit in the Material World

A.R. RATTAN and A.S. SANDHU

THE TERMS 'scientific temper' and 'spiritual values' are of recent origin, though these terms when studied in parts are quite old. The *Oxford Dictionary of English* explains 'scientific' as 'having scientific knowledge or given to scientific study of something'. Whereas it defines science as a branch of study which is either with a connected body of demonstrated truths or with observed facts systematically classified and more or less colligated by being brought under general laws, and which includes trustworthy methods for the discovery of new truth within its own domain. The second part of the term 'temper' is described as mental balance or composure especially under provocation of any kind; moderation in or command over emotions especially anger, calmness, equanimity or actual state of mind or feelings or to bring into a suitable or desirable frame of mind. So the term 'scientific temper' stands for the objective approach or the rational attitude or frame of mind or a wider outlook in a situation where provocation of any kind could cause a bias in the process of comprehension or analysis in a given situation.

Similarly the term 'spiritual values' has been defined. The *Oxford Dictionary of English* explains 'spiritual' as: of or pertaining to, affecting or concerning the spirit or higher moral qualities especially as regarded in a religious aspect. Further, it says 'of or pertaining to' consisting of spirit regarded in either a religious or intellectual aspect, of the nature of a spirit of incorporeal. Where as 'value' has been defined as moral principles or standards.

These terms have been defined variedly. According to *Encyclopaedia of Social Sciences* "Science may be defined as a far flung system of knowledge couched in terms which allow it to serve as a theoretical basis for a practical technique."[1] Further it says that science is not limited to the theory required by man's immediate practical interests or even his immediate practical perspective, first, because all theoretical research, as the very condition of its utility for practice, must transcend the immediate practical perspective.[2] In the *Encyclopaedia of Religion and Ethics* the term 'scientific temper' has been termed as scientific mood. The scientific study of a subject implies a certain intellectual attitude or mood, which need not, however, be regarded as the only way of approaching a subject. Thus the aesthetic or artistic approach and the purely practical approach are not less legitimate than that of the scientific investigator or of anyone desirous of having a scientific knowledge of a subject may be described as a passion for facts (which implies a high standard of accuracy and a detachment from personal wishes); a cautious thoroughness in coming to a conclusion (which implies personal scepticism and self-elimination in judgment and a quality of clearness which implies a dislike of obscurities, ambiguities and loose ends.[3] So, a person with a scientific mood is truthful, courageous and alert. The scientific mood does not imply expert knowledge of any particular science. According to Karl Pearson: "The scientific man has, above all things, to strive at self-eleimination in his judgement, to provide an argument which is as true for each individual mind as his own. The classification of facts, the recognition of their sequence and relative significance are the functions of science, and the habit of forming a judgment upon these facts unbiased by personal feeling is the characteristic of what maybe termed the scientific frame of mind".[4]

The spiritualism or spiritual have been defined, in Philosophy, as the opposite of materialism, i.e., the doctrine that reality is ultimately spiritual in its nature. Cartesianism defines spiritualism as compatible with a dualism which accepts the reality of material substance. Spiritualism has been popularly termed as spiritism where it is not easy to distinguish spiritualism from idealism. Generally these notions are used interchangeably. It may be said, however, more strictly that whereas idealism renders all reality relative to and dependent upon mind, spiritualism regards it as consisting of 'spirits', which are not wholly or chiefly mind's, and so does not make the cognitive process essential to reality. It will follow from this distinction that the same philosophy may be both spiritualistic and idealistic. Berkeley's doctrine, e.g. is idealism in that it denies the reality of materials sub-stance and conceives physical reality as existing only for minds and having for its *esse percipi*; but it is spiritualism in that it composes ultimate reality of spirits, whose *esse* is *percipere*.[5] In fact, the term 'spiritual' is rather ambiguous and may be understood in two ways. It may first be regarded as equivalent to 'mental' in which case the result is Berkeleian idealism. But this equation of spiritual with mental does not seem to be appropriate. In the second sense spiritual is something over and above mental, whereas 'mind' is usually looked upon as a combined whole of cognition, covation and affection, spirit is generally taken to be beyond mental — something objective and impersonal.

A value may be tentatively defined as a conception characteristic of a group which is desirable and which influences a selection from among the available modes and means to satisfy the needs. While values are concepts, they also constitute the basis of action. Value is one of the last or the great philosophic topics to have received recognition, and even now the *Encyclopaedia Britannica* has an article only on economic value. Still it is a growing subject the study of which started only in 19th century. At present the reflection starts from antithesis of 'fact' and 'value' and the difference between the standpoints of 'description' and 'appreciation'. It is widely held that consciousness of value differs in kind from consciousness of fact. It is posterior to the later and represents a reaction upon fact. It is an attitude assumed towards fact, a weighing of fact in relation to an agent, his feelings, his desires, interests, purposes, needs and acts; and it expresses his appreciation (approbation) or reprobation (depreciation) of it in this relation. It follows:

(1) that a certain subjectivity, or, better, a relation to personality is inherent in all values;
(2) that values arise out of the mind's practical attitude when it reacts upon stimulation, and that for a purely theoretic or contemplative view no values would exist; and
(3) that values are something super-added upon the other qualities of objects by the mind, in order to express their relation to its purpose and facts and do not inhere in objects *per se*.

Indeed they may seem to be even more subjective, variable and personal than 'secondary' qualities of objects and hence are often called 'tertiary' qualities. Nevertheless, they are also objectified and projected into objects, when these are regarded as valuable objectivity and *per se*, or when the 'validity' of actual valuations and of existing values is called in question. Hence, 'super-personal' or over-individual and even 'eternal' and 'absolute' values are recognised by many philosophers.[6]

The provisional definition of value as essentially a personal attitude, as a recognition of the supremacy of the category of personality, has maintained itself and proved active to the labyrinth of values. It also renders somewhat nugatory the psychological debates of the Schools of Meinong and Von Enrenfels as to whether values are rooted in feeling, will or desire. For a personal attitude is a concern of the whole man and not of psychological abstractions. If, however, it is thought necessary to pick one among such psychological phrases it is probably best to say that value is a personal attitude of welcome or the reverse, towards an object of interest.[7]

The terms 'scientific temper' and 'spiritual' values can be explained so that scientific temper is a particular bent of mind given to objective study for learning the existing facts or for discovery of new truth. It is not necessarily science but impersonal and appropriate outlook pertaining to the understanding of our surroundings. Whereas 'spiritual values' can be taken as values that have spiritual connotation but the 'spiritual' is not related to supernatural spirit, but something not related to material or personal selfish interests. It is in fact the attitude to judge actions with rationality, so it can help in the eradication of evils persisting in society. This pertains to the higher moral values where society is above the self. The spiritual values can be termed as the science of cognitive values and the realisation that 'truth' is positive value and 'error' the negative one. Logic is applied to study the values, logic, ethic and aesthetics by few philosophers and their studies accept the analogy between these terms and is proved by the conformity of logic with the criteria generally used to distinguish values. The 'spirit' in ancient Indian Literature was the knowledge for the attainment of which emphasis was laid on knowledge. The spirit along is considered the everlasting reality and the infinite mystery of the material world can never be explained merely in material terms. The inquisitive minds encouraged the attainment of knowledge — the knowledge of the everlasting reality. The *Vedas* — as we know them

— originated from *Vid*, to know, and were simply meant to be a collection of the existing knowledge of the day. Moreover the *Rig Veda* was dedicated to the seers, our ancestors, the first Path-finders. It tells how the desire for knowledge crept in the minds — as translated and titled by Max Muller:
'To the Unknown God'!

3. . . .Darkness there was: at first concealed in darkness, this all was indiscriminated chaos. All that existed then was void and formless; by the great power of warmth was born that unit.
4. Thereafter rose desire in the beginning, desire the primal seed and germ of spirit. Sages who searched with their hearts' thought discovered the existent's kinship in the non-existent.[8] So did the *Upanishads* express the desire,

> "From the unreal lead me to the Real;
> From darkness lead me to Light;
> From death lead me to Immortality".

This light is knowledge, the knowledge of the supreme. The supreme is said to be truth, knowledge and eternity, *satyam, jnanam, anantam, Brahma*. The *Brahma* connotes both the truth which is sought and the spirit in us which seeks it. Since god is Truth *satra swarup* the quest of truth is the quest of God or Spirit. Few principles were laid down as the tools of this quest. In Indian philosophy '*Dharma*' was the accepted mode of life, in other words ethical living. If the human action is unrestrained their full values cannot be realised. So as to guide or restraint was *dharma* established. It gives coherence and direction to the different activities of life. It is not a religious creed or cult imposing an ethical or social rule. It is the complete rule of life, the harmony of the whole man who finds a right and just law of his living. This *dharma* was later termed as religion. It must establish itself as a rational way of living. If ever the spirit is to be at home in this world and not merely as a prisoner or a fugitive, secular foundations must be laid deep and preserved worthily. Religion must express itself in a reasonable thought, fruitful action and right social institutions. The aim of religion is to attain a knowledge or a vision of God and the aim of ethics is to re-make human life into the mould of the unseen. . . . It express itself in a burning passion for righteousness and purity. The sense of the spiritual and the longing for righteousness go together.

Righteousness, duty and virtue go together in Hindu attitude of life. The religions, in all the ages and in all parts of the world, though worship God in different forms and names but the essence of all religions is the same. All the religions preach the feeling of equality, liberty and mercy, and forbid lust, exploitation and accumulation of wealth. Thus, the spiritual or religions are not different from ethics. The different virtues of fortitude, justice, love, compassion, self-control are not separate qualities but are the different facets of the personality. Inward awareness, *Satya*, and the life of compassion, *ahimsa*, are the two principal sides of a spiritual life. Christianity preaches four cardinal principles — mercy, pity, peace and love; similarly the *Quran* says: "If you forgive and practise forbearance and pardon, verily *Allah* is also forgiving and merciful." Even the Hindu view of life which sets forth a frame-work to guide the growth of the individual giving four aims of life — *Moksha* (spiritual), *Dharma* (ethical), *Artha* (economic) and *Kama* (emotional) — through four *Ashramas* (stages) of life —*Brahmacharya* (Student), *Grihastha* (householder), *Vanaprastha* (the forest recluse) and *Sanyas* (free super social).

Each person is unique and his way to fulfilment is also unique. It is also true that there is so much common among human beings that we can distinguish certain broad ways to man's realisation — the *karma-marga* (the way of work), *bhakti-marga* (the way of devotion), the *dhyana marga* (the way of meditation) — all these lead to *jnana* (wisdom or enlightenment).[10] Knowledge of reality is to be won by spiritual effort. One cannot think of one's way into reality but only live into it.[11]

Sankara says that one should undertake inquiry into *Brahma* only after he acquires self-control detachment, etc., what he calls *Viveka, Vairagya, Sat-sampatti* and *Mumuksutva*. Moral life is an essential condition for pursuit of wisdom.[12]

The two principles which must govern all group life are the free and unfettered development of the individual and the healthy growth of society. The individual and the society are interdependent. The sound development of the individual is the best condition for the growth of the society and a healthy society is the best condition for the growth of the individual. A dry spirit of detachment and disconnection from immediate surroundings are essential qualities for those engaged in the pursuit of truth. An invincible patience, a content of all little and feeble enjoyments, humility without any baseness on infinite hope and high fearlessness are the qualities that mark the seeker of truth.[13] So this detached, objective method of realising the truth by removing ignorance is free from all sorts of dogma. A spiritual man need not necessarily be a follower of any particular region. Swami Ranganathananda has expounded a similar view:

> "The only way man can deny this truth, says *Vedanta*, is by neglecting it, through spiritual blindness and submersion in his physical organism and its appetites."[14]

A similar opinion was expressed by Swami Vivekananda.[15] It was the parochialisation of the sum total of knowledge of mankind that we can call spirit the ones the other generations could not understand and make it agoraphobically segmented into religious castes, breeds, etc.

The term 'scientific temper', which we have seen, is quite near the spiritual attitude towards life. The *Bhagwad Gita* emphasises the self-less action without the hope for fruit.

(कर्मण्ये वा धिकारस्ते मा फलेषु कदाचन्).[16]

The same volume defines that the worst man on earth is a hypocrite — one who says something else and does something else. As with the passage of time these scriptures became just holy books and numerous dogmas were attached to them, the curiosity to know weakened, similarly did weaken the ethical values as we were ridden in castes, colours and creeds, and desires to have more and more. Though ignorance of the masses is being eradicated with the advance and progress of the country but still the need for spiritual values is being realised because ethical values have gone down, which could be proper guide. It could help to realise and inculcate something which is deep and permanent.

The true scientist is the sage unattached to life and the fruits of action, ever-seeking truth wheresoever this quest might lead him. To tie himself to a fixed anchorage, from which there is no moving, is to give up search and to become static in dynamic world. Science is evolutionary, several existing theories are improved and new ones are formed the great attribute of science is truth by consensus. Science does not believe in revelation. But biologists no longer need thoughts to be explained as processes of science which can explain all of human values but it does not imply to spiritual values. Recently even the scientists have started realising the fact that there is something beyond this physical world. Sir Arthur Eddington expressed the same idea:

> "Physical science has limited its scope so as to leave a background which we are at liberty to, or even invited to, fill with a reality of spiritual import."[17]

So did echo Emerson and Dr. J.C. Bose. Emerson:

> "All science is transcendental or else passes away — Botany is now acquiring the right theory — the *avatars* of *Brahma* will presently be the text-books of natural history."[18]

Similarly said Dr. J.C. Bose:

> "In the pursuit of my investigations I was unconsciously led into border region of physics and physiology. To my amazement, I found boundary line vanishing, and points of contact emerging between the realms of the living and the non-living. . . . By a continuous living tradition and a vital power of rejuvenescence, this land has re-adjusted itself through unnumbered transformations. Indians have always arisen who, discarding the immediate and the absorbing prise of the hour, have sought for the realisation of the highest ideals of life — not through passive renunciation but through active struggle."[19]

Even in ancient works it is explained that we come into existence because of certain biological implications. Biologist was predicting destiny. References to caste and social values is found in '*Gita*'. Only such a culture could produce a man like Gandhi, who thought about various social problems and tried to solve them through methodology rooted in Indian culture, though many people say that the scriptures, like *Gita*, contain many things which are absolete but still Dr. Srikumar, a neurologist, opines that it is possible that the vibrations of the chanting of hymns could have a good impact on mind. Pseudo-sciences accept that vibrations do make an impression on mind. Brain is a good computer with built-in feed-back system. To explain a phenomenon by studying human behaviour can be possible. Group behaviour may be one of the various manifestations. The proper understanding of human behaviour has been a limitation of science, e.g., intuition is a part of spirit, but science could not explain it. Though now it is being accepted that it is the product of a very clever brain. Scientific temper has nothing to do with science. Even scientists behave in unscientific manner. Scientific temper comes more from philosophical background and is nothing else but rationality. All the great saints and philosophers have despised the cruelty shown to the weak, animals and also to subordinate position of women.

Spiritual values consist of several words which can never be explained in words such as, ecstasy, consonance and dissonance, etc. Scientifically these terms can never be defined. Reconciliation between scientific temper and spiritual values is possible because both are the means to realise the spirit, the truth or the knowledge. These can be applied for the betterment of society. As Pt. Nehru had advised,

> "Science has brought about all these mighty changes and not all of them have been for the good of the humanity. But the most vital and hopeful of the changes that it has brought about has been the development of the scientific outlook in man. It is true that even today vast numbers of people still live mentally in pre-scientific age, and that most of us, even when we talk glibly of science, betray it is our thought and actions. Even scientists, learned in their particular subjects, often forget to apply the scientific method outside that charmed sphere. And yet it is the scientific method alone that offers hope to mankind and an ending of the agony of the world."[20]

As he was led into science through economics and politics, he approached all the problems and the life itself scientifically. He believed: "It is science alone that could solve all these problems of hunger and poverty, of insanitation and illiteracy, of superstition and deadening custom and tradition, of vast resources running to waste of a rich country inhabited by starving people."[21] The need of the hour is the realisation of our problems of hunger, poverty and conflicts. To these when we apply the spiritual values and the scientific temper, we can eradicate many of them.

The term, scientific temper, was first coined by Swami Vivekananda who was the pioneer of the Rationalist Movement in modern Indian Philosophy. He once said:

> "I believe in reason, having seen enough of the evils of authority, for I was born in a country where people have gone to extreme in trusting authority."[22]

He mastered all the forms of *Yogas* but he accepted *Jnana Yoga* or *Yoga* through knowledge as the highest one and as a science. He was against dogmatic religion and preferred humanity to be atheistic to blind followers, because, according to him, the "glory of man is that he is a thinking being."[23] The presence of brain system distinguishes man from every other species.[24] What he stressed upon was the need for rational approach. Even Sri Aurobindo believes that knowledge is truth-seeking. According to him, the complete spiritual consciousness not only seeks the Divine but also takes all life and all world activities into the general scope. The spiritualist believes that whatever we see, including social and political institutions, are all works of the Spirit and are realising a definite purpose.[25] Even he believes that materials and spiritual cannot be separated.

Jawaharlal Nehru adopted the expression coined by Vivekananda. He, being a questing mind and having a longing for harmonious world, applied science and scientific temper to study the problems and life itself. He believed that religion must put on the garb of science and approach all its problems in the spirit of science. While supporting secular philosophy he did not favour it having merely material well being as objective and insisted on spiritual values and certain standards of behaviour.[26] Though he did not uphold any particular form of religion, yet he was a deeply spiritual man and delighted in calling himself a pagan. This means that he was opposed to the formal, dogmatic and sectarian aspects of religion. He looked upon science as a means of liberation of man. Science and the understanding it brings are the enemies of prejudice and of inert traditional ideas. Science and technology help to establish a free society based on economic justice and opportunities for all, a society which aims at the cultivation of spiritual values, of the spirit of service, of unselfishness.[27]

Even Gandhi, who is considered to a spiritualistic political leader, had a scientific temper. In him we find both the attitudes — scientific temper and spiritual values — go together. This philosophy of Ends and Means, Truth and *Ahimsa* and his ideal of *Swaraj* leading to the perfection of man and the realisation of the Supreme, the Spirit, the *Moksha* or Truth. Gandhi's philosophy of Ends and Means has a direct relation with his doctrine of Truth and *Ahimsa*. Truth is the ideal of life, it is the goal towards which we must strive. But the way to approach truth is *Ahimsa*. Therefore, for Gandhi, Truth is the end and *Ahimsa* is the means. Truth is God for him. He prefers truth-fearing man to God-fearing. He identified Truth with reality. He accepted that every individual is a mixture of the bodily and the spiritual. He also believes that initially the bodily and the physical aspects were more predominant and that the spiritual went on becoming more and more prominent as the evolutionary process progressed. Evolution, according to him, is a change from the physical to the spiritual. The element of divinity is present in every man and is expressed through reason, conscience and free will. He asserts that if these elements are used in the right manner, man can bring heaven on this earth. And he asked men to follow ethical rules and have moral values. The requirements of a *satyagrahi*, which he expected each one of them to have were — honesty, sincerity of purpose, open-mindedness, discipline, truthfulness, loving but firm, fearless virtuous, selfless and simple in living. This philosophy of *Ahimsa* pre-supposes that a non-violent act is free from hatred, anger, malice and the like. *Ahimsa* for him is not merely refraining from causing injuries to the creature, it stands for certain positive attitudes towards other living beings that one must cultivate *Ahimsa* is nothing but love. Love is a kind of feeling oneness. Love is such a feeling, an energy, that cleanses one's inner life and uplifts him. Such a feeling can help in solving the problems of the day. He calls himself a 'Practical Idealist'. He is practical because he is 'normative' in his analysis of social and political problems.

So we can hope that reconciliation between scientific temper and spiritual values is possible. All efforts must be for spirit, scientific temper, ethics and humanistic values We, human beings, have always been and will always be both spectators and actors in the great drama of life. Science is very close to *Vedanta*. As Swami Vivekananda preached reverence for all the paths — for path of love, the path of *Karma* and even others. He, while advocating the reason, points out that religions, if they are worthy of mention, must stand the test of the science. As the basis of both science and religion is knowledge or reason : there is no essential difference in them except in their application. He regarded modern science as a manifestation of the real religious spirit, for it sought to understand Truth by sincere effort. On the other hand, Einstein wrote:

> "In the materialistic age of our, the serious scientific workers are the only profound religious people. The fate of the human race was more than ever dependent on its moral strength today. The way to a joyful and happy state is through renunciation and self-limitation everywhere."

NOTES

1. *The Encyclopaedia of Social Sciences* New York: The Macmillan Company Ltd., 1957, Vol. 13, p. 591.
2. *Ibid.* p. 592.
3. *Encyclopaedia of Religion and Ethics* Edinberg T & T Clark, Vol. 11, 1958, p. 253.
4. Karl Pearson *The Grammar of Science*, London, 1911, p. 6.
5. *The Encyclopaedia of Religion and Ethics*, Vol. 11, 1958, p. 808.
6. *Ibid.* 12, p. 584.
7. *Ibid.* 12, p. 589.
8. Jawaharlal Nehru *The Discovery of India*. Bombay: Asia Publishing House, 1960, p. 68.
9. N.A. Palkhivala *India's Priceless Heritage*. Bombay: Bhartiya Vidya Bhavan, 1980, p. 6.
10. S. Radhakrishnan *The Hindu View: Dharma & Yoga*, New York: Macmillan Company, 1962.
11. S. Radhakrishnan *The Idealist View of Life*, London: George Allen & Unwin, 1962.
12. S. Radhakrishnan *The Hindu View*, New York: Macmillan Company, 1962, p. 128.
13. Robert A. McDermott (Ed.) *Basic Writings of S. Radhakrishnan*, Bombay, 1970,
14. N.A. Palkhivala. *Op. Cit.*, p. 37.
15. Swami Vivekananda. *Complete Works*, Vol. II, Calcutta: Advaita Ashrama, p. 297.
16. *The Bhagvad Gita*. Chap. II, Shloka 47.
17. Quoted in N.A. Palkhivala. *op. cit.*, p. 6.
18. *Ibid.*, p. 9.
19. *Ibid.*, pp. 8-9.
20. J.L. Nehru *Selected Works*, Vol. 8. 1938, p. 809. Allahabad, Address at the National Academy of Sciences.
21. J.L. Nehru *Selected Works*, Vol. 8, 1937, p. 807. N. Delhi: Orient Longman. Allahabad: An Address to Indian Science Congress, Calcutta.
22. Swami Vivekananda. *A Lecture of Practical Vedanta*, Vol. II.
23. Swami Vivekananda. *Complete Works*, Vol. VI, p. 37.
24. B.K. Lal *Contemporary Indian Philosophy*, Delhi: Motilal Benarsi Dass, 1978, p. 21.
25. D.P. Chattopadhyay *History, Society and Polity - An Integral Sociology of Sri Aurobindo*, New Delhi: The Macmillan Company of India Ltd., 1976, p. 61.
26. Jawaharlal Nehru *Selected Works*, 8, 1938, pp. 809-10.
27. Jawaharlal Nehru. *The Discovery of India*, p. 574.

5

ROOTS OF CONFLICT

FR. T.K. JOHN

SYSTEMATIC TREATMENT of *conflicts* in the society is a modern phenomenon insofar as the tools and categories of the human sciences are being pressed into service in an organised way. Scientific analysis of conflict has become a major feature of contemporary society. Such efforts acquired greater urgency as well as validity after Marx began to interpret conflicts in the modern industrial society on the basis of his economic interpretation of the very historical process itself.

In the following pages an effort is being made to focus upon *contemporary Indian scene*. Therefore, it has a very limited scope and objective. In an unprecedented way India witnessed conflicts and tensions, with great strains upon the social processes and at great cost to the much cherished traditions, beliefs and practices of the society. Some of these conflicts may be referred to so that the reflections below may be properly located:

The first major conflict was with the colonisers of the country. Indian awakening led to systematic articulation of the demands of the people of the country, from the colonial masters, to hand over the freedom and sovereignty of the nation captured by employing dubious methods. Gandhi organised this movement for the restoration of freedom, and the prolonged struggle was characterised by conflicts and tensions. Application of non-violent method by Gandhi won for India freedom.

The second major concern of the country was the recurrent communal tensions. The year preceding Indian independence was marked by conflicts that has communal features. This eventually led to violent eruptions, bloodshed and loss of life and property. The partition of the country did not result in a cessation of the conflict, now called *communalism.*

A third major area of conflict is centred on land. Awakening among the millions of landless agricultural workers and resistance to it by the rich landowners is resulting in violent clashes. The conflict here has economic interests as the cause. Rural unrest in most cases is explained in terms of the growing disparity at all levels, especially between the landless peasantry and the landed rich gentry.

Industrial unrest and labour problems, with accompanying strikes, *dharnas*, lock-outs, often lead to violent conflicts. Here too it is the economic issue that dominates the scene.

Besides, conflicts between ethnic groups with clash of ethnic interests also have been occurring in recent times in the country. Conflicts between adherents of political parties, which sometimes lead to widespread violence, have in some cases affected the very democratic process in the country. These too have caused much concern and anxiety to the collective consciousness of the people.

Factors Responsible for Conflicts

Without claiming any effort at systematic analysis the following factors are recalled as contributing to the origin of conflicts in our Indian society:

1. Absent in most conflict-scenes is the culture of communication. Grievances are seen to be accumulating and one notices a lamentable absence of either a forum at which the conflicting groups could assemble for open exchange in order to acquire some degree of clarity of perceptions. The aggrieved party is often as uncompromising as the party responsible for the oppression. Open discussion, frank exchange, an ability to listen with an open and sympathetic disposition is found to be absent in such situations.
2. A necessary ingredient of a culture of communication is consultation and participation in the decision-making process of a particular group or community. This flows from the very corporate character of the society. Decisions arrived at in the mind of one or few individuals, imposed upon the majority without their involvement in the deliberations that normally precede the decisions, are resented as enslaving impositions

upon the majority.

3. Such deficiencies noticeable in the mental framework operating in conflict situations can be traced to a philosophy of the human person, or better still an absence of a proper philosophy of the human person. Concretely it implies that there is an inability to recognise *the other* as *the other*. A sound humanism will impel each and every one to consider the other at least as an equal, if not even as better than or superior to oneself. On the contrary, close analysis of conflict will reveal that a total negation or rejection of the needs, the just demands and rights of the affected party is responsible for such situations. And, denial of the just rights of the other amounts to a negation of the other as the other. This implies that an exaggerated concept of one-self is operative in such mental framework.

4. One can go still further. Basic to most conflicts is the value system that constitutes and supports a non-egalitarian social structure. Inequality in the society thrives when the individual in the society regards herself/himself as superior to all others. Naturally, this cannot but promote individualism that under-cuts all social and economic relations and transactions. Tensions and conflicts are unavoidable. A high percentage of the conflicts and violence reported in recent times ascribed by sociologists to the steady awakening that is taking place among the so-called 'Harijans' who for centuries were regarded by the upper caste as inferior to them. Suppression of their voices and demands, rejection of their legitimate rights, at least as human persons, are now being questioned and resented. This is accountable for most conflicts in rural areas.

5. Caste system has further aggravated the tension and conflict in the society. Several States in recent times witnessed agitations organised by the upper caste group in the society. This group is consistently demanding the revocation of the privileges or opportunities that were provided by Constitution in order to enable them to regain all surrendered rights and privileges from time immemorial. It was taken for granted that a continuation of the *status quo* enjoyed by the upper caste is their right, and the Harijans should acquiesce and remain where they had been for centuries.

   When these conflicts turned violent legal measures were contemplated and adhered to and not dialogue and communication between the partners. Gandhi would always negotiate with the opponent with the conviction that even the worst enemy has some truth to which the other party has to listen to.

6. Many of the factors referred to above are in a complex way present and operative in most industrial and labour disputes. Unresolved and unjust wage system, unscrupulous exploitation of the weakness and powerlessness of the working class, and a political situation that feeds on such situations do not help resolve the conflict that exists because of these factors. No wonder that violence and bloodshed not to speak of serious breakdown of the peace and order in the society, characterise such disputes and agitations.

Conflict Resolution through Non-violence

From the above considerations it is clear that some very important assumptions or principles have to be honoured if the resolution of conflicts are to take place. And, Gandhi operated on these principles and offers us the way to peace. Wisdom born out of experience has its own credentials. Some of these may be listed below:

Recognition of the Basic Equality of All

Gandhian non-violence is based on his own conviction that all are equal before God. He believed in the basic spiritual solidarity of all on which is based on equality that every individual enjoys and is endowed with. He says:

> "To see the universal and all-pervading Spirits of Truth face to face one must be able to love the meanest of creation as oneself."[1]

Faith in the Goodness of the Other

Faith and trust are among the basic foundations of any healthy society. Social, economic, political and other transactions are conducted on the basis of the trust in others, faith in the goodwill of the other. Industrial and trade goods are dispatched or received on the basis of faith and trust. Social relationships are founded on the trust one has in the other.

In conflict situations it is quite natural that the opponent is regarded as the very embodiment of all evils. There is outright condemnation of all his doings. Even the good qualities are deliberately ignored, concealed or minimised, in order to plead before the public eye for the restoration of violated rights or wounded justice.

However, Gandhi would question this. He would invite his friends to listen to the other side as well. It was his contention that even the oppressor will have grains of truth in him and that could eventually liberate the oppressor from the chains with which he is bound. He had firm belief in the ultimate triumph of truth. One who has faith in the power of truth will have the patience to wait for its full manifestation. By such waiting upon truth, the truth, that is, in the opponent will gather a force and dimension that will eventually lead to amicable solution to the problem that might be vexing the minds and hearts of the victim. Firm belief in the good of the other, even if he/she has offended you, will tide over the tense situation and invite all concerned to adhere to peaceful ways for the resolution of the conflict.

Love for the Oppressor

This is an almost impossible demand. Hostility and antagonism towards the oppressor is our ordinary experience. To minimise the goodness and to exaggerate the weakness of the opponent are normal in most human experiences.

It is to the credit of greatness of Gandhi that he would demand not only not yielding to such propensities natural to the human person, but even loving the opponent in spite of the injustice he has caused. He would demand that utmost consideration and courtesy shown to the opponent is the best human approach to minimise conflict and to promote conditions that will eventually lead to resolution of the conflict. Says Gandhi:

> "If the friend for whom I fast has no love on him, he will not respond. If he has it and responds, it is all to the good. This is how I analyze his act He valued his love for me more than his bad ways."[2]

According to Gandhi this is not only applicable to the human kind but is operational even in nature. To live by mutual attraction and be knit together is the very pattern of nature. Says Gandhi:

"Though there is revulsion enough in nature, she lives by attraction. Mutual love enables Nature to persist."[3]

Role of the Universities

In considering the role of the universities one is entering into a major concern of the contemporary Indian situation. This consideration could be initiated by raising questions that will enable us to achieve some degree of clarification.

What does a university stand for? What is the concept of education that is operational in the programming of the pattern of education in the university? Will the present unfortunate thrust of education that is subordinated to the demands of technocracy be able to recover its identity and create a humanism that will contribute to the growth of the human person rather than the promotion of technocracy with all its enslaving consequences? Will the university become once again the kindergarten for the birth, growth and dissemination of genuine, authentic esteem and appreciation of the human values against the over-emphasised pricing of the products of human labour? As long as these basic values are not consciously affirmed and articulated by frequent exchanges, universities will not be able to contribute substantially to promotion of an integral humanism that will help resolve conflicts as and when these occur.

Two vital considerations urge us to act consistently. First is our past response to a significant recommendation by the well-known Kothari Commission. Taking into account the composite culture of the country and the role of religions in making such a culture, the recommendation aimed at a realistic approach to the problem of communal tension that frequented the religious encounters in certain parts of the country. It was suggested that people of different religious persuasions be brought in closer contact and familiarity with the creeds and tenets of others through study of different faiths. The purpose of such a step is to, first of all, dispel the thick layer of prejudices and ignorance that prevent a true appreciation not only of the faith of the other but even the freedom to have it. This further leads to more integral relationship between members of different communities. This is something that still remains unattended to.

The second is based on the cardinal principle in education, that values are assimilated not by transmission of concepts but by interaction, to propose that inter-religious or inter-cultural praxis be promoted. Only by entering into the home and hearth of the other do we come to know fully the fullness of the other person. Only by actual exchange, contact and familiarity with the religious tenets, economic situation and other facets, will one come to know the other person's values and beliefs adequately. What need is that programmes in the universities are so organised that such interaction through actual live experience be arranged on a regular basis. This could lead to a more healthy atmosphere in which the sources of tension, misunderstanding and the resulting conflicts can be nipped before hand. Such anticipatory steps appear more worthy of our consideration than the fire-fighting pattern of responding to burning issues by means of legislation or police action or short-lived peace marches and such other steps.

Gandhi had an integral vision. Therefore, his idea of non-violence is an outcome of that vision. It can be explained as: the goal of all human quests was pin-pointed as the realisation of the Absolute. The Supreme underpins and envelopes all creation, including the humankind, giving it thus a basic unity and solidarity that is spiritual. All empirical pursuits, experiences and values have a relative hierarchical positioning in the light of the supremacy of the spirit. All knowledge derives its foundation and validity only when this is recognised. With the recognition of these basic values and insights, education, now dominated by an altogether different vision and value system, should be re-organised. The human person and her/his worth, values and concerns then acquire a more honourable position over the present concerns or the regard for human products (technocracy). This will overflow into a healthier social relationship.

Such a vision first of all prevents the accumulation of feelings born out of denied justice and rights deprived. Secondly, even if these outstrip human efforts, application of the principle of non-violence becomes possible. Opportunities are created for facilitating dialogical relationships and communication through which the articulation of the grievances on the part of the aggrieved party and the sympathetic perception of these by the opponent is made possible. This pre-supposes, a trust in the goodness and truthfulness of the human persons.

Close observation of the happenings in the many universities shows that teachers' strike, students' strike, strike by the *karmacharis*, agitations over other internal matters from the list of 'concerns'. Rarely do we her of concerns expressed over violation of human rights, callousness of the nation over the sub-human existence of millions, regression into anti-human practices in the name of religion and for seeking favours from deities, disasters created by the State or society and other grave issues that affect the whole society.

NOTES

1. M.K. Gandhi, *Gita the Mother*, Ahmedabad: Navajivan, p. 156.
2. V.B. Kher, *In Search of the Supreme*, Vol. I, Ahmedabad: Navajivan Trust, p. 324.
3. M.K. Gandhi, *Young India*, 2 March, 1922.

6

WAR AND PEACE AS THE PLAY OF DHARMA: Some Reflections on a Gandhian Paradigm

K. RAGHAVENDRA RAO

THE CENTRAL argument of this article will be that Gandhiji can be studied to extract a specifically Indian theory of war and peace, since it assumes that Gandhiji's thought and theory represented a continuous attempt, in fact, a life-long mission, no less, to apply what he identified as the Indian tradition or civilisation to problems that beset individuals and groups of varying sises and complexity. Of course, this is not to suggest that there was any conscious or deliberate exercise of the kind on his part. Yet, the assumption made seems to give us at least one key to understanding the Gandhian problematic. No doubt Gandhiji did not elaborate in one single text or with any connected texts such a theory, suggesting some definition of war and peace, some analysis of the causality underpinning these phenomena and some prescriptive statements about how to eliminate or minimise the incidence of peace. Indeed, it coule even be argued that Gandhiji articulated an overall theoretical framework in which all human life and thought took the form of a war which had to be fought to attain peace, a peace which did not so much as cancel war as transform it Every Gandhian scholar and student knows that Gandhi's writings present a formidable volume, and that it is not only easy to get lost in it but also to dive back from its depths with not one but several pearls of wisdom pertaining to the same problem. Yet it might be claimed that Gandhiji's *Hind Swaraj*, in spite of its having been over-exploited as a source of Gandhian ideas, would still be a good starting point for building a problematic, tentative but richly suggestive Gandhian theory.

Indian Articulation

The phenomenon of war and its negation, peace, can be, in principle, examined from several perspectives. One could locate them on a wide and sweeping canvas of metaphysics and epistemology. One can merely employ a psychological perspective, invoking some version of human nature. Or one can go even narrower and pin down the political, social, economic or cultural dimensions of the phenomena. Methodologically, too, one can choose from whole range of perspectives from the empiricist-positivist to the metaphysical-normative. Finally, one can use a concept of theory which is separated from practice or a concept of theory which is systematically rooted in praxis. How then, does one understand Gandhi's theory of war and peace in terms of such different frameworks — metaphysical-epistemological, social-scientific, positivistic-normative, abstract-theoretical and praxis-oriented theory? Anyone, who has even a cursory acquaintance with the Gandhian mode of thought, would find it hard to fit it into such categories. Not impossible, perhaps, but frustrating and, in the end, futile. The important reason for this difficulty is, in my view, that the categories I have listed were produced to deal with historical experiences and traditionalities generated elsewhere to take different sets of problematics. To make my point clear, let me take the case of a modern Western classic in political theory, Hobbes, *Leviathan*. But Hobbes is already different from the traditional mode of articulation, though the earlier modes still exercise considerable power over his thinking. If one can separate the secular component from the more theological component from the Hobbesian document, it is possible to see a mode which can be fitted into the categories I have listed earlier. But then does Hobbes really separate the two? Apparently he does in so far as he fails to provide a bridge between the two, excepting the shaky one of natural law. Then why does he go on the theological excursion? He himself provides us with no clear and unambiguous clue.

While Gandhi cannot be easily fitted into the post-Renaissance and post-Reformation European categories of articulation, he can be fitted even less easily into the medieval-Christian mode, though the temptation to do so would be strong and not wholly absurd at that. There are certainly hints of the Christian duality between the body and soul, which is, in the last analysis, cancelled in a theological monism. But perhaps the closest thing to Gandhi in the European tradition is the classical Greek mode, with its strong coupling of the material with the "spiritual", but then the Greek mode constantly returns to its naturalistic moorings, its pantheon of gods, reflecting the human encounter with the natural. No doubt, Plato's commitment to the immortality of the soul may look like an exception, but it remains too exceptional, even whimsical and eccentric, to be called an element articulated in any structured tradition of living and thinking.

Well, why not simply say that Gandhi represents a different mode of articulation, which can be squeezed into the procrustean bed of Western categories but really with no point to it and hence a mode of articulation which can be called broadly Indian? Therefore, before we can go on to construct a Gandhian paradigm, it is perhaps necessary to sketch a preliminary picture of what I take to be the Indian mode of articulation.[1] The essence of this mode is to shun dualities and partialities, vertical and hierarchical frameworks. Though it has its structures of highly abstract and speculative thought, it has always managed to root them in mundane situations of existing. The immortal soul, no matter how high and free it might fly away from the mundane, seldom tries to avoid the flutterings of a soul caged in the confines of ordinary living. In short, the high-sounding discourse on the *atma* and the *parmatma* is never allowed, in the Indian mode, to escape the framework of daily as well as timeless needs of ordinary man, who are, after all, most of mankind. One of the dominant and recurring themes in the Indian mode of articulating life and thought seems to be the framework of four-fold aims of human life[2] — *Dharma, Artha, Kama* and *Moksha*. I think the Weberian stereotype of the spiritual East and materialist West, and the *Moksha*-obsessed and other-worldly image of India, which can be traced in the Western discourse from Hegel to the neo-Weberian Dumont, its climax of absurdity, have to be discarded. While the stereotype of materialist West also is an over-simplification, it has certainly more validity than stereotype India of other-worldly pre-occupation at the expense of the mundane world of everyday reality. It too needs to be significantly modified. I think the more appropriate contrast is not the spiritual East *versus* the materialist West, but the dualistic West and monistic India. In Gandhi, we find a somewhat complex articulation of the monistic or more precisely totalistic view of life. I have used the qualification "complex" advisedly because Gandhi does not straightaway present what I have called a totalistic or comprehensive perspective for man. Rather in his thought such a perspective emerges tenuously and through a tension between two other strands, which Gandhi seems to be welcoming to some extent — the dualistic, body-soul frame, and the stereotypical spiritualistic Indian image. But I do think that the comprehensive or totalistic[3] is the one that Gandhi presents to us as his operational agenda.

Following the formulation of Professor K.J. Shah, it may be suggested that the four objectives of moral code (*dharma*), material welfare (*artha*), body pleasure, not just sex (*kama*) and the post-body concerns (*moksha*), have been conceptualised in the Indian articulation as mutually interactive and supportive, not hierarchical, and that the specific proportionality of any of the four objectives, in any specific individual case, can be variable, but there can be no legitimate case for any individual to discard wholly any one of the four aims of life. Thus, the Indian mode of living and thinking, like the Indian mode of music, combines the opposites into a dynamic and creative equilibrium, the opposites of structure and freedom. Something like the framework briefly sketched is presupposed, even if nowhere explicitly stated, in the Gandhian paradigm of a totality which conceptualises living as a process of relating the self to itself, the self to the otherselves and the self to *prakriti* or nature. Here again a wide variability and creative flexibility is granted, but the broad framework is reasonably well fixed. With this background in mind, Gandhiji was keen on braking the dichotomies between body and soul, body and intellect, man and God, and the individual and the community. Please, note that I am using the Gandhian term, community, not society. I think the term society has non-Gandhian roots in the European history of the bourgeois civil society and the capitalist mode of production. Above all, we must take into account Gandhiji's realism and by that I mean his capacity to grasp the situation on the ground, not from the outside, but from the inside, as it were. This is why Gandhiji was able to bypass the classic Western problematic of the subject-object dissonance. No doubt, it meant some loss, but the Gandhian point is that, on the balance, the loss was more than made up by the gain, as he saw it in the traditional rural life in India.

Non-violent War

I think it very important to realise that Gandhiji began with the assumption that conflict and, therefore, war, was both a natural and an unnatural condition for man. This mystery and paradox lay at the heart of the Gandhian paradigm. Conflict and war was natural insofar as the totality of the human condition presupposed it. In other words, Gandhiji does not deny the dichotomies *per se*, because his realism had to reckon with it, but what he does deny is that it is a condition that cannot be overcome. This position for him was not a subjective problem, and he held that the totality of the human condition presupposed a necessary conflict and a necessary compulsion to overcome it. This is the Gandhian dialectic. Gandhiji rightly saw that war is not identical with violence, because violence was a certain objective, behavioural category. There can be violence but no war. And there can be war and no violence. It is position that derives ultimately from the Gandhian belief in truth and non-violence.

Why does Gandhiji think conflict can arise? First due to the diversity of the human situation, both at the subjective level and the level of larger structures such as society, community, nation, religion and civilisation. This contingency was seen by him as a given, non-negotiable conditionality of our existence. Therefore, as long as humanity does not articulate its life and thought in one mode, there are bound to be serious differences which have the potentiality for conflict and war. But Gandhiji also drew a distinction between such contingent but valid differences and a more fundamental but illegitimate difference between truth and non-truth, God and Devil, good and evil. Therefore, there can be a struggle on both planes. The first level struggle should be muted by mutual toleration at least and, if possible, by mutual understanding. The second type of conflict must be fought — it is the classic Indian *Dharma Yuddha*. There is no backing out of it, as Arjuna was metaphysically reprimanded by his cow-herd mentor, Krishna. Therefore, I think the Gandhian paradigm implies a distinction between a war that is unnecessary and dispensable and a war that must be fought.

The second crucial aspect of the paradigm is that whatever the nature of the war, the method of warfare must be non-violent. Why non-violence? Here the Gandhian point is that one should ask the question: What is the goal of the war? In a superficially utilitarian manner, Gandhiji argues that the overall effectiveness of non-violence in terms of the goal is superior to that of violence. But there is a more fundamental point of *Dharma* involved here. It is that violence will lead to destruction of things, not merely life, and this is something we have no right to do, that is a violation of *Dharma*. We have no right to destroy what we have not created and what we do not even understand, what is not just an isolated piece but a piece in a vast pattern whose meaning we can never grasp subjectively only and whose meaning comes to us through the structures of traditionality, evolved through centuries of tested and lived pain, joy and wisdom. Not only that. We have a duty imposed by *Dharma* to preserve life and living things and existing structures. But then Gandhiji *also* held as central the assumption that we are also under the obligation of *Dharma* to fight the war against evil, violence, and, in fact, against war itself in a sense. If, under certain circumstances, to go to war is a duty imposed by *Dharma* and *Dharma* also imposes the duty not to kill, what is the way out? Put in this Gandhian form, the Gandhian answer will be to fight in such a way that one achieves the goal of defeating the evil but without violating the *Dharmic* injunction not to kill or destroy or violate God who is everything and everywhere. I think it must be emphasised very strongly that Gandhian non-violence is not a call to cease warring for all purposes. But non-violent warfare is a tougher, though more effective, method, in the long run. He was no idle visionary or lotus-eater on this basic issue. He knew the formidable challenge involved in this mode of living and acting, and that is why he developed a technology of non-violent action. It involved rigorous mental and physical discipline. If one could not train oneself for the new warfare and if the war was just and right, Gandhiji advocated the use of violence as a necessary weakness or evil. In other words, if the choice is between efficient and organised violence *versus* efficient and organised non-violence, Gandhiji's categorical counsel would be — non-violence. If the choice is between efficient and disciplined violence and disorganised non-violence, Gandhiji would advise one to go for violence. If the choice is between violence and inaction or cowardice, Gandhiji would most certainly advise the use of violence. But these are hypothetical and pragmatic considerations. Overarching them is the Gandhian counsel that one must do the utmost to wage a non-violent war, which is the only kind of war where the means and ends are not at war with each other.

Rubric of Swaraj

As a social scientist, in the narrow sense, I shall now briefly examine the possibility of the Gandhian paradigm offering some social science payoffs. As we saw at the start of this article, Gandhiji's mode of raising or solving genuine problems is not a mode which reduces them to a mere social context and content. But he is also not given to bypassing or ignoring such dimensions. It is, therefore, not in the least surprising that Gandhiji does relate the capability of waging non-violent war as well as the capability for creating war to the nature of the wider structures in which individual lives and subjective selves find themselves embedded through historical contingencies of time and place. But he also holds out hope that history can be overcome by history-makers in the direction of structures reflecting better the principle of *Dharma*. In short, he seems to suggest that there are overarching historical structures, evolved through centuries, which possess the capacity to minimise (a) the occasions and contexts of conflict both within themselves and with other similar structures and (b) which aggravate conflictual situations and are prone to produce conflictual contexts. Gandhiji called such overarching structures "civilisations", which are wider, more complex, better integrated and more durable than societies or nations or even communities. He knew of at least two such structures — the modern, not necessarily Western, and the Indian. I think it is fair to say that his understanding of the former was perhaps a shade unfair and his understanding of the latter penetrating, whatever one's quarrel with it on points of detail.

Gandhiji maintained in the *Hind Swaraj* that the modern civilisation was more prone to violence, conflict and destruction. By the same token, he held that the Indian civilisation tended to minimise conflicts. I do not want here to offer any extended critique of this position. But some brief preliminary counter-moves are legitimate to prevent the danger of erecting Gandhiji into a mythical monster. In fact, his fallibility was what rounds him up as a genuinely great human being. Being myself a Marxist, I am prepared to see some of his points as valid, but I do think that Gandhiji did not sufficiently separate out the specifics within the Western civilisation. This is not to say that he was too wide of the mark. I think he tends to reduce the Western civilisation to its bourgeois, capitalistic phase. Of course, in the interest of accuracy and in fairness to him, it is possible to argue that he was talking about "modern", not "Western", civilisation, in which case a

Marxist can re-interpret Gandhiji to mean the capitalist civilisation.

Gandhiji's perception and conception of what constitutes Indian civilisation can also arise a number tricky issues. Indian history has had such a long run with so many complex events and persons involved, that any broad reconstruction of it into a structure, called "civilisation", is bound to be problematic. Granting this, one should also grant the need for conceptualising such a structure. But it is to Gandhiji's credit that he has captured some fundamental elements that have been present more or less constantly in Indian life and thought at least since the post-*Vedic* period. The essence of it, yes, but details? I think one should debate the details but one should be grateful to Gandhiji for the insight. But it is also necessary to remember in this connection that Gandhiji did not make the naive mistake of confusing the essence with existence. Existence was the domain of struggle to attain the essence, but the essence was already there as a potentiality. His notion of a vastly decentralised, small-scale, community-oriented, system, his *Swaraj*, cannot be dismissed lightly. No doubt, once again as a Marxist, I should like to complain that Gandhiji saw too much the constant components and not enough the disruptive forces besetting them. But, on the other hand, Marxists have also been guilty of not seeing enough the constants, and hence somersaults and disastrous historical twists, their inability to generate meaningful praxis in the name of an abstract and over-theorised and non-dialentical Marxism! Anyway, the point I want to make here is that the kind of society envisaged under the rubric of *Swaraj* can be shown easily to be less prone to violence and conflict. If that were all the point of *Swaraj*, I think it need not be taken seriously. Gandhiji invests it with more, with a whole range of richly human qualities, totally absent in the modern bourgeois West. Most importantly, the Gandhian message is that ultimately the war of violence cannot be avoided unless we are able to re-structure our context on the lines of *Swaraj*.

Gandhi's Idealism — A Reality

After what may appear to be dense, perhaps even incoherent, arguments and propositions, let me reduce the discussion to simpler statements. First, Gandhiji did not think that war was unnatural or avoidable in a simplistic sense. War was part of human conditionality. However, there were conflicts of a contingent nature which could be avoided or minimised. There were wars of a more fundamental nature involving the question of *Dharma*. Such [illegible] cannot be avoided, and they must be fought. But it is in greater [illegible]ormity, with our own nature and the nature of everything, to wage such a war in a non-violent manner, predicated on a love for the enemy, the goal being not destruction but "re-struction". Third, such a war based on non-violence, which alone conforms to *Dharma*, is not easy, though more effective. Those who cannot employ non-violence, cannot make it an excuse to run away from the war. I think Gandhiji would have loved Arjuna to win his war through non-violence. But being a *Kshatriya* he could not do so, and hence he was justified in fighting the war the only way he knew how. The last point I want to make is that Gandhiji believed that the kind of structures — social, political, economic and cultural — comprising his *Swaraj*, would reduce both the incidence of conflicts and the incidence of violence in handing conflicts. I think in a world where weapons of destruction and occasions to use them are multiplying fast, Gandhiji's idealism may turn out to be the only kind of realism we can afford.

NOTES

1. I am indebted to Prof. K.J. Shah for this insight. It cleared for me many puzzles in our life and thought. Especially our capacity to shift flights of abstraction to utterly mundane and materialistic concerns.
2. I am aware of the alternative three-fold scheme but in essence this does not affect my argument here.
3. Navajivan Publishing House, Ahmedabad, 1938 (1962 reprint).

7

NON-VIOLENCE (AHIMSA): Buddha's and Gandhi's Views

BIMLENDRA KUMAR

IT IS an undeniable fact that men in the world today have been shaken by the tremors of the fearsome holocaust that has envisioned them with nuclear catastrophe. This is by no means a natural calamity, which is beyond human control but this impending holocaust is unfortunately created by power mania of a few autocrats who have thrown the world in a web of chaos.

If we look back into our historical past, we do not discern a period of complete integration or even a workable peace. On the other hand, men were deeply rooted in conflicts arising out of desire and fear, which made the world an inhabitable place. It appears that the great seers like Buddha, Mahavira, Shankara and Gandhi were all fed up with the nature of cyclic suffering in the world through the aeons.

The unity of all life is a characteristic and deeply inspiring feature of all Indian thought. It is the core of the concept of *ahimsa*. *Ahimsa* is far more than non-killing. It is abstention from consciously inflicting injury or causing harm to any person or living creature. It enjoins regard and love for every one.

The Buddha declared that suffering and sorrow which afflict the world are not without a cause, and, therefore, remediable by removing the cause. The Four Noble Truths point the path to *Nirvana* of the extinction of Self (I-ness).

Buddhism arose with its basic principle of well-being for all. Buddha's commandment of '*Bahujana hitaya, bahujana sukhaya*' always remains as an underlying current in all his teachings. It is natural to think that when Lord Buddha thought of eliminating the suffering of all, he had well-being of all at heart. There was no question of harming or injurying any living being. The very idea of well-being of all gave rise to *Ahimsa*. Thus, the concept of non-violence can be defined as the sublime mental state of well-being of all irrespective of any consideration— *'Sabbe satta bhavantu sukhitatta'*.

In a general way, it can be said that the injury is possibly of three types, namely, mental (*manasa*), vocal (*vaca*) and physical (*kaya*). Really speaking, it is a mental one. Body and speech cannot function without the association of mind. A determination of doing anything is made at the mental level first, that is consciousness of doing so and so appears in the mind first and then only it finds expression through different doors and accordingly named as physical and vocal actions. Thus, an action is nothing but a form of consciousness or volition — *'cetanaham, bhikkhave, kammam vadami'*. Refraining injury is an action. Therefore, *Ahimsa* is the name of volition of not doing any harm to anyone.

In the hands of Mahatma Gandhi, *ahimsa*, the sword of self-suffering, became a mighty instrument of large-scale social and political changes. It is a phenomenon of the utmost significance for the future of mankind. Gandhi says:

> "Non-violence is the law of human race and is infinitely greater than the superior to brute force. . . . Non-violence affords the fullest protection to one's respect and sense of honour. Non-violence, in the very nature of things, is of no assistance in the defence of ill-gotten, gains and immoral acts. It is, therefore, in consistent with the possession of other people's countries, i.e., modern imperialism. Non-violence is a power which can be wielded equally by all—children, young men and women or grown up people — provided they have a living faith in the God of Love and have, therefore, equal love for all mankind. When non-violence is accepted as the law of life, it must pervade the whole being and not be applied to isolated acts."[1]

Gandhiji was of the view that a new social order should be established on the bases of *Satya* and *Ahimsa*. Bertrand Russel observes in the Wisdom of the West:

"What are we to do when called upon to obey a law which we find unjust? The question is more alive than ever when blind obedience to our political masters threatens to plunge the world into total destruction."[2]

The only possible answer can be *ahimsa* and *satyagraha*. This is more true today than ever. *Ahimsa* and *satyagraha* go together.

It will be better to point out that though the use of the word *ahimsa* is not very frequent in Buddhist literature, as it is in Gandhian though. Suzuki has rightly observed that there are two pillars supporting the great edifice of Buddhism, *Mahaprajna* (the great wisdom) and *Mahakaruna* (the great compassion). The wisdom, flows from the compassion and the compassion from the wisdom for, the two are one. Both of them are nothing but the attributes of *ahimsa*.

Emphasising the importance of the means as equal to the end, Gandhiji identifies *ahimsa* with Truth, as he identifies Truth with God. He says:

"It is the soul force or the power of Godhead within us. . . . Non-violence without reliance upon that Force (God) is power stuff to be thrown in the dust."[3]

But Lord Buddha never speaks of realising God.

It appears from the text that the Buddha has also conceived an ideal form of social order and wished to put it on the earth with religious ferment and virtuous fragrance. It is the *Brahmavihara*, which refers to a superior and noble way of living, surcharged with internal and external bliss generated by peace and tranquillity. It has four human values, serving as the four firmly footed pillars of the social structure. They are the friendliness (*metta*), compassion (*karuna*), joy (*mudita*) and equanimity (*upekkha*). It is said that each member of the society sow, nourish on the undisturbed surface of mind, the saplings of these four sublime human values and develop them so as to pervade through all the six directions, making the entire atmosphere surcharged with soothing waves of peace and tranquillity. In this background, there will develop a social order where there is neither enmity nor quarrel of any type. Rather there shall prevail the supreme reign of happiness, both internal and external.

Gandhiji expressed the term *Sarvodaya* which means 'the rise of all', for which, all the individuals have to discipline themselves in a manner that let all the innermost elements of the soul rise to the highest level. It means development of the inner strength of all powers within man to the full.

Lord Buddha never believed in the caste system but he distinguished persons on the basis of their deeds. Gandhiji also fought with the weapon of *satya* and *ahimsa* for breaking the casteism in India but in doing so his aim was to remove social disparity which is dangerous for a strong social structure.

Thus, it is clear that apart from so many differences, there lies some similarities in the concept of non-violence (*ahimsa*). Following on the principles of the Buddha and Gandhiji, we can resolve the conflict in the society and establish social harmony among the people.

NOTES

1. Mahatma Gandhi, cited in D.S. Kothari, *Some Thoughts on Science and Religion*, New Delhi. Indian National Science academy.
2. Bertrand Russel, *Wisdom of the West.*
3. M.K. Gandhi, *op. cit.*

8

ROLE OF SATYAGRAHA IN PLURALIST DEMOCRACY

Miss. I. MYLARAPU

Pluralist Model of Politics

INDIAN POLITICS is seen to be developing in the direction of a full-fledged pluralist democracy and for many it is the only type of democracy possible. One of the identifiable images of Indian politics is that it is pluralist.

The pluralist theory states that governmental policy is essentially a compromise between the various interest groups involved, that policy is an outcome of the pressures and shifts in the balance of social and political influence. Here, there are groups of people with common interests arising from occupation, neighbourhood, ideology, ownership and common grievances — who associate together in presence of that interest. Here, the government is seen in theory as suppliers of authoritative rules and values for which the groups strive. There is an assumption of the pluralist that groups in the struggle are able to bring pressure to bear upon the government. With the growing differentiation of the society, new groups enter the arena with demands for help and offers of assistance and are, therefore, not neglected. A further assumption is that politics is not dominated by a single power centre but rather power is dispersed amongst multiple centres of power, none of which is or can be wholly sovereign. Here, no one group is sufficiently powerful to control the output of government in the face of competition from other interested groups. In this way political power and influence are fragmented and no one group or interest is sufficiently strong to be dictator.

At least theoretically it is accepted that over a long period of time, in such societies a great bulk of citisens happens to possess a stable set of democratic beliefs. Most citisens assume that political system is consistent with the democratic creed or that their system is democratic. There is a visible and widespread adherence to the democratic creed. This is produced and maintained by a variety of powerful social processes, e.g., a powerful formal educational system. According to this theory it is accepted that majority of the citisens, or ordinary citisens, remains outside national debates and is apathetic. It is also accepted that there is only ritualistic participation. Voting is only a ritualised affirmation of the psychic dispositions, an act satisfying in itself and closely linked to the primordial and parochial origins of the personality. Besides, this pluralist model is based on scarcity and competition. It resembles a market where formally it gives access to all but what actually happens is that only some privileged groups enter the bargaining arena.

There is an equality of access only, the principle of the formal openness of the public arena to which anyone with the necessary ability can gain access.

India's Pluralist Democracy

India is a country with a nearly unfathomable diversity of languages, sects, castes, religions, regions and cultures. Its citisens are largely illiterate and rural. The population appears mired in traditional superstitions and prejudices and looks incapable of involvement in conscious interest-based activity through organised groups. Its citisens seem incapable of articulating dissatisfaction, appear susceptible to passionate appeals — linguistic, regional, ethnic and religious — leading to outbursts of anger and violence. In short, India looks like a backward country where chaos, disintegration, force and instability must rule.

In contrast to the surface image of Indian society, Indian politics since independence seems unusually stable and sophisticated. The federal democratic form of government has operated successfully over 30 years. Elections are held regularly and all levels of government are open and free. The voter turnout is comparable to that in all Western democracies. It is argued that individuals are now competing for power in an open polity, looking for new sources of support, creating groups and loyalties on new and varied bases. There is certain rise in interest group activities.

But nobody can deny that under this pluralist rubric, there are inequality, exploitation and various other forms of injustices abound in our society — resistance to them should be our duty.

Marginal Groups

In this article attention is being paid to the marginal groups, i.e., to the ignored and disadvantageous sections of the society such as the rural population consisting of small farmers, landless labourers, tillers, tenants, poorer cultivators and Scheduled Castes and Tribes. In the urban areas we may identify the unorganised workers, slum dwellers, unemployed youth as the marginal groups. The religious minority groups may also be added here. These groups we call the marginal groups as differentiated from the well stocked groups, of affluent cultivators and businessmen, which are at a definite vantage point *vis-a-vis* the marginal groups. Some predominant groups are much more politicised than the rest of the population and live in a vibrant political environment of politically conscious ones. They dominate the political, economic and the cultural belief systems and use them in manipulating the lesser groups. For these types of groups, politics as a bargaining arena is real, and policy output of government do reflect interests in them.

Whereas the marginal groups suffer, they are unprivileged in terms of income, education, landholding, good leadership, skill organisational ability and, above all, lack the political consciousness and awareness. They have no patronage, no common language, lack communication and also are not cohesive enough. In short, they lack all the resources need to enter the political arena.

Gandhi had concern for these types of depressed groups and he foresaw that increased educational opportunities could subsequently raise these people in the sphere of politics. But in India this did not happen, 'as in rural India people do not feel politically efficacious, and ritualised voting is predominant'. Even if citisens believe that the vote is an act of public responsibility, this act is possible when the elections present themselves after every five years. Then too voting becomes an effective lever only in the aggregate. Individually by itself a vote is only a periodic affirmation of a segment of the State's policy. A citisen's ability to make the government responsive to his needs and problems rests on channels other than voting.

Failure of Violence

Marches and demonstrations to protest against policies are not adequate. Marches mainly seem the only type of activity in which the underprivileged groups take initiative but usually the number is too small to allow sufficient effect. These groups then experience political impotency and frustration, and being depressed, dejected and disparate become violent and turn to sporadic violence. Once this happens the government springs to action. In order to prevent sporadic violence by these groups and to ensure their loyalty the government typically combines repressive sanctions as well as welfare programmes but if these measures fail to satisfy the groups then they are victims of radical romanticism. As a result they indulge in armed revolts and agitations against some vaguely defined injustice spearheaded by those who lack understanding of the history and cultural situation and usually end, at the best, in temporary ameliorative policies and measures.

The independence movement in India did little to organise the interest of the poor peasants and land labourers.

The development of interest groups during the independence movement was for those who were in ruling positions including the urban capitalists, bureaucrats, intellectuals and professionals.

In India there is a tradition of expecting the government to perform all welfare functions and a traditional expectation that those occupying positions of authority should help ameliorate the ills of underprivileged groups and is a part of the culture defined by the privileged.

More often than not, when a poor peasant, a tenant, or a labourer, approaches a man in authority, an elected official of a career civil servant, he does it with the humility of a petitioner, as a beggar, and not as a democratic citisen who is making his demands and desires. Majority of the people does not have a fair chance as it has economic, psychological, educational and cultural disadvantages. Almost certainly the majority is systematically undermined in terms of effective participation and these people lead an agonised and insecure existence. They would like to demand, for example, adequate power, education, jobs, etc., for satisfying their basic needs. These have-nots are from time to time launching movements often defensive, inadequately organised and based on wrong strategies, taking varied shapes, but always asserting a new determination to fight back and escape the ever tightening noose around their necks.

Struggles doubtless emerge and operate under tremendous difficulties and the hostile atmosphere, lack of resources and the multipronged manoeuvres of the ruling classes to prevent, distort, confuse and repress them. In such a condition extreme violence and violent means seem the only way out. But violence serve no purpose. Violence has always failed in India. In recent times we have seen that violence means always failed to achieve desired ends. Many examples can be given where different groups have resorted to violent means to resolve their conflicts.

The Naxalite movement in India used violent means to resolve their conflicts against rich farmers, moneylenders and local officials. These Naxalites were brave and their movements were violent, elemental and spontaneous, but were, however, not backed by the masses who never liked violence and would never sanction its use. The naxalites sought higher status and issues which were a mixture of political, cultural and agrarian in nature. The Naxalite movement found itself in a disarray. The problems of the small north-eastern States of Tripura, Mizoram, Nagaland can be looked at in the same perspective. All these States have been centres of violent ferment activities, almost all their problems seemed genuine but violent means failed here. The living problem of Punjab today also proves that millions of Indians do not favour terrorism and politics of assassination. The terrorists in Punjab now stand isolated and discredited by the people.

Violence has lost its dynamics and the history of post-independence India has shown that violence and terrorist movements in India could not succeed.

The Gandhian Way Out — 'Satyagraha'

The problem that arises at this point is that if small marginal groups with severe problems have got to survive in this pluralist frame-work and function as viable political functional units, if they want to have a say in the policies of the government and if violence and violent means have failed then what is the way out? The answer to this is that they have to find another way where mass conscious mobilisation is involved and where the limited energies and advantages of these groups will be judiciously used to the advantage and yet not disturb or disrupt the democratic systems in any way. The Gandhian way comes in here. A way that has been inadequately emphasised but which holds out considerable potential in conflict resolution and wherein non-violence plays an important role.

That Gandhi is relevant today and centuries to come is not in doubt at all. If humanity is to progress, Gandhi is inevitable and inescapable. We see conflict around us all the time which is not surprising. What is surprising is the wrong methods adopted to end the conflict which have almost always failed miserably and produced greater conflict. In this way conflicts are seldom resolved. The violence pursued leads to further violence and perpetuation of the problem. The mistaken belief still persists that violence can end conflicts and bring salvation to people.

Gandhi pointed out another way — a new way, and what is more, lived it and showed success. It is for us to understand what it is and use it to our advantage. In this age of consuming fear, this absolutely fearless individual demonstrates to us that there can be a strength far greater than arms and struggles can be fought without bitterness and hatred. This is the most potent legacy left to us. When conflict is the order of the day we ignore Gandhi's ideas, know little about them and are sceptical about them. We fail to realise that we have at our hands an extremely ideal way to resolve the conflict.

Gandhi once said that "man either progresses towards *ahimsa* or rushes to his doom".

The marginal groups in India must realise that in order to survive and survive effectively in this system and if they lack the resources to enter the political bargaining arena then the Gandhian *satyagraha* is the ideal form and probably the only means to the solution.

Human history mostly got accustomed to resistance through violence and bloodshed. It was just here Gandhi intervened and introduced the method of *satyagraha* as a instrument of non-violence. *Satyagraha* is the instrument of non-violent social change. Gandhi's contribution to *satyagraha* lies in the fact that he brought it onto a social plane, no doubt injustice was resisted non-violently but people did it on a personal level. Gandhi tried it on the mass scale.

Satyagraha was to him a technique of action — "Intended to replace methods of violence." It is only when beliefs or impulses or desires are frustrated that *satyagraha* becomes appropriate. *Satyagraha* is a technique of action. It is characterised by adherence to a stated truth by means of behaviour which is non-violent but which includes self-suffering. It seeks to effect change and it operates within a conflict situation. As do all techniques of action for effecting change it employs force but the character and the force of *satyagraha* is essentially different. *Satyagraha* aims at conversion and not coercion. *Satyagrahi* believes that it is not impossible to persuade those in enjoyment of power to part with it willingly under the compelling influence of love. Gandhi believed in mass action and people's power which is collective moral power of masses. Gandhi in *satyagraha* evolved a dynamics of collective action against injustice and exploitation.

Satyagraha is viewed too much from spiritualistic angle, but should be viewed from a strategic and rationalist angle. The principle of non-violence and the instrument of *satyagraha* are the only morally and practically sound methods open to oppressed people. Masses should be adequately prepared to offer *satyagraha.* The philosophy and the implication of this all important technique should be communicated to its mass participants.

In conclusion I would like to say that for all those marginal groups who lack sufficient resources and who are unable to enter the political arena, the only way out for them is to resort to *satyagraha.*

9

PEACE: Individual and Universal

M. TIWARY

PEACE, ACCORDING to early Buddhist tradition, is a psychic phenomenon in the life of a man. It comes into being, as a natural flow, from the first moment of the beginning of the life-process, and expresses itself as manifested or unmanifested due to the accumulated *Karmic-force*. The impact of its two forms is experienced in course of practical life as arising of a series of consciousness, naturally serene or basically distracted. Thus, what we call peace, may be the nearer expression of the *Santa-citta*, a Serene Consciousness, immensely calm, unhindered, pliable, subtle and manifested with all psychic moral components.

Initially, it may be located as a moral psychic unit *Parsaddhi* which mean serenity. It exists with five close associates, namely, *Lahuta* (Lightness), *Muduta* (Mildness), *Kammannata* (Adaptability), *Paqunnata* (Healthiness) and *Ujukata* (Straight Forwardness) and forms a complex unit of six — *Passaddhi-chatthaka*. Up to this stage, it remains as a psychic factor. Further, finding association with other coherent psychic states, it emerges as a consciousness, fully manifesting through mind-door. It is named as *Santa-citta*, a serene consciousness. The arising of such consciousness is the dawn of *Peace*.

Consciousness by its nature is pure and luminous (*pakatipabbhasara*) but it is polluted by in-coming defiling forces. In the situation, it loses its nature and remains enveloped with the layers of pollution. So long it is under such envelopes, it does not breath in or out in its natural way and expresses with internal suffocation as unsteady, restless, flickering and bewildered. It wanders indescriminately to different objects and creates gross attachment with them. It goes on increasing under the blinding influence of immoral layers and as its result, there starts the generation to *Tension* of variegated nature. It gradually pervades and permeates through the entire physical and psychic bodies and makes them saturated with four-fold intoxicants (*asavas*), known as lustful desire for enjoying the sensual pleasure (*Kamaseva*), wrongful maintaining of existence (*bhavasava*), indulgence in heresies (*detthasava*) and nourishing the ignorance (*avijjasava*). In the situation, there is the emergence of a mental chaos, which we name *Absence of Peace*.

How one may be able to remove the state of *Absence of Peace* and generate the state of *Peace*? It is possible only by removal of the layers of pollution and helping the consciousness to emerge in its natural form, pure and luminous. How it is possible? It is, first, by knowing the basic moral and immoral states by a conscious wayfaring through mind; and, secondly, by application of four-fold Noble Exertions (*sammavayama*). Through this process the 14 immoral states and the 25 moral states are understood and their roles are identified. Thereafter, begins the efforts for eradication of the former and helping the faster growth of the latter. How does it proceed? There are five gradual methods for it. They are the (a) *Saddha-vihara*, (b) *Sambara-vihara*, (c) *Pamuka-vihara*, (d) *Pajanana-vihara* and (e) *Brahma-vihara*.

Saddha-vihara

Saddha, in its generic sense, means faith, reverence, honour, etc. In its technical sense, it is a purifacational psychic unit. Its function is to remove the layers of pollution of mind and make it free from defiling forces — (*Samapasadana-Lakkhana saddha*). It inspires further to achieve more higher state of purity. It proceeds with its functions in a subtle graduated way just like the proceeding of a most wise goldsmith for removing the dirt from a fine ornament. To be with such noble effort is the *Saddha-vihara*.

Sambara-vihara

The tension of mind is the natural resultant of developing the delightful desire for relishing the pleasure connected with the senses and their respective objects. Eye, ear, nose, tongue, touch and mind are the six senses. Visible object, Audible object, Odorous object, Sapid object, Tangible object and Ideational object are the six respective objects. Each sense like to enjoy the pleasure connected with its respective object. It creates delightful desire, develops, attachment and results in generation of Tension which hinders the mind and disturb *Peace*. For eradication of the process of generation of Tension, and emergence of Peace, the effort of putting restraints over the wrongful functions of the senses is the only effective remedy. To be with this is the *Sambara-vihara*.

Pamukha-vihara

Pamukha means leaning towards. Technically, it is proceeding towards suppression of hindrances, helping the arising of the constituents of one-pointedness, drawing the mind from different directions, developing one-pointedness on the objects with-form and formless and making it free from pollution, pure, mild, pliable serene, subtle and one-pointed. To remain with such efforts is *Pamukha-vihara*.

Pajanana-vihara

Pajanana means having penetration in the nature of reality and destroying the darkness of ignorance. It is another name of Right Understanding, the dawn of which makes the nature of the conditional things crystal clear as impermanent, subject to suffering and substanceless. In its soothing light one becomes able to curtail the attachment towards worldiness and proceeds towards the attainment of a state of *Desirelessness*.

It is, in other words, going towards a state of *Tensionlessness*. To be with such efforts is the *Pajanana-vihara*. Here it should be understood that beginning from the *Saddha-vihara* up to the *Pajanana-vihara* are the various types of efforts for generating individual peace. A successful and conscious wayfaring prepares a background for emergence of *Peace* universal.

Brahma-Vihara

Brahma means noble, sublime, supra-mundane. *Vihara* conveys the senses of way of living. The *Brahma-vihara*, in this way, is the "Sublime Way of Living". Here Self (*Swa*) is gradually transformed into all (*Para*) and all efforts are directed for the benefit and happiness of all. It proceeds with the practice of four sublime states, namely, Universal friendliness (*Metta*), Compassion (*Karuna*), Un-alloyed joy (*Mudita*) and Equanimity (*Upekkha*) towards being in general with psychic expressions — "Let all the beings be happy". To be with such efforts is the *Brahma-vihara*. With the practice of these sublime states, there shall be the emergence of a state of dual saturation of Peace — Individual and Universal.

10

CONFLICT RESOLUTION THROUGH GANDHIAN STUDIES AND RESEARCH: A Note

RAMJEE SINGH

It's education that forms the common mind.
Just as the twig is bent, the tree is inclined.
— Alexander Pope

IN THE historical perspective, education did always have a function of stabilising authority. Socrates, Gandhi and Paulo Freire are exceptions. Public education generally is to be worked at as a relation of domination and subordination. There are trends of violence in the past history as well as in the present situation. There are physical, communicational, psychical and structural acts of violence in the history of education. This is why we have practically no place for education against violence in our formal curricula. The official elites not only try to neglect and at times frown upon peace-education in the name of ivory-tower academics, but also on the contrary to create violence as an instrument of education which is bound to generate conflict and tension.

In our country, while we have been living in a state of almost constant tensions and in organised or unorganised violence ever since the advent of our independence, we still nurture hopes to solve them by perfecting police machinery and treat it purely as a law and order problem. But our experience reveals that if we increase police force by 10 per cent, the crime and violence rise from 100 per cent to 1200 per cent. We perhaps forget that the roots of violence lie both in our psyche as well as in our worn out socio-economic structure. Our universities, in general, have become degree-oriented dead machines and upholders of *status quo*. This is why, peace education in the formal curricula is in a state of utter neglect. It still remains essentially the concern of the Gandhian constructive workers and peace-activists of a few voluntary agencies.

It took our universities nearly four decades to realise the feasibility and worth of Gandhian Studies and Peace Research as a separate discipline. We may contend that the very concept of peace education is European in origin and content and it has little relevance to the Indian situation. Perhaps, we suffer from a sense of false vanity that India has a rich tradition of peace and non-violence from the Buddha and Mahavira to Gandhi and Vinoba. But it is not worthwhile to know how far Gandhian perspective is being adopted throughout the world slowly but steadily from Martin Luther King to Sokhorav and Walesa.

The Education Policy — 1986 or Programme of Action does not think it necessary to emphasise the need of peace education and Gandhian Studies while dealing with "Higher Education (5.24 to 5.34) or even Open University (5.35 to 5.37)" though it is constrained to admit that "in our culturally plural society, education should foster universal and eternal values, oriented towards the unity and integration of our people. Such value education should help eliminate obscurantism, religious fanaticism, violence, superstition and fatalism" (8.5).

In Indian society today, peace education and Gandhian studies are more relevant than before. We have conflicts and tensions of all types, including war tensions. Communal, caste, regional and linguistic conflicts have become permanent features of our so-called civil life. Naxalism and terrorism including armed insurgency do not seem to die down in the near future. We present a picture of primitive tribalism and sub-nationalism. Continuance of an unjust socio-economic structure on account of political vested interests have only deepened our malaise. On the top, there had been criminalisation of society because there is criminalisation of politics and politicalisation of criminals. For years we have been fooling ourselves that we are civilised. Our civilisation is only skin-deep. This is all the more necessary to work on fundamental lines to eradicate these wrong values.

Education must not only identify the causes of conflict and conditions of harmony but also become instrument of peace. At no time in human history has there been a greater need for understanding peace and considering the use of non-violent means for its achievement. So far, violent means have been considered inevitable for social change or resolution of conflict. But, today, non-violent means are considered not only as an alternative but perhaps the only viable method of conflict resolution. The Marxists who had long adhered to the doctrine of inevitability of war have not only adopted co-existence but have shown preference for unilateral peace ventures. In India, Laldengas and Ghising have taken to the path of ballot instead of bullets. What is required is to infuse the cult of peace and non-violence in the minds of the younger generation. Hence there should be no illusion that Gandhian Studies are only reverential and apologetic. In fact, it is not only suited to our national genius but has also wide global acceptance.

The latest developments, both at the national and international levels, suggest that the idea of Gandhi to form a non-violent army (*Shanti Sena*) to meet the threat of growing and organised violence seems to be quite pragmatic as Central Reserve Police (C.R.P.) or Border Security Force (B.S.F.) have miserably failed to establish peace in Punjab, Nagaland, Mizoram, and Kashmir. Writing in *Harijan* 18th June, 1938, Gandhi's idea of formating such a peace brigade was that *Shanti Sena* 'should substitute the police and the military'. In his Last Testament, Gandhi had clearly visualised a confrontation between the civil power and the police and military power. If the civil power is subdued by the police power, there is no escape from dictatorship. Hence, either we have a strong *Shanti Sena* or an impending military dictatorship.

Peace education and development of *Shanti Sena* are the best guarantee of democracy. It is a tragedy that training in non-violence and association with *Shanti Sena* in the country or participation of peace movements have not found popular and active support among the intellectuals and university community in India. They have been largely the exclusive domain of the Gandhian and *Sarvodaya* workers and a few sensitive souls. India has not seen any powerful peace movements against violence and war during past 30 years. Thanks to the efforts of a few leftist political parties that they have done something in this respect. This only shows the callousness and insensitivity prevailing in the universities.

Perhaps there is an impression that peace studies based on Gandhian lines are uncritical and dogmatic and not worthy for the university education. This is not so. Gandhian concept of peace education and conflict resolution is neither Euro-centric nor it is piecemeal effort. It is not only a mere "criticism of war or violence", neither mere "liberation" from problems of social and economic evils, nor merely a "learning process" in a given educational environment but it is a "life-style movement." It goes to the roots of violence. For example, it rejects the idea of an inherent conflict between man and nature or the inherent evil nature of man. Similarly, it warns us against the ills of over-industrialisation and over-consumption. Mere material welfare of an individual or society at the cost of spiritual and moral development will create conditions of conflict. Similarly, Gandhi and Vinoba had urged to adopt the right kind of religious perspectives by combining science and spirituality to make it an effective instrument of conflict resolution and peace. It was for the university community to ensure adequate and in-depth study and research in the field of "spiritualisation of politics" or "goodness politics" to counter-act the politics of violence, to encourage the study of Economics of Permanence and Peace and Pedagogy of Peace. But the university intellectuals have opted to remain on the ivory tower, with the result universities have flourished without making the new generation even true Indians. The higher a student goes, the further he is removed from his home so that at the end of his education he becomes estranged from his surroundings. He feels no poetry about his home life or love of man. The village scenes are all a sealed book to him. He is also weaned away from his traditional culture and values of peace and harmony. We have failed to revolutionise higher education and relate it to national necessities and problems like growing violence, poverty and social disequilibrium.

It took three decades for the university community to realise the feasibility and worth of having Gandhian Studies and Peace Science even as an optional separate discipline for our students. After 40 years, hardly there are seven or eight centres of Gandhian Studies in the university fold. Whatever little the UGC does to promote Gandhian Studies does so in an apologetic manner because of the name of the Father of the Nation. We have failed to understand its relevance, urgency and paramount need to free our society from growing conflict and violence. Let us not encourage Gandhian Studies as a ritualistic homage to Gandhi but as an urgent academic pursuit of public interest.

11

CURRICULUM ON NON-VIOLENCE AND PEACE

G.P. KRISHNA RAO

SOLUTIONS TO conflicts/wars brought though use of violence or the ones imposed by a stronger party on the weaker party hardly remove the seeds of discontentment. What succeeds on such occasions is the bigger bomb or the bigger stick, not justice or peace. Periods of lull after conflicts can hardly be described as peaceful state.

Conflicts among nations leading to wars of course need immediate attention. However, conflicts arising out of the suffering of the millions due to poverty, discriminations, hatred, vested interests and the various socio-economic conflicts due to large scale industrialisation and urbanisation need greater and deeper attention if we have to achieve lasting peace. Only if we can ensure justice we can have peace, not otherwise.

Can some countries live a luxurious life holding other nations under their dominance without endangering peace? For that matter, can even a section of population hope to lead a high standard of living at the cost of weaker sections and at the same time enjoy peace? These luxuries and comforts cannot but be transitory.

Is real peace possible when the gains of civilisation remain distributed unequally and when the existing social and economic structure perpetuate the same? Is unrestricted use of natural resources conducive to peace specially with an ever growing population? Is the present system of centralised production and trade and commerce conducive to peace? Can campaigns against war or resistance to war by conscientious objectors bring about peace without a fundamental change in our way of life socially, economically and politically? Is peace really attainable when millions go without a square meal a day?

If we want to establish peace, we have to go into these fundamental factors that give rise to conflicts. Though very often individuals and groups suffer due to their own inadequacies to meet situations, in the society as it exists today it is the social milieu that is more diseased and requires appropriate treatment. This may mean even restructuring the society and our methods of resolving conflicts. The wars, big and small, all around us are eye-opener to the reality where we see today efforts are directed towards substituting confrontation with co-operation. This is an evidence that violence and confrontation do not serve the real end.

Our values with regard to functions of family, parents-children obligation, husband and wife roles, system of marriage and its sacramental importance, the objectives and purposes of our schools, the trade and commerce institutions, the employer-employee relations, the obligation of the State and the citisens, etc., are undergoing changes adversely under the impact of technological growth.

Consequently we have to face problems of vagrant children, juvenile delinquency, rising criminality, social vices, general discontentment, bad housing, inadequate food, absence of medical care, etc. Besides these, rapid social change and increase social mobility we weakening kinship and social bonds giving rise to new types of social problems. More children are getting neglected, more old people are uncared, more people are feeling lonely and isolated, neighbours feel as strangers, families are getting smaller both in sise and warmth of relationship. Self-indulgences by individuals and groups are increasing and acquisition of wealth through exploitation is becoming a creed thus promoting worst type of violence. Measures to arrest this trend are vital to live a better and peaceful life. This calls for greater commitment to altruistic values in personal and social life.

Our approach to the poor and needy has been paternalistic, moralistic, rather than humanistic and democratic. Most of our programmes have invariably aimed at making the poor acquiesce to the existing socio-economic conditions. We have been successful in making them more and more dependent, smothering the initiative of the individual and stifling the concept of self-respect. Neither the giver nor the receiver are least worried about this aspect.

The politically conscious section of the poor people is realising that they are being exploited. They are revolting. The only mode before them is the violent way. If we want peace we have to develop a social structure that will eliminate the need for violence to maintain social order at the individual, family and national levels. This only will help to promote peace at the international level. We cannot be autocratic and self-indulgent and violent at the individual and family levels and expect the community and nation to be non-violent and be at peace. What is required particularly on the part of the educated and the elite is self-control and discipline and a sense of social responsibility. We have to change our own attitudes. We love ourselves too much. We must learn to love others. The choice before us is limited. Should we in the name of development opt for affluence for a few and poverty for the rest? The development as we know has led to conspicuous consumption, pollution, violence, strifes, conflicts and alienation. Development has been functional for a few and dysfunctional for the majority, particularly the poor.

The changes that are taking place in China and Russia, particularly the concepts of 'Glasnost' and 'Perestroika', should enable us to keep our eyes, ears and mind open and receptive. It is high time that some of us who believe that the only way to establish socialism or communism is through violent revolution will have to do some rethinking. Today China and Russia and other Communist countries are remodelling their ways, methods and modes.

It is now right time for all of us to think whether non-violent methods are appropriate to reconstruct our life at the individual, family and community levels and whether the non-violent methods would help promote peace at national and international levels.

Non-violent methods need not be accepted just because great men have asked us to do so. We in the universities should critically examine the concept of non-violence for its intrinsic values and accept it only if we are satisfied about its worth and efficacy in bringing about the desired end. What are the basic values in the non-violent mode needs to be elucidated (Please see Appendix).

The universities are expected to provide (i) knowledge and (ii) basic values to its graduates. We are no doubt churning out graduates with degrees (knowledge) but have we been able to inculcate in them values? The corrupt practices, the superstitious attitudes, the autocratic ways, the low scruples of a good number of university graduates in various walks of life and offices go to prove our education system has miserably failed to equip our students with basic values.

Our curriculum in the undergraduate and postgraduate courses in different subjects and professions provide eight to ten papers to impart knowledge but there is no provision in our curriculum to provide knowledge about the basic values. The basic values acquired by some of the graduates should rather be a tribute to other factors like upbringing in the family, social outlook, religions outlook, etc. Should we not think of restructuring our curriculum to provide at least one paper in each discipline (in each academic year) to introduce and to reinforce some basic values based on the concept of social justice, equality, non-violence and peace? This may mean re-adjusting the number of papers in the regular courses.

This seminar will be serving a useful purpose if it could recommend introduction of foundation courses, orientation courses and refresher courses during each year of education to inculcate in the students basic values for promoting social justice, equality, non-violence, peace and allied values.

APPENDIX

BASIC VALUES AND PRINCIPLES FOR PROMOTING A SOCIETY BASED ON NON-VIOLENCE, PEACE, SOCIAL JUSTICE, EQUALITY AND ALLIED VALUES

Some of the basic values and principles that ought to guide us in our day-to-day life have been noted below. These are not exhaustive neither these have been noted in a particular order. Acceptance of these and similar values is the only way open to us to develop an egalitarian, humanistic, socialistic, democratic society based on non-violence and peace.

In the application of these values and principles in different walks of life there are many constraints which we have to overcome. We have to be rational rather than dogmatic in our approach. Of course the line of demarcation distinguishing what ways are rational and what ways are dogmatic is very thin. With determination and patience over a period of time we may learn to mark the thin line of demarcation.

It is also often argued that what was possible for Mahatma Gandhi to adopt may not be possible to adopt by ordinary people. This is also true but as and when more and more people, particularly the young in the universities deliberate what appears impossible today may, in course of time, become possible as well as feasible. We have to learn to adopt and to develop new techniques of promoting and developing a non-violent society based on peace, the only option open to us. This is a challenge before the universities.

Non-violence as an important value should come through realisation. This cannot be imposed on the students. Hence care is to be taken to examine its needs in the present context and help students see for themselves its values and utility as against the other alternatives.

Values and Principles

1. Belief in the worth of each individual.
2. Respect for the freedom of the individual.
3. Realisation of the social responsibility of the individual towards common welfare based on social justice and equality and

responsibility of the community for individuals' welfare.

4. Commitment to principle of simple living, (not poor living) fewer needs, self-discipline, co-operative attitudes.
5. Belief in cohesive social living and development of enduring inter-personal relationships.
6. Need to manage within the resources available and learn to share the resources.
7. A realisation, emphasis only on economic aspects of well-being leads to imbalances in the individual, family, community and the nation.
8. Realisation that human needs consist of physical, social, moral, mental and spiritual aspects. They are interrelated. Undue emphasis on any one aspect is harmful.
9. To develop attitudes of non-exploitation emphasis on quality of life rather than on material well-being.
10. Use of persuasive methods to convey ideas rather than coercive methods.
11. Need for machinery should not make us slaves of machinery.
12. Realise the importance of favoured treatment to the economically, socially and physically handicapped.
13. Develop *lokshakti* rather than *rajya-shakti*.
14. Commitment to safeguarding independence of judiciary.
15. Commitment to decentralisation of political and economic powers.
16. Importance of giving representation to women and youth in all walks of life.
17. Abhor acquisition of power at any cost, by any means, fair or foul.
18. Acceptance of the concept of participatory management.
19. Voluntary acceptance of trusteeship theory in reference to class war. Industry and business should take profit at the current interest rates.
20. Realisation of the need for balanced growth of key, small and cottage industries which help develop healthy communities.
21. Balanced growth of cities and villages on the principle of non-exploitation.
22. Need for conservation of non-renewable resources.
23. Understand that democracy without dissent is meaningless. There should be no scope for tyranny of majority. Neither the majority nor the minority ought to claim a monopoly of right

24. In matters of conscience the majority has no place. The rule of the majority when it becomes coercive is intolerable.
25. "Numerical strength save us of violence when it acts in total disregard of any strongly felt opinion of majority."
26. Minority has a perfect right to act differently from the majority.
27. Where there is no principle involved and there is a programme to be carried out the minority has to follow the majority.
28. The deprived and the dispossessed cannot be calmed and silenced for ever.
29. Willingness to understand the opponent's viewpoints, and respect it as fully as we expect him to respect ours. It is one of the indispensable tests of a healthy public life.
30. "Truth and non-violence are not cloistered virtues but applicable as much in the forum and the legislatures as in the market place."
31. Means are as important as ends, even more important than ends.
32. All social actions should be governed by the principles of selflessness, non-attachment, non-violence and active participation.
33. "In raising our consciousness levels we can use Marx, Gandhi and others as seminal guide-posts not as dogmatic final answers."
34. Strengthen family bonds to elicit commitment to the care of old, children, deviant and infirm within the family.
35. Commitment to strengthen neighbourliness and develop sense of belonging for peaceful community life.
36. Help develop small and healthy communities where social living is marked by cohesiveness rather than develop big cities/megapolis which result in disorganisation leading to various types of violence.
37. Realisation that development as it works today fails to distribute the fruits of development equally. Rich and elite take undue share of development. There is a need for alternative to the present trend of development.
38. Development of attitude of scientific inquiry.
39. Commitment to abolition of untouchability and caste and religious barriers and a commitment to communal unity.
40. Commitment to decent and respectable living for all.

12

INVOLVING UNIVERSITY STUDENTS IN PEACE ACTION AND CONFLICT RESOLUTION

N. RADHAKRISHNAN

MAHATMA GANDHI stands out as the first modern leader who gave serious thought to organise a broad-based People's Movement to combat organised and unorganised violence. He suggested as early as 1938 the formation of a Peace Brigade whose members would risk their lives in maintaining peace, communal harmony and in educating people in their everyday life. He believed that this Brigade would be a substitute for the police and even military some day. He prescribed seven attributes for every member of this Peace Brigade :

1. He or she must have a living faith in non-violence. This is impossible without a living faith in God.
2. The messenger of peace must have equal regard for all the principal religions of the earth.
3. Peace work can be done singly or in groups.
4. The messenger of peace will cultivate through personal service contacts with the people in his/her locality.
5. A peace-bringer must have a character beyond reproach and must be known for his strict impartiality.
6. The Peace Brigade will not wait till the conflagration breaks out, but will try to handle the situation in anticipation.
7. There should be a distinctive dress worn by the members of the Peace Brigade so that they would be recognised without difficulty.

Gandhi called the Peace Brigade of his dream *Shanti Sena (Shanti* means peace and *Sena* means army or brigade). It should have its emphasis on

(1) character building
(2) cultivation of soul force
(3) love of voluntary work
(4) resolve to jump into action in any eventuality
(5) to observe truth, non-violence and non-possessiveness to the utmost of one's ability
(6) disinterested service without desire for results
(7) not to recognise distinctions of class or caste and to respect all religions equally.

Gandhi believed that all these attributes will arm the members of the Peace Brigade (*Shanti Sena*) with inner strength. With a broad-based peace plan it would be possible to achieve a nation-wide peace brigade in every country. This requires that the peace brigade should become a task force after obtaining proper training. To quote Gandhi again,

> "A very small part of the preliminary training received by the military is common to the non-violent army. These are discipline, drill, singing the chorus, flag-hoisting, signalling and the like."[1]

Vinoba Bhave, the walking-saint, took up the idea after Gandhi's assassination. The War Resistors International which held its conference in Gandhigram in South India in 1960 decided to take up the idea and organise an International Peace Brigade. They also decided to train peace workers to be sent to areas of conflicts. A.J. Maste, Michael Scott, Jayaprakash Narayan were behind this move. The Indian *Shanti Sena Mandal* and the International Peace Brigade thus were formed and began functioning well.

Yet the sad fact is no serious efforts are being made to bring the students and youth into the orbit of training in non-violence. The credit of having organised the first group of students in non-violence has gone to Dr. G. Ramachandran, a disciple of Gandhi and founder of the Gandhigram University, in South India, when he introduced *Shanti Sena* training programme in Gandhigram and successfully resisted the introduction of pre-military training programmes. He kept the *Shanti*

Sena at the Centre of the Educational and Rural Reconstruction activities started by the institute. Student and non-student youth, men and women, teachers and other workers showed remarkable realisation of role of the *Shanti Sena* in their everyday life.

The *Shanti Sena* as realised by the Gandhigram Rural Institute is an intensive programme aimed at providing a series of opportunities for the youth to realise the great role they can play. Besides giving them opportunities to know what it means to cultivate non-violence in their personal and public life, it is out-and-out practical involvement in non-violence and not peace making in the traditional sense of the term but realisation of life situations of a wide range. The programme is designed on the basis of the awareness that what the young minds need is exposure to the various problems and inculcation of values in their minds. The aim has always been to integrate peace education and peace action with the main academic programme taking advantage of the willingness of children, student and non-student youth and men and women in the various institutions and service areas of the institute. The idea grew steadily inviting the attention of peace workers and researchers elsewhere.

Dr. Glenn D. Paige, Professor of Political Science at the University of Hawaii and winner of Dr. G.R. Award for the International Understanding (1986), came to India twice to study the working of the *Shanti Sena* and this votary of non-violence was so much impressed by the *Shanti Sena* activities in Gandhigram Rural Institute, that he invited the present writer to introduce the concept of *Shanti Sena* at four international gatherings in December 1984 — one each in Japan, Thailand, Costa Rica and Hawaii — and in six universities in these countries. It is found that the *Shanti Sena* Programme helps young men and women to acquire new insights and each trainee develops a feeling that he/she continues to grow in maturity through his/her involvement, which his/her areas of specialisation for the degree will not offer him/her otherwise. It is this that the *Shanti Sena* seeks to develop. It may be quite possible that these boys and girls will herald a new era of hope and peace some day. Involvement in active peace work and conflict resolution has been an integral part of the training programme. Peace education campaigns, campaign to eradicate social evils, mass rallies against the ever-increasing military expenditure, acting as task-force and rushing relief work during cyclone-havoc, rendering valuable services to forge communal harmony during communal disturbances have been some of the most important items of work undertaken by the *Shanti Sena*.

Conflict Resolution – Three Instances

Let me mention here for illustration three instances in which the members of this University Peace Brigade played some useful role in peace action and conflict resolution.

Inter-Religious Disturbances in Kanyakumari District

Kanyakumari, the southern-most tip of India, is a tourists' attraction. This part of the land is famous for its beautiful paddy fields and religious harmony among the people. Hindus and Christians live with perfect understanding and inter-marriages are common so much so that one can see in the same family members practising both Christianity and Hinduism. In fact religion to them was a matter of purely personal practice. This situation underwent a dramatic change when a dispute over the use of loud-speakers during a festival in a temple in one of the remote villages in this district was blown out of proportion and flared up into a major inter-communal riot, rocking most of the homes and towns. Suddenly the people assumed Hindu and Christian identities. Religious heads participation resulted in many deaths and quite a few villages looted and burnt down in the frenzy which gripped the people. Police, paramilitary forces and voluntary organisations were silent or helpless spectators to the gory act without any human consideration.

All of us in the Gandhigram University, though we were away about 300 kilometres from the scene of violence, were very much concerned and we decided that we should rush to the scene of violence and strengthen peace efforts and prevent further bloodshed and loss of life. As students and staff of a University, we could do only very little in such a conflict. But we were quite convinced that as impartial, non-political and non-religious group of people, not belonging to the area of conflict, we would be able to play at least a small role by touring the riot-hit areas and meeting the religious heads and others to persuade them to come to the table of negotiations. With this limited aim, a team of *Shanti Sainiks*, under the leadership of the present writer, moved to the scene of violence. I quote from the diary we maintained :

> *16-3-1982 :* As first step we thought it would be better if we held informal discussion with those students, staff and others who hail from the areas of violence and disturbances. We thought this

strategy would give us valuable information because these friends would be able to assess the situation in an objective manner. We met 16 persons, some of them students, trainees, staff and workers belonging to both Hindu and Christian religions. We gathered very valuable information from them and we were emboldened to go ahead with our plan when two of them volunteered to join our team.

17-3-1982 : A nine-member team was selected to move to the scene. It comprised two women, one social worker, three teachers and three students. And it so happened there were Hindus and Christians in our group. We spent the whole day in studying all available literature on the district and its people and the back issues of newspapers' cuttings, Press statements issued by different persons, reports by impartial bodies who visited the spots and Government Press releases. This exercise was undertaken as part of the preparation for the team members to acquaint themselves with the issue.

18-3-1982 : Discussion and study of the various aspects of the locality to which we were going continued. We practised a few group songs particularly non-denominational songs. We selected a few songs which extol the uniqueness and greatness of the district. These songs had been composed by a poet who inspired the people during freedom struggle when all the people marched together. This was done with a view to raise nostalgic memories of a glorious past when they lived with perfect harmony.

19-3-1982 : The team met and continued the rehearsal of the songs. Since the team was scheduled to leave next day it was almost a final rehearsal. Dr. M. Aram (V-C), whom we had met before we left for the area of tension, explained the value of persuasion in conflict resolution. He advised the team members to maintain objectivity and impartiality in their approach.

20-3-1982 : We left at 6.0 a.m. after taking a pledge to remain neutral and work for the promotion of peace and establish order in the affected areas. Before we moved out of Gandhigram we offered floral offerings at the Gandhi Pillar in Gandhigram.

The party reached Nagerkoil, the headquarters of Kanyakumari district, around 3.0 p.m. We met the District Collector who was in charge of law and order situation. He advised the team to get the local support of people if the party wanted to visit some of the affected areas, for the people in those areas would look at outsiders only with suspicions. He observed that the real damage done was not to the properties but to the minds of people. The party learnt that they were very keen on restoring normalcy. But fear and suspicions prevented them from coming out and making any positive move. Real bridge-builders were absent form the locality.

At night the party divided itself into two batches and met the principals of the local colleges to seek their help and also to find out whether it would be possible to arrange a peace procession involving students and others and form a Peace Committee of youngmen.

21-3-1982 : The party met the Archbishop of Kotar who was taking rest in a hospital and other Christian friends to know what they thought could be done to restore normalcy.

We next met some of the local leaders of Hindu religion. Most of them appeared agitated. We realised that they were also keen on ending the ugly confrontation. The question was who would bell the cat. We volunteered to mediate between the two groups. Out next attempt was to find out the doves in the group.

The next step was a visit to two of the worst-hit villages from where large-scale migration of population took place. We were informed that it would not be safe to visit these villages and hence advised not to go ahead with our plan. Finally, two persons, a Hindu and a Christian, from Nagerkoil, agreed to join us and take us to the villages. What we saw in one of the villages moved us. A place of worship was completely demolished. The glass-panes and statues in the building were broken into pieces. Remains of the burnt clothes were also seen. A maternity hospital was looted. All the thatched houses were burnt down in the village. When we enquired the reason for such a massive destruction we were told that it is in reprisal of another attack by the other community. The party went to the next village. A cloth store and an electrical goods shop, adjacent to it, were burnt down completely. Thatched houses were set on fire. We also saw a half-burnt places of worship there.

After having studied the situations in both the places the team felt :

1. The police firing (at Mandaikkadu) could have been averted had the police taken precautionary measures, for there were disturbances during the festival the previous year also.
2. The government had not taken proper steps at the appropriate

time to curb violation and deal with the situation with justice and firmness.

3. Both parties suffered heavy losses of property and life.
4. Both parties indulged in inhuman atrocities that brought about great destruction on them.
5. Mutual fear and animosity, instead of amity and tolerance, gripped the minds of all.
6. It was also perceived that both the parties realised that people did not behave as human beings during the clashes.

The following steps were found to be necessary in order to make the people get rid of mutual fear and animosity and create an atmosphere of calmness, amiableness and tolerance :

1. Formation of a committee consisting of members who command love and respect of both religions to go into the details of the clash.
2. Government and non-communal organisations should come forward to take up relief work.
3. Constitution of a permanent 'Peace Committee' comprising religious leaders from all religions and this autonomous committee should act as a mediator and prevent further communal clashes.
4. A unit of the *Shanti Sena* be formed in this area with the co-operation of the principals of local colleges.
5. The Government should enact a law which would ban the use of public address system at places where religious festivals are celebrated.

Next day a meeting of local leaders, voluntary organisations, youth groups, religious leaders and academicians was held at which a committee of 21 persons was formed to (i) assist the local law enforcing authorities, (ii) help remove misunderstanding and fear from people, (iii) to strengthen the local peace committee, (iv) to request the news agencies and press not to publish news items on the basis of rumour or gossip which might inflame passion.

Inter-communal Conflict

Now I shall try to present to you another conflict involving two sections of the same religion (Caste Hindus and the *Harijans*) were involved. This happened in a town (Villupuram) near Madras in 1976. Some unpleasantry between two youths of two communities culminating assumed devastating proportions in the fleeing of almost the entire Harijan population from the village. The Caste Hindus who wielded considerable economic clout felt they had succeeded in driving all their opponents from the town. Tension was mounting gradually and echoes of what happened in this place were heard in other parts of the state as well.

This time it was thought that the woman volunteers of the *Shanti Sena* should be allowed to take a leading role on the basis of the past experience that women are better peace workers than men on certain occasions and what was happening now would be ideally suited to the women trainees to try out. Hence a team of 15 members, led by the present writer, left for the scene of conflict to take up peace work. There were only two men in this group of 15. It should be admitted that when the intention of taking a peace team to the scene of violence was announced, over 200 students expressed their willingness and out of this more than half were women. As we feared, what awaited these girls at Villupuram was a hostile atmosphere. The Caste Hindus had a lurking suspicion that our team was there to find fault with them and force them to agree to a compromise which would result in the eventual return of the Harijans to their moorings. The first experiences were rather very much distressing. But these girls did not give up hope. A few voluntary agencies from other places were also on the scene. We thought it was better to work together and with this aim in mind a meeting of all the agencies was held at which it was decided that the *Shanti Sainiks* would exploit the power of persuasion and would work through the women of the village — an effective method to influence men. To cut a story, in the next three days they succeeded in persuading three of the section leaders to attend a public meeting which eventually led to the formation of a peace committee. It was multipronged attack in which several agencies were involved. While the local leaders were persuaded to adopt an attitude of reconciliation, the *Harijan* leaders were contacted by more acceptable and influential political bosses to come down to the plain and accept the compromise formula. The final settlement under which the Harijans returned after eleven days of anxiety was really a great moment in the lives of all those who participated in the programme. The people who returned after eleven days of anxiety, harassment and fear were greatly relieved to see that their houses were by and large safe and their cattle and other belongings they left behind intact. In a conflict of this nature there would always be the tendency to take away the property of the fleeing party. It must be admitted here that the Harijans who flew out of the village did not have much to be taken way but what even they had was found to be intact. The women volunteers stood sentinel to the property of the people who had left the village. There were tears of gratitude in the eyes of the poor women and appreciation in the Caste Hindus when on the 12th day the party boarded train back to Gandhigram.

Inter-religious Dispute at Vellod

The next major involvement, perhaps a very significant one, relates to a dispute between two religious groups in a village called Vellod near the university campus. It was a hundred-year old dispute which evaded any possible solution despite the best efforts made by the law-enforcing authorities and other mediators. I do not want to be subjective in talking about how the *Shanti Sena* intervened in this village last year when the air smelt of a big conflagration and violence. The *Indian Express* carried a very objective study of what we did in the village. I reproduce below excerpts of the report :

> "Shanti Sena (Peace Corps) of the Gandhigram Rural University is not an ornamental appendage of this institution, just meant for ceremonial parades. It has been, for the past many years, carrying the message of peace and non-violence to the numerous villages that dot the map of Anna District. The village Vellodu lies at the foot of Sirumalai range. The population of around 7,000 earns its living mainly through the traditional occupation of agriculture, nestling in the shadows of the Sirumalai hills, the village has not been spared the stigma of brewing moonshine to augment its economy.
>
> The village had been a thorn in the flesh of Dindigul police, not because of the illicit brew that reportedly flows from the forests of Sirumalai, but for another reason, a century-old feud between its Christian and Hindu population, Vanniars, the largest single community, are divided into Christians, who are in a majority, and Hindus, a little less in number. Religion has not, however, stood in the way of their matrimonial relations. Christian brides taking Hindu grooms and *vice versa* are not uncommon. That much of cordiality and understanding still exist between the two religious groups. But when it comes to celebrating festivals, all this conviviality is thrown to the winds and the two groups remain

daggers drawn. Often tension during festivals reaches a flash point, but saner counsel prevails at the last minute and major group clashes are averted. No other village in the area has figured as many times as Vellod in the police records. Often, during festivals, policemen outnumber devotees at Vellod. Everytime one religious group decides to celebrate a festival, the mood in the village changes. It is not an atmosphere of joy or religious fervour that pervades the village, but a feeling of rancour and anger.

The peace that prevailed was, however, only surface deep and the concord deceptive. As the Chariot carrying the cross began its tour, all the pent up fury burst into a storm. Police, who were present as usual, prevented clashes and brought the celebrations to an abrupt halt, it was five days before the Chariot could continue its journey.

In an attempt to re-start the peace process by Fr. Stephen and Mr. Chinniah, the law enforcement authorities sought the intervention of the Vice-Chancellor of the Gandhigram Rural University, Dr. Devendra Kumar, an ardent adherent to the Gandhian philosophy of non-violence. To the Vice-Chancellor who had dealt with dacoits of the Chambal Valley, this was yet another challenge. Officials of the *Shanti Sena,* with whom the Vice-Chancellor discussed the problem, picked up the gauntlet and with all hope decided to enter the village on a peace mission.

But when they went to Vellod, the reception was far from what they expected. Though they did not expect the villagers to receive them with open arms and anticipated some resentment, they were not prepared for the galling experience. They were treated with not only suspicion but contempt. This was the time when Dr. N. Radhakrishnan, the Director of *Shanti Sena,* and his two colleagues Dr. M.S. Prabhakaran and Mr. William Bhaskar, had to put into practice all that had so far remained only in principles and precepts on peace and non-violence. Lengthy meetings with individuals and groups in tea kiosks, temples and the church resulted in the two groups agreeing to meet in the presence of Dr. Devendra Kumar. This did not mean that all hurdles to a compromise were eliminated. But the *Shanti Sena* official, with the active co-operation of Fr. Stephen and Mr. Chinniah, pursued the process relentlessly, which culminated in a meeting at Gandhigram, represented adequately by both the groups. The meeting decided to appoint a five-member peace panel to go into the problems of the two groups and to make its recommendations.

The bone of contention had been a plot of land in front of the

Easwary Amman temple. There is a raised platform on this plot of land which is used by the Christians to keep the Cross during the festival for people to offer worship. Calling this the Angel's Cottage, the Christians were planning to construct a tower here. But the Hindus prevented this move with all their might.

The peace committee, comprising three Christians and two Hindus, sat day after day for long hours and drew up a three-point peace plan. It had recommended that the plot opposite Easwary Amman temple be declared a common land for use by both the groups and that the foundation dug for the Angel's Cottage should be covered up. But they could erect the cottage in a place, east of the present site.

Hindus were allowed to construct a platform of the same sise as the Angel's Cottage for religious observances. This would be called a peace platform but no idols or religious insignia would be placed on this platform permanently. Christians would also not place permanent objects of worship in the Angel's Cottage. Both the platforms would be used only during festival. At the initiative of the *Shanti Sena* the committee also called for the withdrawal of all criminal and civil cases from the village pending before courts. If agreements alone could bring about peace and harmony, this world would not be what is today. A strong will is needed to fulfil the provisions of such accords in letter and spirit.

The people of Vellod have already demonstrated that they have the will and courage of their conviction to ensure lasting peace in the village. On New Year's day both groups got together to celebrate the day and usher in an year of peace and understanding. Fr. Stephen acclaimed the accord of a 'holy writ' while Mr. Chinniah described it as the golden chapter in the annals of the village. The Vice-Chancellor and the officials of *Shanti Sena* hail it as a major break-through in rural development, in that the accord has been able to achieve the foremost prerequisite for progress — peace and understanding. Dr. Devendra Kumar said this accord could be a model for other villages similarly afflicted. *Shanti Sena* can legitimately feel proud that it has helped to bury a hundred-year-old feud and put the village on the path to progress."[2]

NOTES

1. M.K. Gandhi, *Satyagraha*, Ahmedabad: Navajivan Trust, 1951.
2 *Indian Express*, 20 February, 1988.

13

SOCIAL SERVICE FOR UNIVERSITY YOUTH

K.D. GANGRADE

THE EDUCATION Commission rightly said that the destiny of India is now being shaped in her class-rooms. This is no more rhetoric. In a world based on science and technology, it is education that determines the level of prosperity, welfare and security of the people. On the quality and number of persons coming out of our schools and colleges will depend our success in the great enterprise of national reconstruction whose principal objective is to raise the standard of living of our people.

Thus, education as an investment in human resources plays an important role among the factors which contribute to economic growth. It secures returns in the form of skilled man-power geared to the needs of development and also creates the right attitudes and climate for development. It seeks to create an environment of discipline, harmony, understanding and team-work which is conducive to the implementation of production plans. Both for accelerating economic development and for improving the quality of the society, it is essential that we should establish a firm and purposive link between education and development.

The present educational system is, however, responsible for increasing the deplorable gulf between the educated and the uneducated classes, between the intelligentsia and the masses. The intelligentsia should try to become a real service group striving to uplift the masses and no become a parasitical group living for itself and perpetuating its own privileged position. Our traditional "elite" as a whole — with some noble exception — had no close ties with the masses and the new "elite" created by modern education also remained largely aloof from the people, except during the struggle for freedom under Mahatma Gandhi, when he was able to inspire large number of educated and well-to-do persons to identify themselves with the interests of the masses and the country as a whole. But when the struggle for freedom came to an end with the attainment to independence they again tended to move away from the people. It is, therefore, imperative that a close link is forged between the educational programme and the needs of the society. The universities and training institutions should identify themselves with the economic and social environment and develop a sense of commitment of the task of meeting the needs of the society.

For this purpose the Education Commission recommended that some form of social and national service should be made obligatory for all students and should form an integral part of education at all stages. The Commission hoped that this would become an instrument to build character, improve discipline, inculcate a faith in the dignity of manual labour and develop a sense of social responsibility.

To sum up, the main aims of the Social Service is to provide opportunities to the teachers and students to gain valuable practical experience from such service and to break down the walls that now divide institutions of learning from the life of the common people.

Objectives of the Social Service

The objectives of Social Service under two broad categories can be classified are :

A. Overall Objective.
B. Specific Objectives.

Overall Objective

The overall objective of the Social Service is educational. Service to the community is the activity through which this objective is sought to be attained.

Specific Objectives

The more specific objectives of the Social Service are to arouse the student's social conscience and to provide him with the opportunity :

1. to work with and among people;
2. to engage in creative and constructive social action;
3. to enhance his knowledge of himself and the community through a confrontation with reality;
4. to put his scholarship to practical use in mitigating at least some of the social problems;
5. to gain skills in the exercise of democratic leadership;
6. to gain skills in programme development.

In consideration of the objectives of the scheme a major question that should receive our attention relates to the emphasis and orientation of the service programme. Do we see the scheme as primarily providing opportunities for growth and for constructive work to the students or do we look upon this as a means of mobilising students for meeting community needs? We should be clear about the service and eucational goals of the programme as these represent two types of emphasis which must be kept in mind in planning service activities by students. It is true that students cannot be considered as merely instruments for meeting community needs. Yet it is community needs and the effort to meet them that give relevance to student activity. To the extent that we take community needs into account we have to provide students special skills to render the type of service most needed by the community. We may have to organise "capsule" type of short-term courses to equip them with programme skills to be useful to the community. These skills acquired by students may help some of them in becoming self-employed after graduation.

At the same time, too great an emphasis on the service to the community by students can be self-defeating. It may result in setting up false criteria for judging the usefulness of student service programmes. In part, at least, this usefulness would lie in what the student himself gains out of his effort to be of service to the community. From this point of view it is essential to select carefully the tasks that are assigned to student groups. They must have the potentiality of enabling a student to benefit by the new skills he has acquired, to derive satisfaction from the achievement of clear though limited, goals and from the experience of working with others on projects useful to society.

In brief all the programmes and activities that are to be undertaken by the students should be primarily aimed towards giving educational experience to the participating students. Meeting the needs in the community is important but it cannot be regarded as a primary goal. The experience of working in programmes under the scheme may deepen students knowledge of subjects learnt in the class-room.

Programme Planning and Development

The development of programmes and projects is central aspect of the Social Service. The emphasis in programme planning and development should be that:

(a) any activity whether of small or great social significance must be the expression of genuine interest of the students;
(b) the activity should be specific and known to be within the capacity of the students, thus providing an opportunity for immediate satisfaction and evident progress;
(c) the activity must be a stimulation for further related activity; and
(d) it must provide opportunities to the students to be participating citisens in the world of today and tomorrow.

The most important principle in programme planning is that the students should be helped to plan their own programmes. This does not mean that staff adviser does nothing. Rather it means that he works with the students at their own level and helps them to develop a programmes in consonance with their interests and needs.

There are three principal elements in the programming process: the students, the teachers, and the programme content. Each of these elements, however, has many components. The students have their interests and their needs, their special abilities, their relationships with each other and with the teacher, their particular norms and values related to their family and community life. The teacher has his professional knowledge and skills, his special abilities, his role as the representative of the college and as the bearer of the values and norms of the college and of society as a whole. The programme content has its inherent potentialities for meeting the needs and interests of the students and for maintaining or changing the norms and values of the group, the community and the society.

The interaction of these three elements is essential in programme planning if the social service is to provide a meaningful experience for its members. All these elements are important and have place in the process. It is inevitable that in any particular situation one element may be more prominent than others. At times the students are dominant; at times the teacher is more in evidence; and sometimes the content takes the first place.

In the properly functioning programme process, no one element is permanently emphasised at the expanse of the others; instead, constant shifting of emphasis takes place according to the needs of students and communities. It is the integration of the three elements of programme that produces stable and satisfying result.

A variety of programmes can be developed under the Social Service for the students. A suggestive list of programmes is given in Appendix. Broadly speaking these programmes can be listed within the following categories :

1. *Institutional Work* — The students may be placed in selected welfare agencies to work as volunteers.
2. *Institutional Projects* — Improvement of campuses; construction of play fields, swimming pools, etc.
3. *Rural Projects* — Eradication of illiteracy, minor irrigation works, agricultural operations, health, hygiene, sanitation, development of rural roads, etc. This may be done by adopting villages with 10 to 15 km of colleges.
4. *Urban Projects* — Adult education, welfare of slum dwellers, training in civil defence, setting up of first-aid posts, hospital work, etc.

The programmes of the Social Service should be sufficiently attractive and challenging so as to motivate the students to join the Scheme.

Conditions for the Success of the Project

The college may prepare and take one or several projects under the Social Service Scheme programmes. A project is a planned undertaking the points about the project to be borne in mind are : the nature and content of the project, its objectives, organisation, personnel and budgetary requirements.

The actual implementation of the projects will present many

problems and challenge to intelligence of the teachers, students and the administrators. Gordon Alloport, a well-known psychologist, has suggested following points to make a project successful:

(a) They should meet the genuine need of the community or the particular group which they are meant to serve and their value should be apparent to the community as well as the workers.
(b) As far as possible, the local community should be given an opportunity to participate in the planning and execution of the work.
(c) They should provide ample opportunity for work by the unskilled participants also.
(d) While the manual work should be realistic and strenuous, it should be held within reasonable limits so as to allow adequate room for other aspects of the programme — educational and recreational. Unless the programme is well balanced, it will not be able to sustain the interest of the kinds of youth who are to be drawn into the scheme.
(e) The leaders and the staff should be given adequate training, theoretical and practical, in the various functions which they will have to perform.

Discovering and arousing interests

Sociological, psychological and educational studies have revealed that there are general forms of interest for people of various chronological ages and of different educational, occupational, cultural, economic and other groupings. The teacher should start programme planning keeping in mind the assumed interest of the students. He should, however, not regard them as fixed programmes which students must follow. This will limit the operation of the decision-making process and restrict the participation of the students.

Interest finders, check lists and other devices may be used to help the students state their interests directly or indirectly. The expressed interests of students may only reflect items with which the members are familiar or for which the college has facilities. In any case, by trying out various activities and observing and analysing the reactions of the students to them, the teacher will be able to discover if these activities are in fact of real interest to students.

The discovery of assumed, expressed and implied interests should help the teacher to develop programmes which will be sufficiently attractive and suit the requirements of all students who wish to enrol themselves in the Social Service Scheme.

National integration

One of the by-products of the Social Service Scheme will be the promotion of national integration among students. The inter-state camps, national and regional conferences and seminars will give opportunities to the youth to live and work together. These will foster in them bonds of friendship and may help in breaking the narrow regional and local feelings.

The students through these programmes will have a better understanding and appreciation of the diversity of Indian culture.

APPENDIX

PROGRAMME FOR THE SOCIAL SERVICE

I. Projects in the area of Education

1. Helping younger students with studies.
2. Organising science clubs.
3. Organising a library and/or a book bank.
4. Organising exhibitions.
5. Fund-raising for educational activities.

II. Projects in the area of Recreation

1. Making, renovating, collecting and distributing toys, picture-books etc. to children in institutions, including hospitals.
2. Conducting play groups for children.
3. Organising competitions and contests.

III and IV ** ** **

V. Camp Projects

1. Work Camps (road building, well-digging, etc.).
2. Children's summer camps with college students as group leaders.
3. Day camps for urban areas.

Points for Selection and Placement of Students

1. Student background and equipment.
2. Motivation of students.
3. Activity Preference.
4. Time availability.
5. Agency expectations.

Some Considerations in Activity Planning
(*Whether Activity Calls for*)

1. Individual Effort — Group Effort.
2. Concurrent (Part-time) work — Vacation (full-time) work.
3. Short Duration — Long Duration.
4. Work with people — Work with materials.
5. Starting a new project — Collaborating with an existing project.
6. Raising own resources — Using resources of other agencies.

14

EDUCATION AND CHARACTER BUILDING:
Role of Gandhian Institutions

R.P. MISRA

"I WOULD feel that if we succeed in building the character of the individual, society will take care of itself. I would be quite willing to trust the organisation of society to individuals so developed.

I would try to develop courage, strength, virtue, the ability to forget oneself in working towards great aims. This is more important than literacy; academic learning is only a means to this great end."

— *Mahatma Gandhi* (1932)

THE ABOVE quotation sums-up the role of education in character building. No nation can progress and attain great heights unless it is managed by men and women of character. Such leaders will emerge only in societies where education is not limited to intellectual pursuits but also to character building. This is more so in countries like India where history has been punctuated by two hundred years of alien rule. Societies uprooted from their past often go through a crisis of character before they see Light of new era of stability and peace.

All attributes of a good character are not universally accepted. After all, what is good or bad is to a great extent determined by culture. In fact, the two are inseparable. Yet, there are qualities which are recognised in one form or the other in all cultures as indicators of good character. We may call them qualities of the heart, head and hand.

Bartrand Russel has defined an ideal character as one which possess *Vitality, courage, sensitiveness*, and *intelligence*. This is exactly what Mahatma Gandhi said in 1932 (see quotation above). *Vitality* is a physiological characteristics which is always present where there is perfect health. It promotes pleasure in feeling alive, interest in the outside world and the power of hard work.

Courage means absence of fear and the power to control fear. The test of courage has been crudely behaviouristic. Gandhi said that only one, who adheres to truth and non-violence, can be courageous. It has much to do with the inner strength.

Sensitiveness comes from sympathy which in turn comes from the feeling of human brother-hood. A sensitive person cannot eat while millions are hungry, cannot live in luxury while millions are in misery. He feels sympathy even when the sufferers are not near and dear persons and even when suffering is merely known to the occurring, not sensibly present.

Intelligence is the last of the four qualities which go with good character. Ignorant people have never been compelled to change their mental habits and have often stiffened into and unchangeable attitude. The instinctive foundation of the intellectual life is curiosity with open-mindedness.

A community of men and women possessing vitality, courage, sensitiveness and intelligence, in the highest degree that education can produce, would be very different from any thing that has hitherto existed. The question is how can it be done?

The search for the policies and programmes has been on in India for many decades. Commissions, Committees, Symposia, Seminars, etc., have been held in hundreds. Perhaps we have made some progress. The efforts have not gone in vain but we have not reached that critical stage where change gets internalised and self-propelled. Perhaps we need a different approach. Perhaps, the very premises of our thinking rests on a shaky foundation.

Educational Channels

A major lacunae in our analysis lies in our over-emphasis on the formal channels of education for achieving our social goals. We rarely realise that the educational processes begin right from the day, a child is born or may be the day life enters the womb of the mother. Much of the personality of man is shaped during the first five years of his childhood. Parents, family members, neighbours and even strangers are his teachers. They educate him, informally, about the ways of the society and the expectations they have from the child when he grows into a man.

As the child grows to adolescence, his informal contact circle widens and he starts seeing a more complex world wherein his parents are only a small part. He also sees the contradictions in what he learnt from the parents and what he learnt elsewhere. Not only this, he sees contradictions between what his parents say and do.

While he sees these contradictions widening, he goes through, if at all, the formal channels of education — the schools and colleges. What he learns through these channels is partly designed to widen his knowledge about the physical environment and partly to make him a better citisen. He learns history, geography, civics, economics, mathematics, sciences, etc. He learns about greatmen of the world and the equally greatmen of his own country. He finds that there are great qualities which made men and women great in the past. But he also sees that much of what makes people great is being violated by the people around him including his own teachers. Thus, he finds contradiction in what the school teachers and what the society taught.

Those, who pursue formal education further, might get to the stage of self-discrimination. But for a great majority, formal education is only a short interlude in life to be remembered not for learning but for a different experience — an experience of utter irrelevance. It is this group of people which constitutes a majority in the world — developed countries not excluded.

The character of the people is thus not so much shaped in schools and colleges, as in the larger society through informal education. The first teacher is the mother, then the father, then the family members and then the larger community. It is the character of the mother, the father, the family and the community which plays a vital role, particularly, because even the teachers in the formal sector of education were also once children. Education and character building can go together only if both informal and formal channels of education are geared to character building as much as for knowledge building.

Educational Environment in India

Let us look at the educational environment of India. In matters of formal education, India cannot be proud of itself. Two-thirds of its population is still illiterate. And if one considered only those who have at least 5th standard education, then we must bend our heads in shame. This has been our achievement since 1947!

Of course, there are reasons why we lag behind. Nothing happened without reasons. The real reason, however, is that we have not paid attention to primary and secondary education to the extent we were expected to. Nor we are paying the expected attention even today, our New Educational Policy notwithstanding. Our emphasis has been on urban elite education, leaving the vast countryside high and dry. We will be hard put to locate even one government primary school in each of the 400 or so districts of India which can match a good urban school — public or private. A rural primary school is a concern of none. The participatory democracy has now been replaced by representative democracy in villages tearing the village community into pieces. School is not the concern of the village community. The official inspectorate which once kept the system going even though at a low-key, is now rendered ineffective partly because of political interference and partly because of its own degeneration. The new teacher is no more proud of his profession. In fact, the whole system now rests on heaps of fictitious data on enrolment, etc.

In a forward looking society, the best institutional building in a village should be a school. One can see this in countries like Japan, Korea or even China. In India most primary schools will have no buildings, and those, which have, can be recognised from a distance because it would be the most delapidated one. What is worst, many villages have no land for future buildings. The village *Pradhan* and the *Lekhpal* have joined hands to dispose of every piece of land, not infrequently, to those who already have land. In fact, the damage to the village land and village community done during the past 40 years will far exceed anything done during a century before.

True, we have made remarkable progress in may sectors. Agricultural productivity has gone up but the dependence of rural people on land has remained almost static while the contribution of agriculture to GDP has secularily declined to now 37 per cent. Rural areas have gone poorer. Increasing population without adequate educational facilities has remained bottled in the rural sector. A small spill over to the urban centres has made them places of slums and squalor. May be, it is the fear of higher rate of rural-urban migration which has kept rural education a neglected field.

Coming now to the non-formal educational environment, we see the situation to be depressing for a great majority of children, both in rural and urban areas. The children are not taught on how to be good; they learn by experience how to survive in a hostile environment. These children are born and brought up in environment of fear and scarcity in an environment of uncertain future or, should we say, a hopeless future. The character that emerges from such an environment is centred on "beg, borrow or steal". It is not on human brotherhood, truth, non-violence, etc., extending from the family to the larger world beyond. The unfortunate part of the story is that nothing serious is happening to see a ray of hope in the future.

What can be done?

The analysis presented above is not new. It is not that these things have happened unexpectedly. In fact, nothing else would have been the outcome of a model of social development we charted out after independence. Imperatives of the situation of early 1950s forced us to go the way we want. Perhaps we did not have much elbow room for manoeuvring. Rising population and declining land resources forced us to opt for a technology which was essentially anti-poor, particularly in the absence of any meaningful social reform. Gandhiji, who could have exerted moral pressure to do otherwise, died within six months of independence.

Now we have reached a stage where fundamentalism has gripped our mentality to the full; where newest technology has no place for those who are illiterate and poorly educated; where past policies (not only in India but all over the world) have started coming in the way of any future progress. There is chaos; a feeling of desperation; a psychology of fear and an environment of conflict and war. We have money to buy arms, but not to invest in schools, we have to augment production for export but we have no money to invest in sectors which will give employment to our people on mass-scale. Technology has become *Bhasmasuri* in character.

The representative democracy, of which we were so proud, has failed to deliver goods. In fact, it has become non-functional. People have lost faith in it. The situation is so serious that no more than 25 to 30 per cent of people would go to the polling booths for casting their votes, if they are not physically carried by the candidates. All over the world, not more than half of the total eligible voters exercise their right to vote. The representative governments have lost credibility, as have the socialist governments which also claim to be representative.

In such a difficult situation, there appears to be only way out. That is the Gandhian way. Not India alone, but the whole world has to re-assess Gandhi and his model of human society. This assessment has to be critical. We need not accept things only because Gandhi said it. In fact, Gandhiji's whole life was nothing but an experiment. He was a social scientist who believed in experimentation. And whenever his experiments gave different results, he did not hesitate to change his views.

Let us take the broad scenario which Gandhi built for the future. It is a dynamic scenario and hence not anti-developmental. Within this broad frame of reference, we have seen his educational programme. In Gandhian Scheme of Education, both formal and informal sectors are taken into account and given due importance.

His school system was linked to a living village society — which meant a society which would be equitable, self-reliant, self-governing and imbued with a participatory democratic ideals. The education itself will concern itself with the *Head*, the *Heart* and the *Hand*. It has to begin from home. So the parents have to be taken care of and involved in the whole process. School, in his scheme of things, could not be taken out of the total rural social system. The same applied to urban areas.

The Catalysts

The catalysts for a new education system could be the Gandhians and Gandhian institutions. Let the charity begin at home. There are hundreds of voluntary agencies in the country running educational programmes and quite a large number of them Gandhian in orientation. What is the condition of the schools they are running? How many of them can be said to have developed an integrated system as Gandhiji envisaged? In fact, the tragedy today is that most of the Gandhian institutions are being run on most un-Gandhian lines. If Gandhiji's followers have lost the track, how can we expect a government working under great stresses and strains to keep its mind cool!

What we need today is a large number of voluntary agencies wedded to Gandhian concept of education to work independently or with government agencies to change the educational pattern and to make it worthy of a culture that India is. Of course, there is need for change in government policies and in many other things which will come if new avenues are opened up for the future.

Participatory democracy relies heavily on voluntarism and voluntary agencies. The representative democracy has penetrated even the tiny village. It is not going to be abolished. Its ill-effects can be tempered by the equally penetrating voluntary agencies. The followers of Gandhi and all those, who want peace and harmony in society, have to come forward for the voluntary work particularly in the sector of education. Then and then alone we can hope to create a situation in which education can become a means of character building and social change.

APPENDIX

LIST OF PERSONS WHO PARTICIPATED IN THE NATIONAL SEMINAR ON "CONFLICT RESOLUTION THROUGH NON-VIOLENCE: ROLE OF UNIVERSITIES"

1. **Dr. S.K. Aggarwal**
   Department of Geography, University of Delhi, Delhi.
2. **Dr. Christopher Benninger**
   Director, Centre for Development Studies and Action, P.B. 843, Deccan Gymkhana, Poona.
3. **Sandhya Chaudhary**
   Department of Gandhian Studies, Panjab University, Chandigarh.
4. **Shri Davendra Bhai**
   Centre for Science for Villages, Wardha, Maharashtra.
5. **Meena Dutta**
   Department of Gandhian Studies, Panjab University, Chandigarh.
6. **Prof. K.D. Gangrade**
   Pro-Vice-Chancellor, University of Delhi, Delhi.
7. **Dr. Chandan Gupta**
   Institute of Emotional Management, Delhi.
8. **Fr. John**
   Vidya Jyoti, Raj Niwas Marg, Delhi.
9. **Dr. Suman Khanna**
   Lecturer, Mata Sundari College, Delhi University.
10. **Dr. D.S. Kothari**
    Chancellor, Jawaharlal Nehru University, Mehrauli Road, New Delhi.
11. **Prof. M.K. Machwe**
    Department of Physics, University of Delhi, Delhi.

12. **Prof. S. Malhotra**
Department of Gandhian Studies, Panjab University, Chandigarh.
13. **Prof. R.P. Misra**
Director, Gandhi Bhavan, University of Delhi, Delhi.
14. **Shri Kapil Deo Misra**
Journalist, 169/10, Sadar Bazar, Pratapgarh, U.P.
15. **Shri Diwan Singh Nagpal**
Department of Gandhian Studies, Panjab University, Chandigarh.
16. **Dr. Jai Narain**
Department of Gandhian Studies, Panjab University, Chandigarh.

Resource Persons

17. **Dr. B.N. Pandey**
Vice-Chairman, Gandhi Smriti and Darshan Samiti, 5-Tees January Marg, New Delhi.
18. **Prof. V.N. Pandit**
Department of Economics, Delhi School of Economics, University of Delhi, Delhi.
19. **Dr. Rashmi Sudha Puri**
Department of Gandhian Studies, Panjab University, Chandigarh.
20. **Prof. N. Radhakrishnan**
Gandhi Gram Rural Institute, Gandhi Gram-624302.
21. **Prof. K. Raghavendra Rao**
Yamuna Bharti, Kalyan Nagar, Dharwad, Karnataka.
22. **Prof. Jafar Raza**
Department of Urdu, Allahabad University, Allahabad.
23. **Prof. Moonis Raza**
Vice-Chancellor, University of Delhi, Delhi.
24. **Prof. Indira Rothermund**
Centre for Development Studies and Action, P.B. 843, Pune.
25. **Prof. B.K. Roy Burman**
Centre for the Study of Developing Societies, Rajpur Road, Delhi.
26. **Miss Kanchan Saxena**
113, Garhi Peer Khan, P.O. Chowk, Lucknow, U.P.

27. **Dr. J.D. Sethi**
    Professor, Department of Economics, University of Delhi.
28. **Prof. K.J. Shah**
    Karnataka University, Dharwad, Karnataka.
29. **Dr. Gauri Shankar**
    Institute of Gandhian Studies, P.O.B. No. 1116, Rajghat, Varanasi, U.P.
30. **Shri Kalika Prasad Shukla**
    Advocate, Vivek Nagar, Pratapgarh, U.P.
31. **Shri Suresh Narain Shukla**
    Department of Agro-Economic Research Centre, University of Allahabad.
32. **Dr. Ramjee Singh**
    Prof. and Head, Department of Gandhian Thought, University of Bhagalpur-812007.
33. **Dr. K.S. Subramanian**
    Institute of Emotional Management, Delhi.
34. **Prof. G.R. Sundar**
    Deputy Director (Prog.), Gandhi Smriti and Darshan Samiti, New Delhi.
35. **Prof. Mahesh Tiwari**
    Department of Buddhist Studies, University of Delhi, Delhi.
36. **Shri Raj Narain Tiwari**
    Vice-Chairman, Nachiketa, Allahabad.
37. **Dr. V.K. Tyagi**
    Department of Geography, Shaheed Bhagat Singh College, University of Delhi, Delhi.
38. **Dr. Rafiq-Zakaria**
    Sealand, 41, Cuffe Parade, Bombay.

Students

39. **Vivek Singh**
    C/o The Director, Institute of Gandhian Thought & Peace Studies, Gandhi Bhavan, Chathem Lines, Allahabad University, Allahabad.
40. **Sanjay Kumar Rai**
    Allahabad University.

41. **Mr. Mannawwarul Haq**
    Sir Ziauddin Hall, Aligarh Muslim University, Aligarh-202002.
42. **Mr. A.R. Myrthong**
    History Department, North-Eastern Hill University, Mayurbhanj, Nongthymmai, Shillong-793014.
43. **Parag Mitra**
    Andhra University, T-V/4, Port Officers Qrs. Maharani Peta, Visakhpatnam-530002, A.P.
44. **Mr. D. Jaya Raj**
    Andhra University, 23-9-44, Rajappa Naidu Street, Visakhapatnam-530001, A.P.
45. **Deoniti Prasad Sinha**
    Delhi University, 326, Mansarover Hostel, Delhi-110007.
46. **Anil Dutta Mishra**
    Delhi University, 326, Mansarover Hostel, Delhi-110007.
47. **Ms. R. Neeraja**
    Venkateswara University, Thirupati, A.P.
48. **Shiva Dhawan**
    Deptt. of Philosophy, Delhi University.
49. **Ravi Sharma**
    Deptt. of Adult Education, Delhi University.
50. **Miss Suman Sharma**
    Gargi College, Delhi University.
51. **Atul Sondhi**
    Deptt. of Buddhist Studies, Delhi University.
52. **Miss Ritu Khanna**
    Deptt. of Social Work, Delhi University.
53. **Miss Vanita Saran**
    Delhi University.
54. **Sunil Naidu**
    Deptt. of Mathematics, Delhi University.
55. **Anand Maru Lobo**
    Goa University, 456, Lamaravel Do Na Paula, Goa-403004.
56. **Ulhas V. Gawandi**
    Goa University, Parse Pedne, Goa-403512.
57. **Ms. Bhagya Shree**
    C/o H.L. College of Commerce, Gujarat University, Ahmedabad-380009.

58. **Arun Kumar**
C/o H.L. College of Commerce, Gujarat University, Ahemadabad-380009.

59. **Ms. Aparna Jain**
Himachal Pradesh University, Jain Biscuits Store, 36, The Mall Road, Shimla-171001.

60. **Shyam G. Menon**
University of Kerala, Kovalam, Mulvana Junction, Trivandrum-6950378.

61. **Rajesh G.**
University of Kerala, T.C. 1/754, Insulin, Kumarapuram, Trivandrum-695011.

62. **R. Kanan**
Deptt. of Gandhian Studies & Ramalinga Philosophy, Kamraj University, Alagar Koil Road, Madurai-625002.

63. **A. Annamalai**
Deptt. of Gandhian Studies & Ramalinga Philosophy, Kamraj University, Alagar Koil Road, Madurai-625002.

64. **Vardesh T. Hiergange**
Karnataka University, House No. 38, Ashwin Koppatank, Dharwad-580008, Karnataka.

65. **Sanjay B. Shettennavar**
Karnataka University, Room No. 247, Shalmala Hostel, Campus, Dharwad-580003.

66. **Shailendra Kumar**
Lucknow University.

67. **Km. Rajni Srivastava**
Lucknow University.

68. **Shri A. Prafullo Kumar Singh**
Manipur University.

69. **Shri M. Ibungomacher Singh**
Manipur University.

70. **Mr. R. Srinivasan**
II M.A. (Economics), University of Madras, Madras-600005.

71. **Mr. Sarbari Sen**
Madras University, 8, Vijay Flats, Balaji Avenue, II Street, Madras-600017.

72. **Mr. Jamshed A. Siddiqui**
Aligarh Muslim University, 131 Mohd. Habib Hall, Aligarh-202002.
73. **Mr. P. Harish**
Osmania University, R. No. 92, ECHI, Osmania University Campus, Hyderabad-500007.
74. **Mr. Y. Pardhasardhi**
Osmania University, R. No. 30, NRSH, Osmania University Campus, Hyderabad-500007.
75. **Ms. D. Suting**
History Department, North-Eastern Hill University, Mayurbhanj, Nongthymmai, Shillong-793014.
76. **Shri Deshbandhu Tyagi**
University of Rajasthan.
77. **Shri M.L. Avasthi**
University of Rajasthan.
78. **Ashok R. Rattan**
Deptt. of Gandhian Studies, Panjab University.
79. **Amardeep Sandhu**
Deptt. of Gandhian Studies, Panjab University.
80. **Miss Indira Mylarapu**
University of Poona, 13/242, Mira Society, Shankar Shet Road, Pune-411037.
81. **Bothara Abhay Gulabchand**
University of Poona, C/o Prof. Ms. K.A. Parekh, 7, Panch Pandav Society, Pune-411016.
82. **Rakesh Kumar Sharma**
Sagar University.
83. **Ms. Nilima Sharma**
Sagar University.
84. **Biswajyoti Panda**
Utkal University, C/o B.B. Panda, IPS, J.O. Qr. No. 21, Maitree Sarani, Cuttack-750001.
85. **Snigdha Tripathy**
Utkal University, C/o Shri S. Atha, Qr. No. D-3/4, Irrigation Colony, B.J.B. Nagar, Bhubneswar-751014.
86. **Ms. Ira Upmaneyu**
D/o Shri R.K. Sharma, Near B.D.O. Office, Kendaghat, Distt. Solan, Himachal Pradesh.

INDEX

CONFLICT RESOLUTION THROUGH NON-VIOLENCE

VOLUME TWO

DEVELOPMENT WITHOUT DESTRUCTION

List of books published under Gandhian Studies and Peace Research Series

1. Gandhian Model of Development and World Peace, **R.P. Misra**
2. Conflict Resolution Through Non-Violence : Role of the Universities (In 2 Vols.), **K.D. Gangrade** and **R.P. Misra** *(eds.)*
   Vol. 1 : Science and Ethics, **K.D. Gangrade** and **R.P. Misra**
   Vol. 2 : Development without Destruction, **K.D. Gangrade** and **R.P. Misra**
3. The Social Philosophy of Mahatma Gandhi, **K.S. Bharathi**
4. Gandhian Humanism, **Mohit Chakrabarti**
5. Gandhian Holistic Economics, **Shashi Prabha Sharma**
6. Gandhian Spiritualism : A Quest for Essence of Excellence, **Mohit Chakrabarti**
7. Gandhian Perspective on Population and Development, **A.K. Sharma**
8. Thoughts of Gandhi and Vinoba : A Comparative Study, **K.S. Bharathi**
9. Economic Philosophy of Mahatma Gandhi, **Shanti Swarup Gupta**
10. Political Thought of Mahatma Gandhi (The), **K.S. Bharathi**
11. Gandhi and 21st Century, **Janardhan Pandey** *(ed.)*
12. Gandhian Philosophy of the Spinning Wheel, **Mohit Chakraborti**
13. Gandhian Satyagraha : An Analytical and Critical Approach, **Ajay Shanker Rai**
14. Gandhi and His Religion, **(Lt. Col.) P.A. Raju**
15. महात्मा गाँधी विचार वीथिका, **एस.पी. अग्रवाल**
16. Poverty of Gandhian Philosophy, **Himansu Roy**
17. Right to Equality in the Indian Constitution : A Gandhian Perspective, **Shashi Nath Saraswati**
18. Meditations on Gandhi : A Ravindra Varma Festschrift, **M.P. Mathai, M.S. John** and **Siby K. Joseph** *(eds.)*
19. Politico-Economic Ideas of Mahatma Gandhi : Their Relevance in the Present-Day, **Sukhendu Mazumdar**
20. Moral Lessons from Gandhi's Autobiography and Other Essays, **K.D. Gangrade**
21. Fire Sans Ire : A Critical Study of Gandhian Nonviolence, **Mohit Chakrabarti**
22. Gandhian Alternative (Volume 1 : Towards a Gandhian World Order), **Suresh Misra** *(ed.)*
23. Gandhian Alternative (Volume 2 : Nonviolence in Action), **Savita Singh** and **Bharati Misra** *(eds.)*
24. Gandhian Alternative (Volume 3 : Socio-Political Thoughts), **Anil Dutta Mishra** and **Sushna Yadav** *(eds.)*
25. Gandhian Alternative (Volume 4 : Economics Where People Matter), **V. K. Natraj, Kamlesh Misra** and **Neeru Kapoor** *(eds.)*
26. Gandhian Alternative (Volume 5 : Education for Human Development), **Suresh Misra** *(ed.)*
27. Gandhian Approach to Development Planning, **Ram Vinod Singh**

GANDHIAN STUDIES AND PEACE RESEARCH SERIES - 3

CONFLICT RESOLUTION THROUGH NON-VIOLENCE

Role of the Universities

VOLUME TWO

DEVELOPMENT WITHOUT DESTRUCTION

K.D. GANGRADE
and
R.P. MISRA

CONCEPT PUBLISHING COMPANY, NEW DELHI 110 059

ISBN: 81-7022-310-5 (Set)

ISBN: 81-3022-312-1 (Vol. II)

Reprinted 2007
First Published 1990

Published and Printed by
Ashok Kumar Mittal
Concept Publishing Company
A/15-16, Commercial Block, Mohan Garden
New Delhi-110 059 (INDIA)
Phones : 25351460, 25351794 *Fax* : 091-11-25357103
Email : publishing@conceptpub.com

PREFACE

A SET of twentyeight papers presented in the national seminar on Conflict Resolution through Non-Violence: Role of Universities (organised by the Gandhi Bhavan, University of Delhi in February 1989) have been published in two volumes. This is the second volume consisting of papers dealing with the conflicts generated by the development styles in vogue today. They throw light on the origin and nature of the conflict, identify the victims of the conflicts; and point to the paths to resolve the conflicts.

In theory, development aims at enhancement of welfare of the people. In practice, it has been found to generate a variety of side-effects which tend to rob the very freedom, liberty and living space of man. The problem is not with the development concept *per se* but with its style, approach and methodology. The non-violent economy which Mahatma Gandhi prescribed presents an alternative style of development which is sustainable, humane and liberating.

The papers included in this volume touch upon the theory and practice of development and advocate the Gandhian concept of humanised development wherein the micro-spaces become the foundation of a new social order. In this order, it is not the trickle down processes from above but the capillary action from multitude points from below which generates development. It is the strength of these micro-spaces or communities which alone can guarantee a peaceful and sustainable progress of human kind.

We are grateful to the authors of the papers for sparing time for this purpose. We are particularly thankful to Geoff Harris, Raja Jayaraman, and J.A. Camilleri who permitted us to reprint their papers published earlier by the University of New England, Australia.

We gratefully acknowledge the assistance rendered by our colleagues at Gandhi Bhavan in organising the Seminar and editing of the volume.

Gandhi Bhavan
Delhi-110 007

K.D. GANGRADE
R.P. MISRA

PREFACE

CONTENTS

LIST OF TABLES

TABLES

LIST OF CONTRIBUTORS

Christopher C. Benninger
Director, Centre for Development Studies and Activities, P.B. 843, Deccan Gymkhana, Poona.

Joseph A. Camilleri
Reader in Politics, La Trobe University, Melbourne.

K.D. Gangrade
Pro-Vice Chancellor, University of Delhi, Delhi.

Geoff Harris
Senior Lecturer in Economics, University of New England, Armidale, Australia.

Raja Jayaraman
Senior Lecturer, Department of Sociology, University of New England, Armidale, Australia.

S.L. Malhotra
Department of Gandhian Studies, Panjab University, Chandigarh.

R.P. Misra
Director, Gandhi Bhavan, University of Delhi, Delhi.

V. Pandit
Department of Economics, Delhi School of Economics, University of Delhi, Delhi.

A.K. Rattan
Department of Gandhian Studies, Panjab University, Chandigarh.

Prof. Moonis Raza
Former Vice-Chancellor, University of Delhi, Delhi.

Indira Rothermund
Centre for Development Studies and Action, P.B. 843, Pune.

B.K. Roy Burman
Centre for the Study of Developing Societies, Rajpur Road, Delhi.

Amardeep S. Sandhu
Department of Gandhian Studies, Panjab University, Chandigarh.

1

CITIZENS OF A WOUNDED EARTH IN A FRAGMENTED WORLD

MOONIS RAZA

IT IS most appropriate that the "new beginnings" have opened up the trail towards earth citizenship in the twilight of a new dawn. The domain of the earth transcends the anthropocentric orbit of the world. This conceptual distinction is of the essence. While the world has been too much with us in the corridors of time the mother earth, *Gaia*, has been deeply wounded by the distortions of the biblical injunction urging the homosapien to "have dominion over the fish of the sea, and over every living thing that moveth upon the earth". While the concept of the world as the home of man has encouraged molestation and rape of the earth since the neolithic times; the concept of the earth as the planet of life calls for harmony between human and non-human off-springs of *Gaia*. The "new beginnings" of the yester-year have inexorably led us to a crucial element of the new Weltanschauung — that of the earth citizen, the man in nature, who shares citizenship in the republic of the earth with the rooted grass and the flying bird, the microscopic bacteria and the gigantic elephant, the thirsty sand dune and the torrential river, the mountain peak and the ocean deep. The restricted view of the world, with its frontiers as well as boundaries and its countries as well as States, needs to be replaced by the all encompassing view of the *Gaia* — the mother earth of the solar family in the Milky Way of the expanding universe.

The most effective constraint in the received conceptualisation of this interactive relationship, which clutters clear thinking, pertains to the inability of current thought structures to break from the Cartesian dichotomies and assimilate as well as transcend the dualism between matter and energy, wave and particle, quantum and field, living and non-living, plant and animal or material and spiritual. The assertion of the monist view and a holistic approach should, however, not be mistaken, as Bookchim points out, "for a spectral oneness that yields cosmic dissolution in a structureless *nirvana*". The wholeness is not a bleak undifferentiated "universality" that involves the reduction of a phenomenon to what it has in common with everything else. Nor is it a celestial, omnipresent "energy" that replaces the vast material differentia of which the natural and social realms are composed. To the contrary, wholeness comprise the variegated structures, the articulations, and the mediations that impart to the whole a rich variety of forms and thereby add unique qualitative properties to what a strictly analytic mind often reduces to "innumerable" and "random" details.

Humanisation of Nature and Naturalisation of Man

The starting point of our odessey towards earth citizenship must be the recognition of the unity of nature, a rejection of dichotomised models and the assertion of an essentially monist position. The fragmentation of the holistic into the realms of nature and culture or between the worlds of man and that of his non-human environment leads to a situation wherein each segment of knowledge ends up, in its own specifically sophisticated manner, with an aspectual, distorted and limited vision of that which is, definitionally, total — dissected limbs of a cadaver being mistaken for the integrated, living, ever-changing system of interdependencies.

The monist view of objective reality is contingent upon the recognition of this unity, operationalised through the mechanism of interactions between social man and non-human nature. The essentiality of man and nature is based on "man as a natural being and nature as a human reality". Since the naturalisation of man and the humanisation of nature proceed simultaneously through man's interaction with nature, human history may be viewed as the continuation of and a qualitatively new stage in natural history — the two constituting a differentiated unity. Man interacts with non-human nature, transforms it and himself gets transformed in the process.

In the process of transforming nature and himself, social man moves from the realm of necessity to that of freedom, in the sense in which Spinoza conceived the latter as "recognised necessity". It may, however, be noted that "freedom does not consist in the dream of independence of natural laws, but in the knowledge of these laws, and the possibility this gives of systematically making them work towards definite ends. Freedom and necessity are not, therefore, mutually exclusive categories. Freedom should not be confused with the "self-determination of the spirit" or the so-called "freedom of will" which puts it outside the purview of the compulsions of nature. Neither should necessity be equated with mechanistic determinism, which negates the role of human will and considers the action and behaviour of man as the function of objective nature alone.

To the extent that man does not understand the process of nature through social practice, he is in the realm of blind, unrecognised necessity; to that extent he is unfree, a slave crouching in awe and supplication before the rising sun or the mighty mountains. Also as long as he fails to perceive how absolute is the necessity of maintaining the integrity of his habitat, he would continue to crouch in awe before the eco-disruptive products and processes of an entirely ersatz civilisation, and be a willing slave to the god of consumerism. "Necessity is blind only in so far it is not understood." As man marches onwards on the basis of understanding natural laws and systematically making them "work towards definite ends", he steps into freedom though continuing to be within the gravitational field of necessity, which no longer remains blind but becomes an instrument of conscious social practice. The hold of necessity continues, nevertheless. In fact, it becomes more and more rigorous with every technological advance — with every step towards freedom. With rudimentary knowledge about the property of stones and elementary acquaintance with the laws of Applied Mechanics, the palaeolithic tool-maker became relatively free *vis-a-vis* his hominid ancestor; but was still at the mercy of nature — the vagaries of climate or the ferocity of predatory animals. The modern tool-maker in the Hindustan Machine Tool factory has extended the orbit of his freedom by recognising and utilising a far larger number of very much more complex laws of nature. As Krichoff puts it : "As (man's) bonds become more numerous, they also become more elastic. Civilisation has lengthened his leash and padded his collar so that it does no gall; but the lash is never slipped". Looked at thus, freedom only transforms the nature of the role of necessity; it does not weaken it. The freer man becomes, the more he recognises the chains that bind him. Paradoxical it may appear, but the more free we are, the less free we become. The chains of necessity cannot be broken; they can only be utilised through social practice. Even if we conspire with fate a *la Omar Khayam*, we cannot "shatter it to bits"; but we scan certainly transform the external world of nature "Closer to our hearts' desire" by cognising the laws that govern it.

The realm of freedom is the Noosphere, the sphere of the planet earth which has been 'humanised' by rational human activity. The traditional division of the planet into the lithosphere, hydrosphere, atmosphere and the biosphere may interest the hydrologist, the meteorologist and the geologist, but these layers enter into human affairs not separately but in intrinsic relationship with each other. When the alluvial fan in a Himalayan valley gets transformed into a system of terraces, when the mighty torrents are tamed to fertilise the thirsty earth, when a new crop rotation system is evolved to take advantage of a short growing season. When a wrong grazing practice leads to deforestation — then the segments of the lithosphere, the hydrosphere, the atmosphere the biosphere get synthesised and transformed into the noosphere — the realm of cognized necessity.

The anthropogenic elements in this interactive system of interdependencies are crucially important not because man is the "principal inhabitant of the planet" as Cholley put it, or because he, of all living things, has a divine soul, as Ritter would have wanted us to believe, but because and only because he is the creator of the noosphere. He alone, among the known species of the planet, does not just adapt himself to non-human nature but actually interacts with it; who is not only a passive element but is an active factor in the eco-system; who does not only vegetate and survive within the orbit of blind necessity but operates within the realm of freedom, cognizing laws of nature so as to transform it. And yet, as the evolving crisis would show, there are very definite limits which he can dare to transcend only at his peril. Recognition of these limits would be the recognition of necessity today which would entail nothing less than freedom from illusive affluence for a tiny minority of the human race and at the same time from pangs of inexhorable deprivation for the rest.

The noosphere — the sphere of man-nature interaction — may be viewed as a triangle of forces. Nature provides the base, lays down the limits of freedom and indicates the direction along which optimum appropriation through social labour is possible in the long run. Technology aids natural processes, bends them to human (or shall we say humane) purposes, modifies them and thus extends the range of freedom. Institutions are either conducive to or restrictive of man-nature interaction. The development process unfolds itself through integrating the anthropogenic and the non-human components into a system of interdependencies. Unless the concept of the eco-system, as a holistic complex of interdependencies, subsumes within it this anthropogenic component, operationalised through the triangle of forces in the development process, it would cease to be the concept of the system and would flounder in the quicksands of its own inadequacies. On the other hand, if this concept comes to terms with social man, it can become the most significant of the unifying conceptualisations of objective reality.

The concept of the earth citizen is rooted in the eco-system and this intellectual construct has emerged in the sphere of idea as a timely corrective to the academic tradition of the post-industrial society based on the disaggregation of the totality into facets, aspects, parts or fragments for deeper study and analysis, thereby engendering the knowing of more and more about less and less till one finally ends up by knowing everything about nothing. The gap between the essentially holistic character of the objectively existing system and its fragmented cognition through disaggregated analysis has already become a serious constraint and has led to a crisis in knowledge. It is the experience of history that, at such critical moments, unifying principles emerge which provide the basis for a Weltanschauung, an integrated view of totality. The four-element, four-humour universe of Hippocrates-Aristotle-Ptolemy, the Newtonian principle of gravitation and laws of motion, the theory of evolution of Darwin, the dialectical and historical materialism of Karl Marx and E-MC^2 equation of Einstein may be considered to be such unifying principle of knowledge, emerging on the scene as synthetical constructs integrating disaggregated findings into a system of ideas and bringing the entire spectrum of sciences into their orbit of influence. It is being suggested that the concept of the eco-system is a unifying principle of this order which, though rooted in all the sciences, still transcends them. It provides the closest conceptual approximation to the integrated complexity of objective reality and may, therefore, serve as the basis for the most relevant ideology for the contemporary world.

Like all the significant ideas of science, the scientific conceptualisation of the eco-system, which is a recent product of the intellectual crisis of the post-industrial society, is rooted in a pre-scientific tradition of great chronological depth and is, in fact, embedded in the basal psyche of the homosapiens. The system of animistic and totemistic beliefs, characterising the proto-idelogoly of the palaeolithic age, was based on a unity of all that exists and transcended the duality of the biota and the abiota, of the animal and the human, of the material and the spiritual. The worship of the Mother Goddess, which has been the sub-stratum of the spiritual ideas of the agricultural peoples all over the world, was similarly rooted in a holistic view of the Universe, which subsumed the man-nature dichotomy into a broader unity though in an inverted form. The mysticism of the Orient, which continues to wield considerable influence over the mind, resolved the subject-object, man-nature contradiction through a monist view of reality. The modern concept of the eco-system has such a distinguished percentage. Just as science has arisen out of magic; so has this scientific conceptualisation emerged from pre-scientific intellection by assimilating within it the kernel of truth in the latter and rejecting its pseudo-spiritual claptrap, by moving from the realm of false consciousness to that of consciousness.

A proper development of this concept, both epistemologically as a model of the universe and methodologically as an analytical tool, has to contend with the continuing rigidities of the fragmented hierarchies in knowledge. While the social sciences have moved towards a certain degree of internal cohesion, the world of non-human nature is still alien to it, at best producing unnecessary noise in their sophisticated computer programmes. The agricultural economist would rather not dirty his hands with the soil—this nauseating residual in his regression model, which cannot be wished away. The incapacity of the natural sciences to go beyond the rigid limits of their sub-system is no less alarming. The internal integration of the natural sciences has at best produced the science of ecology. In their just concern with the autotrophs and the heterotrophs, the ecologists tend to forget that homo-sapiens constitute a category qualitatively different from the other heterotrophs, that their explanatory system is incapable of accounting for the behaviour of social man; that they are asking only limited questions and can, therefore, get only inadequate and partial answers. At best they recognise man as an element in the *man-and-nature* syndrome and have shown a unique incapacity to recognise the reality of *man in nature*. They fail to see that rationality of man is as much natural as the irrationality of the monsoon wind, the chernozem or the xerophyte. The unifying concept of the eco-system has arisen to break the constraints imposed by the complementary inadequacies of the soical and the natural sciences. While the former cannot come to terms with the animality of men, the latter cannot come to terms with his humanity.

It is only by correcting the distortions of fragmented models that the nature of the development process can be properly understood. Let us reiterate that development is operationalised through a triangle of forces, wherein nature lays down the limits of freedom and indicates the direction of optimal advance, wherein technology extends the area of freedom within the general orbit of necessity and wherein institutions are either conducive for or restrictive on man's interaction with nature through technology. The eco-crisis of the contemporary times is a consequence not of a technology gone berserk but of an institutional frame, which is no longer capable of coping with it. The crisis calls not for a stoppage of technological advance but for a new world order — a just equitable and humane world order which can regulate man's relation with non-human nature as well as man's relation with man.

It is only by viewing the development process in the manner described above that we can steer clear of two erroneous strategies, namely, (i) the strategy of 'development' at all cost, leading to eco-destruction, and (ii) the strategy of rejecting development in the name of ecology. Within the conceptual frame presented above, the ecology-development contradiction is a false contradiction. The laws of nature not only impose constraints on but also point to the direction of optimal development. Unless this dual relationship between the ecological correlates and the development process is fully recognised, one tends to get neckdeep in the morass of 'hippie' ecology, the spurious environmental concerns of the 'flower people' for whom nature is a virgin which should not be violated through human intervention. The latter view, under different hues and colours, is being assiduously sold to the Third World by some of the ideologues of the developed countries. The situation is rather ironical. The advice not to proceed along the path of development through proper resource utilisation comes from those nations who are themselves the major culprits of eco-destruction through the dysfunctional monopoly of natural resources in an international system of inequalities, wherein 20 per cent of the world population is permitted to misuse 80 per cent of its resources, and wherein the city of Chicago alone is allowed to consume more oil than the second most-populous country in the world. The anti-development injunctions that are being issued for the benefit of the innocents of the Third World by the prophets of doom of the Club of Rome, or the dons of MIT and/or Sussex are really intended to widen the North-South gap and perpetuate the poverty and misery of the bulk of humanity. Our concern with ecology within the framework of an eco-systemic approach is directed to optimising (and not maximising!) development so as to extricate our people from the vicious stranglehold of hunger and poverty; for, in the Third World, hunger continues to be a most potent pollutant — an eco-destructive force of tremendous magnitude. It destroys man, the earth citizen, an important component of the contemporary eco-system. Those who rightly lose their night's sleep over the fate of a blighted tree or a faded flower should sometimes also look at the bloated bellies, sunken eyes and the skinny arms of hungry children!

The Contemporary World: Integration, Differentiation and Fragmentation

The concept of an earth citizen, as an element of the wounded eco-system becomes still more complex if it is seen in the context of the simultaneous process of integration, differentiation and fragmentation of the modern world. The problems of coming to terms with the globalisation of society needs to be satisfactorily solved with a view to bridge the gap between parochial perceptions of narrow minds and the concerns of a one-world reality. The spread of modern industrialisation had already towards the beginning of the 19th century replaced the aggregate of closed or semi-closed systems of the pre-capitalist formations by a loosely integrated world market. The peasants of Asia and Africa, living for millennia in the isolated small world of petty production, were used to natural calamities such as floods and droughts, cyclones and earthquakes but were for the first time exposed to blind forces of the market which they did not know. The suction mechanism of international exploitation extended its tentacles to the remotest hamlet and united the developed and the underdeveloped in a world economy. Advances in transport and communication during recent years have further strengthened such trends, have brought the entire world to our doors and have made everybody everybody's neighbour. Walls have crumbled; and ideas ride the winds. A poem, created on the the Left Bank today, provides spiritual sustenance to young scientists in the Silicon Valley or Novosibirisk the next day. The findings of a research project in the Kolar mines reach Trieste in minutes and become inputs in the work of a Nobic laureate, whose words are heard with bated breath in Tokyo, Princeton and Oxford over the week-end. The agro-biological researches in Mexico provide the basis for the green revolution across the oceans in India and Pakistan. The heartbeats of the young in Europe become faster on the Indian *sitar*. The world has become one indeed!

The integration of the globe should not be confused with its homogenisation. The jean-clad, hamburger eating, coca-cola drinking, hashish smoking young men and women with vacant eyes roaming around the bylanes of large cities the world over constitute the thin layer of froth over the multi-splendoured sub-stratum of profound meaning in all traditions over the globe. Unity lies in plurality; not in the negation of it. Development is a process in which integration and differentiation are dialectically united, being contingent upon each other. The unicellular amoeba is neither integrated nor differentiated. The complex human organism is both. While homogenisation is the function of the breaking up of identities and their assimilation in synthesised melting pot products, integration is articulated through a multi-level and hierarchical system of interdependencies. Homogenisation, in fact, is the anti-thesis of integration. One has not to be less of an Indian to be more of a man; one has not be less of a Pathan to be more of a Pakistani. Universals exist through specifics; and specifics acquire deeper and wider meaning through universals. They make each other possible and sustain each other. Brothers Karamazov are so deeply Russian that they transcend their Russianness and become universal. Semetna's "My Motherland" sings of the pride in his mother or his country or in the mother earth or the Milky Way or the expanding universe or all of them at the same time; for the lilt of the Valtava in the opening bars of the symphony is so like lullaby as well as the music of the stars! The Blue Danube of Strauss, the 01' Man River of the Negro spiritual, the Ganga *Maiya* of Indian folk lore — aren't they the specific forms of the same universal. The mystic search for the river in a drop was based on a dialectical relationship between the whole and the part — of unity in diversity and of diversity in unity articulated by the simultaneous integration of the differentiated and the differentiation of the integrated.

Education of our times has to come to terms with the specific without becoming parochial, philistine and mundane; and with the universal without becoming other — worldy, ethereal and divine. It should become human and humane, the conscience of mankind, smelling of the earth and yet grazing into the stars.

Differentiation needs to be distinguished from fragmentation. Differentiation articulates and reflects diversity, fragmentation generates and sharpens disparity. While differentiation of an integrated world is a function of development, fragmentation of the world has been a function of the development of a few have nations proceeding along and causatively linked with the underdevelopment of the mass of mankind. This is the most agonising tragedy of our times; for development like freedom is indivisible. The industrial revolution marks the watershed in history. The surpluses generated by the sweat and toil of people all over the world, since then, were swallowed up by the ruling classes of a few nations through colonial suction mechanisms to build industrial empires and to transform the rest of the world into their raw material appendage and a market for their goods.

The fragmentation of the world between the industrialised North and the agricultural South has created a serious clevage in the rural-urban continuum. North is becoming increasingly non-rural with most of its population living in urban settlements; South is being transformed into a large aggregate of villages inhabited by most of the rural population of the world. The percentage share of the population of the more developed countries who inhabit their urban settlements goes on increasing at an alarming rate and getting concentrated in fewer and fewer megalopolises. The North is threatening to become one large urban connurbation — the cruel and sick city with the anomie and loneliness of an alienated humanity, the windowless silos full to the brim with discarded hopes and nameless fears, the concrete jungles inhabited not by neighbours — neither love nor hate, neither friends nor foes, but by faceless non-persons: data units of an animated demography. Was it for this that prometheus brought fire from the heavens and Vishnu churned the oceans!

There are three altars in this big city — one each for the revered gods of an industrial capitalism run amuck — economies of scale, economy of agglomeration and economies of urbanisation. The industrial revolution ushered in the era of the factory city, smoke belching chimneys rising over working class slums, the refuge for expropriated peasantry in an alien world. Viewed in the context of history, the emergence of the industrial city was a positive step in the right direction. It converted the vertical shift in the work force from the primary to the secondary sector into horizontal mobility from the rural to the urban settlement. The city was thus an instrument of history and the three-fold economies provided the *raison d'etre* for this historical process.

The scientific-technological revolution of our time has, however, transformed the situation qualitatively. The micro-chip has taken quite a bit of the wind out of the sail of the economies of scale. A highly skilled white aproned workforce of two figures working in a villa within a park may produce higher value added then a blue collared workforce of four figures breathing polluted air in the jungle of chimneys of a four-acre factory. It is not being suggested that the small is always and necessarily beautiful. The argument is based on the realisation that the scientific-technological revolution has made it possible for economies to be available along the whole spectrum of scales. It is, therefore, not surprising that the North is increasingly shifting the resource-based, large-scale polluting industries to the South and is concentrating instead on the innovative highly skilled, R & D-based systems wherein the laboratory imperceptibly merges into the production line. The "clean" scientific-technological revolution, unfolding in the North, is pushing the polluting industrial revolution into the South. By the time the North is in the 21st century, the South would be struggling into the 19th century.

The autonomy of the shopping plaza from the residential neighbourhood and of the latter from the industrial area has already been made possible by qualitative improvements in short-range transport. The home computer has brought about an information revolution; and interconnected terminals of large systems make it possible for same economies to become available in small and medium sized settlements as well. The perspective for the 21st century is, therefore, not necessarily of cannibal megalopolises swallowing up smaller specimens of their own species but of a balanced and humane system of settlements where the large, the medium and the small flourish in symbiosis. There is too much of urbanisation in the North and too little in the South. The polluted city of the North and the filthy village of the South are two sides of the same coin. The former is sick with affluence, the latter is diseased with poverty. The former has the paunch of the over-fed, the latter has the bloated belly of the scurvy stricken; the former needs slimming, the latter needs nutrition. Glorification of the former is inhuman and romanticisation of the latter is cruel. There is no escape from one to the other. The blacks in the blind alleys of Harlem as well as the hippies in the suburbs of Kathmandu have learnt this bitter lesson the hard way.

Education of the future must contribute to the resolution of the contradiction between the integration of the globe and its fragmentation. The fracture in the human condition brought about by the hammer strokes of industrial capitalism must be healed in the interest of not only those who have been at the receiving end but for mankind as a whole. Educational policies must be intrinsically intertwined with the basic structural changes without which the new international order would remain just an idle dream. It must correct the perspectives of those who search solace in the spurious spirituality of poverty as well as those who seek meaning and purpose at the consumerist counters of affluence. Education of the future must combine the sophistication of the city with the earthiness of the village and thus restore the rural urban continuum in the living style of mankind.

In the light of the significant role that education has to play in fostering the new international order, it is really surprising that the models of the Club of Rome, the Japanese Club of Rome and of Leontiev have no place for education. Unless this serious limitation of our futurological models is removed, the world may get broken up in three fragments instead of two, as has been pointed out by a United Nations Educational Scientific and Cultural Organisation (UNESCO) study:

> "This means that without basic structural change (the New International Economic Order), we shall end up with the world divided into three types of countries; at the bottom, countries with primary (basic) education doing extraction work and subsistence labour; in middle, countries up to the level of secondary (including vocational) education doing some simple processing; and at the third and top level, countries where everybody is a university graduate working highly in research-intensive industries with large science and technology components."

The tragedy of the modern era is that the Third World is already getting fragmented into the Third and the Fourth; and the developing into the less and the least developed. Education is unfortunately playing a key-role in this process of inequalisation. The dream is becoming a nightmare!

2

EARTH RAVAGED: The Fall-out of Human Evolution

A.S. SANDHU & A.K. RATTAN

Far-reaches of Human Time

THE HUMAN lineage has now been traced back to over two million years. Pithecanthropus erectus, the 'erect ape man', since determined to have lived half a million years ago, was not the intermediate he was thought to be, at the time of his discovery, but a rudimentary human inhabitant of Java. Australopithecus of South Africa, named 'the southern ape', is now recognised hominid. When the Leakey's later found its famous and vastly old fossil at Olduvai it was placed in the human family tree as Zinjanthropus — 'East Africa man' found by the Potassium Argon clock as living 1,750,000 million years ago. The course of human evolution has been distinct from that of the anthropoids and began its particular direction before a time of which we have knowledge, perhaps, it has been suggested, to diverge before the apes began.

In spite of the fact that man lacks powerful jaws and teeth of apes but still is one of the most omnivorous of creatures. He eats, likes and is able to digest a great variety of foods and is not driven thereto by famine as civilised observers have concluded at times from their own fastidiousness. The human stomach and intestines are extraordinarily competent and tolerant, somewhat limited in ability to consume raw starch in quantity. Sensitive to lack of iodine and of high intake of salt, mankind suggests an old affinity to the sea. Needing to drink often, the more so in the drier and warmer air, man could not range far from fresh water. This most naked of warm-blooded creatures, thin and sensitive of skin lacking fang, claw and horny extremities, was restricted to a particular habitat outlined in his anatomy and physiology. An African origin is generally accepted, present evidence favouring East Africa. The physical geography of equatorial eastern Africa is not greatly different from that of millions of years ago.

Tools and Man

From the earliest Pleistocene time man has been a user of tools, though they have not been exclusive to him. Professor W. Kohler has shown that some primates can occasionally improvise a tool to meet a given situation. But a chimpanzee has not sufficient foresight to be able to shape a stone or a stick for use in an imagined future, and as far as lower beings are concerned it is difficult to say how much of their planned work is due to inherited co-operation and how much to real evolution of the possibilities in a special case.

However, we must accept that man without some kind of tools would be an impossibility. Concerning the study of ancient tools we are nearly in the same situation as a linguist or a geologist. The Linguist must build exclusively upon signs that are not immediately understandable, and the geologist has to consider what the conditions were when his ammonite died and was embedded in some sort of clay. The ammonite is just as mute as the hieroglyph or the casual tool, but the tool has the advantage that it may be copied as a model and treated in systematic experiments in order to learn something essential about its use.

A collection of facts and an analysis of characteristic traits are equally necessary for an ethnologist, a historian and a natural scientist working on material from ancient times. However, an object collected without a historical background will often require another form of treatment. A purely heuristic classification may reveal important phases of its development, especially when one pays attention to apparently unimportant details such as relics preserved from stages when environmental conditions were different.

Relation of Shape and Material to Environmental Conditions

Obviously a certain adaptation to geographical conditions is reflected in the character of tools and implements as well as in other man-made elements of the environment. A threshing sledge is characteristic of dry climates and a flail would be used in temperate zones, for you have to thresh the corn in the barn because of rainy weather in autumn and snow in winter. The mould-board plough is unfitted to arid conditions but necessary when a tough matted sod needs to be turned over. The coulter to cut this sword is, therefore, characteristic of the plough not of the ard. The blade of the grass-scythe was developed to its full sise in the northern half of the Roman empire not in Africa or Asia. The longest scythe blades are in English Museums. But tools also reflect topographic at differences. In Scandinavia the wheel plough was not generally accepted in north of the plains of Scania. The spade is used in may places where there is not enough space to manoeuvre a plough, although the plough is not otherwise the implement generally used. The Kafirs in the Hindukush plough with an ard when possible but near the fairly broad U-shaped valleys suitable for ploughing with an ard are V-shaped valleys with terraced sides. On the small terraces the seed is covered by means of a fork-shaped traction shade; one woman digs the spade into the ground and another pulls it up, this process being repeated until all the seed is covered, after which water is led through the irrigation system among the terraces.[1] Alexander Fenton has mentioned that questions of demography may some time influence the manner in which hand-tools are used or adopted.[2]

Man's Occupance of the Soil

Since man's achievement of humanity with the deliberate and conscious use of tools in the early Pleistocene, the soil has been continually modified by human activities soils have been destroyed and created. They have been a source of food and other raw materials. Man has altered the soils he has occupied both, directly, by economic activities such as ploughing and digging clay for bricks, and indirectly, by changing such soil forming factors as vegetation, drainage and micro-climate.

High and Low-Energy Environments

On a world-scale we can distinguish between high and low energy environments.[3] In low energy environments soil erosion by natural agents is rare because local relief is slight, rain-storms are of low intensity, the waste mantle is stable and vegetation cover is continuous.

High energy environments are characterised by considerable local relief, intense rain-storms, and large-scale mass movement. As a result of these characteristics soil erosion by natural agents is a frequent occurrence, and today is often greatly aggravated by human action. This distinction between high and low energy environment is important because it makes clear that under certain circumstances soil erosion is a natural phenomenon — the "geologic norm" of Lowdermilk and Sharpe.[4] In high energy environments where natural soil erosion occurs it is extremely difficult to disentangle the human and natural causes of erosion. Today some of the most difficult problems in land management occur in high energy environments, and research into the history of land-use soils and geomorphology is only slowly enabling us to distinguish between natural erosion and humanity aggravated erosion.[5]

Under a continuous vegetation cover in low energy environments, soil erosion proceeds so slowly that it does not interfere greatly with the normal processes of soil formation. Human actions, by changing vegetation, by altering the structure of the soil with cultivation, by damming rivers and digging new drainage channels, thus altering the slope of the land and the water channels running across it, are, therefore, potent causes of soil erosion.[6]

Crucial stages in man's changing relationships with the soil are nine in number :

1. The first use of fire.
2. The domestication of plants and animals.
3. The invention of irrigation.
4. The creation of soils, for example, by terracing or draining swamps.
5. The widespread use of iron plough shares and coulters, and iron spades, which enabled sod, grassland and heavier soils to be extensively cultivated.
6. The spread of commercial economies — in antiquity as well as in modern times.
7. The improvements in European agriculture in the post-medieval period and with Europe, an expansion overseas, the spread of temperate European practices to other areas.
8. The increasing mechanisation of agriculture which began with steam traction in the 19th century but has increased many-fold with the heavy diesel engines of the mid-20th century.
9. The increasing urbanisation and industrialisation of human

societies, with large areas used for non-agricultural purposes, including recreation, and increasing pollution of the total environment with waste materials.

Early Changes

In early times, and until recently amongst those people who retained simple food-gathering economies, modification of the soil by man must have been mostly indirect and unintentional, being induced largely by vegetation changes, many of them caused by fire. There would have been selective use of plants for food, fuel and house construction, and a wide range in type of plant material used — bark, bast, leaves, stems, roots, fruits and tubes. For religious and economic reasons certain plants might well have been specially protected against damage from grazing animals and over-utilisation as happened more recently in parts of West Africa and China, for example.[7] An estimate of the changes brought about over a very short period of time can be obtained by studying, for example, surviving Australian aborigines but the effect of such changes being made annually or seasonally over a long period of time is more difficult to assess.

Intensive use of such trails, especially around waterholes in drier areas, may have modified both vegetation and soils to such an extent that the surface of the soil would have become compact and impermeable with virtually no surface vegetation so that surface run-off would have increased and local erosion ensued.[8]

Cumulative modifications of vegetation by all these means would have favoured grasses and shrubs at the expense of trees, especially in areas marginal for tree growth as along the dry edges of the tropical forests or in drier mid-latitude areas such as the central and western United States. Regular burning of forests is known to reduce the amount of organic matter and nitrogen in the soil, thus reducing its fertility.[9]

Since the domestication of plants and animals there has been increasing intensity of utilisation of natural resources, caused not only by increasing number of the human population but also by the increasing material complexities of human cultures.

European Influences

Within the past five centuries local sequence of occupance has everywhere been interrupted by the intrusion of Europeans. The transfer of temperate European farming techniques to the warmer and drier parts of the rest of the world has had dramatic effects. Tobacco planting had exhausted many soils in Virginia by the middle of the 19th century, by which time the upland cotton lands of Georgia were also dissected by gullies.[10] The dust bowl of the drier western States developed alarmingly during the 1920s and 1930s, less than a century after much of the land had been first cultivated by the European settler.[11] Even in areas climatically more akin to those of Europe the new settlers often allowed land to deteriorate rapidly. Along the fertile banks of the St. Lawerance the habitants practised intensive cultivation of wheat and other crops, but neglected to replenish the soil with manure, and failed to allow land to lie fallow. As a result by the 1980s much of the land which had been continuously cropped for 20 years was completely exhausted.[12] Such is the case with mycorrhiza which were introduced into Australia with living plants in pots.[13]

New and larger machines have not been entirely advantageous in all environments. It is especially fortunate that in most of the agricultural areas of North America and Western Europe, where larger and heavier machinery has been developed, soils have been structurally strong and stable. Such effects as compaction caused by the concentrated operation of farm machinery between tree rows have been shown to be relatively short-lived in orchards in southern England.[14] Elsewhere, in areas where soils are structurally weaker and less stable the widespread use of heavy machinery has brought new problems.[15] Such ploughing allows too much evaporation of valuable moisture and induces the formation of an impermeable plough pan at the base of cultivation, hence making the soil less permeable to the often heavy intermittent rainfall, and again increasing soil erosion.

Soil Erosion

Over much of the low lands, primary deciduous forest was replaced intermittently from neolithic times onwards by crops, grass or heathland. Evidence for soil erosion, presumably induced by human activities, has been recorded on many archaeological sites elsewhere in Britain. Alluvial deposits in the forecourt of the Monamore neolithic chambered cairn at Lamlash, Isle of Arran, are probably eroded podzolic B_2 horizon material, washed down slope in the third millennium B.C. as a result of human activity uphill from the cairn.[16] In Ulster, Pollick and

Waterman have described the way in which occupation on a Bronze age habitation site at Downpatrick was interrupted at least in part by spread of hill-wash, of sandy boulder clay.[17] Occupation resumed above. This layer but was itself overlain by three to four feet of hill-wash, which must have been formed rapidly since the junction between the occupation layers and hill-wash was very sharp. Presumably this erosion was the result of woodland clearance and cultivation of the slopes above. A major cause of this increased liability is probably the intensification of arable cropping during the past 10-20 years, which has been made possible by the wide spread use of chemical fertilisers. Erosion following a grassfire on the limestone uplands of Derbyshire was also described in some detail.[18] Clearly, however, the balance between man-maintained pasture and bare limestone is tenuous indeed.

Problems of Irrigation

Improvement is of necessity a continuing process. Irrigation, without maintenance of drainage, can lead swiftly to the production of saline soils impossible for cultivation especially if no crop rotation or inter-cropping is practised. In the coast-lands of southern Turkey one can find areas which were reclaimed from marshland 10-15 years ago and then cultivated continuously with cotton and irrigated, but not drained, so today they are too saline for cropping. Probably, the largest area in the world today where salinisation problems occur is in the West Pakistan.[19] Man's use of the soil has been a chequered process in the attempt to feed an evergrowing population on a limited area of the earth's surface.

Adaptation to Environment

The argument that the environment controls directly effect man is, at its simplest, geographical determinism and like all simple causal explanations for human behaviour to stand up to testing yet the belief that some influences on human affairs come directly from the physical environment is so persistent that the intellectual exploration of these problems remains attractive. Although our society has now acquired tremendous capacities to alter the landscape, some explanation of the impact of the physical environment as a complex variable on social life is important. We have studied the effects of altitudes on the Oxygen levels of the atmosphere and the consequences of these levels either for the performance of athletes or the lung capacity of Andean peasants.[20] Nonetheless something important is missing in these equations, they overlook the fact that human behaviour is soical and, therefore, has to be learned, we never so act merely as biological pawns buffeted by external forces. All human life is soical life. Every society has, as one aspect of its social matrix, means of adaptation to its environment. These means represent one part of its solution to the problems of survival. They consist of techniques and desired objectives and both are learned. Even the capacity to learn has to be learned. Societies are variable and rarely stable. They affect each other in complex ways and adapt to physical or biological world with many distinctively different solutions to common problems.

These considerations lead to the fact that problems of adaptation are social. In consequence it follows that explanations about variation in adaptive processes and about adaptive innovations — which is an isomorphic statement — are to be looked for in variation of other elements of sociological systems, and not in changes of either ecological or biological systems.[21] Over the past 40 years there has been a substitution of Israeli Jews for Arab Palestinians; here we have two different communities living side by side in the same environment. These community differences are so striking that we could say, justifiably, that members of each community looked at and, therefore, lived in different physical environments.

The Current Problems of Environment

Mankind in its course of cultural evolution has come to a stage where man has realised that the fall-out of his own development impedes him from further progress. It is in the wake of the realisation that man has turned to what may be called the side effects of evolution.

Pollution: What is pollution? We often act as if the answer to this question is self-evident, and indeed it is in the more exaggerated cases. If we mean the presence of impurities in a system, everything is constantly polluted, since trace amounts of foreign matter are found in the purest substances. That would necessitate the introduction of the concept of hazards' levels of contaminants, which vary widely among different substances. A different approach might consider what compromises we would be willing to make in terms of acceptable levels of pollutants in order to preserve certain aspects of life-style. In any case, the complex connection between pollution and the quality of life we, as consumers, desire ought not to be overlooked.

Health Effects: Pollution affects human health and comfort in a number of ways. Under some circumstances, it brings overt clinical disease or even death. More commonly, however, it produces lesser effects, such as difficulty in breathing and impaired lung function from inhalation of polluted air, irritation of eyes, nose and throat, unpleasant tastes or odours, psychological and behavioural effects.

Excessive Air Pollution for Short Periods (Acute Episodes): Hazards from atmospheric pollutants have been demonstrated most vividly in episodes of acute exposure. There are many reliable reports of individuals of small and even large groups made ill or even killed by occupational or accidental exposure to toxic fumes. The glaring examples of this are Chernobyl and Bhopal gas tragedies where thousands lost their lives. Everywhere such accidents are caused by toxic fumes, vapours, pesticide aerosols, smoke or high concentration of dust. A few community catastrophes have resulted from combinations of fog, temperature inversion and air stagnation coupled with unusually large amounts of ordinary combustion produced atmospheric pollutants. In these rare but tragic episodes, fatalities occurred predominantly among the elderly and those with pre-existing cardiac or pulmonary diseases. Certain communicable diseases, such as tuberculosis, influenza and the common cold, are transmitted by airborne micro-organisms.

Prolonged Exposure to Ordinary Urban Air Pollution: Attempts to identify possible effects of ordinary urban air pollution on longevity or on the incidence of serious diseases have been inconclusive. Special attention has been focused on lung cancer which is known to be closely associated with tobacco smoking, and with the inhalation of rodon, other radio-active materials nickel carbonyl chromates asbestos and other chemicals. These are consistent findings of a greater incidence of lung cancer in the cities than in the country, and it is possible that urban air pollution is an contributory factor in this disease but its role is uncertain except in special situations, such as proximity to industrial plants that handle the known carcinogenic materials. Urban atmospheric pollution can aggravate asthma and some other chronic respiratory illnesses and can cause transient eye and respiratory tract irritation. Evidence from animal studies suggests that exposure to air pollution may increase susceptibility to pulmonary infections.

Water-borne Pollutants and Health: A century ago, our population was ravaged by water-borne diseases among which typhoid, fever, cholera and dysentery were conspicuous. These tragedies led to today's water treatment methods which, when applied, control adequately most disease producing bacteria. Viruses, such as those of hepatitis, remain a problem. Chemical pollutants in water sometimes threaten human health. Substantial contamination of ground-water with nitrates derived from sewage or from fertilised farm fields has been reported in several States. Drinking water with nitrate nitrogen levels above eight or nine Pbm, which are occasionally reached, may cause Methemoglobinemia in infants.

Pesticides and Human Health: The tremendous growth in the variety and use of organic pesticides since World War II have caused concern as to their possible effects on human health. Exposure occurs chiefly from ingestions of foods, from direct skin or respiratory contact during use and from inhalation of air-borne materials near treated areas. Chlorinated hydro-carbon and phosphate ester pesticides have been detected in many surfaces and in amounts ranging up to a few parts per billion. These small concentrations are not known to be a threat to human health. On rare occasions, high concentrations of pesticides appear in potable waters, usually as a result of industrial discharges. Human illness traced to pesticides in public water supplies has not been reported, but examples from domestic well contamination may have occurred.

In the bodies of green-house workers, spray pilots and others who have received occupational exposures, the level of pesticides is higher than in most of our people. These workers sometimes show marginal or definite impairment of important bodily function as a result of pesticide exposures.

Effects on Other Living Organisms: Man is but one species living in a world with numerous others; he depends on many of these others not only for his comforts and enjoyment but for his life. Plants provide the principal mechanism whereby energy from the sun can serve the earth's inhabitants. In doing so, they maintain the oxygen content of the air and the basic habitat and food of animals and men. Micro-organisms, bacteria, algae, fungi and protozoa, perform a myriad of essential functions including the purification of air soil and water, and the recycling of nutrients. Animals serve man as great converters, changing plant stored energy into forms of food he prefers and supplying him with a wide variety of materials — leather, furs, oils and pharmaceuticals, ivory and pearls, bristles and wool. Many in fact are beneficial — some as pollinators, others as predators on harmful forms, some as makers of silk and honey. As contributors to happiness and the quality of life, plants and animals provide opportunities for enjoyment of natural beauty, for hunting, fishing, gardening, scientific study, entertainment and the satisfaction of our human curiosity.

In the control of pollution, plants, animals and micro-organisms are useful in two ways. First, living things, especially micro-organisms, have a capacity for absorption and decomposition of pollutants resulting purification of air, water and soil. Second, many species of organisms each with its own particular range of sensitivity to each pollutant stand as ready-made systems for environmental monitoring and for warnings of danger to his environment.

Because living things are independent and interacting they form a complex dynamic system. Tempering with this system, though sometimes necessary, produces results which are very damaging. Many of the effects of pollution fall into this category.

Kinds of Effects on Organisms Other Than Man: Pollution affects living things in many different ways: In high concentrations, the sulphur dioxide in stack fumes kills trees and crop plants. The mixture of pollutants in urban smog damages spinach, tobacco and other valuable plants. Domestic sewage and animal wastes can act as fertilisers stimulating the growth of algae but creating unfavourable conditions for game fish heating of rivers and lakes by return of waters used to cool industrial processes or power plants can favour some living forms and devastate others. Soils and water can be polluted by radioactive materials derived from weapons' testing, from industrial release or from naturally contaminated fertilisers or spring waters. Once in soils or water, the radioactivity may then become concentrated in organisms. Sediments released into streams or lakes can reduce the supply of light for plants, and smother fish, eggs and other useful forms.

The effects of pollution on livestock and crop plants often show up clearly and cause farmers quickly notice and impairment of health or yield. Effects on wild forms are not likely to be detected and are harder to measure. Disappearance or catastrophic diminution of a wild population often occurs before the effects of a pollutant are recognised. The effects of pollutants on living things are usually complicated and seldom well understood. Organisms are subject to many different pollutants at the same time, pollutants that may enhance one another, partially compensate for one another or act side-by-side.

Pollutants tend to reduce the number of species and to make the relationship of those that remain less stable. It reduces the variety and abundance of wild life serving our recreation and enjoyment. Pollution is the common problem of the rich and the poor countries alike, because it was conceived in the womb of development with affluence and it begins with increasing the sensual desires of human beings.[22]

Impairment of Water and Soil Resources

Excess Fertility in Waters: Many streams, lakes and estuaries have received such large quantities of mineral nutrient, originating in the sewage of domestic animal wastes, that they have become filled with objectionable growth of algae and other water plants. These cause deterioration of water quality, making it unsatisfactory for domestic, industrial, recreational uses for fish and wild life. Nitrates and phosphates, derived from human and animal wastes, detergents and animal fertilisers are the most noticeable causes of over fertilisation of water, though other nutrients may possibly be important.

Soil Pollution: Soil pollution impairs the yield or the quality of farm products, and can contribute to subsequent air or water pollution. Long-term pollution of soils has resulted from repeated application of copper, arsenic or lead in insecticides, fungicides or fertilisers. The accumulation of poisonous metal has been so great in some orchard soils that it hampered their capacity to raise any useful crop for many years. Herbicides may persist in the soil and damage crops months or years after application. Since most herbicides have a relatively short life in soil, long-term losses of soil usefulness are not likely. Radioactive substances derived from uranium in some phosphate ores may survive the manufacturing process and persist in the finished commercial phosphate fertiliser.

Air Pollution: Air and water are the two boons of nature to all living beings. But due to the use of chemicals and burning of fossil fuels, the poison of carbon dioxide, nitrogen oxide and other piosonous gases have spread in the atmosphere. In Berlin large number of children suffer from pseudocrap in winters due to the concentration of polluted air in certain places. Air pollution has, besides human beings, started affecting plants. The forests of Europe, Canada and the United States have become the victims of acid rains. The famous Black Forest of Alps too is seriously effected. Air pollution threatens the forests in three ways:

(i) The pernicious gases, acid elements mixed in air destroy their leaves and destabilise the internal process.
(ii) Acidification affects the soil.
(iii) Increase carbon dioxide in the atmosphere.

Deterioration of Materials and Urban Environments: Air-borne soot deposits on buildings, clothing and automobiles raise the maintenance costs by necessitating frequent cleaning and makes our lives more dingy and depressing. The particles of soot that dirty our cities also lower visibility, obscure attractive views and give graycasts to our days and make travel more disastrous. The unpleasant odour of a rendering plant, the noise of jet air plane or of the other fellow's transistor radio, disorderly jumbles of autohulks, unsightly trash in a dump all are irritating offensive.

Climatic Effects of Pollution: Carbon dioxide is being added to the earth's atmosphere by burning of coal, oil and natural gas at the rate of six billion tonnes a year. By the year A.D. 2000 there will be about 25 per cent more CO_2 in our atmosphere than at present. This will modify the heat balance of the atmosphere to such an extent that changes in climate, not controllable through local or even national efforts, could create possibilities of counter-vailing changes by deliberately modifying other processes that affect climate.

Deforestation: The forests are the banks of oxygen and sinks of carbon dioxide for human kind. As the man has started consuming forest wood for purposes other then fuel add shelter, the forest areas have been denuded. The hills with thick forests have been stripped off as the commercial exploitation began. Since last century this process has been too fast. Deforestation had devastating effects in the United States on agriculture. The forests, covering 800 million acres, were felled to meet the requirements of development leaving only 55 million acre. A study by Wes Jackson reveals that in US four million farmers had to leave agriculture in the past 50 years as it is no more a profitable job.[23]

Environment and the Energy Dimension

The evolution of man has been boosted in the recent years by the exploitation of our natural resources for the production of energy. It is this energy that is instrumental in our cultural evolution and our adaptation of the environment to ourselves. The pursuit of these energy sources has led to exploitation of our non-re-cyclable energy generating fossil fuels in addition to the ruination of environs via various pollutants. It is against this we shall search for alternatives.

Men have long dug in the earth for materials that produce power but only recently have they begun on any significant scale to tap the immense energy source lying all the while beneath their feet — the great heat stored in the depths of the earth. Emanating from the earth's crust in the form of natural steam, this geo-thermal energy can be utilised to generate electricity by a direct and simple method that requires no fuel, no heavy boilers and no high dams. Only in the last few years has the economics of this form of power in competition with the other energy sources been clearly proved.

The World's Biggest Nuclear Plant

This great potential is based on the fantastic practically inexhaustible heat still being generated in the earth. Geo-thermal power is derived from the world's biggest nuclear plant — the earth itself. The scientists are of the view that by cooling the earth's centre even by one degree Fahrenheit would run all the existent power plants for 20 million years. This estimate is based on the study of surface conditions of hot springs' steam leaks and geysers.

Down to Earth's Mantle

The next big step is towards deeper wells, which have an electrifying effect on production. The first round of wells drilled in the Big Geysers was shallow one, between 500 and 2000 feet deep, the second round went down to about 5000 feet or nearly a mile. This added depth increased the average power output per well from 3,000 to 10,000 kWs. Such subterranean architecture could move geo-thermal energy into a scale with nuclear power, and make cheap energy available all over the world.

Vanishing Flora and Fauna

Man's parochial and anthropocentric view of his surroundings has led him to ruin ecological balance causing ruin and devastation of the other species. Many a plants and animals are extinct, thanks to man's selfishness. Even now attempts could be made to salvage our vanishing co-existors.

Wildlife Management in the National Parks

The purpose of preservation of native animal life is to conserve the scenery and the natural and historic objects and the wildlife therein and to provide for the enjoyment of the same in such a manner and by such means as will leave them unimpaired for the enjoyment of future generations. The goal of managing the national parks and monuments should be to preserve, or, where necessary, to recreate, the ecologic scene as viewed by the early generations. As a part of this scene, native species of wild animals should be present in maximum varieties and reasonable abundance. Protection alone, which has been the core of park service wildlife policy, is not adequate to achieve this goal. Habitat manipulation is helpful and often essential to restore or maintain animal numbers. Likewise, populations of the animals themselves must sometimes be regulated to prevent habitat damage, this is especially true to ungulates.

Insofar as possible, animal populations should be regulated by predation and other natural means. However, predation cannot be relied upon to control the population of larger ungulates, which sometimes must be reduced artificially. Excess game that does not leave a park must be removed. Trapping and transplanting has not proven to be a practical method of control, though it is an appropriate source of breeding stock as needed elsewhere.

Preserving Vegetation in Parks and Wilderness: Objectives of Preservation

Since vegetation is never static, preservation must consist, in effect, of managing change. Consequently, it is necessary to determine exactly what the objective is and thereby to determine how much change and what kind can be tolerated.

One of the most common objectives is to keep park lands green or, in arid lands, green and golden. Fire protection is considered the principal means to this end. The fact that vegetation protected from fire may change completely in a relatively short period has rarely been considered, because administration and public have not appreciated that this can happen.

Probably, the next most common objective to the preservation of certain favoured dominant species within the vegetative complex is the fact that certain successional stages may be fast disappearing and that the overall vegetative structure may be changing, within rather broad limits, is usually ignored as long as the dominants remain dominant and the general appearance of the landscape is not altered. Change that does not interfere with the effective display of the dominant species has, in general, been acceptable.

A less common but still popular objective is the preservation of particular successional stages. Most often this objective has reflected a desire to preserve a piece of virgin forest to native grass-land and generally has involved a climax phase of vegetation, that is a condition of dynamic equilibrium in which species on position remain more or less constant.

Today, many wilderness supporters argue that we should leave large areas of vegetation to change as they may, that man should keep his hands off and let nature run the course unimpeded by controls against fire, insect and disease.

Compatibility of Objectives

Many preservationists consider management *per se* to be an unwarranted interference with nature by man. This need not be true. Management consists merely of those actions that are necessary to achieve one or more objectives, whatever they may be even if the objective is "no management". Probably, incompatible objectives are much more widespread in current efforts to preserve vegetation than is generally recognised because change in vegetation can proceed for many years without the public or even by the park administrator responsible for its preservation.

Zoos: Their Changing Roles

The expansion of urban populations now makes it necessary for zoos to educate the generations growing up without any natural contact with wild creatures. Except at the zoo, the opportunities to know or even to become interested in wild creatures are largely vicarious for most city-dwellers. Yet, the opinions of these urbanites may ultimately shape the future policies of conservation in this country. Seen in this light the educational challenges to the zoo naturalist and the conservationist are identical.

Zoos and Conservation: One the reasons for the exhibition of live animals is to encourage the visitors, to become more deeply concerned with their surroundings and to take advantage of local and the out-of-doors wild life. It is customary for biologists to urge those who can to seek animals in the wild, to hike and to visit national parks, but it is evident that such visits in great quantity will finally destroy these wild seas. The fragility of many animal and plant communities subjected to human pressures in some of the national parks has become all too evident[24] and the real value of the zoo's role in this context is to act as a partial substitute for visits to natural areas and to fulfil certain functions of parks in the field of environmental education and conservation.

Nevertheless, zoos are frequently and inaccurately accused of depleting wildlife populations. Until the boycotts of arangutans (Pongo pygmaeus), first initiated in the United States in 1962, zoos did contribute to the precarious status of this species, but evidence is lacking to show that collecting pay zoo has been of major importance to any other animal population although zoos have also restricted their importations of giant tortoises and monkey eating eagles. The problem lies elsewhere. The U.S. Department of the Interior reported importations for 1967 totalling 74,304 mammals (62,526 of which were primates largely for laboratory study), 203,189 birds, 405,134 reptiles, 137,679 amphibians and 27,759,322 fish.[25] Zoos required not more than a fraction of one per cent of this number, and most alarmingly the total number of live mammals and reptiles imported for the laboratory, pet and zoo trade are but a fraction of the number represented in the trade in hides and animal products.[26]

No significant captive stocks of endangered fish or amphibians are being bred in zoological parks, but the San Diego zoo has been notably successful with one particular reptile, the Galapagas tortoise (Testudo elephantopur), and successfully hatched 17 young tortoises from 1961 through 1965.[27]

Current successes arouse curiosity about lost opportunities, and a review of the responsibilities that the past five centuries of exhibition would have posed to modern collections of birds is instructive.[28]

A researcher examined the 162 extinct birds with captive propagation potentials in mind.

Today, there are promising scientific developments at several large zoos in the form of more or less independent research institutes. The biologists in an institute connected with a zoo may have a few, if any, responsibilities for exhibits, yet they can benefit from the stimulus of the living collection and from association with experienced curators. The National Zoo in Washington, perhaps, is most easily utilised for comparative studies on a broad spectrum of species, its special facilities can provide an important supplement for intensive field investigations of a particular species and can suggest new approaches to old problems. As an urban institution and a source of diminishing wild creatures, the zoo seems destined to fulfil an increasingly important role in education, conservation and research.

Population and World Economic Development

"In the long run, the lack of adequate species and resources is logically certain unless fertility is reduced to improve a ceiling on rising consumption than to lower the availability of food per consumer and ultimately to cause a rise in death rates. These conclusions all follow from the mathematics of geometric increase. . . . At the current growth rate the population of the United States should outweigh the earth in 2,500 years".[29]

Implications

Various studies have suggested that if population were stationary instead of growing by three per cent per year it would have at its disposal for informing the State of the existing population, current productive power and per capita income amounting to something like 20 to 25 per cent of national income under *ceteris paribus* conditions. The precise magnitude of this figure depends upon the economic significance of differences in age composition and the relevant wealth population ratio. It affords a rough measure of the current cost of a two to three per cent yearly rate of population growth. The magnitude of this cost together with the disadvantages from the stand-point of education of an unfavourable age composition suggests that countries like Brazil which require larger populations for the optimum exploitation of their resources can progress more rapidly if they reduce their annual growth rates of population from the present two or three per cent to, say, one per cent.

In most of the world, persisting population growth constitutes most serious long-run threats to the continuing improvement of man's material lot. Because of the existence of limitational factors, if only that of suitably situated space, there is a limit to the extent to which populations can grow in any country or in the world as a whole. It is sometimes argued that fertility will never endanger man's standard of life, since men, having acquired a standard, are unwilling to surrender it, whether to population growth or to other income depressants. This argument overlooks a more fundamental, ethical and eudemonic issue posed by population growth. However, it ignores the fact that resources currently used to support the costs of population growth might otherwise serve to augment welfare per capita. It fails to ask to what degree maximum welfare per capita should be more nearly realised if those preferring population growth, whether in the United States or elsewhere, were required to support more of its costs than at present. It neglects the fact that in much of the world living standards already are desperately low and will prove hard to raise even if the stock's wings were clipped.

By the End of The 20th Century

Science and technology will advance more in the next 10-15 years than in all the millennia since man's creation. By the century's end man will have achieved a growing ascendency over his physical being, his earth, his planetary environs.

The primary reason is man's increasing mastery of the electron and the atom from which it springs. Through this knowledge he is capable of transforming everything within his reach, from the infinitesimally small to infinitely large. He is removing the fetters that for more than a million years have chained him to the earth, limited his hegemony over nature and left him prey to biological infirmities.

Food: The western nations by the turn of the century will be able to produce twice as much food as they consume. New approaches — the protein enrichment of foods, genetic alteration of plants and animals accelerated germination and growth by the electronic means will be widely used. The ocean itself, covering seven-tenths of the earth surface, will systematically be cultivated for all kinds of plant crops and fish-floating sea farms.

Raw Materials: Chemistry will create further substitutes for existing materials, transmute others into new forms and substances and find hitherto unsuspected uses for the nearly 2,000 recognised minerals that lie within surface of the earth. The rocks that crust the earth contain potentially extractable quantities of such basic metals as iron, copper, aluminium and lead. The ocean abounds in a variety of chemicals.

Energy: The energy at man's disposal is potentially without limit. One pound of fissionable uranium, the sise of a golf ball, has the potential energy of nearly 1,500 tonnes of coal, and the supply of nuclear resources is greater than all the reserves of coal, oil and gas. Increasingly electric plants will be nuclear and atomic energy will be a major power source particularly in the underdeveloped areas. Small atomic generators will operate remote installations for years without refuelling. Electronic generators converting energy directly to electricity will light, heat and cool homes, as will solar energy. Many areas of the world may also draw power from the thermal gases and fluids within the earth's mantle. Ultimately even more powerful energy sources will be developed, the example of nuclear fusion, the tapping of heat from deep rock layers.

Health: The electron has become the wonder weapon of disease and disability. Ultraminiature electronic devices implanted in the body will regulate human organs whose functions have been impaired — the lungs, kidney, heart — or replace them entirely. By end of the century medical diagnosis and treatment will be indicated by computers, assembling and analysing the latest medical information for use by doctors anywhere in the world.

Genetics: New and healthier strains of plants and animals will be developed. Transmitted defects of the mind or body will be corrected in the genes before life is conceived. If cancer proves to be genetic or viral, it may be destroyed at the source. Then appear in fact to be few ultimate limits to man's capacity to modify many forms of living species.

Air and Space: Around the earth, a network of weather satellites will predict with increasing accuracy next season's, floods and droughts and extremeties of heat and cold. It will note the beginnings of typhoons, tornadoes and hurricanes in live for the disturbances to be directed or dissipated before they reach dangerous intensity. Ultimately, the development of world-wide, long-range meteorological theory may lead to the control of weather and climate, space will become hospitable to sustained human habitation. Manned laboratories will operate for extended periods in space expanding our basic and practical knowledge about the nature of the universe, the plants and earth. Permanent bases will be established on the more habitable planetary neighbours and from these a stream of televised reports and radioed data inanimate and conceivably also living matter, will flow to earth. In doing so, science will give new validity to Alfred North Whilehead's profound observation that civilisation develops "by extending the number of important operations we can perform without thinking about them". Man's mind will then be free for the creative thinking that must be done if the impact of science is to harmonised with man's enduring spiritual, social and political needs.

NOTES

1. A Gailey and A. Featon (eds.), *The Spade in Northern and Altantic Europe*, Belfast, (1970), p. 207.
2. A. Feuton, Material Culture as an Aid to Local History Studies in Scotland, Journal of Folklore Institute 2, iii, (1965), p. 334.
3. Cited by Bruce Proudfoot in *Man's Occupance of the Soil*, p. 8.
4. W.C. Lowdermilk, "Acceleration of Erosion Above Geologic Norms", *Trans. American Geophysical Union* 15, (1934), pp. 505-09.
5. For a general survey of present knowledge see L.D. Stamp (ed.), *A History of Land Use in Arid Regions; Arid Zone Research*, 17, UNESCO, (1961)
6. S.L. Vendrov, *"Geographical aspects of the problem of diverting part of the flow of Pechora and Vychegda rivers to the Volga Basin", Soviet Geography*. 4, vi, (1963), pp. 29-44.
7. R.S. Rattray, *Ashanti*, Oxford: Clarendon Press, (1923), pp. 121-32.
8. A.S. Thomas, "The Tramping Animal", *Journal of British Grasslands Society*. 15, (1960), pp. 89-93.
9. For a general discussion of effects of forest fires see K.P. Davies, *Forest Fires, Control and Use*. New York, McGraw-Hill, (1959).
10. R.H. Brown, *Historical Geography of the United States*, New York: Harcourt Brace & World, (1948), pp. 133-34.
11. Maps of Soil erosion in U.S.A. have been published in *Soil, the yearbook of Agriculture* 1957, U.S. Department of Agriculture, p. 307.
12. W.J. Eccles, *Frontence 'The Courtier Governor'*, Toronto: McClelland and Stewart, (1959), p. 6.
13. L.D. Prayor, "How important is my corrhiza to introduce conifers?", *Australian Journal of Science*, 20 vii, (1958), pp. 215-16.
14. D.A. Holland, "Environmental modifications resulting from the culture and grubbing of trees". *Journal of Applied Ecology*. 4, (1967), pp. 353-62.
15. Willimott, *Conservation, 'Survey of the Southern Highlands of Jordon'*, London: U.K. Ministry of Overseas Development, (1964), pp. 64-7.
16. J.C.C. Romans, 'Soil Analysis'. *Proceedings, Soc. Antiquaries Scotland*, 1963-64. 97, (1966), pp. 30-4.
17. A.J. Pollock and D.M. Waterman, "A Bronze Age Habitation Site at Down Patrick Ulster", *Journal of Archaeology*. 27, (1954), pp. 31-41.
18. T.D. Ford, "A Recent example of soil erosion on the Derbyshire Limestone", Cited by Bruce Proudfoot. op. cit.
19. H. Schroo, "Notes on the Reclamation of Salt-affected Soils in the Indus Plain of West Pakistan". *Netherland Journal of Agriculture Science*. 15, (1967), pp. 207-30.
20. C. Monge, "Biological basis of human behaviour' in A.L. Kroeber (ed.) *Anthropology Today*, Chicago, (1963).

21. An early statement of this purposive and sociological approache is given by the concept of 'telesis' in L.F. Ward, *Pure Sociology*. New York, (1903), pp. 457-576.
22. Sunderlal Bahuguna, "The Crisis of Civilisation and the Message of Culture in the Context of Environment in *Gandhi Marg*. No. 104. Nov. New Delhi, Gandhi Peace Foundation, (1987), p. 458.
23. *Ibid.*
24. S.A. Cain, In *Future Environments of North America*, F.F. Darling and J.P. Milton (eds.) Garden City New York, (Natural History Press, (1966), pp. 53-54.
25. U.S. Department of the Interior news summary 19 Feb. 1968. The U.S. Government Printing Office, (1968), Washington, D.C.
26. W.G. Conway, *Animal Kingdom*. 3, 21, (1968).
27. C.E. Shaw, *Oryx* 9, 122, (1967).
28. J. Vincent, "List of birds either known or thought to have become extinct since 1600". Institute Union.
29. A.J. Coale and E.M. Hoover, *Population Growth and Economic Development in Low-Income Countries*, Princeton, New Jersey: Princeton University Press, (1958), pp. 330-31.

3

FRAGMENTATION AND INTEGRATION:
The Future of World Politics

JOSEPH A. CAMILLERI

THE INTERNATIONAL political and economic system is undergoing substantial transformation, involving new patterns of fragmentation and integration, both of which point to areas of increasing vulnerability in international relations. Conventional wisdom might suggest that integration is stabilising whereas fragmentation heightens instability. The reality, however, is far more complex for these fragmenting and integrative pressures are closely interconnected and mutually reinforcing.

To illuminate these interactive processes and their implications for the future of international society I propose to examine the recent evolution of the system of sovereign States on the one hand and the continued development of the world market on the other.* These two systems, at least in their modern form, have histories stretching over the best part of five centuries, although that historical process has accelerated rapidly since the scientific and industrial revolutions of the 17th and 18th centuries, and even more rapidly since the Second World War. The nation-State and the national economy represent the point of intersection between these two systems and the locus of new patterns of integration and unification on the one hand and fragmentation and differentiation on the other.

* This is a preliminary outline of a much larger project on which Jim Falk and I are currently working and which will eventually be published as a book by Edward Elgar.

System of Sovereign States

The Roman Empire and its successor, the Holy Roman Empire, partly because of the territorial spread of the imperial system and later because of the universal moral order presumed by Christendom, had nurtured the idea of a world society. But with the growth of the absolute monarchies and the subsequent rise of nationalism, the concept of an international community was discarded in favour of a world of separate and sovereign political communities. This system, which was formalised by the Treaty of Westphalia in 1648, has been labelled by Hedley Bull the "anarchical society",[1] that is, a society of States which, though jealous of their sovereignty and, therefore, not subject to common government, are nevertheless conscious of certain common interests and common values and of the need to share in the working of common institutions.

With the increasing complexity of relationships and needs, of beliefs and institutions, ushered in first by the Renaissance and Reformation and later by the scientific, technical and industrial revolutions, there emerged a new pattern of collective identification. Increasing literacy, higher levels of numerical, technical and general sophistication, the development of market relations, increasing mobility and communication leading to urbanisation, and the consequent need for a common linguistic medium and script gave powerful impetus to the national principle.[2] Amidst turbulent social, economic and political change, nationalism became the vehicle for sharing past glories and grievances and future hopes, dreams and ambitions. Nationalism brought about the coincidence between culture and Statehood through the emergence of the nation-State.

In its modern guise, in Europe as much as in the post-colonial world, the State assumed an emancipatory role. It was expected to ameliorate social and economic deprivation, to protect vulnerable peoples, liberate oppressed and colonised populations, to oversee a new model of economic development that would usher in an age of progress and prosperity. Representing the interests of the whole nation, it would maintain its autonomy from competing interests and classes, and where necessary use its coercive powers to implement policies in pursuit of the common good. Written constitutions were in part intended to give effect to these principles. This is not to say that nationalist rhetoric ever fully reflected political reality. In any case, as Gellner and others have observed, the coincidence between State and nation has been at best partial. The world currently comprises some 200 States with at least 800 nationalist movements and more than 7,000 potentially assertive ethnic communities. Nationalism, the cultural instrument that has done so much to achieve the cohesion of the State, is increasingly challenging the stability and legitimacy of the modern State.

Of course, most separatist movements lack the numerical, economic or military strength to achieve their separatist objectives. They are, thus, driven by their very commitment to ethnic self-reliance to seek allies among other dissident groups at home and abroad. They may also enlist the support of foreign States which, for a variety of motives, may have an interest in eroding the authority of the national government. In this sense the internationalisation of ethnic conflict may by said to accentuate the vulnerability of the State system.

Now, it has been argued that separatist and revolutionary movements are themselves intellectually and organisationally imprisoned by the State system since they are committed to wielding power, whether it be through the disintegration of an existing State or the substitution of one political system for another. This conclusion is not, however, altogether accurate for it does not take sufficiently into account the yearning for communal decision-making and the implicit "withering away of the State" which inspires the ideology of many of these movements. In any case, even if it were true that political opposition to the State is often premised, at least conceptually, on the principle of Statehood, the fact remains that an increasing slice of political life, domestically and internationally, overflows the boundaries of the State system. In this sense the nation-State is being undermined form within by the very concept of *nationhood*.

But the demand for greater autonomy is by no means confined to ethnic minorities. It is common to all groups in society which experience a sense of relative deprivation, often accentuated by the visible discrepancy between steadily rising expectations and the system's lagging capacity to satisfy them. This is not to suggest that established structures are facing imminent collapse, but simply to underline the sharpening conflict of values and the progressive delegitimisation of State morality. In this respect, it is worth noting that trade unions, student and feminist groups, ethnic, cultural, religious and other sub-national organisations can form coalitions within national boundaries, and also develop formal and informal relations with their counterparts in other countries as well as with international institutions. Such interaction, assisted by the increased mobility of people and messages, can often take place even when governments define it as illegitimate. The efficacy of global communications has provided ethnic, cultural and political conflict with an international dimension which transcends the boundaries and jurisdiction of the nation-State.

The World Market

Side-by-side with the emergence of the sovereign national State has been the internationalisation of economic activity, a trend that has been a distinguishing feature of capitalist development for more than a century and a hall.[3] For Immanuel Wallerstein the capitalist world economy has an even longer history stretching as far back as 1450, when the crisis of feudalism gradually gave way to a geographic expansion of the division of labour. With the advent of European imperialism other economic systems were either eliminated or absorbed into the European economic order.[4] With capitalist industrialisation we have seen the progressive institutionalisation of trade, financial and technological exchanges across national boundaries. Since the turn of the century the industrial and financial growth of the large corporation has enabled it to integrate the advances of the physical and social sciences and apply them to the creation of "a new structure of international industrial organisation and a new international division of labour."[5]

The period since the Second World War has been the rapid increase in the export of capital with transnational corporations developing a highly sophisticated brain and nervous system capable of connecting widely differentiated products and divisions, and geographically distant affiliates and subsidiaries. The end result has been the increasingly cosmopolitan organisation of the productive process, and the transnational mobility of capital, labour, finance, information and expertise. Paradoxically, the national State has played a critical role in the emergence of an increasingly integrated world market.

It is the State which establishes the legal conditions for property relations, regulates the business cycle, manages the labour and land markets, provides credit and subsidies to industry, funds scientific and technological research, organises transport and communication systems, and maintains social cohesion by offering a range of welfare and social services.[6] The institutionalisation of trade, financial and technological exchanges across national boundaries would not have been possible without State intervention in the economy. In the aftermath of the Second World War, the American super-State performed a global stabilising and co-ordinating role — not only militarily but economically and ideologically — which made possible the rapid growth of capitalist interdependence.

It would not be far-fetched to argue that the internationalisation of trade, finance and production has become synonymous with modernity. Critical to the entire process has been accelerating technological innovation. The global span of the mass media and the development of almost instantaneous systems of data processing and transmission have played a vital part in the globalisation of economic activity. The worldwide transportation and communication networks, the international governmental agencies and the transnational corporations have combined in an integrated, mutually inter-locking system — the world market. The inner logic of this system now permeates almost every national society whose economic and political life is as a consequence made dependent on external pressures which it can scarcely influence let alone control.

Progress centres on the unifying power of the world market and the industrial muscle of the imperial powers that gave rise to it has become the dominant image of change. In this sense modernity has become synonymous with market-oriented growth. Both East and West, North and South, despite ideological differences and economic disparities, experience the effects of the same technocratic model of development where management, programming, information control and militarisation are made to co-exist with economic and social dislocation, political instability and psychological and military insecurity. This polarisation, a *systemic imbalance*,[7] is most strikingly reflected in Third World societies where the contradiction is between privileged elites that benefit from modernisation and the peasant and urban masses that are devastated by it. The hierarchy of military power and the threat of nuclear extinction are perhaps the ultimate expression of the fragmentation of the globe. The myth of economic and military modernity continues to hold sway but the success of the image rests not on its intellectual and moral force but on a new form of cultural imperialism dressed as rationality and self-interest.

Relationship between the World Market and the System of Sovereign States

The logic of the world market does not operate in an institutional vacuum. It is embedded in a web of national, international and transnational institutions that endow it with organisational potency and legitimation. Among these institutions none is more important than the State or to be more precise the system of sovereign State. Here, I am largely in agreement with Wallerstein who argues that the State system is one of the three pillars of international political economy. Together with the core-periphery division of labour and the world market, it sustains capitalist commodity production. It concretises through legal, diplomatic and military arrangements the distribution of power on a global scale but also provides the crucial mechanism for the organisation of economic production and exchange within and between different sectors of the world capitalist system.[8]

But the system of sovereign States is by definition a fragmented system. The whole exercises no authority over the parts. It does not represent a universal moral order. It is the interaction of competing, often discordant, wills. In the post-1945 period, the American State, by virtue of the economic and military power at its disposal, was able to act as the organiser of the world capitalist system and to preserve its integrity in the face of internal and external threats. The restructuring of the world's trading and monetary systems was complemented by the establishment of a network of military alliances which ensured the strategic and economic integration of their members under undisputed American leadership.[9]

But American power, which contributed to an unprecedented expansion in the accumulation of capital, also sowed the seeds of future competition and is now in visible decline. Not only has the Soviet Union achieved nuclear parity with the United States, but the Europeans and Japanese have effectively and perhaps irrevocably undermined American economic supremacy. The ensuing rivalry between the major trading and financial centres makes it impossible for new political structure to emerge capable of regulating the world market. To give but one example, in the area of international finance States have attempted to regain control over their financial resources either by imposing restrictions on trade, by applying exchange controls, by unilaterally re-aligning the value of their currency or by raising interest rates. Such partial or temporary measures, however, have normally served to fuel speculation or given added impetus to the financial revolution. International institutions are increasingly acting not so much on behalf of any one State or group of States but on behalf of anonymous market forces.

It would not be far-fetched to argue that a state of anarchy has characterised international economic relations since 1973. The periodic economic summits of the leading Western industrial powers have proved entirely ineffectual in reconciling competing interests and policies with respect to growth, inflation, currency alignments and interest rates. Yet the demise of the American imperical order and the emergence of a new era of imperial rivalry have not impeded the transnational expansion of capital. If anything, the trend is towards accelerating interpenetration of national economies and increasing pre-eminence of world market forces.[10]

Here it is worth reflecting for a moment on the nature and intensity of the current economic crisis. For we are not merely witnessing a profound change in the global balance of economic power. The other side of the equation is the crisis of stagflation — a sharp decline in rates of growth coupled with high inflation and unemployment — which has in varying degrees gripped most parts of the industrialised Western world since the early 1970s. The economic, political and environmental constraints on growth have compounded the difficulties of national economic management and made it increasingly vulnerable to the strategies of transnational capital.

In the current economic crisis the re-organisation of the capitalist system is proceeding through increasing concentration of ownership and control; rationalisation of production through re-structuring of labour processes and introduction of labour displacing technologies; re-location of much industrial activity from the core to the semi-periphery (i.e., to the newly industrialising countries); a multi-faceted campaign for increased privatisation and de-regulation of the economy. all of this reflected in and reinforced by a new ideological orthodoxy intent on changing the cultural and political environment and thereby facilitating and legitimising the above strategies.

What emerges from the re-organisation of the world economy is the growing centralisation and internationalisation of capital. Yet this apparent unification of the world co-exists with, indeed contributes to, a far-reaching pattern of uneven development. An increasingly integrated world economy, while reinforcing the North-South cleavage, at the same time creates a new structural divide within all countries often on the basis of wealth although race, gender, religion and ethnicity can also become important instruments of division.

How then does the integration of the world economy and the interpenetration of national economies, which it implies, interact with the fragmented system of sovereign States? Part of the answer lies in the efforts of transnational capital to seek international competitive advantage through the agency of a particular national State. For example, American, Japanese and European corporate interests are currently locked in fierce competition, whether in the agricultural, manufacturing or financial sectors. They are all attempting to buttress their positions by seeking the support of their home States. State intervention, whether it takes the form of subsidies, tax concessions, or devaluation of the currency, is seen as the necessary condition for the achievement of corporate advantage.

In any case, a point is soon reached where the disruptive effect of competition creates a need for co-ordination without which the continued internationalisation of capital may itself be in jeopardy. Accordingly transnational capital is obliged to rely more and more on international governmental institutions (e.g., World Bank, International Monetary Fund, Bank of International Settlements, Organisation for Economic Co-operation and Development, International Atomic Energy Agency) which can perform a co-ordinating and moderating function. The policies of these institutions act as a further constraint on national sovereignty.

The erosion of sovereignty is particularly evident in the case of Third World countries many of which have accumulated large foreign debts that have made them highly vulnerable to the stringent requirements of the International Monetary Fund. But the negative impact on national sovereignty is equally apparent in First World countries. Evidence of this is provided by the monotonous regularity with which social democratic governments in Western Europe, Australia and New Zealand, ostensibly committed to full employment and social welfare policies, have had to jettison their pre-election programmes in order to comply with OECD orthodoxy.[11] The national state continues to intervene to facilitate the re-structuring of the economy, the rationalise competition and maximise competitiveness, to lessen the violence of the crisis, to counteract the tendency to self-destruction. But in performing these interrelated functions the State is responding to contradictory global pressures pushing simultaneously towards integration and fragmentation rather than to a coherent set of autonomously determined national priorities. In that sense the sovereign State is the indispensable agent in the development of the world market but also its primary victim.

The State System in Crisis

By virtue of its fragmented character the system of sovereign States has always been prone to the use and threat of force. But since the advent of total war the military edifice on which national security is said to rest has acquired unprecedented proportions in terms of the human and financial resources devoted to its construction and preservation. Yet the security it delivers has become progressively more elusive.

Contemporary structures of militarisation reflect not only traditional inter-State rivalries but industrial and technological pressures that underpin what has been variously described as the military industrial complex, the steel triangle or the contract state.[12] I am referring here to that loosely structured coalition of converging or overlapping interests in which are represented the armed services, industry, finance, the legislative and executive organs of government, the mass media, the scientific and technological professions and even unions, and which have a stake in high and rising levels of military spending. Particularly important in this respect is the technological momentum of militarisation, which crosses the boundaries of the civilian and military sectors of the economy and operates to a greater or lesser degree in both industrialised and developing societies.

Warfare and preparation for war, particularly in the nuclear age, would seem to be antithetical to the accumulation of capital. The use of force risks the destruction of all commodity production, or at the very least the severe disruption of the free flow of labour, capital and money.[13] On the other hand, the internationalisation of capital and the development of a world market that penetrates and dominates entire industries, regions and nations inevitably provokes ideological, political and economic resistance. The very attempt to contain or neutralise such resistance often necessitates the use or threat of force as indicated by the succession of colonial wars and wars of intervention that have characterised much of contemporary history.

The two World Wars represent a different and more complex phenomenon which revolves principally around the collision of rival national capitalisms. With the advent of nuclear weapons a comparable military collision would prove suicidal, hence the desperate attempts to enhance the credibility of the mutual threat system through such concepts as flexible response and nuclear violence is open to question. In any case the threat of nuclear war-fighting. Whether a system of mutual deterrence based on brinkmanship can indefinitely keep the strategic balance below the threshold of nuclear extinction has not diminished but encouraged the incidence of conventional hostilities in many parts of the Third World. At the same times, commercial incentives have combined with bureaucratic and technological pressures to ensure the application of nuclear fission to civilian purposes which has in turn facilitated the horizontal proliferation of nuclear weapons.

Military technologies and their spin-offs produce not only instruments of war but commodities on the world market which form a key link in the chain of transnational production, exchange and finance. Modern weapons are not simply instruments of Statecraft. They are complex systems involving research and development, testing, production, transportation, storage, servicing, inspection, a continuous process of technical modification and refinement, marketing and advertising, in short a web of commercial, financial and administrative transactions. They are pawns in a fiercely competitive market. Militarisation is at the interface between a single international division of labour and a multiplicity of sovereign States.

In the era of Cold War politics, the mutual threat system represents an attempt by the two super-powers to extent their political control beyond their respective territorial boundaries, to divide the world into two opposing camps, to impose bipolarity on a global scale.

Each of the two blocs justifies its existence and ensuing military and political integration by asserting that it is necessary for the security of its member States and the preservation of the values to which it adheres. In practice the integration of each bloc, in particular military integration (i.e., network of bilateral and multilateral agreements on the establishment of bases, stationing of troops, joining military exercises and adoption of joint strategies), has ensured the primacy of the super-power. More than that, the web of alliance arrangements has mirrored and reinforced the economic penetration of the super-powers inside the boundaries of their allies. In other words, it has occasioned a steady erosion of national sovereignty. In the case of the Soviet Union penetration has often involved the use of physical force (e.g., Hungary, Czechoslovakia, Afghanistan) and led to an explicit formulation of the concept of 'limited sovereignty'. Economic penetration has been particularly relevant in the Western camp, although the United States has not hesitated to resort to force as part of a global interventionist strategy designed to secure docile client States in many parts of the Third World.

The process of integration unleashed by the Cold War has been countered in part by the intermittent re-assertion of nationalist sentiment in allied States, resulting in tensions within the two alliance systems, verging at times on outright revolt (e.g., Mao's China, Gaullist France, Dubcek's Czechoslovakia). Not surprisingly, the fluctuation between Cold War and *detente* is, therefore, closely related to the to-and-fro movement between integration and fragmentation. *Detente* is in part a lever used by allies to facilitate the re-assertion of their sovereignty. The Cold War is a lever used by the super-powers to re-assert their imperial dominance.

The effects of militarisation are not, however, confined to the international arena. For the militarised State is likely to target its fire power as much on the domestic population as on the external enemy. Allegedly, in the interests of national unity, but often more as a way of diverting attention from social and economic ills, the State will exploit religious, linguistic or ethnic differences and unleash a reign of terror on vulnerable groups, castes and communities. Violence and civil war are thus instruments for the re-assertion of elite dominance.[14] Particularly in the West, the terrorist threat has become a convenient peg on which to hang a new array of legal powers that often cut across established civil liberties and are, more often than not, used to contain political unrest and suppress social movements. Although the axis of conflict, legal setting and ideological justification may vary considerably from country to country, the State's heavy reliance on the use or threat of force is a common feature of the political landscape in First, Second and Third World countries, and is in each case exacerbating the economic, cultural and ethnic fragmentation of society.

Nor are human rights and democratic traditions the only casualties of militarisation. Economic inequality and environmental degradation are also an integral part of the process. Militarisation is perhaps the most visible sign — though by no means the only one — of the widening gap between the promise and performance of the modern State. Theoretically, the nation-State is meant to act as the protector of human rights, of national culture, of the national economy. In practice because of the centralisation and militarisation of the State, on the one hand, and the integration of the national economy into the world economy, on the other, it has become increasingly difficult for the State to represent the community or preserve its independence.

The bureaucratisation of the modern State, which the world market dictates and reinforces, fosters alienation and withdrawal and thereby undermines the meaningful exercise of sovereignty. In this context we understand by sovereignty the principle that within the community the State exercises the sum of political power and represents the supreme political authority. Applied internationally, the function of the concept is to express the principle that the State recognises no higher external authority. In the contemporary period the cultural basis of nationalism has been decoupled from economic decision-making. As a result of the increasing inter-penetration of national economies, the State appears less and less able to exercise national sovereignty in either the internal or external sense. This phenomenon is especially acute in the dependent societies of the Third World but is equally evident in the industrial world, for here the process of economic integration is, if anything, more advanced and pervasive. Moreover, the nationalist principle has been weakened by the emergence of highly integrated alliance systems where the legitimising principle is ideological (i.e., serving the interests of the imperial power) rather then national.

Furthermore, the capacity of the modern industrial State to guarantee minimum universal standards of health, education and employment is increasingly problematic. In the case of Third World societies, where the State was seen in the aftermath of political independence as the instrument of development and nation-building, it is now widely recognised that the actions of the State reflect the interests of dominant castes, classes and elites, transnational corporations, international financial institutions and other metropolitan centres of power. There is diminishing faith in the ability of the newly independent States to challenge credibly effectively the premises and structures of the existing international economic order. The growth of strong internal security systems points to the failure of the State to maintain the confidence of its citizenry, to the mounting crisis of legitimacy.

Discontent and Revolt

Despite the very significant institutional, technological and ideological differences between the First, Second and Third Worlds, indeed between countries within each of these three worlds, there is evidence to suggest that the scope for domestic participation in most contemporary States is limited and generally in decline. Under the mutually reinforcing impact of domestic and external pressures the State is unable to satisfy the conditions of individual responsibility and mutual aid and co-operation necessary for the democratic process. the State, still widely regarded as the major institution for the organisation of human affairs, is finding it increasingly difficult to allay the deeply felt insecurity, that is the instinctive human response, to the growing signs of economic, military and ecological instability.

In conditions of increasing uncertainty and vulnerability, the State's competence and authority are increasingly under challenge. The natural reaction of the State is to expand its powers as a means of regaining control. In this sense, it would appear that under the combined impact of integrative and fragmenting influences we are witnessing the simultaneous weakening and strengthening of the State.

The challenge to the State is most strikingly evident in the development of those struggles and movements that are giving expression and responding to acute and widely shared insecurities. On the one hand, these movements are propelled by an appreciation of the increasing unity of human existence. On the other hand, they reflect a sense of "frightening vulnerability" to processes and institutions that are alienating, oppressive and ultimately "exterminist".[15] Slowly but cumulatively they have given rise to a trenchant critique of the modern State and of the prevailing doctrines of economic rationality. This critique represents a revolt of conscience, a re-assertion of normative discourse. Yet, it is not for that reason a purely subjective phenomenon. It is also premised on an analysis of objective conditions and is embryonically present in a great many new organisational forms and practices. The rise of non-State actors and processes, particularly at the sub-national and transnational levels, have given new life to the notions of personal and local autonomy on the one hand and of world community on the other.[16]

Imperial dominance, that is dominance of the institutions that currently underpin the world system — in particular the world market and system of sovereign States — is being weakened by the phenomenon of imperial conflict (East-West) and imperial competition (rivalries between European, Japanese and American capital). But imperial decline has also been weakened by the emergence of resistance movements in the First World (e.g., peace/anti-nuclear, ecological, feminist, consumer, human potential/self-awareness movements), the growth of dissent in Eastern Europe (e.g., Solidarity in Poland) and liberation and self-determination movements in the Third World. These movements have been successful in changing the political agenda, in re-defining the goals of peace, disarmament, development and environmental balance and in calling into question the present international division of labour and the Cold War basis of world politics.

Despite diverging ideologies, strategies and organisation styles, contemporary social movements share the same perception of a future increasingly under threat, in which the established economic and political institutions seem less and less able to prevent the crisis from crossing the threshold to disaster. In other words, these movements, united by a common understanding of an increasingly fragile world, are waging diverse but interrelated struggles inspired by a new vision of the future. They are in the process developing a new political culture, mapping out the ground for cultural liberation and political resistance.

Rejectionist movements, it is true, have yet to mount a comprehensive challenge to the *status quo*, let alone to construct a credible alternative to the present organisation of human affairs. They have yet to develop a coherent cultural and political framework around which it is possible to build a new sense of autonomy and solidarity. On the other hand, it may be that useful groundwork has already been done and that the defining principles and structures of an alternative world order are, however dimly, beginning to emerge. The critical question becomes: Is it possible given the present historical conjuncture, on the one hand, to permit and encourage diversity that does not degenerate into fragmentation and violent confrontation and, on the other, to avoid unification and integration of a kind that conceals domination and thrives on alienation and inequality? To re-phrase the question: What is the potential for fashioning equitable, peaceful and sustainable institutions that respect and foster identification with local community yet recognise emerging global connections and responsibilities?

The answer presumably lies in a new form of politics that reconstitutes the meaning of both power and authority, encourages devolution and decentralisation of decision-making, not least in the economic arena, but that locates citisenship in a planetary setting in both spatial and temporal terms. Decisions must be made in a way that recognise the larger interests of the human community and reconcile the conflicting demands of present and future generations. The task is to grasp the universal history that is in the making, yet with due attention to the particular histories that are the legacy of individual civilisations, communities and cultures. As Richard Falk has observed, "the universalisation of communications, trade and knowledge flows should not be allowed to become a recipe for the homogenisation of world culture"[17] Here one must be at pains to question the presumed universality of Wester civilisation, and, in particular, the subordination of all history to the institutions and ideology of progress associated with the rise of the West.

The emerging awareness of the unity of the human experiment must be grounded on the contribution of different histories, in particular those of colonised peoples and societies. Nor can one exclude the rich insights and perspectives of significant traditions within the West that have consistently challenged Western intellectual and political orthodoxy. That is perhaps the main function of the "anti-systemic" movements to which we have referred, and which are best placed by virtue of their histories and philosophical disposition to build bridges between nations and civilisations. Only a new cosmopolitan culture, that gives due recognition to the needs of both society and personality, is likely to provide the basis for a new political and ecological stability. This new cultural synthesis will need to combine "the profound eastern sense of the unity of man and cosmos as reflected in *Vedantic* and Buddhist philosophy, with the Western passion for freedom, self-mastery and creativity."[18]

The question remains: What is to be the institutional setting for this new cultural project? No comprehensive answer to this question is yet possible, but one may safely assume that a new political order will need to harness the residual emancipatory thrust of the State and nationhood, but at the same time contain and eventually eliminate the oppressive, exploitative and hegemonial ends to which they have been put. What is proposed is not the abolition but transformation of the State in a way that restores and extends the sovereignty of the body politic. To use Kothari's phrase, "the transformation of the State must be achieved through the transformation of civil society not the other way around."[19] Thought the State will for the foreseeable future have to continue to perform certain centralised functions, many existing functions could be devolved to other political spaces in civil society, and even residual functions could be performed in concert with local and international institutions.

What perhaps needs to be understood is that civil society is not synonymous with the nation. Civil society exists locally, nationally and internationally. It follows that the nation-State must be situated within a larger frame-work that includes both the local and communal levels of organisation, on the one hand, and a transnational framework of communication and co-ordination, on the other. An alternative world order that avoids the current pitfalls of fragmentation and integration must develop processes which weave together local, national and transnational loyalties and institutions. Different levels of organisation are required to meet different needs and/or values. The local level can most effectively achieve autonomy and direct participation whereas the national and international levels may be necessary to achieve principles of equality and re-distribution. The national and international levels are also required to achieve "socially valued economies of scale". Each level of organisation should integrate within its decision-making processes the other two levels and the principles which underpin them.

The underlying principle at each of the three levels of decision-making is democratisation. The advantage of stringently applying the democratic principle at every level of organisation is that it slows down the process of social, economic and technological change, thereby making the wide range of problems associated with this change more manageable. At the same time democratisation automatically reduces the scope of the profit motive and substantially qualifies the market as an allocative mechanism. Democratisation of the decision to invest, that is of the allocation of human and financial resources, lies at the heart of a re-structured political economy. Democratisation, by intruding normative criteria at the centre of the policy-making process, is also a considerable constraint on bureaucratic rationality and on the creation and expansion of large bureaucratic empires.

Regrettably there are no easy solutions. What is envisaged is a period of prolonged cultural, structural and ecological re-construction. The project may take decades to mature; it carries no guarantee of ultimate success but the objective and subjective conditions for its genesis are already with us.

NOTES

1. Hedley Bull, *The Anarchical Society: A Study of World Order*. London, Macmillan, (1977), pp. 13, 46.
2. See Ernest Gellner, *Nations and Nationalism*, Oxford, Basil Blackwell, (1983), pp. 35-8.
3. The argument that a "world economy" already existed in sixteenth century Europe is outlined in Christopher Chase-Dunn and Richard Rubinson, "Toward a Structural Perspective on the World System". *Politics and Society*, 7, 4, (1977), pp. 455.
4. For a fuller analysis of the historical process see Immanuel Wallerstein, *The Capitalist World-Economy*, Cambridge, Cambridge University Press, (1979), pp. 1-36.

5. Stephen Hymer, "The Multinational Corporation and the Law of Uneven Development", in J. Bhagwati (ed.), *Economics and World Order from the 1970s to the 1990s*, New York, (1972), p. 114.
6. The diverse functions of the State and the crisis to which they give rise have been examined by numerous authors. Of particular interest are Jurgen Habermas, *Legitimation Crisis*, Boston, Beacon Press, (1973). James O'Connor, *The fiscal Crisis of the State*, New York, St. Martin's Press; (1973). Suzanne de Brunhoff, *The State, Capital and Economic Policy*, London, Pluto Press, (1978). J.E.S. Hayward & R.N. Berki (eds), *State and Society in Contemporary Europe*, Oxford, Martin Robertson, (1979). Boris Frankel, *Beyond the State? Dominant Theories and Socialist Strategies*, London, Macmillan (1983).
7. J.A. Camilleri, (1976). *Civilisation in Crisis: Human Prospects in a Changing World*, Cambridge, Cambridge University Press, pp. 22-26.
8. I. Wallerstein, "Semi-Peripheral Countries and the Contemporary World Crisis", *Theory and Society*, 4, Winter, (1976), pp. 461-84.
9. For a discussion of the shift from 'imperial hegemony' to 'imperial rivalry' see Joseph Camilleri, "The Advanced Capitalist State and the Contemporary World Crisis", *Science and Society*, XLV, 2, Summer, (1981), pp. 130-58.
10. Giovanni Arrighi, "A Crisis of Hegemony", in *Dynamics of Global Crisis*, London, Macmillan Press, (1982), pp. 65.
11. Ralph Miliband, John Saville, Marcel Liebman and Leo Panitch (eds), *Socialist Register 1985-86: Social Democracy and After*, London, Merlin Press; also Joseph Camilleri, *After Social Democracy, Arena*, 77, (1986), pp. 48-73.
12. Gwyn Prins (ed), *Defended to Death*, Harmondsworth, Penguin Books, (1983), pp. 133-68.
13. Mary Kaldor, "Warfare and Capitalism"in *Exterminism and Cold War*, edited by the New Left Review, London, Verso, (1982), p. 264.
14. Rajni Kothari, "Masses, Classes and the State", *Alternatives*, XI, 2, (1986). April, p. 176.
15. E.P. Tompson, "Notes on Exterminism, the Last Stage of Civilisation", *New Left Review*, No. 121, (1980). May-June.
16. Richard W. Mansbach, Yale H. Ferguson and Donald E. Lampast, *The Web of World Politics: Non-State Actors in the Global System*, Englewood Cliffs, N.J., Prentice-Hall, Inc. (1976); Robert O'Keohance and Joseph S. Nye (eds.), (1972). *Transnational Relations and World Politics*, Cambridge, Mass., Harvard University Press.
17. Richard A. Falk, "Solving the Puzzles of Global Reform", *Alternatives*, XI, 1, January, (1983), p. 54.
18. J.A. Camilleri, *Civilisation in Crisis*, pp. 193; see also R.B.J. Walker (ed), *Culture, Ideology and World Order*, Boulder Co., Westrew Press, (in particular essays by R.B.J. Walker) (1984).
19. Rajni Kothari, *op. cit.*, p. 183.

4

SOCIAL AND ECONOMIC COSTS OF MILITARY EXPENDITURE IN DEVELOPING COUNTRIES

G. HARRIS

INTRODUCTION

ECONOMISTS BRING some fairly distinctive questions to the study of social science issues. First, whilst they are aware that there are many plausible ideas around (e.g., that economic growth will lead to a reduction in poverty), they will want to ask whether this is the *best* way of achieving such an objective. This is often approached by the concept of cost effectiveness, where the benefits of some policy cannot be measured precisely, but the costs can so measured. The economist will ask, for example, 'what is the cheapest (most-effective) way to bring these 10 million people out of poverty ?'. The various policies will then be examined and evaluated, and the results provided to policy-makers. Non-economic factors, it should be noted, may well preclude the choice of the cheapest methods.

Inherent in this approach is another aspect of the economists' role — that of providing estimates of the costs of any proposed policy. Many developing countries, for example, desire to be self-sufficient in food. It is easy enough for policy-makers, with nationalistic fervour running high, to pass legislation banning food imports. The economist, however, will want to estimate the costs associated with all the implications of such a decision, which may include, for example, increased imports of fertilisers and machinery, higher cost food for urban consumers, demands for increased wages, etc. There are many good ideas around: an important role of the economist is to estimate the costs of potential policy decisions so as to enable policy-makers to make more informed decisions. This chapter endeavours to do this in respect of military expenditure in developing countries.

Data on Military Expenditure

There are several agencies which exclusively provide data on military expenditure in annual publications: the Stockholm International Peace Research (SIPRI), which publishes *World Armaments and Disarmament: SIPRI Yearbook;* the United States Arms Control Disarmament Agency (ACDA), which publishes *World Military Expenditures and Arms Transfers;* and the London-based International Institute of Strategic Studies (IISS), which publishes *The Military Balance.* In addition, there are more general sources of social and economic data, including the World Bank's *World Development Report* and the International Monetary Fund's (IMF) *Government Finance Statistics Yearbooks,* which include military expenditure data. Major problems, however, exist as regards the accuracy of the estimates of military expenditure. Such sources often use each other's data and produce substantially different estimates. The important issue of data reliability is discussed by Nicole Bali (1983) and Blackaby and Ohlson (1982).

With these warnings in mind, we now turn to some data. Table 4.1 contains military expenditure data for 19 Asian countries for the most recent available year. Whilst there is danger in using data for a single, possibly, unrepresentative year, these data appear to reflect reasonably accurate typical magnitudes of reported military expenditure over the past few years. The unweighted average of military expenditure as a proportion of Gross Domestic Product (GDP) is 4.3 per cent for all countries. Those countries with above average expenditure cause no surprises given the potential conflicts in which they are concerned. The given proportions for Malaysia and Singapore, on the other hand, may be understood in terms of their ability to afford high military expenditure.

Military expenditure as a proportion of Central Government Expenditure (CGE) averages 16.3 per cent, with the Far East group again higher than South Asia. The range of the proportions, particularly in the South Asian group, is very large, reflecting two major determinants of the sise of military expenditure. Alternatively, the data may be

TABLE 4.1: **Indicators of Asian Military Expenditure**

	Military expenditure as a proportion of GDP, 1984	*Defence expenditure as proportion of CGE,1983*	*Defence expenditure per capita (US $ 1982*
1	2	3	
South Asia			
Afghanistan	3.5[1]	n.a	n.a
Bangladesh	1.6[5]	9.0[2]	2
India	3.2[5]	20.0	8
Nepal	1.0[4]	5.4	n.a.
Pakistan	6.2[5]	34.8	21
Sri Lanka	1.7	2.4	n.a.
Average of South Asia	2.9	14.3	10
For East			
Brunei	4.5[3]	n.a.	n.a.
Burma	4.3[1]	19.0[4]	6
China	n.a.	11.9	9
Hong Kong	1.0[2]	n.a.	n.a.
Indonesia	4.5	11.7	19
Japan	1.0[5]	n.a.	87
North Korea	12.3[5]	n.a.	92
South Korea	5.1	31.9	110
Malaysia	8.1[5]	15.1[4]	144
Philippines	2.0[5]	13.6	18
Singapore	5.8	18.5	373
Taiwan	6.1	n.a.	193
Thailand	5.0	19.8	38
Average of Far East	5.0	17.7	99
All Asian Countries	4.3	16.3	80

Sources: Data in column 1 are from SIPRI, 1986. pp 244-45, and refer to the most recent year for which data are not classified as uncertain. The exception is Indonesia for which all data are classified as uncertain. Data in column 2 are derived from the World Bank and refer to the most recent year (normally 1983) for which data are available. The Chinese figure is from SIPRI, 1986 p. 219. Data in column 3 come from IISS 1984-85, PP. 140-41.

Notes: 1 = data refers to 1979; 2 = 1981; 3 = 1981; 4 = 1982; 5 = 1983; 6 = 1984.

arranged in terms of the levels of GNP per capita, as in Table 4.2. These data suggest that low income Asian countries spend as high a proportion of CGE on the military as lower middle income countries, but the former figure is heavily influenced by the weight of India and Pakistan. A more general conclusion is that as countries become better off in terms of GNP per capita, they allocate a higher proportion of CGE to the military. The obvious exception is Japan, which has been a relatively modest spender on defence.

TABLE 4.2: **Military Expenditure by Income Group**

	Number of countries	*Military expenditure as a proportion of GDP*	*Defence expenditure as a proportion of Central government expenditure*	*Defence expenditure per capita (US $)*
Low income[1]	8	3.1	15.1	24
Low income (excluding India and Pakistan)	4	2.0	5.6	n.a.
Lower middle income[2]	5	6.0	15.0	72
Upper middle income[3]	4	5.0	21.8	209
Japan[4]		1.0	n.a.	87

Source: As for Table 4.1

Notes :

1. i.e, below US $400 GNP per capita in 1984; these comprise the six South Asian countries, plus Burma and China.
2. i.e., above US $ 400 and below US $ 1,700 GNP per capita in 1984; these comprise the remaining Far East countries except Malaysia, South Korea, Hong Kong, Singapore, Brunei and Japan.
3. i.e., between US $ 1,700 and US $ 7,260 GNP per capita in 1984; these comprise Malaysia, South Korea, Hong Kong and Singapore.
4. Japan's GNP per capita in 1984 was US $ 10,630. Brunei's GNP is high but not available.

In real terms, Asian military expenditure increased by an average of a little over six per cent per annum in the decade 1976 to 1985, compared with a world figure of 2.6 per cent. This raised Asia's share (excluding China) of world military expenditure form 5.4 per cent in 1976 to 6.6 per cent in 1985. The share of military expenditure in

China's budget has fallen consistently since the mid-1970s, and in 1984 and 1985 was 11.9 per cent. Although the data are regarded as uncertain, Chinese military expenditure in constant prices appears to have fallen by about a third over the period.

There further preliminary points deserve to be made. Information as to the *composition* of military expenditures is not readily available at any useful level of disaggregation. Data for 48 developing countries indicate that a very high proportion (three quarters or more) of annual military expenditure goes in operating costs (i.e. personnel and operation/maintenance). This means that military expenditure in developing countries is not principally spent on imported weaponry but on recurrent expenditure which, incidentally, makes it difficult to make large cuts in military expenditure in the short-term. Second, military expenditure data are of limited value in measuring military strength, since the same expenditure might produce forces of quite different size, training, morale and sophistication. The principal interest of this article, however, is the possible socio-economic consequences of military expenditure, for which purpose the data are crucial. The composition of military expenditure, as well as the uses to which forces are put, is likely to have important implications for its social and economic impact.

Third, whilst generalisations across countries are unavoidable in a article like this, they are potentially misleading. What is true for one country at one point of time may not be true for the same country at another point of time, let alone other countries at other times. In many respects each developing country is unique, and deserves to be studied on its own. With respect to the military, the nature of its role varies substantially between countries: in Malaysia, it has a strict military function whereas in Indonesia up to a third of military personnel work in other government and departments. The strategic situation, too, varies greatly and explains a good deal of the variation in military expenditure, both in total and in composition. India and Pakistan allocate enormous government resources to military forces as a result of their long-term dispute over Kashmir. The Philippines, on the other hand, has no hostile neighbours (nor land boundaries) and also hosts U.S. bases at Subic Bay and Clark Field. It is, therefore, able to use its armed forces almost entirely to deal with internal opposition.

Some Benefits and Costs of Military Expenditure

The main benefits and costs of military expenditure (and these presumably increase as military expenditure itself increases) are listed in Table 4.3. We examine these in this section, bearing in mind that all are likely to have been true for at least some countries at some point of time. What we will be trying to ascertain is whether they are generally true and, if so, whether the results achieved could be more cost effective.

TABLE 4.3: **Benefits and Costs of Military Expenditure**

	Benefits		*Costs*
1.	Protection of society from internal and external aggression	1.	Reduced growth via the impact of military expenditure on savings and investment.
2.	A socio-economic environment conducive to investment, to growth and to the alleviation of poverty.	2.	Reduced expenditure in other expenditure categories.
3.	modernisation of skills and attitudes	3.	Greater likelihood of war.
4.	Spin-offs to other sectors of society	4.	Greater likelihood of internal oppression.
5.	Public services and works.	5.	Greater likelihood of military takeover.

Benefit 1 : The primary justification of military expenditure is that it protects the nation from external and internal threats. This is a goal about which economists cannot quibble, but they will want to ask some questions. (An important non-economic question here is: Whether it is the nation or the group of people whc make up the government who are being protected ?). In particular, economists will want to look at different ways of achieving security, and to estimate that costs of each alternative. Policy-makers may then be better able to choose between these alternatives.

Benefit 2 : The most important economic benefit of military expenditure is that, by limiting both internal and external threats, it provides a socio-economic climate conducive to investment, and thereby to economic growth and the reduction of poverty. There is, no doubt, a general truth in this contention: investment, from both domestic and foreign sources, it generally regarded as essential in order to secure a respectable rate of economic growth, and re-distribution is easier in the context of high growth. There are, however, a number of questions which need to be asked.

If the reduction of relative and/or absolute poverty is a fundamental objective of developing country governments (and there would be many who would dispute this, despite the rhetoric), are there not more cost effective ways of achieving it ? It may be that growth might be stimulated more by government investment expenditure on education and infrastructure than by spending on the military to create a favourable environment, for private investment. In any case, some would dispute that growth significantly benefits the poor. The basic needs' approach is based on the premise that the benefits of growth will not trickle down to the poor to any degree, and that governments should, therefore, meet basic needs of food, shelter, education, health services etc. by direct provision. Finally, it may be that disarmament talks could lead to a less threatening external environment and thus act as an alternative to military expenditure. Such talks are likely to be more cost effective than military expenditure.

Cost 3, 4 and 5 : The availability of military forces may worsen rather than improve socio-economic stability. It may be that governments will be tempted to settle external differences of opinion by the use of force rather than by negotiation (*cost 3*); the military, which may, in fact, control the government, could push strongly for such a response. Internally, the existence of a strong military may be anything but stabilising given the possibility of a military takeover (*cost 5*), and military governments have a poor record as regards their treatment of opponents (*cost 4*).

Cost 1 : There has been an important over the past ten years about the impact of military expenditure on economic growth. It has been widely assumed that high defence expenditures act so as to reduce growth. A comprehensive study by Emile Benoit (1978), covering 44 developing countries over the period 1950 to 1965, concluded that military expenditure acted as a positive stimulus to growth. How might a high defence burden promote growth ? Indirectly, said Benoit, an increase in the defence burden will have small but positive effects on investment and the inflow of external resources which promote growth. There are also several direct means by which defence expenditure might influence growth, the first being by an improvement in human capital. Such an improvement may come about through the feeding, clothing and housing of people, the provision of education and training and the inculcation of attitudes and aptitudes which may stimulate growth (*benefits 3*). For instance, the military may encourage national cohesiveness as opposed to tribal or regional loyalties. Another possible impact is that defence forces may undertake public works which may have important benefits to the civilian population, and may carry out such nationally useful activities as mapping and surveying (*benefit* 5). Benoit admits that the evidence of the stimulus to growth from such factors is 'imprecise, anecdotal and difficult to evaluate'.

This is no doubt that such positive effects have operated for some countries at some periods of time but it is arguable as to how generally they operate. Take, for example, the training of people in skills which they could later use to the benefit of the civilian sector. We would need to know whether the military was in fact training people in skills which were in short supply in the civilian sector, whether the skills learned were fairly easily transferable, whether those who were trained actually left the military before retirement and, if they did, whether they indeed used their skills in the civilian sector ? Whilst the answers to such questions for some countries at sometimes has been positive, I doubt that they would all be so for many countries now. Therefore, such justifications of military expenditure may be invalid. More fundamentally, we could ask our cost-effective question.

If we want trained personnel, is training via military service the cheapest way of achieving this ? Almost, certainly, the answer to that is on, although it may be argued that the military is performing a number of roles in society, of which training is only one.

The more sophisticated criticisms of Benoit fall into two categories — matters, which he did not take into account (or take sufficiently far), and aspects, where his results are alleged to be incorrect. Several researchers have recalculated the correlation coefficients between defence expenditure and growth for different groups of countries and different time periods. Such studies are consistent in reporting either no relationship or a negative one. This result is not surprising given the level of aggregation involved. Indeed, an important criticism of the correlation approach is that it is unlikely to be very revealing about the relationship between processes as complex as armament and economic growth, where countless interactions occur continually.

Considerable work has subsequently been carried out using more sophisticated explanatory models, in particular examining the simultaneous nature of the relationship between growth, savings/investment and military expenditure. The general conclusions (e.g. Deger and Smith, 1983) are that savings are negatively related to the level of defence expenditure (i.e., high military expenditure is associated with lower savings). This indirect negative effect on savings and thereby on investment is considered sufficient to outweigh the potentially positive impacts of effects — the modernisation and technological spin-off effects.

Benefit 3 : Modernisation effects incorporate the attitude and skill-changing impacts of military service mentioned above. Again, it is not sufficient to conclude that these are positive without investigating whether the same result could have been achieved by other, cheaper, means.

Benefit 4 : Spin-offs to other sectors of the economy may be important. For instance, new technologies may be introduced into the country to produce or maintain defence equipment. Again, we would not want to take this benefits simply at face value. What other effects may result ? Is skilled manpower, for example, diverted to a military-related industry, and, if so, what is the effect of this on the productive activity in which these people were previously employed ? The only examination of the impact of technological spin-off (Deger and Sen, 1983) was carried out for India, a country with a very large military-industry base, and in which any technological spin-off would be revealed to best advantage. The conclusion of the study, however, was that such spin-off made insignificant contributions to economic growth.

Cost 2 : There has been widespread concern that the substantial defence expenditures incurred by developing countries have important opportunity costs in terms of reduced expenditure elsewhere, particularly on education and health. It is self-evident that government expenditure on any activity means that those particular funds cannot be spent on other, possibly highly desirable activities. It is also clear that low income countries typically spend a greater proportion of CGE on military than they do on education-and-health combine. However, it seems to be believed that military expenditure may have some special ability to divert government funds away from other activities, i.e., defence expenditure increases are financed by reduced government expenditure elsewhere. This would be an easy enough proposition to test if total government expenditure was constant between years, in which case gaining and losing sectors would be readily identifiable. However, since total government expenditure typically increases from year to year, it is faster or slower growth of expenditure in the different categories which is the norm. To identify trade-offs in such a situation is not straightforward (Harris et al., 1987).

Two points of some importance should first be understood. The first is that if income is not spent on defence, only a small part of it (Benoit estimates about one-fifth) is likely to go into 'productive investments'. He notes that optimum civilian programmes for growth would no doubt make a much greater contribution [but] . . . 'one must compare the defence programmes with their objectively probable substitutes, not with their optimum substitutes, if one seeks to estimate realistically their opportunity costs and net benefits'. Thus, the negative impact of defence expenditure on growth via investment may not be as great as is usually supposed.

Second, education and health expenditures, for example, have important investment components, i.e., they provide a stream of returns into the future. It has been argued that military expenditure is more a consumption expenditure, with immediate benefits, rather than any long term positive impact; benefit 2, however, certainly has a long-term perspective.

Three methods may be used to establish whether trade-offs exist. First, using cross-section data, it should be possible to discern whether relatively big spenders on the military are relatively small spenders on, say, education and health (and *vice versa*). Second, the effect on central government expenditure increases or cutbacks on, say, defence, health and education allocations may be examined. If a trade-off existed, it might be expected that defence expenditure would gain more or lose less relative to other expenditure categories during times of CGE expansion or cutback. It has usually been assumed that defence is less vulnerable to cutback than social expenditures. Third, time series data for individual countries could be employed. For example, education expenditure as a proportion of CGE (as the dependent variable) could be regressed against other variables including defence expenditure as a proportion of CGE. A significant negative coefficient would provide support for the view that a trade-off existed, i.e., it suggests that a rise (fall) in the defence expenditure causes a fall (rise) in the education expenditure variable.

Studies using each of these approaches in an attempt to identify trade-offs between defence and education/health have been unable to provide much evidence of trade-off. That is, it does not appear that defence expenditure is competitive with health and education, although it clearly must be with other expenditure categories. There are, however, several problems with these approaches. First, the data on which the studies are based are subject to important limitations. Second, there are important problems involved in adding together highly diverse societies and averaging the outcomes, as many of the studies mentioned in this section have done: longitudinal studies of single countries have considerable methodological advantages. Third, differences in the composition of expenditures between countries (or within countries over time) can result in different impacts, which trade-off studies do not pick up. In health, for example, policy initiatives such as a switch to preventative medicine and/or non-brand medicinals could result in health standards rising whilst health expenditures were constant or even falling. It is interesting to note in this connection that the most important of all preventative measures — clean water and sanitation — do not ordinarily fall within health budgets.

Despite the general conclusions of previous research, there is no doubt that expenditure allocations to health, education and the like could be increased if defence expenditure was reduced. Case studies of the CGE allocation processes in individual countries would be useful in order to understand how defence expenditures might be re-allocated.

We may sum up our consideration of the costs and benefits of military expenditure as follows:

1. As a general statement, the presence of strong military forces may provide stability and thereby encourage investment, growth and the alleviation of poverty (benefit 1). On the other hand, a strong military may be de-stabilising in several ways (costs 3, 4 and 5).
2. Whilst the military has positive impacts with respect to modernisation of attitudes, the development of human capital and provision of public works (benefits 2, 3 and 5), it seems likely that these could be achieved by more cost effective means.
3. Spin-off from military to civilian industry seems to be insignificant (benefit 4).
4. Military expenditure has negative net effects on growth because of its large negative effect on savings and investment (cost 1).
5. Expenditure on the military means that some government financial resources are available for other expenditure categories (cost 2).

Financing Military Expenditure

Another aspect of military expenditure is its financing, which may come from domestic sources (taxation or borrowing), or from foreign sources (borrowing or aid). To the extent that financing derives from the two domestic sources there will be opportunity costs, in terms of foregone private and public consumption and investment. We considered the public aspect of this in our examination of trade-offs and also saw that military expenditure is likely to retard growth by reducing domestic savings, both public and private. However, a good deal of military expenditure is financed by foreign borrowing.

One of the most significant changes in the position of developing countries during the 1980s has been the massive increase in net foreign indebtedness (in US dollar terms) and in debt service ratios (the ratio of debt repayments to exports for any one year). These increases have resulted from sharp increases in the domestic interest rates of the creditor countries which have moved through to existing and new debt incurred by debtor nations; and the rapid appreciation of the US dollar, in which currency most international loans are written. This foreign debt problem has a number of links with military expenditures one study estimates that at least 20 per cent of new foreign debt incurred by LDCs since the mid-1970s was used to purchase weaponry. High levels of military expenditure make the containing of budget deficits difficult and may require further borrowing and/or disrupt debt service payments. Interest rate increases in creditor countries are in part due to large budget deficits and these are partly attributable to high levels of military expenditure in those countries.

Conclusion

The main conclusion of this article is that allocations of high proportions of CGE to the military have important social and economic costs to developing countries. These appear to outweigh the benefits, and are likely to rise in future as the proportion of CGE/GNP allocated to military increases. Unfortunately, the prospects for reduced military expenditure (except as a response to short-term macro-economic stringencies) seem to be fairly remote. The most recent *SIPRI Yearbook* (1986: 347) suggests that arms control in developing countries has been 'heading up a dead-end street for many years'.

What can be done? At a personal level, we must not allow ourselves to be daunted by the prospect of a long and tedious struggle. Those, needing some encouragement, are recommended to read a recent article by Frank Blackaby, a former director of SIPRI (Blackaby, 1986). There have been successes in this general area such as the abolition of the slave trade, and the outlawing of chemical weapons and germ warfare, and there do seem to be prospects for reductions in nuclear weapons. Second, Australia *could* have a useful role to play in promoting disarmament in its region, particularly if it is able to extricate itself from some of its present policies, including the presence of American bases and uranium sales to France. It is too much to expect neighbouring countries to take Australian regional disarmament initiatives seriously whilst we continue with such policies. New Zealand has a much more credible position. Related to this is the question of Australian weapons' exports. These currently amount to $ 250 m a year and go principally to the Middle East and South-East Asia; their massive expansion has been recommended in a recent government report (the Cooksey Report) which has been discussed by Atkinson and Kettle (1987). There may be some economic justification for such exports, just as there is for uranium exports. But the economist is not a policy-maker, and morality should always take pre-eminence over economics, which is why presumably we don't produce addictive drugs for export. If Australia has any aspirations to be a force for peace, it must act to remove or avoid policies which will justify other countries paying no attention. Such removals will have a cost in dollar terms: if the economists can estimate the cost, will policy-makers take the appropriate moral decisions?

REFERENCES

Atkinson, J. and Kettle, St. J. "Defence and the dollar". *Australian Society*. February, (1987), pp.23-26.

Ball, N. Measuring Third World Military Expenditure: A Research Note, *World Development*, 12(2), (1984), pp. 157-64.

Benoit, E. Growth and defence in developing countries, *Economic Development and Cultural Change*, 26(2), (1987), pp.271-80.

Blackaby, F. Peace research and the Stockholm International Peace Research Institute (SIPRI), Peace Research Centre, Australian National University, *Working Paper* No. 3, (1986).

Blackaby, F. and Ohlson, T. Military Expenditure and the Arms Trade: Problems of Data, *Bulletin of Peace Proposals*, 13(4), (1982), pp.291-308.

Deger, S. and Sen, S. Military Expenditure, Spin-off and Economic Development, *Journal of Development Economics*, 13(2), (1983), pp.67-83.

Deger, S. and Smith, R. Military Expenditure and Growth in Developing Economies, *Journal of Conflict Resolution*, 27(2), (1983), pp.335-53.

Harris, G., Kelly, M. and Pranowo, Trade-offs between Military Expenditure and Health/Education Expenditures in Developing Countries, *Journal of Peace Research* (1987).

5

HUMANISING DEVELOPMENT: Promises, Problems and Prospects

R.P. MISRA

INTRODUCTION

MAN IS the measure of all things. It is not the power of a nation-State — economic or military — nor industrialisation, urbanisation nor modernisation: it is the happiness of man that ultimately counts. The development of a country must, therefore, be seen as the sum total of the satisfying lives of millions of men and women who constitute its citizenry. The final goal of development is to obtain a life worth living.

Thus far, there is no controversy. The current debate on development is not centred on this final goal. It centres on two questions:

(a) What constitutes a life worth living, and
(b) What means should be adopted to achieve it?

Three schools of thought, with some interfacing ideals and ideas, deserve our attention. According to the first school, "a life worth living" is one which has the highest per capita income possible; which has the maximum range of consumer goods; which values this in terms of money and whose relations are contractual and formal. It sees no limits to economic growth as there could be no limits to human ingenuity in the control of nature. The second school sees increasing poverty in the midst of plenty as a sign of limits to what economic growth can achieve and, therefore, advocates increased emphasis on equity, i.e., the strategies of economic growth must have built-in sub-strategies which distribute evenly the fruits of growth to nations and peoples who are unable to benefit from the grinding mill of growth. It is estimated that, if the current trends continue, there will be a greater number of poor people in the world in A.D. 2000 than in 1981. A number of strategies have, therefore, been suggested for reversing this trend before it is too late. The third school advocates a steady state (or zero growth) economy once material welfare has reached a level beyond which it can add nothing to human welfare in real terms. It is against consumerism and all that is considered "a must" for the so-called modern economy — specialisation, concentration, centralisation, maximisation and the de-humanisation of work. It calls for a culture-specific development process wherein economic growth is subordinated to the dictates of "a life worth living".

Within each of these three schools there are divergencies in approach. Some look at the issues from an international perspective, others from a national perspective; some are more utopian than others while still others are realistic in varying degrees. The main object of this article is to review concisely how these three schools of thought look at the concept of development. The article does not aim at offering a new model for development; it only hopes to clarify some of the issues pertinent to the ongoing debate. Given the present world order, the depth of poverty prevailing in the underdeveloped countries, and the increasing social disruption in the developed countries, it does, however, lean towards a more humanistic approach to the development process.

DEVELOPMENT PROCESSES IN HISTORICAL PERSPECTIVE

Enough has been written on how economic development was triggered-off in Europe, then in the United States and later in the Soviet Union, as a consequence of the Industrial Revolution in England and the Netherlands. It is still, however, an engima for all those who are in search of a "General Theory of Development". A peculiar cluster of events in specific circumstances, which were neither anticipated nor planned, took place. Maybe some of those events took place elsewhere too, but not in the same sequence or in the same setting as that which led to the Industrial Revolution in Europe. We may never know what caused the Industrial Revolution, but, even if we do, it would have only minor significance for planners and policy-makers now — for it is impossible to recapture or transplant specific historical processes from one country to another.

Protestant ethic, we were told in our school days, was the prime mover. It meant frugality, individualism, love of freedom, a scientific attitude and so on. But now we are told that the Confucian ethic is also good because Japan, the Republic of Korea and Taiwan have also succeeded in developing their economies. China has made good progress and Vietnam was able to defeat the United States, the greatest military power in the world. If, for some reason, India's economy started to grow at an accelerated rate, the Hindu ethic may also be added to this list. One wonders why the Catholic ethic has not yet been mentioned because resource-rich Brazil and Mexico are indicating signs of growth, and why has Islamic ethic not yet been accredited for the growing economies of the oil-rich countries of West Asia? What it really means is that we really do not know what generates development. We can only interpret the event after it has taken place. The social sciences are still methodologically too weak to predict the course of human destiny.

For the industrialisation of the non-industrialised world it is not necessary to create the same conditions which prevailed in England and the Netherlands prior to the Industrial Revolution. The entire social economic history of mankind since this epoch-making change has become our common heritage. The heritage is part and parcel of the new environment in which social and economic development is being attempted in the developing countries. The Soviet Union, though late in launching industrialisation, devised a new social organisation to meet the challenges of the time as the United States had done much earlier. Japan is a classic example of a truly unique style of development, purely national in character. There is, thus, no ethic involved. Each culture provides avenues and opportunities for social and economic changes; for peace and war; for self-destruction or a life really worth living.

What cuts across all so-called ethics in the process of economic development triggered-off by industrialisation is the access to resources (natural and financial) and technology. Any country which has both of these in abundance can become a mighty industrial power within half-a-century. It need not take 200 years to industrialise itself, nor does it need to employ the Protestant ethic, the Confucian ethic or the Islamic ethic.[1] To talk about ethics is to avoid the main issue which hinders the economic development of less-developed countries in Africa, Asia and Latin America.

Just 200 years ago, there were no marked differences in the economic well-being of different people throughout all parts of the world. The level of development in the way it is conceived of today was definitely low, but it does not mean that people were necessarily less happy than they are today (happiness is after all, a state of mind). In these 200 years, more than half the population has regressed to a stage where it does not have enough to eat; a quarter of the world's population is only just managing to meet the bare essentials, while the remaining quarter suffers from the burden of affluence. Herman Kahn said that all will be prosperous within the next 200 years[2] but since he said that, three years ago, the gap between rich and poor has further widened.[3] Data indicating the increasing disparities among rich and poor nations, as well as the increasing inequities within nations, are too well-known to need repeating here.

This unprecedented inequity is the aftermath of the Industrial Revolution and the pattern of economic growth it triggered-off. It is not the chain of events which led to the Industrial Revolution which facilitated this inequity but the sequence of events which resulted from it which became responsible for widening opportunities for people at all levels of society. But had it not been for the colonial penetration of Africa, Asia, Australia and Latin America, the story of economic development would have been very different. The idea of bringing up this issue is not to caricature the Industrial Revolution or Western-style economic development but to suggest that such development could not have taken place without the following prerequisites:

1. Occupation by force of vast resource-rich lands in the Americas, Australia, Siberia, South Africa, etc.
2. Colonisation of agriculturally rich countries from which raw materials could be obtained and to which manufactured goods could be sold at prices determined by the colonial power; and
3. Obstructing the spread of Industrial Revolution to regions outside Europe and Anglo-America.

Extraordinary though it may seem, no nation lacking an abundant natural resource base or extensive colonies rich in resources has become industrialised except where it chose to become an indirect colony of a super-power. Included in the resource-rich countries are United States, Canada, Australia, New Zealand and South Africa. These are countries which were incorporated in Greater Europe; they were not colonised in the same way as the countries of Asia and Africa. The case of Latin America is similar, although not exactly the same. It must be mentioned here that Japan, the only nation to catch up with the West, is no exception to this. One doubts whether Japan could have done all it did in the pre-Second World War period without its overseas colonies.

Quite a few nations, rich in petroleum resources, are industrialising fast, despite various hurdles, direct or indirect, put in their way by the industrialised countries. These countries have become rich not because of any Industrial Revolution in the sense that it occurred in the West, but by gaining control of their oil wealth hitherto denied them by the West. One is struck by the fact that all the so-called middle income countries (according to World Bank classification) are the resource-rich countries, and all the very poor countries which are categorised as low income countries are resource-poor countries.

The Republics of Korea and Taiwan do not have rich resources of their own. But in these cases because of their very peculiar place in the East-West confrontation, investment resources from the United States and Japan especially, flowed into them after 1950. Their economies are almost completely integrated with those of the West. The share of foreign capital in the Republic of Korea's economy is staggeringly high by any standard.

Thus, when Europe started developing, it had the resources of the whole world at its disposal and at a price determined by it. It also had the whole world as its captive market in which to sell its goods and, above all, it had the Americas, Asia, Australia and part of Africa to send its excess population. It was a few entrepreneurs who started the process of industrialisation but within a century it had engulfed the entire population. History was so written that every European was endowed with Protestant ethic and was, therefore, a hero. Some of the historical jokes that were written at the time, such as Columbus being the *discoverer* of America, persist to this day, in our textbooks and encyclopaedias.

This is not to suggest that it was rich resources which triggered-off the Industrial Revolution. Far from it, the idea being advanced here is that once the Industrial Revolution took root in its rudimentary terms, it was the abundance of resources together with ample markets which made European nations what they are today. Europe (including the USA) became the core region of the world to which resources came from the periphery. In turn, manufactured goods went out to the periphery, setting in motion an exploitative interdependence between Europe and the colonies.

What the newly independent countries of Asia, Africa and Latin America need today is the cessation of, if not the reversal of, this exploitative relationship. Now that a few of these countries have developed their economies to the level whereby they can threaten a nuclear holocaust to protect their national interests in terms of the above-mentioned relationship, the need for a change is more pressing than ever and implementing such a change is possibly the greatest challenge facing the world community today.

Is it possible to evolve a new world order whereby the fundamental interests of the developed countries are well protected and yet the exploitative nature of their relationship with the developing countries is removed, giving way to a co-operative one? Can the developed countries lower their expenditure on lethal armament manufacture and aimless pursuit of growth and transfer part of the saving to developing countries to aid in their industrialising processes — not so much in order for them to challenge the developed nations but in order for them to begin the self-sustaining development process? The answers to these questions will determine the shape of the world in the years to come.

Development Debate and the Challenges of the 1980s

The model of economic development which emerged after the Industrial Revolution assumed resources to be provided. This assumption was derived from the real context in which the capitalist mode of production expanded during the two centuries prior to the Second World War. While the Industrial Revolution changed the mode of production,

> from the Enlightenment of the 18th century sprang the idea of the perfectability of man, the product not of any divine intervention but of a deliberate social process. . . . And, notwithstanding the traumatic experience of the 'Industrial Revolution' in Britain, the notion of progress as a continuing process, the product of man's ingenuity and purpose took root in society well before the middle of the 19th century.[4]

The notion was further strengthened as science and technology released the latent power of the human mind to usher in new processes of production modes of transportation and communication and increased trade through colonisation and subjugation of other nationalities abroad.

The belief in an economic panacea for all the ills of mankind and faith in science and technology as the twin-engines to generate economic growth were further strengthened in the first half of the 20th century. And apart from some problems and occasional backslidings, the growth engine did perform well. The fuel (external resources) was so abundant, the mechanical system, thanks to science and technology, so perfected, and the market for products so wide open (the whole world was a captive market), that nothing could misfire. Abject poverty, which had been the lot of the European masses, was almost eliminated by 1940, minor pockets here and there notwithstanding. The basic material needs of all the people were largely met, although relatively speaking only a few were rich.

The disparities in personal income, assets and earning capacities were rationalised on the grounds that those who organised production — the capitalists, the managers, the entrepreneurs, and the technocrats — had to get their due rewards. Whatever was left should belong to labour. But as production zoomed further, and labour became more organised, these disparities narrowed down considerably to make even the common man realise that nothing could be achieved without continued economic growth.

The October Revolution in the Soviet Union in 1917 produced a new model of economic growth. It was through State capitalism, run and managed by the labouring class (proletariat), the growth was promoted. Marx predicted the natural death of Western capitalism because of its inner contradictions. The labouring class would one day rise to take over the system. Marx prophesised that the growth engine would then run faster and smoother and man would become fully emancipated socially as well as economically, from the clutches of capitalism. Thus, Communist ideology too put its faith in economic growth, although its ultimate goal was to create a New Man.

The Second World War culminated in the defeat of the Axis powers. It also ended old-style colonialism. There were three reasons for this. In the first place, the colonies which were rich and where the white man had established in numerical superiority (USA, Canada, Australia, New Zealand and parts of Latin America) were already free. Those in Asia and Africa were, by then, so poor, overcrowded and weak that they were not worth the trouble as colonies any more. They had served their purpose well. Secondly, the colonial powers were so weakened and disgusted with the war that they did not have the courage to fight against the rising tide of nationalism in the colonies. And those who had the temerity to fight ultimately had to beg for a peaceful withdrawal (for example, the French in Indo-China, the Portuguese in Africa and the British in Kenya). And finally it was feared that any further delay in granting independence to the freedom movements would drive the nations closer to the Soviet Union — an allied power during the Second World War, but an adversary during the ensuing Cold War period.

As soon as the colonies attained independence, barring a few, they adopted the Soviet mode of planning, but the Western mode of production. These plans invariably aimed at rapid economic growth. Quite a few of them also called for a variety of institutional reforms, but in operational terms this boiled down to one aim — the fastest possible economic growth. Some countries envisaged 15 per cent growth, others were more realistically aiming at seven per cent. But no country aimed for less than five per cent growth, which entailed a doubling of the GDP in 14 years.

The growth mentality became so pervasive that it acquired synonymity with virtue. If a country's economy was slow-moving, it was because it could not manage itself; its people were ill-prepared, politically naive, uncultured and corrupt. But if the growth rate was high, then there was something great in that country. A military dictatorship of the worst form acquired virtue if it could promote growth, no matter how many people it put in jail without trail or how many people were shot dead without even a preliminary hearing. And a country following a liberal democratic or socialist path became an outcast if it failed to push up the growth rate high enough to be considered respectable. Economic growth and development became synonymous terms and countries were labelled as developed or underdeveloped purely on the basis of their achievements in terms of GDP and per capita income.

Economic growth became the standard measure or power, strength and virtue, not only at the international level but also at the national and sub-national levels. One of the major weapons of opposition parties (wherever they existed) against the ruling party was the low rate of economic growth, and since low and high were qualitative and relative terms, one could always accuse the other of a poor performance. Today, economic growth is the most powerful ideology that governs societal behaviour in the developing countries.

Despite the heroic efforts of the developing countries in the post-Second World War period to accelerate the growth rates of their economies, the gap between rich and poor countries continues to widen. The rich are becoming richer and the poor are becoming poorer in real terms. While the growth men still assert that

> . . . two hundred years ago almost everywhere human beings were comparatively few, poor and at the mercy of the forces of nature, and 200 years form now, we expect, almost everywhere they will be numerous, rich and in control of the forces of nature.[5]

The fact is that today there are more poor people in the world than there were yesterday, and each day the burden of world poverty is not only spreading fast horizontally but growing fast vertically. The growth men say that in the long run every country will be equal and rich, but the developing countries new feel that they will disintegrate as nation States or be colonised by the same group of countries which released them from bondage just a decade or so ago if current trends continue. It is a question of tomorrow, not 200 years hence.

More and more countries have now come to realise that given the capitalist model of development, they cannot accelerate economic growth without substantial investment in farms and factories. But the investment resources are mostly concentrated in the developed countries. Developing countries also realise that the political independence they gained did not emancipate them economically and they have to continue functioning in an international economic and political frame-work which favours the rich countries at the cost of the poor ones. In order to benefit from this framework they have to give up much of their political independence and are forced to all themselves completely with one of the super-powers. Many developing countries have already taken this course of action.

While the developing countries have faltered on the economic front, the development countries have not done well on the social and environmental fronts. There is growing disillusionment due to the over indulgence in materialistic pursuits leading to environmental deterioration and social disruption. The disillusionment is further heightened as the growth engine has slowed down, even in developed countries, generating inflation and unemployment to unprecedented levels in recent years.

While the search for viable strategies to accelerate economic growth continues in the developing countries, two very visible trends have emerged in the developed countries. While the European countries, perhaps because of their age and maturity, are keen to participate in a dialogue to evolve a more equitable economic order, in the United States the tendency is to try to preserve the *status quo* at any cost, which, in effect, means maintaining the supremacy of the United States in all spheres of life.

During the 1950s, almost all developed countries extended economic assistance to the developing countries in the form of grants or concessional loans. The amounts were never large enough to be called a massive transfer of resources. But even those amounts have decreased. Realising that some of the developing countries were entering the market as manufacturers, the developed countries have now put various kinds of indirect barriers to protect their sagging economies. Added to this is an inequitable international economic order which still favours the developed countries.

Thus, one of the reasons why the resource-poor developing countries have not been able to fairwell in matters of economic growth is not necessarily because they are incapable of handling their problems. It is largely because the international context in which they are trying to develop does not allow them to grow fast. The conditions of development are the opposite of those which the West European countries and the United States faced in the 19th century. This explains largely the deepening economic and social crises in many of the developing countries.

Something else has also happened which makes the situation worse. Even though poverty among the masses continues to increase, the economies, of the developing countries have not been at a complete standstill. Some progress has been made. Much of the benefit accruing from its progress had, however, gone to only a small minority of the educated elite, viz., industrialists, businessmen, contractors, government servants, employees of private firms and, of course, politicians. It happened in the developed countries too, in the early stages of their development, but the resources were so abundant, and opportunities for the export of goods so favourable that this minority group expanded rapidly to cover the entire population within a span of 100 years. The same cannot be expected to happen in the developing countries now for the reasons already explained.

Apparently the developing countries chose a misfit model for their development. For, a development model, to be considered good or bad, depends entirely on the situation and context in which it is applied. The Western capitalistic model gives good results only so long as the resources are cheap and the markets are wide open. Neither of these two conditions exists today. However, the realisation on the part of the developing countries that they chose mistaken models for their development has yet to occur, it seems. But more and more countries, and more and more people, are now questioning the efficacy of this model for development and have started searching for other models more appropriate to their specific conditions.

At the same time the anti-growth movement has become stronger in the developed countries. It started with the concern about environmental deterioration and resource depletion. Increasing pollution of air, water, soil and foodstuffs and a deterioration in the whole quality of life; the looming scarcity of mineral energy and other resources; the headlong rush to consume them, in the manufacture of more and more goods which add nothing to the quality of life of people; all these factors started a trend towards questioning the wisdom of continued and unlimited economic growth.

In 1955 von Neumann remarked:

> "The great globe itself is in a rapidly maturing crisis — a crisis attributable to the fact that the environment in which technological progress must occur has become both undersized and under-organised . . .
>
> In the first half of this century . . . this safety . . . was essentially a matter of geographical and political *Lebensroum*: an ever broader geographical scope for technological activities, combined with an even broader political integration of the world. Within this expanding framework it was possible to accommodate the major tensions created by technological progress.
>
> Now this safety mechanism is being sharply inhibited; literally, and figuratively, we are running out of room. At long last, we begin to feel the effects of the finite, actual size of the earth in a critical way.
>
> Thus, the crisis does not arise from accidental event or human errors. It is inherent in technology's relation to geography on the one hand and to political organisation on the other . . . in the years between now and the 1980s the crisis will probably develop far beyond all earlier patterns. When or how it will end — or to what

state of affairs it will yield nobody can say"[6].

The growth proponents mounted a counter-attack to prove that the technology which generated pollution could also de-pollute it and that the resources were not as exhaustible as they first seemed to be

> "the potential for feasible technological fixes or solutions to important issues such as energy, pollution, safety and health should not be underestimated, although it frequently is. The astonishing history of science and technology in the 19th and 20th centuries shows that solutions to the physical needs of society have usually become rapidly available when those needs were perceived as urgent and feasible. Whether for armaments, commerce, exploitation, travel or recreation, technology and affluence delivered remarkable solutions within a reasonable time period".[7]

It was argued that, for continued technological progress, economic growth was a necessity, just as for technological progress continued economic growth was essential. The two were inseparable. As Herman Kahn asserts:

> "We firmly believe that despite the arguments put forward by people who would like to "stop the earth and get off", it is simply impractical to do so. Propensity to change may not be inherent in human nature, but it is firmly embedded in most contemporary cultures. People have almost everywhere become curious, future-oriented and dissatisfied with their conditions. They want more material goods and covet higher status and greater control of nature . . . they believe almost certainly, correctly, that it is technologically and economically possible for them to achieve these goods".[8]

or to quote Lewis:

> "We do not know what the purpose of life is, but if it were happiness, then evolution could just as well have stopped a long time ago, since there is no reason to believe that men are happier than pigs or than fishes. What distinguishes men from pigs is that men have greater control of their environment; not that they are more happy. And on this test, economic growth is greatly to be desired."[9]

The contention of the growth men is that disparities in achievement are the unavoidable cost of development. There is no need to be alarmed. They would be very much reduced, but never evened out, in due course of time. The faster the growth of the economy, the shorter the time necessary for inequities to be brought to tolerable levels. As such there is hence a case for accelerating growth in the developing countries through increased penetration of capital and technology from the developed countries and, therefore, less emphasis on distribution. Industrialisation and urbanisation are the twin processes which accelerate growth and both are dependent on capital accumulation and technological innovation.

The single-minded pursuit of economic growth may produce war; it may increase inequalities among people; it may generate undesirable social and environmental side-effects; and it may produce a hedonistic, materialistic culture. But all these are the costs one has to pay because once the GNP is high all the aberrations can be removed by using part of the growth for corrective measures. "The West need not apologise for industrialisation, even is industrialisation on occasion produced or made possible aggression. Almost all successful societies have been aggressive at one time or another".[10]

The anti-growth lobby has, however, continued to expand of late, not so much because of fear of pollution or depletion of natural resources, but more because of a realisation of the social effects of continued accent on economic growth

> "In consequence of the technological eruption in the West there are today almost no institutions embedded in tradition through which love and respect can easily and regularly be given vent. While revelling in sexual permissiveness, we are inhibited in the expression of love for our fellows. Surely there was never a time in history when, between men, it was more awkward to express, and more difficult to experience, an unalloyed affection. From the pangs of such frustrations man's lust for power currently distils its frenzy, and sparks his hopes with technological fantasies that can only remove him further from fulfilment. The resulting despair begets a craving to pierce more wantonly the seemingly repressive integument of the social order, a craving expressed in the fevered search for novelty and excitement which is fostered and met by commercial interests. One result of these combustible forces is the popularisation of sexual display and abandon and, inevitably, also a

> growth in the taste for sadistic violence and obscenity.
> To punish mortals the gods grant their wishes. But whether seen as nemesis or not, the vision evoked by this interpretation of events is a frightening one: that of Western civilisation, the civilisation of the Enlightenment, the civilisation of Science, a civilisation born of high hopes and auspicious heralding, today frothing with power and glee — and being piped gaily to the brink of the abyss. And all that yet might stay the fatal plunge lying in the mud, discarded and in decay.[11]

While the growth men are looking beyond earth's lithosphere towards the ocean floor, the moon, the other planets of the solar system and even to the stars for resources needed for future economic development, the anti-growth men would first like to make this earth a better place to live in before colonising other celestial bodies. They advocate a zero-growth economy for the developed countries, the reconstruction of the disrupted social fabric; diversion of resources and technological progress towards the non-economic aspects of life. For the developing countries they advocate a new style of development which attacks the poverty syndrome directly; meets the basic needs of the people first; and generates a variety of humanistic trends in the society. It is also contended that a nation with a low growth rate and a low per capita income can maintain a very favourable standard of living for its people, just as the reverse can also be true.

While the debate continues, and becomes further intensified, the governments in developed as well as developing countries continue to pursue the mirage of economic growth: The developed countries because they want to acquire more power to enable them to hold on to whatever they amassed through exploitation in the past, and the developing countries because they need power to get out of the stranglehold of the developing countries. They all tend to believe that *power comes from the barrel of economic growth.*

Approaches to Humanised Development

Before moving further, it is important that to define the meaning of humanised development. For the purpose of this article, humanised development is that process of societal change which has improved the quality of human life for the immediate as well as the long-term good. The quality of life has to be seen from all relevant perspectives — not only from the economic angle. Which aspect receives prominence, when and for how long would be determined by specific circumstances. An attempt is made here to discuss a few of the approaches.

The Pragmatic Approach: *Something which will Work*

An increasing number of scholars in the developed as well as in the developing countries favour a position between the capitalistic and Marxian approaches. They can be called pragmatists because their particular styles of approach have emerged from the realisation that,

(a) accelerated growth is just not possible, as the conditions for such growth are no longer favourable,
(b) that whatever small growth does take place in the developing countries is being cornered by the top 10 to 25 per cent of the population, leaving the poor relatively poorer, and at times absolutely poorer, and
(c) the socialist revolution which can bring about a drastic change in the system is not the immediate future in most countries.

The idea, therefore, is to evolve strategies which will improve the conditions of the poor, at least slightly so as to make them more vocal and demanding.

These approaches do not challenge the capitalist mode of production but advocate a more socialist mode of distribution. They advocate a number of institutional reforms in favour of the poor, principally land reforms. For all practical purposes, the advocates of these approaches do not want any revolutionary change in the system. Instead, they want the system to re-adjust itself in response to new challenges, and quicken the process of development for those who have been left behind in the past.

The various paradigms of these approaches accept economic growth as essential for improving the lot of the poor. They suggest policies, strategies and other mechanisms through which the fruits of growth could be passed on to the poor countries and their peoples. This could be done by helping the poor both on the production and consumption fronts, and by instigating them to unite as pressure groups to demand a greater voice in decision-making.

The New International Economic Order: One of the paradigms takes national States as units and tries to remove those features of the existing world order which work against the developing countries. The contention is that the existing world order was evolved at a time when much of the world was colonised by the Western world and hence was unable to assert its own viewpoints. Today's world stands divided between the rich North and the poor South leading to a new global human *problematique* rooted in:

— the pervasive dualism of the world along the North-South axis;
— a fundamental disequilibrium in the world economy arising out of underlying structural maladjustments and affecting all regions of the world;
— a state of instability in the world political process arising from continuing asymmetry between the world's regions, together with a growing challenge from less-privileged regions to the centres of economic and political power and intensifying pressures for a new international order;
— enveloping all other sources of conflict, the conflict over resources and life styles, with the North wanting to preserve and even enhance its standard of living, and the South wanting to achieve minimum living standards for which it would need access to resources and institutions — many of which are located in the South — over which the North has acquired control and hegemony;
— penetration into the Third World of alien life styles of the industrial advanced societies and their concomitant structures of production and technology, producing in its wake a structural crisis, growing disenchantment among the people and new sources of conflict within and between third World countries;
— new dimensions in the increasing militarisation of the world political process with (a) some countries of the North responding to the perceived threat from the South to their economic and political power and life styles by new doctrines of military hegemony and pre-emptive warfare against the Third World, and (b) the elites in many countries of the South making up for their economic and political failure by resorting to military aggrandisement which, incidentally, is often used for repressive measures at home — the two aspects together making for an endemic state of insecurity at all levels, and a complete distortion

of the development process;

— as a result of these various phenomena, a growing confrontation waged in defence of the global *status quo*, at both national and international levels, but essentially triggered by policies pursued by major Northern powers against the South through protectionism, resource diplomacy, doctrines of "defence' against the Third World, and attempts to sow the seeds of fragmentation in the Third World through aggressive salesmanship of military hardware, technology and models of life style and development;
— fragmentation and turmoil in the Third World arising out of mass awakening and frequent shifts and turnover of elites.[12]

In order to come to terms with some of these problems, the United Nations declared 1960-69 as the First Development Decade. A decade when, hopefully, international co-operation would greatly strengthen the industrialisation processes in the underdeveloped countries of the Third World. The Second Development Decade (1970-79) called for a direct attack on poverty. Neither of these aims were fulfilled, as neither goal was achieved. The Third Development Decade launched in 1980 is unlikely to yield better results, given current indications. But these and other international efforts have made the problems of underdevelopment clearer and better understood. Enormous amounts of work done by the Club of Rome, World Order Model Project, Dag Hammarskjold Foundation, Cepal and many others have produced enough documentary proof and rationale for a New International Economic Order. The Brandt Commission Report[13] had set the stage for a North-South dialogue, in Mexico.

The direction of thinking could be gauged form the following excerpts from the Scheveningen Report entitled, "Towards a New International Development Strategy":

> The development of Third World countries will remain an unfulfilled goal if they remain unable to secure a share of resources commensurate with their development needs, due to unfair competition from industrialised countries. Conversely, Western life-styles and their demonstration effect on the South must be restrained if maldevelopment is not to become totally globalised. . . . there is need for a system of international accountability of each State for the impact of its national development, or maldevelopment, on the development of other nations. This again is especially relevant to

rich and powerful countries having disproportionate access to, and use of, world resources and pursuing a life-style and technology that produces the bulk of environmental hazards for the world. Such a concept of accountability is no less relevant to the richer classes within societies . . . there emerged from this ethical perspective for development an appreciation of the international obstacles to an alternative development strategy. These obstacles are largely institutional in respect of financial transactions, trade barriers, technology transfers and control of communication and information channels. In each of these areas the responsibility and accountability of the industrialised countries must be stressed . . . major elements of the North have moved along the path of confrontation by resorting to protectionism, resource diplomacy and doctrines of defensive warfare against the South, as well as through attempts to fragment the South through its sub-militarisation. In response, the South is left with no option but to match this confrontation by internationalising collective self-reliance, engaging in its own version of resource diplomacy and trying to work out new global coalitions of interest that derive strength from divergencies of interest within the North and its incipient fragmentation.

Within this overall context of confrontation, and indeed as an instrument of global structural transformation (which is also the aim of the confrontation), it should also be possible to enter into negotiations with the North. The principal aim of these negotiations should be to change the rules governing international flows of trade, money, finance and technology. The effective functioning of international institutions dealing with economic transactions should also be demonstrated, and collective self-reliance should emerge as a forceful determinant of the new development strategy.

The new international development strategy and its frame-work of negotiations should aim at a few key issues and adopt them as its priority policy and negotiating targets.

1. It should above all aim at two key elements of national self-reliance in the Third World and eradicate the obstacles facing them: sustainable production of domestic food supplies and endogenous capacities of developing, acquiring and adapting technology.
2. It should provide the concept of development with new and different cultural roots by drawing upon alternative modes of

civilisation; in particular, is should push forward the eradication of illiteracy and racism, and should move towards a fully worked out code of conduct on control of international mass media and information networks.

3. It should incorporate demilitarisation as a development object and should initiate moves towards a step-wise and time-bound programme of disarmament and demilitarisation, for without progress in this front progress on economic and political aspects of development, the environment, the achievement of collective self-reliance and transformation towards the NIEO will always remain problematic.
4. It should pay more attention to the present waste and maldistribution of development resources — especially food, technology and energy — and should aim at effective means to increase the command of Third World countries over such resources.
5. It should aim at full participation by the Third World in the management of all global commons which are outside the scope of national sovereignty over resources, all of them to be dealt with under the comprehensive framework of the 'common heritage of mankind' at the present historical juncture.
6. Within the context of the policy priorities outlined above, the strategy should promote negotiations — made meaningful by the increased collective countervailing power of the Third World — to complete the unfinished agenda of United Nations Conference for Trade and Development (UNCTAD) V: namely, to establish a restructured international frame-work for trade, monetary and financial co-operation which should accommodate the different economic and social systems and patterns of development prevalent in the world community and which would be based upon institutionalised democratic processes of consultation and decision-making. This framework should include:

   * international measures to regulate the activities of transnational corporations in the fields of trade, money, finance and technology, including effective codes of conduct, backed up by comprehensive national legislation in both home and host countries;

* a trading system which makes room for the growing industrial capacity of the Third World and which also provides a sound base for the world commodity economy;
* a monetary system, which ensures greater stability, helps to control inflation, provides for better and more equitable methods of creating and distributing reserves and of adjusting to both deficits and surpluses, and promotes resource flows to the Third World;
* a system of financial transfers for development based increasingly on automaticity and operating according to universally acceptable and socially responsible criteria, as is the case within nations;
* as part of the latter, a system of international taxation, which should be universal, progressive and start at low rates, and which could be initially applied to the use of the global commons and also levied on internationally undesirable activities e.g., arms expenditure or trade, pollution, accumulation of destabilising exchange reserves.[14]

Strategies to help the Poor in the Developing Countries: The New International Economic Order would assist the developing countries in getting a better share of world resources, but such an order is not likely to come about in the near future. A number of strategies have, therefore, been suggested by international agencies and individual scholars and development specialists to improve the deteriorating lot of the poor in these countries.

One of these strategies calls for creating more employment opportunities for the poor. The ILO was the main rotary of this strategy. The emphasis was on projects which were labour-intensive and also added to the permanent assets of the community. New Intensive Rural Employment Programmes were launched to cover almost all sectors of the rural economy — crop farming, horticulture, animal husbandry, social forestry and irrigation. In the urban areas, the programme concentrated on the informal sectors of the economy — petty traders, retailers, blacksmiths, carpenters, etc. They became eligible for loan-assistance for banking institutions. It was argued that all such people had aptitude and ability, but they lacked the capital to complete with the formal sector.

Whatever its other limitations, the employment programme did help a few who otherwise would have never been helped. But the problem was so complex and all-pervading that a single programme with limited resources could do precious little.

Around 1974, Chenery suggested enhanced investment in projects (usually of small-scales) which related directly to the poor — education, health, credit and agriculture. He argued that the poor should have more capital to earn sufficient income to meet their basic needs. If their consumption pattern improved, they would demand goods which were produced in the large-scale sector. Thus, that sector would also benefit indirectly from investment in the activities which helped the poor both in urban and rural areas.

Then came the famous Basic Needs strategy. This strategy also emerged from an ILO mission. There were, however, a number of other proponents of this strategy, mostly based in the developed countries (Hans Singer, Emerij, J. Grant, Paul Streeten, and many others).

The idea behind the Basic Needs approach was simple to begin with but it became complex and unmanageable as more and more of its supporters climbed into the band-wagon. It was suggested that as the economies of most developing countries were growing at a slow rate the living conditions of the poor should remain miserable for a long time to come. Moreover, the benefits of even that slow growth were being cornered by the upper classes. As there was no hope of any structural change in these societies, a better strategy would be to aim at meeting the basic needs of the poor. It was also felt that it was easier to get international assistance for this purpose, than for industrialisation, for example.

The basic needs programme laid stress on food, nutrition, health, education, particularly literacy, clothing, shelter and the organisation of the poor. Sri Lanka was cited as an example of a country which had enhanced the quality of life of its people far above that of most developing countries even though its per capita income was low. It gave free or subsidised food to all those who were poor and provided social services at nominal cost, or sometimes at no cost. It was argued that the basic needs of the poor throughout the world could easily be met by an additional foreign aid of just (US) $ 15 billion.

Because foreign assistance was available, very many of the developing countries renamed their social service programmes as Basic Needs Programmes. On the intellectual front, books and articles have appeared since 1974 defining basic needs (sometimes seeming to include almost everything under the sun); They have at times suggested elaborate methods of identifying and planning for the supply of them, outlining ways of moulding all human activities to fit in with the Basic Needs approach. These writings continued until the developing countries began to get suspicious about the format of Basic Needs. It was suspected that the whole approach may have been a strategy devised to divert their attention away from the increasingly vocal clammering for a New International Economic Order. Basic Needs programmes continue to be important components of national plans but they are no longer accepted as viable strategies for development.

Among the other strategies to reach to poor, John Mellor's thesis of "Agriculture First" and Waterston's thesis of "Integrated Rural Development" deserve mention. Since the bulk of the poor in the developing countries live in rural areas, Mellor suggests that priority be given to agriculture and agricultural development. The other strategy is known as Integrated Rural Development, elaborated by Albert Waterston in the mid-'70s. He found that the Green Revolution, resulting from large-scale investment in agriculture, helped only those who had large land-holdings. But the majority of the rural inhabitants in the most densely populated developing countries was either of small holders or landless. They did not benefit from the Green Revolution. Waterston, therefore, suggested an integrated approach to rural development with attention given to the following six elements:

1. involvement of small farmers and landless labourers in labour intensive production;
2. rural works programmes in minor projects to create permanent assets including infrastructure;
3. introduction of labour-using rural industries in processing of agricultural products, production of intermediate goods for agricultural production and manufacture of locally needed consumer goods using local raw materials;
4. self-reliance;
5. creation of an organisation cutting across various ministries to take up development tasks; and
6. region planning with accent on development of a hierarchy of development centres linking the villages with the capital city.

Waterston pointed out that none of these would be of much help if land reforms are not taken up seriously by the governments of the developing countries.

There are two more strategies which deserve attention here. One of them is the human resource development strategy propounded by Irma Adelman in 1975. This strategy is slightly different from those discussed above in that it gives prominence to industry, and technology. A pre-condition for this strategy is the re-distribution of productive assets. She give examples of Japan, the Republic of Korea and Taiwan in this regard. The government must ensure that assets acquired by the poor are not snatched back from them again.

Adelman advocates the creation of human capital through crash programmes for literacy, education and training. As a result of the heavy investment in human capital, economic growth may slow down. This may lead to protest and social upheaval. She, therefore, suggests that a strong government, even a dictatorial one, may be necessary to control the situation. Once the human capital is developed, the country should launch a labour-intensive industrialisation process. Countries, like India and China, will produce largely for their own markets but smaller countries would produce for the international market. The mass employment so generated would create additional demands which, in turn, would lead to more production and employment.

Then there is what one may call the strategy of self-reliant development. According to the proponents of this strategy, the causes of increasing unemployment and poverty in the developing countries can be traced back to their dependence on the developed countries. Only hard work and a sense of achievement can make a country mobilise itself for nationhood.

> This is, of course, considerably harder. But it is precisely the shared experience of hardship which has always proved to be by far the most reliable tool by which people have acquired the common features identifying them as members of the same group. Indeed, self-development is not merely an effective alternative way of nation building. Historically, as Marx would phrase it, it was the primary way. Every country, that is today fully developed, economically grown up and emotionally mature, has gained its status not by jumping in infantile contemporary fashion on the shoulders of somebody else's experience. Every one of them gained it by single-handedly wresting it from forbidding hostile environments in personally suffered trail, error, blood and sweat and toil and tears.[15]

More Humanistic Approaches — *The Search for a New Meaning of*

Development: A growing number of development thinkers does not consider the growth with equity approach a lasting solution to the major development issues in question. According to them, development means far more than the discipline of economics can comprehend. Development is something which makes life more satisfying. To equate it with economic growth amounts to saying that money is the measure of all things.

One school of thought has concentrated on challenging the very idea of continuing economic growth as a desirable phenomenon. While the other sees a humanistic style of development emerging out of the current confusion over development theory and practice. Those in the first school believe that they are physical and social limits to growth, which are being reached in the developed countries. As an illustration, two authors, who have contributed greatly to the current topic are quoted:

Mishan opens his most recent book, *The Economic Growth Debate*, with a question: Does money buy happiness? The rest of the book is an answer to this question. His answer is no, but he adds that money does buy something. It buys food, shelter and clothing and other needs without which man cannot live. These needs must be met far above the mere survival level. But once they are met, money buys very little. It is the other human urges which gain in importance then, but which cannot be evaluated in terms of monetary value. Man can still be most unhappy in the midst of material plenty if these other urges are not fully satisfied.

Mishan lists 14 constituents of a good life:

1. Food and shelter
2. Health
3. Nature
4. Leisure
5. Instinctual enjoyment
6. Security
7. Love and trust
8. Self-esteem
9. Kith and kin
10. Customs and mores
11. Role and place
12. The moral code
13. The great myths
14. Personal freedom

And he contends that only a few of these can be bought with money. The rest fall in the social realm; they are determined by factors other than growth.

But even if it could be said to economic growth that it expands un-

> ambiguously the options open to the consumer, it would not follow that men should be regarded as being better off. For one thing, these options refer only to the amounts and varieties of goods available to the average person in his capacity of consumer. In his other roles, as worker, citisen, member of the family or part of the larger community, the individual may not be faced with more options as a result of continuing economic growth. . . . What is more, even if . . . economic growth continues, it is plausible to believe that a stage will be reached beyond which greater levels of output will add virtually nothing to his well-being. This is so not only because a point of satiation exists even for the most acquisitive animal, but also because, in high income societies, an individual's satisfaction comes to depend less on his absolute income and more on his income relative to the incomes of others, . . .[16]

Fred Hirsch in *Social Limits to Growth* touches on similar issues and tries to answer three of the oft repeated questions by economists:

1. Why do people desire economic advancement even though it produces disappointing results for those who achieve it? (most, if not all of us).
2. Why is there so much concern with distribution when we know that in the long run everyone can raise his level of living by more production? and
3. Why is there so much State interference in economic areas in modern times?

He refers to these as three paradoxes. (a) the paradox of affluence, (b) the distribution compulsion, and (c) reluctant collectivism.

> My major thesis is that these three issues are interrelated and stem from a common source. This source is to be found in the nature of economic growth in advanced societies. The heart of the problem lies in the complexity and partial ambiguity of the concept of economic growth once the mass of the population has satisfied its main biological needs for life sustaining food, shelter and clothing. The traditional economic distinction between how much is produced, on what basis and who gets it then becomes blurred. The issues of production, of individual versus collective provision, and of distribution then become intertwined.[17]

Hirsch suggests "that the prime economic problem now facing the economically advanced societies is a structural need to pull back the bounds of economic self-advancement. That, in turn, requires a deliberate validation of the basis of income and wealth distribution and that these economies have managed to do without in the transition period that is ending".[18] Tinkering with the system here and there to bring it back to health would not work. What is needed is a new way of thinking and new way of looking at the system of production and consumption, with distribution as a central point.

The issue at stake is, however, not only the physical and social limits to growth, but also of "should growth be equated with development". And if not, then what does development mean. Both growth and development signify continuity. Should the economy ultimately come to a standstill? Does it mean that the evolution of the world should stop? If not, then what would be the direction of this evolution?

In answer to this question. Denis Goulet says:

> Whatever other purposes development may have, it has for all groups at least the following objectives:
>
> — to provide more and better life-sustaining goods to members of societies;
> — to create or improve social conditions of life in some way related to a perceived need for esteem;
> — to free human communities from servitude (to nature, to ignorance, to man or other communities, to institutions, to beliefs, to techniques of development, etc.) considered oppressive so as to release them for positive self-actualisation.[19]

Others, such as Everett Hagen, have given similar universal values. In his most recent writing, Alvin Toffler[20] questioned the very bases of current theories of economic growth and suggested a gradual emergence of a new "wave" which integrates the achievements of the first and second "waves", i.e., the agricultural and industrial civilisation. The third "wave" will provide man opportunities to progress in the realm of science and technology, yet remain human. Toffler's arguments are incisive and convincing, although his style is journalistic and he tends to make generalisations which are rather sweeping.

> The Third Wave brings with it a genuinely new way of life based on diversified, renewable energy sources, on methods of production that make most factory assembly lines obsolete; on new, non-nuclear families; on a novel institution that might be called the "electronic cottage"; and on radically changed schools and corporations of the future. The emergent civilisation writes a code of behaviour for us and carries us beyond standardisation, synchronisation and centralisation, beyond the concentration of energy, money, and power.[21]

Even if the seeds of change are not exactly as Toffler sees them to be, he does suggest an alternative goal of that almost undefinable term "development". According to him, economic growth is not a goal which human societies can pursue forever and at all stages of their evolution. It has been a goal for a transitional period. And that period has already ended in the developed countries and most eventually end for the currently developing countries too. The industrialisation process in the developing countries cannot be stopped. It will go on incessantly albeit slowly, partly because there is no clear alternative to it and partly because the poor cannot wait for too long. It is to be hoped that the industrialisation processes, beginning in these countries, will stay clear of the materialistic and superfluous aspects of growth which have hallmarked the industrialisation processes of the developed countries. A new approach may soften the rigours of economic growth.

The Spatial Approach to Humanised Development

Development has also been seen from the perspective of space. The way in which space is organised internationally or internationally reflects the changing relationship between man and nature and man and man. All societal values and institutions have their reflections in the way space is organised. Thus, space is not something which can be equated with nature; it contains a variety of societal processes, including the mode of production and distribution.

As the spatial patterns and structures exhibit societal patterns and structures, each societal change brings about an appropriate change in space, the reverse is also true. The man-space nexus also changes as man's perception of space — resulting from new values he acquires — changes. Development is a process of change which a society decides to carry out within itself and in its relations to the outside world. It affects both the people and the space. It is this societal process which gives rise to different human personalities and to equally different structures in space, which together generate a new societal process.

Development can thus be seen as a spatial transformation process. A feudal society will have one type of spatial organisation, a semi-feudal society another and a capitalistic society a third one, while an egalitarian society will have still another. By studying the spatial organisation we can understand the nature of the society. We can also predict the nature of the spatial organisation by understanding the nature of the society.

The current emphasis on distribution of the fruits of economic development has its implications for space. If the natural resources are more evenly distributed; if the productive forces are not concentrated in a few hands; if the political power is not centralised, the spatial organisation and structure of human activities will be different from the present ones, prominently exhibiting core-periphery relationships. The land boundaries would change; the size and architecture of buildings would be different and the location of various activities would exhibit more egalitarian traits.

Gandhi once said, ". . . earth provides enough to satisfy every man's need, but not every man's greed". The greed-based spatial organisation would be completely different from the need-based spatial organisation.

One of the major byproducts of growth-oriented development is the loss of community. Sociologists and anthropologists have their own meaning of community, but it is inseparably linked with the concept of space. The community consists of a people who share common experiences and values, and who are independent; they known each other well and have respect for each other. They take common decisions on several issues which affect their lives.

The spatial range of such a community cannot be too large. People must live within a radius of a few kilometres. The change in the mode of transportation and communication does not make any difference because one of the fundamental bases of a community is face to face communication. It is a human need, apart from anything else. As the spatial extent increases, the interaction among the people becomes specialised. It is then no longer a community. It becomes a region or a nation.

Self-reliant development has to start from the community. Unless the spatial organisation is so articulated that such communities both in rural and urban areas are revived and activated, the end result with always be a dependent style of development. Beyond the community, then, one has the region, and then the nation, finally the world. The whole world is a community of men and women struggling hard to escape their own myths and prejudices. But the local community, which constitutes the basic unit of all higher level communities, is the prime mover of self-reliant development from below.

Unfortunately, this concept of community is not the fundamental basis for the division of space for developmental purposes. In humanised development processes, the spatial organisation will require thorough change to enable each member of the local community to look inwards for guidance and support. At present, everyone is looking outwards, breaking whatever is left of the community to fragments.

Concluding Remarks

What we have discussed above is in the realm of hope. There are many models and many more ways of looking at development. But the question is: How are these models going to be implemented? Who is going to bell the cat? People with power and authority have vested interests in the system, as it is at present. Who would wish to destroy or knowingly weaken himself, human nature being what it is?

One may question the growth men on many accounts, but they are the ones who are the heroes today. It is they who are the opinion-makers, providing the tools and techniques for continued economic growth, moreover, the growth men have been in the field for over two centuries. They have not been there in vain. Without them much of humanity would have remained in bondage. They are not men to be despised and hated.

Three-fourths of humanity are still living below the poverty line. It clearly needs economic growth to remedy this situation. True, the developed countries no longer need rapid economic growth, but this does not mean that the whole world has reached a stage where growth is no longer needed. Yet, at the same time, it is clear that we cannot maintain economic growth in the old classical style indefinitely, without damaging our cultural, social and environmental heritage. The need for re-thinking is very much here and it is good that so many people have been thinking and writing about this issue over the past few years. These writings have now created favourable public opinion but have yet to take hold in the minds of those who make the vital decisions regarding economic growth and who are captives of the systems they preside over.

It will take time. What is needed is more literature, more discussion and more conferences to convince even those who do not want to be convinced. We must also remember that, apart from periods of catastrophe such as war, societal changes have not taken place in a year, or even two years. It is hoped that a nuclear conflagration will not be necessary to transform growth into a humanised development process.

NOTES

1. Within 25 years of his birth, a boy, whose parents still live a very primitive life-style in the backwoods of Arunachal Pradesh in eastern India, was able to pilot a sophisticated jet bomber in the Indian Air Force. He was neither imbued with the Protestant Ethic nor the Hindu Ethic, the Confucian Ethic or the Islamic Ethic. It was the Machine Ethic and the basic capacity of all human beings to adapt to new conditions through learning and unlearning processes which transformed this young man.
2. Herman Kahn et al. *The Next 200 Years* London: Associated Business Programmes, (1976).
3. Herman Kahn, *World Economic Development: 1979 and Beyond* New York: Morrow Quill, (1979).
4. E.J. Mishan, *The Economic Growth Debate: An Assessment*, London: George Allen & Unwin, (1977). p. 25.
5. Herman Kahn, *World Economic Development* p. 2.
6. John von Neumann, "Can We Survive Technology?", *Fortune*, June, (1955). pp. 236-37.
7. Herman Kahn, *World Economic Development*, p. 240.
8. *Ibid.*, pp. 23-24.
9. W. Arthur Lewis, *The Theory of Economic Growth* Homewood, Ill.: Richard Irwin (1955). p. 421.
10. Herman Kahn, *World Economic Development*, p. 441.
11. Mishan, *The Economic Growth Debate*, pp. 266-67.
12. "Towards a new International Development Strategy: The Scheveningen Report", *Development Dialogue*, Dag Hammarskjold Foundation, Uppsala, 1980:1, pp. 56-7.
13. Willy Brandt Commission, *North-South: A Programme for Survival*, London: Pan World Affairs (1980).
14. "Towards a New International Development Strategy", pp. 61-64.
15. Leopold Kohr, *Development Without Aid* Llandybie, Carmarthenshire: Christopher Davies, (1973). p. 11.
16. E.J. Mishan, *The Economic Growth Debate*, London: George Allen & Unwin, (1977). p. 29.

17. Fred Hirsch, *Social Limits to Growth* London: Routledge & Kegan Paul, (1977). p. 1.
18. Fred Hirsch, *Social Limits to Growth*, p. 190.
19. Alain Birou, *Towards a Redefinition of Development*, Oxford: Pergamon Press for OECD, (1977).
20. Alvin Toffler, *The Third Wave*, New York: Bantam Book, (1980).
21. Toffler, *The Third Wave*, p. 10.

6

GANDHIAN PATH TO PEACE

RAJA JAYARAMAN

"Non-violence . . . is a rule of conduct for society if it is to live consistently with human dignity and make progress toward the attainment of peace".*

—*Mahatma Gandhi*

INTRODUCTION

THE MAJOR feature of Gandhian approach to peace is that it cannot be achieved unless use of violence in the form of physical injury (*himsa*) is eschewed in settling human conflict and is replaced with non-violence (*ahimsa*). The term non-violence should be understood not just simply as absence of physical injury, but as an active force of love (*prem*) towards fellow creatures including humans, animals and plants.

Mahatma Gandhi was fully aware that human social interaction encounters many situations of conflicts and tensions. He accepted equally that "societal systems all over the world are imperfect, and many forms of social injustice, discrimination and inequality prevail". However, for Gandhi the means used for correcting various social and personal imperfections are as important as the ends themselves. If 'establishing peace is the objective (end), then the means used to achieve it must be such that they do not negate its intrinsic value'.

Gandhi believed that violence (war) begets violence and that

* This is from a booklet entitled, *The India of Gandhi* published jointly by the Ministry of Tourism, India Tourism Corporation, and UNICEF, November, 1982.

violence cannot liberate violence. It cannot also liberate human beings from social justice. Those who advocate violence to combat injustice merely contribute to it.

The fundamental question in Gandhian approach then is 'how to find peaceful means of resolving conflict?'. With a view to fully understand Gandhian path to peace, I propose to examine the following: first, the sources of Gandhi's ideas; second, the essential feature of his notions of non-violence and *satyagraha* (Truth Force); third, the uses of Truth Force in practice and, finally, the importance of Truth Force in the present day world.

Sources of Gandhi's Ideas

Gandhi was aware that neither the Hindu classics such as *Bhagavad Gita* and *Ramayana* nor contemporary Indian practices condemned war unconditionally or preached the need for non-violence in inter- and intra-group relations. However, Gandhi saw Hindu religion not in a static form, but as something 'which is dynamic and evolving'. He used traditional Indian concepts, but their meanings were considerably enlarged and at times modified. For instance, the idea of non-violence, which went back into the Indian tradition and was found in Buddhism and in Jainism as well as in the Hindu tradition, gave Gandhi an enlarged meaning. He made it as a societal and community obligation from what had been traditionally a personal duty. The ascetic ideal of self-sacrifice (*tapasya*), which the saints of India expressed in its most rigorous form, Gandhi used it to social ends. To him the real end of self-sacrifice and self-restraint was not withdrawal to the forest, but deep involvement in societal issues. On the whole, the Indian traditional concepts supplied Gandhi with acceptable symbols, but he gave them new meanings. In this, as Dalton observes:

> "Gandhi's motive was not to subvert his religious tradition but to reconstruct it, hence his 'instruments of cultural change' were not 'history and science' but religion itself, and associated symbolic forms".[1]

While Gandhi was no doubt influenced by his Indian background, he did not wish to shut himself off by other influences. He once wrote:

> "I do not want my house to be walled in on all sides and my win-

dows to be stuffed. I want the cultures of all lands to be blown about my house as freely as possible. But I refuse to be blown off my feet by any . . . Mine is not the religion of the prison house. It has room for the least among God's creation. But it is proof against insolence, pride of race, religion or colour".[2]

In this context, the influence that Christianity and some modern Western thinkers had on him needs acknowledgment. In the Sermon on the Mount, Gandhi read the injuctions to love enemies and not to resist evil by violent means. From his two favourite writers, Ruskin and Emerson, Gandhi took over many ideas including the idea of utilising military heroism and discipline for peaceful ends. Tolstoy's quest for Truth and his dissatisfaction of modern civilisation, with its inherent violence and falsity, struck a sympathetic cord in Gandhi.

Writers have argued concerning the importance in Gandhi's philosophy of Western or Eastern influences. It must be clear from what has been presented so far that Gandhian path to peace and non-violence is a synthesis of both Eastern and Western traditions. Without his Indian religious, social and cultural notions the content of his philosophy would have been different. Had he shut himself off from the West, or the other, his mass political action would not have had the impact it had in Indian society.

The Essentials of Truth Force (*SATYAGRAHA*)

Gandhi coined the term *Satyagraha* during the Indian resistance movement against discriminatory laws in South Africa. He preferred this term as against the term 'passive resistance' because '*satya* (Truth) implies love and *agraha* implies firmness or force' and these two aspects together 'form' the basis for social and political action.[3]

The three essential pillars of Truth force are: *Satya* (Truth), *ahimsa* (non-violence) and *tapasya* (self-sacrifice and voluntary suffering).

Truth (Satya)

The first pillar in Gandhian path to peace is the notion of truth. Gandhi conceived life to be an experiment with truth. According to him human beings must continually search for truth; for truth, he came to believe, 'is God'. However, Gandhi equally believed that no one person or community had monopoly over truth. The reason for this belief comes from his firm conviction that human beings, conditioned as they are by their earthly existence, are not capable of knowing the absolute truth. For this reason no one person or community or society has the right to employ violent means to reach truth. Gandhi believed that violence carried an implicit judgement on other people that 'contains a finality' that no person 'is fit to impose' upon others. The perpetrators of violence through their action set themselves up as judges of as who is to live and who is to die. But, according to the concept of truth in the philosophy of Gandhi, human beings are not fit to pass final judgement on such an issue of life and death for they are trapped by their subjective reality. Thus, the concept of truth, in the philosophy of Gandhi, is that of plural and relative truth. Besides, the Gandhian notion of truth is to be judged in terms of the fulfilment of human needs. Such truth would be destroyed through the use of means that violate human needs.

Non-violence (Ahimsa)

The second essential notion in Gandhian philosophy is non-violence, which means non-injury. To put it more positively, it can be taken to mean love or active goodwill. Non-violence is predicated upon the belief in the sacredness of life and can be understood as an action based on refusal to do harm. It also means refusal to allow harm and injustice to exist, not just physical harm alone. In other words, non-violence not only suggests that one acts in a manner that will not harm anyone, but that one strives to root out injustice in the world. However, non-violence is not the end, but a means to the end of search for truth. Gandhi once wrote:

> "*Ahimsa* is not the goal. Truth is the goal. But we have no means of realising truth in human relationships except through the practice of *ahimsa*".[4]

Gandhi firmly believed that non-violence was never the path of the cowardly. "It is not a passive state, but is positively action-oriented; it does not avoid conflicts, but seeks to face the resolve them. The philosophy of non-violence stresses that it is not only violent actions that are themselves unjust and, therefore, must be avoided, but that sometimes inaction can contribute to injustice. Non-violence is a philosophy of means. In this approach it is assumed that means and ends are inter-connected, and that unjust means cannot bring about just ends". Gandhi said:

"The means may be likened to a seed, the end to a tree; and there is just the same inviolable connection between the means and the end as there is between the seed and the tree".[5]

Self-Sacrifice and Voluntary Suffering (Tapasya)

The third aspect of the Gandhian approach to peace is the willingness to voluntarily undergo suffering and sacrifice. The *satyagrahi*, i.e. one who practises *satyagraha*, undergoes self-suffering (*Tapasya*) not for his/her own sake, but as a demonstration to an opponent of one's seriousness of purpose in any conflicting situation. Self-sacrifice can demonstrate the *satyagrahi*'s sincerity, for only to the extent that one is sincere about one's convictions would one be willing to undergo sacrifice on their behalf. One's ability and readiness to suffer allows one to resist injustice. The refusal to submit to injustice often involves suffering and sacrifice. However, Gandhi, as Bondurant points out, has "emphasised the need for discrimination in inviting suffering and sacrifice. Submission was never an element of this concept. Submitting to humiliation should be strictly resisted . . . In every case a *satyagrahi* must refuse to do that which his conscience forbids him to do and must preserve the dignity of the individual though it means loss of property or even life.[6] Because of the high risk involved in any struggle against injustice, the *satyagrahi* must possess the positive attribute of not only love and goodwill (*ahimsa*) but also courage.

In waging *satyagraha*, one is not prepared to yield the position one holds to be the truth. However, one remains open to and invites the persuasive attempts of one's adversary, and is prepared to depart — either totally or partially — from one's original position if persuaded that one is in error. Again, in any *satyagraha* one distinguishes between one's adversary and his/her role in the struggle. Though in any *satyagraha* the clash of relative truths is involved, the *satyagrahi* seeks a resolution that will satisfy the needs of both parties to the conflict. It is the essence of the *satyagraha* that this seeking of a wider truth judged in terms of human needs cannot be done through violence, which negates human needs and destroys life. In *satyagraha* there is the implicit belief that violence itself is a form of injustice. *Satyagraha* operates against injustice, not as such against people who practise it. The *satyagrahi* is not against the adversary in conflict, but is against adversary's unjust acts.

To sum-up, the quintessence of Gandhian path to peace is the rejection of the use of force over resolution of conflict. Since Gandhian notion of *satyagraha* rejects physical violence as the ultimate instrument of justice, it has been called as "the moral equivalent of war". According to Horsburg, Gandhi's *satyagraha* meets the following criteria to qualify as a moral substitute to war:

1. That it is a method of resistance distinct from war.
2. That it does not suffer — or suffers in lesser degree — from the moral deficiencies of war.
3. That it can be used in all the circumstances in which a resort to war has usually been held to be either necessary or permissible.
4. That it offers at least some prospect of being effective when used in those circumstances.[7]

Gandhi himself was fully convinced that *satyagraha* could generate sufficient moral and spiritual force to transform the world. It was also his belief that it would be enough for the release of this moral force if only "one person" were possessed fully by the truth force (*satyagraha*) just "as one General is enough to regulate and dispose of the energy of millions of soldiers who enlist under his banner even though they know not 'the why and wherefore' of his dispositions".

Truth Force in Practice

Any discussion on *satyagraha* in practice is largely about its effectiveness as a means of establishing justice, equality and freedom. In this context, one point which needs to be kept in mind is that although Gandhi believed in the effectiveness of non-violent methods of social and political action, his commitment to the principles of *satyagraha* did not rest upon this belief. In other words, Gandhian philosophy relied more on the means rather than on the ends. Keeping this in mind, it is necessary to stress that Gandhi insisted that *satyagraha* must never be employed frivolously without just cause. In South Africa, where Gandhi first started his *satyagraha* movement, the struggle had been against legal discrimination of the Indians on the ground of race. After he returned to India, Gandhi embarked on a series of *satyagraha* which were directed not only against alien (British) rulers but also against his own fellow countrymen who practised various forms of social and economic discriminations.

It is not my intention to offer here a detailed analysis of Gandhi's *satyagraha* campaigns in India.[8] However, a few examples will illustrate Gandhian philosophy and techniques of non-violence used for establishing just objectives or ends. For Gandhi a *satyagraha* campaign should crystallise around some truth — or, rather, it must embody some aspect, admittedly partial, of universal truth. In the Vykom Temple Road *satyagraha* (1924-25), for example, the object was to vindicate "the right of every human individual to pass along a public road without discrimination on the basis of Caste" for here the Harijans had been forbidden to use the highways around the temple.[9] The means used in establishing this "truth" were that of non-violent demonstration, self-suffering by *satyagrahis* opposed to discrimination and persuasion of opposition to abandon discrimination. In the Bardoli campaign of 1928, the "truth" objective was "the granting of an impartial enquiry into the enhanced assessment of land tax imposed on peasants by the Government of Bombay".[10] The methods employed in asserting the truth in this case were non-cooperation, civil disobedience and social boycott. The two cases presented above were directed mostly against local authorities within India. However, Gandhi's other campaigns such as the *Satyagraha* in 1919 against Rowlatt Act and the famous Salt *satyagraha* of 1930-31 were directed towards achieving larger political and nationalist goals.

The Gandhian *satyagraha* is basically a group or community movement; at times, as in the Salt *Satyagraha*, a mass movement. Gandhi envisaged the involvement of the whole community and the whole nation to high degree in its non-violent defence against injustice, oppression and discrimination. He did, however, conceive of an individual form of *satyagraha* that might be used on some occasions. For instance, the undertaking of a fast by one or more carefully selected individuals might be an efficacious, as well as non-violent, means of exposing the public to practices of untruth. However, as Bondurant points out, Gandhi "warned against the indiscriminate use of the fast and was well aware that often there is violence behind such fasting".[11]

Finally, another important aspect of Gandhian non-violent action is the involvement of *satyagrahis* in constructive social and community welfare works, which Gandhi insisted must always accompany the somewhat "negative" forms of *satyagraha* such as non-cooperation and civil disobedience. In India, Gandhi centred his constructive welfare work on such things as promotion of Hindu-Muslim religious harmony, village and handicraft industries and improvement in the status of women and Harijans. In the final analysis, Gandhian *satyagraha* is not merely a philosophy of non-violence; it is also a technique for the constructive resolution of human conflict. It does not aim at the elimination of conflict from social relationships. Conflict is admitted as a built-in element of the human situation. But conflict, Gandhi maintained, could be directed into creative, non-violent channels provided there was a proper understanding of the means necessary for this purpose. Thus, Gandhi's path to peace is not a perfectionist ethic or a counsel of meek submission or withdrawal, but an effective tool for the collective achievement of practical objectives.

Importance of Truth Force

It has been claimed by some writers that Gandhi's *satyagraha* is something peculiarly Indian, indeed peculiarly Hindu, without appeal to people from other social and cultural environments. Although some of the Gandhian concepts and techniques may need modifications, if they are to become easily acceptable outside India, there is ample evidence from Gandhi's *satyagraha* movement that non-violence as a means for resolving conflict was not so narrowly circumscribed as some of Gandhi's critics maintained. It was adopted by the Muslim Pathans under the leadership of 'Frontier Gandhi', Khan Abdul Ghaffar Khan, who founded in 1929 an organisation on the Gandhian model known as *Khudai Khidmatgar* (Servants of God). In America, Martin Luther King, Jr., effectively used the Gandhian non-violent protests in the Black Civil Rights Movement in the 1960s. There have been other significant non-violent protests in the world including the ones against totalitarian regimes. As Sharp points out:

> "It is . . . sometimes possible to organise resistance even while under the heel of totalitarian repression. The fact of the matter is that non-violent struggles have been waged against the Nazis and also in Communist nations, although they were not led by people who necessarily believed in and expounded the moral philosophy of non-violence. . . . To cite a few cases, such action (strategy of non-cooperation) was employed to a significant extent in both the Danish and Norwegian resistances against Nazi occupation. It was used in the East German uprising of 1953, during the 1956 Hungarian revolt and in the Soviet political prisoner camps".[12]

To conclude, Gandhi believed that human social conflicts could not be eliminated altogether, but resolution of them could be achieved through non-violent means. 'Justice, equality and freedom are laudable goals or ends, but if violent means are used to achieve them, then the means adopted would be self-defeating.

The proponents of non-violent methods believe that it is both moral and practical in human affairs. For them, non-violence has to become a way of life. As Pelton points out:

> "People must come to regard all human beings as their brothers and sisters. Non-violence means that we do not violate anybody. It means that we do not exploit or oppress anybody. Non-violence means that we regard life as too sacred to be destroyed for any reason. But, beyond that, it means that we do not tolerate injustice anywhere or to anyone, what we do not turn our backs on the sufferings of others. Non-violence means active goodwill toward all people".[13]

Today, there are many people who notice injustice, discrimination and oppression in the world, and they believe that they can root them out through violence, terror and war. There are others who seek to protect their self-interest and, out of fear of loosing it, resort to violence and terror. Like people, nations go to war with so much self-righteousness, with such a noble sense of fairness, justice and determination for peace. Again, like people, nations are blind to the historical experience that wars between nations have not ended wars, that physical violence has not brought about enduring world peace. "The peace", as Pelton observes, "is far more than and far different from, a lull between wars".[14]

He further says:

"We must conceive of peace as an activity, not as an end-state. For too long, peace has been equated with the absence of conflict. This formulation of peace is inherent in the mistaken notion that was can end war. For, without the development of non-violent means, the next major conflict can only lead to war once again. Once we realise that conflict will always be with us, we can understand that peace must be found in the means we use to wage conflict".[15]

Finally, let us reflect what truth there is in the words of Martin Luther

King, Jr: "One day we must come to see that peace is not merely a distant goal that we seek but a means by which we arrive at that goal. We must pursue peaceful ends through peaceful means. How much longer must we play at deadly war games before we need the plaintive pleas of the unnumbered dead and maimed of past wars?"[16]

NOTES

1. D. Dalton, "The Gandhian View of Caste, and Caste after Gandhi" in *India and Ceylon: Unity and Diversity* (ed.) by Philip Mason, Oxford University Press. London, (1967). pp. 159-81.
2. M.K. Gandhi, *Young India*, 1 June, (1921).
3. M.K. Gandhi, *Satyagraha in South Africa*, S. Ganesan, Madras, (1938).
4. M.K. Gandhi, *Harijan*, 23 June, (1946).
5. M.K. Gandhi, *Non-violent Resistance*, Ahmedabad, Navajivan Publishing House, (1951).
6. J.V. Bondurant, *Conquest of Violence : The Gandhian Philosophy of Conflict*, University of California Press, Berkely, (1971). p. 29.
7. H.J.N. Horsburg, *Non-Violence and Aggression: A Study of Gandhi's Moral Equivalent of War*, Oxford University Press, London, (1968). p. 20.
8. For a systematic study of some *satyagraha* campaigns in India, please see Bondurant, *op. cit.*, especially chapters 2 and 3.
9. For a step by step analysis of this *satyagraha* campaign, see Bondurant, *op. cit.*, pp. 46-52. The term 'Harijan', which Gandhi used to refer to untouchable Castes in India, means God's people or children of God.
10. See Bondurant, *op. cit.*, pp. 53-64.
11. *Ibid.* p. 37.
12. G. Sharp, "The Technique of Non-violent Action" in A. Roberts (ed.) *Civilian Resistance as a National Defence*, Stackpole books, as quoted in L.H. Pelton, (1974). *The Psychology of Non-Violence*, New York, Pergamon Press, (1968).
13. L.H. Pelton, *Ibid.* pp. 267-68.
14. *Ibid.* p. 267.
15. *Ibid.*
16. M.L. King, Jr., *Where Do We Go From Here: Chaos or Community*?, Bantom Books, New York, (1968).

7

GANDHIAN WAY OF RESOLVING GROUP CONFLICTS THROUGH SATYAGRAHI SOCIALISM*

INDIRA ROTHERMUND

> I have claimed that I was a socialist long before those I know in India have avowed their creed. But my socialism was natural to me and not adopted from any books. It came out of my unshakable belief in non-violence. No man can be actively non-violent and not rise against social injustice no matter where it occurred.
>
> — *Mahatma Gandhi*

IN THE midst of global peace and anti-nuclear movements and a growing realisation of the problems of management of natural resources and preservation of environment world over, a paper on the Gandhian way of resolving indigenous group conflicts would appear to be reversal of global interest-based dimensions. India is also beset with tremendous problems not only of economic poverty but of spiritual poverty, erosion of moral values on a massive scale, rise of terrorism, environmental destruction and so on, all this demands a fresh approach, a rethinking of a Gandhian alternative. And Gandhi said — "For me the path of salvation leads through unceasing tribulation in the service of my fellow-countrymen and humanity"[1] and he insisted that his life is one indivisible whole and all his activities run into another and they all have their rise in his insatiable love of mankind. By practising non-

* Originally the term was used by Acharya Javdekar.

violence step by step from the nearest to the remotest, we learn how to make friends with all; Gandhi was thus interested in generating love that establishes a continuity of interpersonal relations. Interpersonal relations with the individual at the centre are not structured as a pyramid with the apex dominating the bottom. Gandhi says:

> "In this structure, there will be ever-widening never ascending circles. Life will not be a pyramid with the apex sustained by the bottom. It will be an oceanic circle whose centre will be the individual always ready to perish for the village, till at last the whole becomes one life composed of individuals . . . sharing the majesty of the oceanic circle of which they are integral units".[2]

This metaphor of ever-widening concentric circles signifying interdependence is based on the philosophy of the essential identity of all, and this is the core of Gandhi's socialism, it is *satyagrahi* because it is based on holding fast to Truth (*Sat* or God). This concept of *Satyagrahi* — non-violence can be gradually universalised if it is practised with an awareness of the oneness of all, as Gandhi asserted — and his socialism is metaphysical as it is based on the perception of the identity of God, man and the world as expressed in the Indian Upanishadic monistic philosophy of non-dualism. This is the basic pattern underlying Gandhi's approach to life and his concept of socialism. A few strands of his idea of socialism are discussed within the short span of this chapter. His thinking can be compared to Indian music wherein the variations are built around a *raga* with the basic core remaining the same, namely, the belief that the universal life force is at once immanent and transcendent. This is explained in the *Chandogya Upanishad* with the ontological expression *Tat tvam Asi* (That thou art) which establishes that the human soul, the essence within (*Sat*), is the trans-individual Self, the Brahman, which is described by Gandhi as "Truth (*Satya*) is God". The *Upanishadic* philosophy of identification, in its basic elements, is by no means limited to the circles of educated theologians but it has penetrated all of India".[3]

Gandhi and Marx

Gandhi's belief in the immanent unity of all human beings was often put to test whenever he had to face the problem of conflicts arising in the course of events that tended to disturb the inherent equilibrium of individual action and social order. He still had a strong faith and conviction that the spiritual unity did ultimately provide a sound foundation for one's thought and action and that *Satyagraha* was his only means of dealing with such recurrent problems. Marx also faced the problem of reconciling the idea of man as an individual with the notion of a society. He argued that the society should not be treated as an abstraction which would then appear as a separate *sui generis* entity to be confronted with man as an individual. According to Marx:

> "man is a social being and all his activities are a manifestation and confirmation of social life. Man as an individual and man as a species are not distinct, man is not individual man but species being".

To him, the human species and society seemed to be co-terminous. Being social thus becomes an inherent quality of man — his generic character. The quality of a social being is treated by Marx as man's generic nature, since in actuality man has acquired it as a member of the societies. This makes it difficult to account for differences among various societies. As the quality of being social is inherent in every man he just projects it by thinking of himself as a member of the society and thereby re-confirms his social being. This unity of man as a species and society is shaken by death which singles out man as an individual. Marx tries to explain this by asserting that it is only the particular individual, a definite part of the species which is mortal.[4]

This problem, in contrast, does not arise in the Gandhian thought since the individual has already transcended the discreteness of individuation as his soul is a part of the transcendent and immanent Brahman, i.e., supreme consciousness. Death is *Moksha* — salvation — which means, according to Indian thought, the transfiguration of the whole man into the Supreme Being. Gandhi always based his ideas on such spiritual convictions that those who are striving for the good of others, even after salvation from the worldly life, go on doing good to the world in conjunction with the Divine universal spirit.

Gandhi explained how individual-salvation and social emancipation can be simultaneous. He says:

> "Willing submission to social restraint for the sake of the well-being of the whole society enriches both the individual and the society of which he is a member . . . if one man gains spiritually,

> the whole world gains with him, and if one man fails, the whole world fails to that extend".[5]

This emphasis on the interdependence of man, transcending his own separate will and the common moral entity, may be compared with the Marxian idea of man's spiritual development and self-emancipation being inseparable from the development of society.

According to Marx:

> "the individual is caught up on the material relations of production and he can become a "fully human being" by freeing himself from the bondage of alienation, "by changing and humanising the existing socio-economic realities through revolutionary action".[6]

Marx claims that the alienation of man is rooted in the work process and division of labour which together pave the way for private ownership, and that "total man really grows when, in the classless society, the life of the individual and the life of society are no longer in opposition to each".[7] Man's self-realisation is possible only when he frees himself from all kinds of alienation. Marx deals with the question of alienation thus:

> ". . . as along as a cleavage exists between the particular and the common interest, as long, therefore, as activity is not voluntarily but naturally divided, man's own act becomes an alien power opposed to him, which enslaves him instead of being controlled by him".[8]

With Marx, alienation is not a spiritual phenomenon, as in the case of Gandhian philosophy, but it is existential having its roots in the concrete conditions of social life; it is the social fate of man. Gandhi holds that man alienates himself from the fundamental essence by losing sight of it due to avarice and because he does not practise self-purification and does not strive for self-reform. Man does not progress by outward emancipation but by inward sublimation. Gandhi, therefore, looks for the source of alienation of man not in the material conditions of life but in man's ignorance about the identity of all life, the consciousness about which he can gain through *Sarvodaya*,[9] and renunciation. This he expressed in the following words:

"All that we see in this great universe is pervaded by God. Renounce it and enjoy it or enjoy whatever he gives you, do not covet anybody's wealth or possessions."[10]

According to Gandhi, the act of renunciation which is stressed here is not a merely physical act but "represents a second or new birth. It is a deliberate act — not done in ignorance. It is, therefore, a regeneration. . . . Do not covet anybody's possession.[10] The moment you carry out these precepts you become a wise citizen of the world living at peace with all that lives.[11]

Sarvodaya*

The idea of interdependence and service to the fellowmen is expressed by Gandhi by the term *Sarvodaya* or good of all. The philosophy of *Sarvodaya* rejects the utilitarian principle "greatest good of the greatest number", because the utilitarians do not admit of any self-sacrifice or renunciation. It may, however, justify the elimination of minority rights for the sake of an abstractly conceived majority. For this reason Gandhi adopted the term *Sarvodaya*, which means literally "the rise of all" (Sanskrit word *Sarva* meaning all and *udaya* - rise, which implies a heightened awakening or a process of 'conscientisation' towards the inner depth of humanity rooted in the essential oneness of all. In the endeavour to achieve the good of all the individual has to discipline himself in a manner that lets all the inner-most *Satvika*** element of his soul "rise" to the highest level. It means development of the inner strength, of all powers within man to the full. This ethical ideal hinges upon the principle of self-purification.

As a believer in the oneness which is immanent in all the diversity of the universe, Gandhi 'seas all with an equal vision'. Therefore, he was vitally concerned with idea of brotherhood between different com-

* The concept of *Sarvodaya* was first used by Gandhi as expressing the idea of the good of the whole humanity which he found in Ruskin's *Unto This Last*.

In fact, he entitled Ruskin's book as *Sarvodaya* (M.K. Gandhi, (1954). *Sarvodaya*, Ahmedabad, Navjivan, edited by B. Kumarappa).

** *The Bhagvadgita* (VII 12-13) speaks of the creation constituting of entities evolved from the three *Gunas* (Modes of nature), *Sattva* (goodness), *Rajas* (energy or activity) and *Tamas* (evil or darkness).

munities, Gandhi interpreted *Atma*/Ram (the Indian term for God) as being essentially the same as the metaphsical identity or *Vedanta* monism. Nehru explains this idea, while writing about Vivekananda, he says:

> "He preached to monism of the *Advaita* philosophy, the *Vedanta*, and was convinced that only this could be the future religion of thinking humanity. . . . The *Vedanta* idea was of the solidarity of man and his inborn divine nature".[12]

This conceptual scheme is not a monopoly of philosophical schools, it is assimilated by ordinary people and it gives direction to individual and social life.

This phenomenal level of individual and societal harmony underlying the concept of *Sarvodaya* cannot be given a name or be fully stated, but it influenced the people who were culturally related to Gandhi's way of thinking. Therefore, from personal harmony it was only a step to social harmony which is based on the Indian concept of Vedanta monism.

In order to realise this inherent essence, according to Gandhi, the individual has to discipline himself in a manner that helps to accept the idea of social restraint.

His idea of "social constraint" is not Rousseau's willingness of man to agree with all to submit himself irrevocably to the general will of society as a whole. In Rousseau's thought the individual seems to acquire a dual character inasmuch as he can use his "particular will" to his own advantage, but, as a member of a society, "wills of common good" and being a unit of this he acquires a common identity. But, for Gandhi, the individual has already transcended the discreteness of the individual since his soul is a part of the transcendent and immanent Brahman — the Supreme Being. There is no question of an agreement as in Rousseau's social contract to agree to give up a part of his own will, the individual in Indian thought just has to follow his *dharma*.

The word *dharma* would stand not only for righteousness or duty, but also for the universal ordinance by which the cosmos is sustained. *Dharma* may be translated at "ontological ethics".[13] Radhakrishnan says:

> "*Dharma* gives coherence and direction to the different activities of life. . . . It is the complete rule of life, the harmony of the whole

> man who finds a right and just law of his living. Each man and group, each activity of soul, mind, life and body, has its dharma.[13]

This being so, no outside force is necessary to make man follow his own *dharma* but his own efforts to conduct his life as a *yajna*; and social harmony will not be difficult to achieve, this, according to Gandhi, is a *tapasya* (penance). If man realise that it is his *dharma* to give up part of his own right for the good of all, there is no need of collective coercion. Similarly, if all collectively follow their own *dharma* the individual will not be forced to give up his private judgement.

The individual, following his own *dharma*, can also make "the common will" right; this does not depend on his whim or fancy but on his acceptance of his *dharma*. From this act of following his own *dharma* in a society the individual transcends his own separate will and becomes a part of the common moral entity. It is a dual process, wherein the society responds to this act of the constituent unit, by following the *dharma* of the society as a whole, because of *swadharma* of each member of the society constitutes the collective *dharma* of the society and gives coherence to its activities. The pulls and counter-pulls enacted through *dharma* by the individual and the society give stability and also hold in balance the two spheres of rights and responsibility, and usher in *sarvodaya*.

Harijans

The emphasis on *Sarvodaya*, good of all, has profound implications for resolving caste conflicts. One has only to recall the atrocities committed on the Harijans during recent years in order to think of Gandhi's way of turning the spotlight on the discrimination practised against untouchables, by naming them Harijans and fasting for them. Characteristically, Gandhi says:

> "All the religions of the world described God pre-eminently as the Friend of the friendless, Help of the helpless, the rest of the world apart, in India who can be more friendless, helpless, or weaker than the 40 million or more Hindus of India who are classified as untouchables".

However, Gandhi was aware of the fact that the word 'Harijan' alone would not bring about the change in the status of the untouchables, but he wanted to remove the stigma of reproach implied by the term untouchable.

The new term 'Harijan' transcends the situationality and acquires a symbolic aura, and it expands the universe of discourse and becomes more relevant to the real problem of social transformation. And, Gandhi suggested by naming the untouchables as Harijans or children of God (*Hari*), he wanted to bring home to the upper castes the egalitarian core of Indian philosophy discussed above and which Nehru referred to as "the old pedantic ideal of the life force, which is the inner base of everything that exists." This reluctant reverence with which Nehru terms his concept as an "old pedantic ideal" indicates that this philosophy of identity of all life is to the Hindus an intimate and ever present thought, an "inner memory". With this in view, Gandhi expects all to whom he addresses, specifically the Hindus society, to expand their mental horizon by incorporating the content of the term 'Harijan'. If they comprehend the inherent equality which the term unfolds, he believes that this would create a basis for resolving harmoniously any conflicting situation arising out of the discriminating attitude of the higher castes towards the untouchables.

Recently, however, the untouchables (*Dalits*) have been expressing their reluctance to accept the name Harijans as they believe it implies an "upper caste arrogance"; it is argued by their spokesman, on their behalf, that they prefer the term *Dalit*. However, the term 'Harijan', as used by Gandhi, is in fact more appropriate for a true understanding of the problem. Untouchability, it hardly needs to be pointed out, is an evil that has a basis not only in the social but also in the religious practices. Gandhi, by using the term 'Harijan', emphasises both equality of all Indians before law and before God.

For Gandhi the idea of equality as a purely secular concept is incomplete, for, it does not question or enter into a dialogue with the other, more durable mode of thinking and behaviour, namely, religious. Untouchability, as an extreme and inhuman form of inequality, derives its sanction from inhuman religious beliefs and practices. It requires more than a secular concept of equality to challenge it. The use of the term Harijan thus implies the acceptance of not only the assertive secular power to 'Harijans' but, more importantly, their claim to human dignity. All persons are created equal by God (as *Harijans*), and some of them are made unequal by man-made laws (as in this case by the customary laws of the *Dharmashastras*), legitimacy of the latter has to be questioned. And to do this a purely positivist and secular concept like '*Dalit*' is plainly inadequate. Instead a counter-concept should be rooted in a higher and more universal form of religion's sensibility.

Besides, it was his identification with them which bridged a great gap. It was not a random identification, but an identification of a central strategic importance; Gandhi, the national leader and a caste Hindu himself, voluntarily decided to live with the untouchables to become one of them in appearance and in the standard of living. This identification had a revolutionary influence upon the caste system, which had deteriorated into a system of social discrimination.

However, one could not take for granted that this impact would have an everlasting effect, Gandhi himself was aware of this limitation. Therefore, he started a new weekly called *Harijan* devoted to the campaign of the removal of untouchability, because the felt that, in this matter, education and the like should be presented with all the possible vigour. In addition, Gandhi urged the Government of India to facilitate the passage of Ranga Iyer's Untouchability Abolition Bill, and he was keen to start public propaganda in support of the measure.

Besides, as he considered temples as "an integral part of Hinduism", he was convinced that one single act of allowing Harijans to enter temples will purify Hinduism and will open hearts of both caste Hindus and Harijans to meet each other on the basis of mutual harmony. In his words, 'the message of economic and educational uplift would touch only those to whom it is personally directed'. This proposition, he believed, can easily be understood by those who, like him, accept temples as an integral part of Hinduism as churches and mosques are of Christianity and Islam; it is not necessary that every Harijan should at once enter the temples, it is enough and is necessary that he knows he has acquired that right.

Ironically, Constitutional safeguards have proved ineffectual in encouraging social change and in grappling with the new realities of the problem of untouchability. The Constitutional provisions of 1950 and the programmes pursued by the Government, which contained egalitarian provisions and equality of all citizens, are described as mere 'palliatives offered to the aggrieved sections . . . meant to create a liberal progressive image of the new-born Indian State in the outside world'. Of course, Gandhi himself was aware that compulsion (as implied in the Constitutional provisions) can neither remove untouchability nor safeguard Hinduism. Sustained moral and cultural values cannot be forced by legislation, nor can they be achieved by a forced restructuring of society unless there is 'a change of heart'.

Therefore, Gandhi emphasised,

> "the caste Hindus, having created a class of outcastes, have up to the present day been treating them in a most irreligious and brutal manner and should now sooner or later atone for it".[14]

This atonement, he said, consists of meeting them as they are and treating them with an egalitarian attitude, behaving decently with them, it is only a small acknowledgement on the part of the society of the grave injustice that it has done to the Scheduled Castes over the millennia. At the same time, the upper caste youths who do very well in the examinations find that they are overlooked in favour of Scheduled Castes even though the latter get lower marks in examinations. Thus, the constitutional safeguards have become a double-edged weapon, and there are no dedicated workers who would translate the import of these legal provisions to both the Harijans and the caste Hindus. One may as well ask whether the statute books have only provided 'the truth of privileges' to the Harijans and forced them to remain isolated sections of society instead of being absorbed into the mainstream of Indian life? But, can we summon the courage and imagination to re-examine the true comparative merits of the two words 'Hari-jan'? Do we need an Attenborough to lead us to seeing Gandhi in a new light?

There seems to be no easy way of solving the dilemma with which we are faced today. The success or failure of any movement to lessen the chasm between Gandhi's Harijans and the caste Hindus, and to eradicate the 'caste factor' from people's consciousness and from our political life, depends on the right type of workers and the right type of leadership, which may not necessarily have a political commitment as such but which is dedicated to the cause.

Trusteeship

Further, Gandhi's assessment of inequitous inequalities and the accumulation of wealth in the hands of a few led him to the concept of trusteeship or holding private property as a trust. This idea of decentralisation of economic power includes devolution of political as well as economic power to the people. Gandhi's proposals are based on a vision of reconstructed polity and a regenerated society in which the path of *Satya* and the cultivation of *Ahimsa* are carried to the fullest. In fact, this new ideology of trusteeship was rooted in his own social philosophy, giving it a larger intellectual perspective with its modern nuances. He believed that it was possible to convert the property owners, if they believe it to be their *dharma* to be he 'caretaker' of the property in trust for the common good; trusteeship is, therefore, looked upon as 'a non-violent alternative' to State ownership. Within the Hindu social system with a strong commitment to the doctrine of *dharma* the concept of trusteeship if likely to find some roots. *Dharma* as the cosmic law or intological ethic is close to Indian traditional definition of religion as *Dharma*, and it gives coherence and direction to the different activities of life. *Dharma*, properly understood, can establish the harmony of the whole man that will surge out like oceanic waves reaching the whole humanity outside.

Understood as an ideological struggle, trusteeship is founded on *Satyagraha*. Therefore, if the capitalists are not willing to accept trusteeship nor give up exploitation, Gandhi would suggest an 'ideological struggle through *Satyagraha*'. Acharya Javdekar described this attempt a non-violent transformation as "*Satyagrahi* Socialism", because it is built on truth and non-violence. But Gandhi did not try to build a system. When asked if the property owners would be willing to give up the larger part of their wealth, he says:

> "When an individual has more than his proportionate portion he becomes a trustee of that portion for God's people. . . . As for the present owners of wealth, they would have to make their choice between class war and voluntarily converting themselves into trustees of their wealth, they would be allowed to retain the stewardship of their possessions, and to use their talent to increase the wealth, not for their own sake, but for the sake of the nation and therefore, without exploitation".[15]

This concept of trusteeship affects not merely ownership including distribution of income, but it extends to labour disputes and claims, is often criticised as being an utopian concept, Gandhi is labelled as a failure. It is Gandhi's firm conviction that "human nature is not fixed and immutable, and every man has limitless possibilities for good of life". Gandhi, therefore, never gives up the hope of changing the heart of the owners of property and transforming them into trustees; he maintains that "*Satyagraha* can rid society of all evils — political, economic and social".

His ideal of trusteeship is accepted by some Indian Marxists as the non-violent step towards socialism. As Gandhi suggests, socialism is a beautiful word, in socialism all the members are equal, none low, none high. To quote Gandhi,

> "Socialism is as pure as crystal. It, therefore, requires crystal-like means to achieve this. . . . Therefore, only truthful, non-violent and pure hearted socialists will be able to establish a socialistic society in India and the world. To my knowledge there is no country which is purely socialist. Without the means described above the existence of such a society is impossible".

To conclude, like Saint Simon and Fourier, Gandhi hoped to achieve the metamorphosis of the existing inequalities by peaceful means. Gandhi never loses faith in powers of universal persuasion. Precisely, because he was aware of the hatred and suspicions dividing the rich from the poor that Gandhi wanted to avoid violent revolution by means of trusteeship. He did not share the belief of Marx that 'the violence produced by the ills of society would purge society of these ills'. Gandhi would like to build socialism on the foundation of 'conversion of human nature through service and love!

NOTES

1. *Young India*, December 31, 1931.
2. M.K. Gandhi, *India of My Dreams*, (Ahmedabad, Navajivan) (1947). pp. 26-27.
3. Indira Rothermund, *The Philosophy of Restraint — Mahatma Gandhi's Strategy in Indian Politics*, (Bombay, Popular Prakashan) (1963). p. 45.
4. E. Fromm, Das Menschenbild bei Marx (Frankfurt), (1968). pp. 116-17, also T. Huttomore Rubel (Ed.), (1971), *Karl Mark's Writing's — Socialism and Social Philosophy*, (Penguin).
5. M.K. Gandhi, *My Religion*, Navajivan, (1955), p. 124.
6. Damodaran, K., "Marxism and Alienation", *Mainstream*, May 4, (1968). p. 12.
7. Garaudy, R., *Karl Marx*, London: Lawrence & Wishart (1964). p. 75.
8. Sarkar, S., "Marx and Man", *Mainstream*, March 28, (1968), p. 20. Also Istavan Mezaros, *Marx's Theory of Alienation*.
9. Rothermund, I., *op. cit.* p. 25, (Sarvodaya means the good of all or the "rise of all", as explained later.)
10. Indira Rothermund, *op. cit.* p. 56.
11. Gandhi, M.K. *Hindu Dharma*, *op. cit.*, pp. 41-42.
12. *New York Times*, Sept. 7, 1958, Quoted in Indira Rothermund, *op. cit.*, p. 35.
13. Indira Rothermund, *op. cit.*, p. 46.
14. *Ibid.*
15. M.K. Gandhi, *Harijan*, February 23, (1947).

8

CONFLICTS, PARADIGMS AND ECONOMIC DEVELOPMENT: Some Gandhian Perspectives

V. PANDIT

INTRODUCTION

GANDHI'S ROLE as a political leader is universally known. It is also widely recognised that the unique mystique of his leadership lay in his ability to forge politics with a moral force. All the same it is sometimes overlooked that Gandhi's approach to different problems concerning individuals, nations or society in general arose from an integrated view of life. Interpretation of his views taken in isolation or torn out of context has therefore led to considerable misunderstanding.[1] Since political freedom to Gandhi was not an end but a necessary means to achieve economic social and moral reconstruction he dwelt in depth on all these aspects particularly in the context of India.

While many facets of Gandhism have been studied in considerable detail his economic philosophy has unfortunately remained relatively neglected.[2] The main reason for this has been that economists immersed in an entirely different mainstream — in content as well as in methodology — and used to a compartmentalised approach to social problems could not visualise Gandhi's ideas as constituting more than a moral philosophy unrelated to economic problems. On the other hand those with some appreciation of Gandhi's economic philosophy could not translate it into a methodology familiar to the mainstream economists nor constructively break away from this mainstream methodology.

The present chapter is neither a critique of the prevailing economic orthodoxy nor a full-fledged analysis of Gandhian views on economic development. Lying somewhere between the two it is only a modest attempt to look afresh at some basic elements of Gandhism in the light of development experience during the recent decades as well as some new approaches within economic analysis. Out purpose is more to stimulate interest in a reappraisal of Gandhi's economic philosophy than to present a fully articulated viewpoint. It is quite natural that views expressed here are shaped in the context of Indian experience over the past four decades though explicit reference to facts and figures is generally avoided.

Since our focus is on conflict two points need to be made at the outset. First, we note that it is customary to regard resolution of conflict as an objective of social policy. While there is no disagreement about this we need to distinguish between short run and long run objectives. Conflict resolution is in our view only a long run phenomenon — with all the mystique and evasiveness that the term 'long run' may evoke. It will not be wrong to claim that few, if any, conflicts get resolved in the short run. In the short run we are therefore more concerned with "conflict management' than with 'conflict resolution' — the latter being kept in view as a long run objective. By the term conflict management we simply mean attempts (i) to narrow the area of conflict and (ii) to transform one kind and level of conflicts into another kind and level. Second, we need not necessarily regard conflict by itself undesirable. Conflicts may often be symptoms of the underlying dynamics of change in the right direction. It may frequently be even desirable to encourage conflict in order to force social and economic transformation.[3] It is of course, clear that the desirability of the outcome is critically dependent on how the conflict is managed in its different phases.

Economic Paradigms and Systems

Conflict of economic interests has perhaps been the most obvious aspect of social life from times immemorial. Even today economic conflict continues to dominate other types of conflict either explicitly or implicitly. How has civilised society then tried to understand and manage these conflicts — in theory and in practice.[4] Without going into details we recall that economic thought over the past century has been dominated by two major paradigms. The first, which may be regarded as the mainstream owes its articulation of Adam Smith's celebrated book, *The Wealth of Nations*. The second paradigm which has played a prominent role in world affairs during this century is enshrined in Marx's epoch-making work *Das Kapital*.[5]

At the risk of over-simplification the central themes of the two paradigms, subsequently referred to as *Laissez faire* Liberalism (LL) and State controlled Socialism (SS) respectively, can be stated very briefly. While LL places faith in the market mechanism based on perfect competition SS believes in the capability of the socially controlled state machinery. The two paradigms are not confined only to economic affairs but are associated with alternative political and social systems. However, neither of the two systems is to be found in its pure from anywhere in practice. Instead, we have a fairly wide variety of mixtures such as welfare state, democratic socialism and mixed economies.

Under LL conflict management is entrusted to the market as an institution aided by the forces of supply and demand — the visible manifestations of Smith's "invisible hand". Actions and decisions of the individuals are coordinated by the market leading to the tranquillity of "equilibrium". Every economic agent is assumed to be "rational" in the sense that he is solely concerned with and motivated by his self-interest. Consumer's actions are intended to maximise their level of satisfaction and producers strive to maximise profits. On the other hand, in case of SS the state in its wisdom makes centralised decisions which are in the best interest of the society as a whole. The presumption is that the state has all the relevant information needed for decision-making and is capable of executing all its decisions without fear or favour.

As stated above, we do not intend to undertake an extensive critique of economic theory and the resulting economic systems as they operate. All the same it is necessary to make some observations arising in the context of conflict management. Considering LL first, can one say that a competitive equilibrium is a state in which conflict has been minimised and that this state is the most desirable under the given circumstances? In several situations the answer may be in the affirmative. But in many others the answer is a clear 'no'. Unfortunately, most situations arising in the context of development of poor countries fall in the latter class. Pareto optimality which characterises competitive equilibrium may be relevant where basic physical needs are satisfied but not so when people get priced out of the market for even such things as a square meal, medical care or a roof on one's hand.[6] This kind of optimality may in a sense indicate efficiency but it serves no purpose in evaluating the social desirability or otherwise of different outcomes.

Further problems arise because the notion of rationality[7] which is at the very root of all calculations in the mainstream economics is conceptually limited as well as empirically inadequate. This is in part because academic disciplines including economics take a partial and fragmental view of human affairs. It is also in part due to the exclusive focus on goods and services that satisfy physical needs. We shall return to this point subsequently in section 'Rationality and Efficiency'. As regards socialism the situation is no better as individual preferences, not to mention non-materialistic aspirations, are completely overlooked. Consequently, the issue of conflict is assumed away. The state is, as mentioned above, presumed to be in possession of all information as well as capable of implementing all decisions fairly. It does not seem to be an exaggeration to say that the standard tools of the mainstream economic theory are of only limited use in conflict management in the context of economic development.

We must hasten to add that the caricature drawn above of economic thought — in theory, philosophy and practice — does not represent the discipline faithfully in all its details. The prevailing doctrines have indeed been subjected to severe criticism from within and frequently. A lot has been written on the inadequacies of the concept of Pareto optimality as a guide for policy formulation and evaluation. Possibilities of what are termed as market failures, empirical invalidity of the postulates underlying the market mechanism etc., have often been highlighted by economists. A particular mention must be made of the work of Sen who has questioned the notion of rationality of which stands the edifice of economic theory.[8] Similarly, the recent years have witnessed a re-evaluation and reinterpretation of socialist thought and practice.[9]

In the context of economic development it is gratifying that economists have moved a few steps away from their earlier strongholds by recognising the importance of many things other then per capita food shelter and clothing. That GNP is a poor index of social welfare has been well recognised by economists for a long time but attempts to quantify entities like distribution of income, land, wealth, access to health services and educational facilities, and to incorporate specific issues of policy relating to these into economic analysis is relatively recent.

The fact that economists are increasingly concerned with the wider umbrella namely "quality of life" as the determinant of social welfare is indeed a welcome development.[10] All the same it would be wishful to think that much dent has been made into the prevailing orthodoxies. A measure of "soul searching" which alone can lead to radically new modes of analysis has yet to take place on a wide enough scale. Though questions have been raised about the prevailing paradigms the difficulties in finding acceptable alternatives appear to be insurmountable at the moment.

Record of Development and Conflict

It is now nearly four decades since a large number of erstwhile colonies — which now constitute the third world — regained political freedom and launched a concerted effort for economic and social development. Most of them, like India have adopted, the path of mixed economy hoping to combine the advantages of socialist economy and liberal polity. How far these hopes have come true is for anyone to see?[11] It is true that most of these economies have had rates of growth in GNP substantially higher than those observed for the preceding several decades. It is also well-known that several of these countries have had a spectacular increase in the volume and variety of production raising per capita incomes multifold. It is however, not equally well-known that such growth, as has occurred has varyingly taken a heavy toll of the environment, social institutions, household tranquillity as well as individual freedoms.

It will not be an exaggeration to say that the predominant part of the third world is still steeped in poverty and deprivation in absolute as well as in relative terms.[12] High unemployment rates, incidence of hunger and disease in the country side, spreading urban squalor widening disparities and growing alienation are still the main features of the Third World as a whole even though there are pockets of visible modernisation and economic prosperity. Economic and demographic projections for the coming decades hardly give reason for optimism with regard to the future of man in a collective sense. It appears to us that development has gone astray[13] mainly because it has not been able to manage the major conflicts in a desirable manner. The particular perception and the manner of managing conflicts has led to the adoption of wrong priorities in almost all countries.[14]

The arena of conflicts that have arisen during the process of economic development in different countries and in different situations is so large that it is hard to list such conflicts and harder to discuss them in any depth. We may, however, subsequently single out a few that appear important to us and also relevant in the present context. To some extent these are also interrelated.

First, there has been a continuing conflict between economic and non-economic objectives. For example a widely debated issue relates to the trade-off between economic growth and a variety of objectives commonly termed social justice. There is similarly a conflict between employment and productivity, between conservation of non-renewable resources and increase in the levels and style of living.

Second, there are controversies regarding the scale of production and the associated structure of organisation. This also involves implicitly conflicts not only between small and large industry or between labour intensive and capital intensive techniques but also between the central metropolis and the rural hinterland.

Third, the nature and extent of government intervention albeit control too has been the focus of debate all over the third world. A related question in this context has been the degree of centralised decision-making. The reconciliation of conflict between different group interests and the role of lobbies operating in the corridors of power.

Finally, a prominent issue in the development theory and practice has been the one relating to international trade. To what extent should the objective of economic independence and self-sufficiency be pursued as a goal at the cost of economic efficiency is the central issue here.

Basics for a Better Foundation

It is easier to find faults even with what may be an established paradigm as well as to have hindsights on the mistakes that might have already occurred. To spell out clearly a coherent and feasible alternative is, however, not equally easy. Fortunately, as stated earlier we have not set that as the purpose of this modest attempt. The objective is only to draw attention to some ideas of Gandhi in relation to conflict management and development.

Two things seem to be the most important in the present context. First, Gandhi was greatly influenced by the vedantic principle of *advaita*, i.e., non-duality. This shaped his so-called wholistic approach to all human affairs, and even beyond. Absence of compartmentalisation is indeed the most fundamental aspect of his views on social problems. Second, but no less important, is Gandhi's concern with the individual as the primary entity in all spheres. Let us consider these two things at some length.

It has become quite common in academic as well as in policy forums to take a fragmented view of problems and to deal with these one by one in isolation of each other. Typically, economists take social, legal and political institutions as exogenously given. Other social scientists adopt the same attitude in their respective disciplines. This is in sharp contrast to Gandhi's way of looking at social, economic, political and educational institutions not only as interacting with each other but also as parts of a larger single entity.[15] This is precisely why for him political independence was not an end but a means to economic development and national reconstruction in all spheres.

This integrated approach is important because a lack of it leads to an imperfect understanding of conflicts and a diminished ability to manage conflicts in the sense mentioned earlier. Many development problems become chronic and vicious largely because they are posed and tackled in isolation. In most countries the development programmes have failed to involve people at the grassroot level precisely because of the compartmental approach. As a consequence, it is not uncommon to see the intended beneficiaries of such programmes as indifferent witnesses having no say in identification, designing or execution of even small local projects.[16] Mass involvement was important to Gandhi as a means to what he termed *Sarvodaya*.

Turning now to the second principle it is sad to observe how much we have got accustomed to thinking and analysing issues in terms of aggregates carrying labels relating to castes, religions, economic classes and the like. While categorisation does sometimes serve a purpose, an excessive concern with labels is an obstacle to the correct understanding of conflicts and problems. To deprive man of his individuality is tantamount to focing him into a pattern and to diminish his self-respect. Unfortunately, it has become far too common to view people only as members of one group or the other rather than as "themselves". There is, consequently, less inclination shown or effort made to understand each other as individuals.[17]

Prima facie there are two compelling reasons why focus must be on the individual. First, it is obvious that individual is the more permanent entity than the group he is affiliated to, simply because affiliations are subject to change — in principle and in practice. Second, a deeper reason is that some important dimensions of human existence get blurred in aggregates. In particular, things that relate to man's inner life — with which Gandhi was much concerned, are meaningless in a collective sense. Since conflicts basically belong to this realm attempts to manage interpersonal or interclass conflicts only at the aggregate level are not at all sufficient. This is undoubtedly basic to Gandhi's conceptualisation of non-violence, *sarvodaya*, trusteeship and social justice.[18] Moreover, it is at this micro-level that these ideas have the greatest possibilities. If a beginning is not made there the success at aggregate levels is unlikely. Only those who are at peace with their own self can manage conflicts at wider social levels.

Rationality and Efficiency

The most widely employed criterion to reject anything that does not conform to the established rules of the game is that of rationality as enunciated by mainstream social scientists. All modes of analysis and blue-prints of action are subjected to this criterion. In economics specifically the notion of rational behaviour arises directly from utilitarianism, i.e., the belief that individuals must and do always strive to maximise utility, an euphemism for what pacifists would hold as almost synonymous with selfishness. How valid is this basic postulate which is the cornerstone of all economic analysis? To answer this we have already alluded to the work of Sen. His critique of utilitarianism is basic and some of his remarks are worth quoting in the present context.

> " . . . Agents may have preferences about their preferences, i.e., to mould their own preferences. . . It involves 'a battle with oneself' that is marked by all kinds of feints, ruses and strategic devices . . . "

As if to sharpen the anti-utilitarian argument, Sen goes on to add " . . . people frequently do the unselfish thing . . . "[19]

This is extremely important in the present context because the psyche of pain and pleasure, of happiness and unhappiness go considerably beyond the "basket of goods and services". The view that happiness depends, as it were, not only on what your state, actually is but also on what you think that state to be cannot be dismissed lightly.

Correspondingly, the concept of rationality needs to be widened in evaluating individual actions as well as in designing policies. Gandhi's is this wider notion and whatever it implies. There are no doubt problems of measurement but these are no harder than those that appeared to bedevil utility theory in its early phases.

Next, we consider another important criterion widely applied to economic problems — one that is of more direct and particular relevance to economic development, namely, "economic efficiency". This concept is mostly used to pure technological terms under the assumptions of perfect certainty and competitive market structure. Moreover, costs and benefits are measured only in terms of tangible outcomes or, at best inclusive of factors that are easily quantifiable.[20] Here again, the basic problem is that economic issues are not viewed in their total setting. Considering the present context let us confine this discussion to the question of the scale of production — a theme very important to Gandhi's economic philosophy and his approach to conflict management.

The well-known "economies of scale" argument has led policy-makers to favour large scale production — the hallmark of modern industrialisation under capitalist as well as socialist economic systems of the contemporary world. On its own ground the efficiency argument justifying mass production is in most cases unassailable provided we are concerned only with the short run and only with pure technological considerations. Cost calculations underlying the argument here overlook two things. These are:

(a) uncertainties which arise with regard to the long run as well as for other reasons, and
(b) costs and benefits which cannot be translated into pecuniary terms.

Conflict is germane to both these aspects. Let us consider these in the reverse order.

To begin with, it must be appreciated that technology operates within a milieu of which man and the associated organisational structure are an integral part. Thus, technology cannot be isolated form the wider human consideration. It is well-known to social scientists and to economists in particular that technology determines the pattern of income distribution and the structure of production. It also implicitly specifies several other things such as marketing, packaging and transportation requirements. Now, it is here that conflict arises even in simple economic terms. The need for conflict management is imperative.

Taking cognizance of uncertainty mentioned earlier takes us into deeper issues. But unfortunately, this is one of those problems which modern economic theory deals with in depth — both at the micro level as well as at the macro level. It has been very rightly accepted that uncertainty is an unavoidable phenomenon. If arises in part due to the inherent nature of things and in part due to the inadequacy of information that could in principle be available. This inadequacy is in turn due to the fact that gathering of information is costly in terms of money, time and effort. In economic theoretic terms information is not a free good.

The foregoing discussion points to the necessity of recognising organisational and informational efficiency along with the conventional technological efficiency. It is our view that both organisational and informational efficiencies on the one hand and the magnitude of conflict on the other feed on each other. Further, we put forth the proposition that these inefficiencies and conflicts increase with the scale of production in particular and sise of the system in general.

The necessary implication of the forgoing proposition is that there is less conflict in smaller systems so that gains in non-technological efficiency may very well exceed losses in technological efficiency caused by smallness. Taking a somewhat different but important context one may ask why there is less endogenous or spontaneous conflict in (smaller) rural communities than in (larger) urban communities.[21] The reason for this must be sought in the fact that misinformation, uncertainty, sense of insecurity, alienation and the resulting negative psychic impulses have a grater scope to thrive in larger communities.

Patterns and Possibilities for Development

In the preceding sections we have discussed some features of economic condition in the third world — pointing out the major issues of conflict. We have also outlined a few elements of Gandhian perspectives in relation to these conflicts and development problems in general. In the remaining two sections it is intended to bring the different threads together in order to draw implications for development policies. However, these are in the nature of what one may call loud thinking in the sense that they do not constitute a complete and self-contained outline of an alternative.

Before we draw any specific conclusions it will be useful in this section to have an overview of the historical and contemporary development of nations in order to form some judgement about the prospects for today's poor countries. The taxonomy of development suggests that the contemporary world consists of five broad types. The one that concerns us directly is the set of countries that are very poor, growing at a moderate pace and not endowed with any particular resource of critical importance. The other four types are:

(a) the highly developed countries — most of which come under the umbrella of OECD,
(b) socialist countries in eastern Europe which are called CPE (Centrally Planned Economies),
(c) newly industrialised high growth countries referred to as NIC, and
(d) oil exporting countries i.e., OPEC.

A few points regarding world economic development need to be underlined as follows: Most countries in the OECD have grown in a historical setting characterised by domestic as well as international inequities both working in favour of their development. Further, while they offer reasonable standards of living even to the lower echelons of the society, their staggeringly high per capita incomes are accompanied by considerable distress at the individual level in non-material terms. CPEs have made remarkable progress in standards of living as well as in evolving an egalitarian society, reduction in crime and progress in certain other spheres. But a serious victim in such countries has been the free mind.

NICs, which have hit the headlines for the past two decades for their unprecedented increase in per capita GNP are typically small sized economies. They have been helped by massive external aid, and a political economy which allowed multinational corporations to play a vital role in their development. It is hard to visualise either a continuation in their high growth performance for a long time or a repetition of this feat in other third world countries particularly the large ones. Finally, we have OPECs which have suddenly jumped the fence of join the club of prosperity by virtue of their special endowments. How much of growth and equity they will eventually achieve is to be watched?

The remaining countries of the world are sometimes referred to as the fourth world. But in our taxonomy, they qualify for the term 'fifth world'. We have earlier commented on the state of affairs in these countries. Recalling that and the brief overview of the history of development given above two points emerge very clearly. First, countries in this fifth world have, over the post four decades followed a course of development which has made no dent into the problems inequality and employment. Moreover, there is little hope that the lot of the lowest echelons in the society will be blessed with even the basic needs over the next half a century. Second, it is also clear that it is not possible, nor in our view desirable for these countries to follow the path that has resulted in prosperity for countries in the remaining four categories. A radically new approach must therefore evolve without any further loss of time.

Some Broad Conclusions

Fortunately, man is endowed with the ability and the will to think, to experiment and to experience. He has, from times immemorial been in search of a civilised social order through a process of trial and error. By its very nature the process may have sometimes led to undesirable alleys but the movement has on the whole been in the right direction. No wonder that diehard supporters of what we termed LL have over time conceded some ground to SS and the latter itself is in a melting pot, groping for new solutions. It is indeed remarkable that the counter-revolution in Eastern Europe has by and large been orderly and non-violent.[22] This should be an eye opener to those who pooh-pooh Gandhi's non-violence as a non-starter impotent in consequence and impossible in practice. That the fifth world of our concern, which has, in most cases, undergone one non-violent revolution in the late forties or early fifties will now have to undergo a non-violent counter revolution seems to be unavoidable.

Following from the discussion so far, it appear that the salient features of this counter revolution will have to be as follows: These are clearly interdependent and in keeping with the spirit of the paper must be viewed as parts of the same single package.

(a) First and foremost, the excessive preoccupation with the rate of growth of GNP or per capita income must yield to an increased emphasis on raising the quality of life. This will include efforts to secure greater equity, increased expenditure on health, housing and meaningful education and a concerted attempt to maintain ecological balance. *Antyodaya* and other similar programmes initiated by the government in part of India were steps in the right direction but lacking in the required measure of commitment. *Janasaviya*, the recent similar step taken in Sri Lanka is very promising. It is hoped that the programme will not be given up as unpractical even before it receives a fair trial.

(b) Second, policy-makers must resist the temptation to go for unnecessarily large showpiece projects for irrigation, power generation as well as all types of industrial ventures. Smaller projects should be able to use more local resources, generate more employment with less dislocation and, generally invite greater participation of people. In a wide variety of instances they would be feasible as well as efficient in the sense discussed earlier.

(c) Third, the much publicised role of trade as the key to economic growth is unwarranted. Clearly, all countries cannot have a trade surplus. Perhaps we should judiciously distinguish between trade that is necessary for natural and technological reasons and trade that may appear to be desirable on the basis by hairspitting economic calculations. The latter kind brings in its wake not only increased uncertainties and conflicts but also, as Gandhi visualised, the dangers of dependence, exploitation and imperialist tendencies. Even internal trade must be minimised so that greater effort and resources are devoted to commodity production and essential social services.

(d) Fourth, government intervention is not by itself undesirable but the important thing is the motivation for such intervention and the style of its execution. Unfortunately, the record so far has not been encouraging. But if there is greater and effective decentralisation of decision-making in a democratic manner what may formally be called government intervention should in fact be collective decision-making at the grass roots level.

(e) Fifth, increasing militarism that we observe in all countries is no assurance for either domestic or external peace. High military expenditures in the fifth world are not only ill-motivated and encouraged by internal and external powers that be but also fatal for such countries, with or without economic growth. To limit such expenditures must receive a high priority.

(f) Finally, a basic presumption throughout this chapter is that

> values not only do matter but are also worth fighting for collectively as well as individually. Unfortunately, it has come to be somewhat cynically accepted that values are extraneously given. Sometimes, however, it is conceded that values have meaning and scope for improvement only collectively. This is not at all a sustainable view. Values can and must begin at the individual level. This has not so far been adequately emphasised. The mode and content of education has concentrated exclusively on how to "make a living" neglecting how to "live a life". A reorientation of education must begin with emphasis on the basic human values of love, truth, non-violence, peace and right conduct fully integrated with the secular education of the highest quality that is at present receiving attentions.[23]

We have not explicitly related the above suggestions to conflict management but in the light of the earlier discussion it should be clear that this is implicitly present in and important to each of these.

NOTES

1. A very good example of this is the writing of Arthur Kostler. See for example his book, *Lotus and the Robot*.
2. The last decade has however witnessed an increased interest in the subject. See for example, A. Das, *A Foundation of Gandhian Economics*, Allied, Bombay, (1979). B.C. Das and G.P. Sethi, *Gandhi Today Gandhi Peace Foundation*, New Delhi, (1978). V.T. Patil (ed.), *Studies in Gandhi*, New Delhi, (1983), and V.K.R.V. Rao, *Gandhian Socialism*, and the writings of several notable authors like R. Diwan.
3. Mass movements led by Gandhi himself since the early twenties are examples of conflict creation.
4. It is interesting to note that early thought in the West is attributed to what are called 'Churchmen' for whom economic affairs were part of life subject to moral values. In ancient India Kautilya's *Arthasastra* similarly propagated the philosophy that all material preoccupations must be sanctified by a concern for higher values and pursuits.
5. For convenience we shall refer to the former as *laissez faire* liberalism (LL) and the latter as state controlled socialism (SS).
6. Socialism fares better in this limited context as it is not governed by the anonymous market forces.
7. For an extensive and recent discussion of rationality in economics see Barry Hindess, *Choice, Rationality and Social Theory*, London, Unwin Hyman, (1988).
8. See his "Rational Fools: A Critique of the Behavioural Foundations of Economic Theory", *Philosophy and Public Affairs*, Vol. 6, pp. 317-44. We shall

return to this point in some detail in section in Rational and Efficiency of this Chapter.

9. A remodelling of the socialist world which has begun with unexpected enthusiasm is evidence of a continuing search for better social and economic order and an example of transformation of conflicts.
10. An innovator in this area too is A.K. Sen, (1981). See for instance his *Poverty and Famines*, Oxford, Clarendon Press, and several related works. See also various contributions in T.N. Srinivasan and P.K. Bardhan (eds.), *Rural Poverty in South Asia*, (1988). Columbia University Press, New York.
11. Students of chemistry know for sure that when two elements are combined the result is either a chemical compound which may exhibit properties entirely different from those of the two elements or a mechanical mixture which will possess *all* the properties of both the elements.
12. This is borne out by several studies. See, for example, Srinivasan and Bardhan, *op. cit.* and an early study by M. Ahluwalia, N. Carter and H.B. Chenery, World Bank, *Growth and Poverty in Development Countries*, Washington D.C.: (1979).
13. We are deliberately not saying that development policy has failed. For, success or otherwise has to be judged in relation to the intended objectives. Since growth of GNP has been set as the major objective in most countries, economic policy has been successful in varying degrees.
14. Two examples one can readily think of in this context are (i) each country owns and operates an international airlines enterprise, and (ii) each country spends a prohibitive sum of money on the so-called defence establishment.
15. In this basic sense Gandhi's approach is very akin to that of Marx something not generally appreciated by mainstream acedemics.
16. To the extent that countries like China have taken an integrated view or the development problems facing them they have been able to achieve greater involvement of people, the recent events notwithstanding.
17. It seems to be correct to claim that this adds to conflicts on the one hand and on the other prevents us from properly understanding and managing conflicts. The way communal violence is often treated by the media, the government and even by the investigative commissions is a good example of this.
18. An indepth exposition of these concepts from an economic view point by one of the most renowned economists is to be found in V.K.R.V. Rao, *Gandhian Socialism*, Bombay: Bharatiya Vidya Bhavan, (1972).
19. A.K. Sen, "Rational Fools: A Critique of the Behavioural Foundations of Economic Theory", *Philosophy and Public Affairs* Vol. 6, pp. 317-44. See also A. Hirschman, *Shifting Involvements: Private Interests and Public Action*, Oxford, England: Martin Robertson, (1982).
20. It is important to note that if people were democratically involved in project selection and evaluation their revealed preferences would help to overcome the quantification problem in, at least, some cases.
21. Exogenous and organised caste and community based rural violence should not be taken as a refutation because we are talking of endogenous or spontaneous conflicts.
22. At this stage it is hard to be definite about the motives underlying these changes. It is hoped that the pursuit for free mind has been the more important objective than the passion for consumerism. In case this is not so, the counter

revolution will prove to be like jumping from the frying pan into the fire.

23. This need not be rejected as infeasible because such an orientation is already being carried out at some institutions. A spectacular example of such institutions is the Sri Satya Sai Institute of Higher Learning in Andhra Pradesh. Despite hurdles the record of achievements has been remarkable even over a short span of less than a decade.

9

DEVELOPMENT AND DISPLACEMENT

K.D. GANGRADE

WITH THE advent of freedom, India faced many problems. As the task of immediate relief and rehabilitation of refugees was on the way to completion the government began to think in terms of rebuilding the country and re-awakening the people in slumber.

This made the government adopt planning as a way and method to deal with the complicated problems and change the lives of the people. Thus came the Five-Year Plan — a model of human patience, skill and endeavour; a documented account of the national resources, both human and material, and suggestions for their optimum utilisation. A constructive revolution had begun, and, as part of a series of development schemes, national as well as State, the government began to acquire land for various purposes, either to build dams or set up industries, or even to provide house-sites for urban people.

The schemes in themselves claimed to be well-conceived, and contained provisions for compensation to former owners and for rehabilitation of people uprooted by the acquisition of land. But, experience shows that most of these schemes are very ill-conceived in regard to rehabilitation of the persons concerned. This often leads to disintegration of communities.

Small Republic

It is intended to discuss here a case study of various problems that arose in a village community as a result of acquisition of land at Krishnapur, a village situated 24 km from a metropolitan city on a main road which has been served by a development block since 1952. There is a regular bus service connecting the village with the city. The village has about 158 households with 948 people, which can be divided among the various castes as follows: *Jats* (peasants) 60; *Chamars* (shomakers) 35; *Bhangis* (sweepers) 30; *Brahmins* (priest-scholars) 15, *Khatis* (carpenters) 5; *Nais* (barbers) 3; *Banias* (shopkeepers and moneylenders) 2; and *Gadarias* (shepherds) 2.

The local residents say that in the national uprising of 1857 all the people of the village, except a single Brahmin, fought against the British. Brahmin gave shelter to a high British military official and kept him away from the wrath of the people and thus saved his life. The Britishers succeeded in suppressing the revolution and later took away all the land from the villagers who had taken part in the "Mutiny". This land was subsequently given to the Brahmin as a reward for his services. Since then all land in the village has been owned by that person's family, and at present it is owned by five brothers. Most of the *Jats* who survived the battle had no option but to accept the tenancy of the Brahmin landlord. This changed the role of the *Jats*, who had been the dominant land-owning caste in the village. They became subordinate to the Brahmins economically as well as socially. Some of the families of *Chamars* and *Bhangis* were also given land for cultivation.

The economic status of the majority of the people, except the landlord family, is the same. They are divided into closed groups on caste basis. Each caste has its own social norms which are strictly followed by its members.

The most important unifying factor among the members of the same caste seems to be the *hukka* (hubble-bubble). All the members of the same caste smoke freely from the same *hukka*. Members of other castes cannot have a smoke through the pipe but through the *chillum* (in which the tobacco is put).

Marriage

Villagers are supposed to marry within their caste group but not with a person from their own village. At an earlier period, the condition of the village and the bad treatment given to the people by the landlord were such that the villagers of other areas would not marry off their daughters into this village. They claimed that marriage into such a village would be like sending their daughters to prison. This decision led the people of the village to stand against the landlord and to refuse to do *baigar* (forced labour). As a result, the *Jat* and other lower castes in other villages decided not to ban marrying their daughters into the village. Not so with the Brahmins, however, and the effect of this has been very serve.

Land Required

The village has about five individuals who are quite important and enjoy the confidence of members of their caste. They are Pandit Chander from the Brahmins, Narain Singh from the *Jats*, Garib from the *Kumhars*, Tara Chand from the *Chamars* and Dayal from another caste. Brahmins hold leadership positions in the village, and their leader, Pandit Chander, had been the *Sarpanch* of the village *Panchayat*.

The cultivated area in the village is about 4,200 *bighas*, half of which is across the road. The whole of the village land belongs to Pandit Chander and his family, but some of it has been cultivated by 25 other families which have worked on the land for the past 60 years and have been paying *lagan* (revenue) to the landlords. The rate of *lagan* had varied from six *annas* to two rupees in the beginning, but past year it was raised from two to five rupees per *bigha*. Not content with the small income from their land and fearing that they might lose it under the Zamindari Abolition Act, the landlords were able to persuade a government department to take their village land (2,645 *bighas*) for a government project (hereafter named Project X). The tenants were not at all aware of this, and were shocked when the construction material for Project X was unloaded on their standing crops. Subsequently, they were served notices to vacate the land immediately. The transaction meant that 25 families of *Jats* and 26 families of *Chamars* were rendered landless. The village was also deprived of pasture land for its cattle. Further, the fodder which the whole village received from this area was no longer to be available. About 11 Jat families had some land on the other side of the road, but deprived of their other holdings their income would fall below the subsistence level. The rest of the people, mainly artisans who did not follow agricultural pursuits, were also affected.

Sons of the Soil

The *Patwari* (land recorder) informed the villagers that the land had been acquired by the government and henceforth they were nothing to do with it. Following this action Narain Singh and a few others appealed to the Chief Minister to use his good offices and to save the village from a calamity, because the acquisition would deprive them of their cultivable and pasture land. If the project is finalised the villagers would be rendered jobless. They also wrote that a senior government officer had visited the village but nothing had been done so far. In reply, the Chief Minister's Secretary wrote to Pandit Chander, the *Sarpanch,* that he had instructed appropriate authorities to arrangement for early payments of compensation to the owners.

During the same period the Harijans (*Chamars*) of the village had written to a Harijan promotional agency (hereafter named Agency B) in a nearby city for help. There was no response from the agency. As the social worker had become very friendly with the villagers, Tara Chand and others approached him for help. He got in touch with Mr. Bhola, the government official, who had visited the village and knew about the land acquisition. As a result he and the social worker went to Agency B and met the general secretary, Mr. Mansukh, who denied help as a matter of policy of Agency B in such situations but gave hope to assist due to their keen interest. In the meantime the villagers went to the State Development Minister and explained to him that the acquisition of their land would result in their starvation. The Minister's reply was that the government needed the place for a project and so it had been acquired. He did not assure for any relief but promised to 'look into the matter'.

On Mr. Mansukh's person request, the Minister visited the village. At that time Mr. Mansukh and the social worker were also present. The Minister was shown the standing crops and he promised that these would not be touched. Then the villagers asked for permission to plough the land for the next crops but refused saying that it would be illegal and obstructive.

In consultation with the villagers, Mr. Mansukh prepared a written memorandum of their problems and sent is to the proper Minister. The difficulties of the villagers were explained and data regarding the cultivated land given. It was stated that the villagers did not want to come in the way of national development, and three suggestions were submitted:

1. The cultivated land should be spared and in its place certain other barren land in a nearby village should be used;

2. The villagers should be given alternative land;
3. Quick and adequate compensation should be paid to the villagers to enable them to buy land in some other area.

In addition, the Minister was asked for an appointment when the problem could be discussed. For 15 days Mr. Mansukh did not get such an appointment, and as time for the next crop was slipping away the villagers became more and more restless, and decided to hold a meeting in order to plan the next steps.

Minister's Regret

Narain Singh and Tara Chand said at the meeting that its purpose was to decide what further steps should be taken in connection with the land problem. One villager suggested that they should all go to the Chief Minister, who, he felt, was the only person who could help. "We should go to him with all our children and cattle and ask him to decide this way or that". Tara Chand said that since Agency B had written to the concerned Minister it was best to talk to him. Narain Singh also supported this and said that it would be best for the villagers to go to the Minister with a copy of the application already sent to him through Agency B. All agreed with the proposal.

The Minister told them that he knew of the case and was very sorry for what had happened. He said he was unaware that so many people would be put to inconvenience and assured the villagers that he would write to the Chief Executive Officer and other officials and do whatever was possible. He also said he would send an engineer and his private secretary to visit the spot to see if anything could be done. The villagers returned full of hope and confidence.

The next day the engineer and the Minister's secretary visited the area. They later informed the secretary of Agency B that it was not possible to leave any major portion of the land for the villagers. At the same time taking land in another village and leaving the cultivable land in this village was impossible, because such a change would seriously affect the construction programme of the project. They referred, however, to a small block of land on one side of the project which would not be used immediately.

The villagers heard nothing for the next seven days. They were getting impatient as the time for ploughing the land was fast slipping away. They wanted a quick decision. During this period the villagers were informed that the crops on the side of the road should be harvested within the next 24 hours.

Village Meeting

Narain Singh and Tara Chand thought it was better to meet the Chief Minister before doing anything. Tara Chand suggested that they should start ploughing the land and in case of resistance should offer *satyagraha* and get arrested. Narain Singh thought it would be better to have a village meeting at which to decide on the next step. It was evident at the meeting that the villagers had become desperate. It was decided that they should see the concerned Minister first and ask with reference to their earlier meeting, his final decision.

They met him in the evening and were told that there was no need for them to have come after such a short interval. He had written to the Chief Executive Officer and others who would have to decide the whole matter as the land had been acquired through them. The villagers numbering about 25 (including two women) went from there to the residence of the Chief Executive Officer of Project X, who received their application and said he would look into the matter.

During this period Agency B had written to the Chief Minister and the Chief Executive Officer explaining the whole situation and asking for a sympathetic consideration of the case. In reply to this letter the Chief Executive Officer wrote that a reply had been sent to the Minister. He also said that in early deliberations concerning Project X attention was drawn to the fact that the land was cultivated and that its acquisition would cause difficulties to the cultivators.

Land for Tillers

In reply to the proposal of the general secretary to acquire land on the other side of the village for distributing among the displaced persons, the Chief Executive Officer stated that such an acquisition was not possible under the Land Acquisition Act of 1894, which provided for the payment of compensation in cash only. He also asserted that he was exploring the possibilities of any other way in which land could be given to the cultivators. He said the Project X authorities had themselves sought to change the location of the project in order to leave cultivated land untouched, but they found that no such change was possible.

Villagers Held

Mr. Mansukh wrote to yet another government official explaining the problem and asking for his consideration. He received a reply to provide a detailed account of the whole problem and the various stages through which it had passed.

The villagers began to cultivate the land, though some among them were taken into police custody for this. The district board chief warned the police officials not to harass the villagers as they had permission to cultivate the land which was not under present project construction.

Orders

The letter received by the villagers informed them:

(i) that about 200 *bighas* of land would be given back to the villagers,
(ii) that orders has been issued that the police would be removed from the place,
(iii) that the villagers would be allowed to use the land only up to April, after which they would have to vacate it,
(iv) that they should try for compensation through the Controller for Compensation.

Long Struggle

The villagers met the Controller in connection with the land acquired by Project X. For this he suggested that an application be made and gave some hope that he would help them. He also visited the village. The villagers sent an application along with the names of the villagers who were ready to work as peons and labourers on the project. Their request was granted, and they were given preference in the recruitment of peons and labourers for the project.

After about three years' struggle the villagers succeeded in getting work on the project and checking that the entire compensation did not go to the landlord. They had to fight in the court to get the compensation as they were owners of the land according to recent land reforms, but the landlords had manipulated the deal in such a way that all compensation money had been ordered to be given to them.

Schemes Needed

An experience such as this makes people apathetic and indifferent to development works in the national interest. Land acquisition work should proceed in such a way that it does not disturb and destroy communities. All acquisition cases should have detailed schemes of rehabilitation of the displaced persons including their training and absorption in the newly started development projects. The social worker was very much struck by the suggestion of one villager that they should have some shares in the new industries, housing colonies, etc., to ensure regular and continuous income. They should also get proper counsel in regard to investment of their money, either by organising co-operative societies or individual enterprises which they could easily handle. In the absence of such thoughtful schemes a large number of people have to pay a heavy price for our unplanned acquisition of land and developmental activities.

10

APPROACHES TO DEVELOPMENT

R.P. MISRA

JUST FOURTY years ago, all those who mattered in development — politicians, academics and planners — appeared to know what development meant and how to achieve it. There was a mood of confidence, assurance and urgency. There were instant solutions — decolonisation, economic aid, industrialisation. There were theories and strategies galore — often contradicting each other, yet accepted ungrudgingly as they were the products of some of the most brilliant minds of the time. The West was the model of development: where else could development theories come from!

Today, 30 years later, the success euphoria of the past has given place to despondency, confusion and stalemate. The developers are still there, and so are the development theorists and planners. But they all concede that development is not as easy as they thought it to be and that there is no panacea for underdevelopment. It is realised that the road to development is tortuous; that development is not economic growth alone, and that many of the issues which were debated in the past were not the real issue when seen in the light of the problems being faced by the less-developed countries (LDCs) today.

This chapter reviews the progressive shifts in development paradigms, examines the relevance of the major development debates of the past three decades and underlines forces and issues which would shape, direct and dominate the development scene in the coming decades.

The Changing Meaning of Development

Man sees God in his own image. And so it is with development. As

God means different things to different people, so also the meaning of development differ from man to man. It is person-specific, situation-specific and time-specific. Yet, like the concept of God, the concept of development also transcends these specificities. There is something universal about it which is subsumed in or hidden behind the mundane meanings it acquires in day-to-day life. It is this universality which is now emerging as the main current of development thinking. The increasing realisation that there is something amiss somewhere is nagging us all, and hence the growing criticism of the development style of the past.

Development is not a recent phenomenon. It has always been there. Humanity would not have reached the present stage, had there been no development. It is the conscious and institutionalised attempt at societal development, that is, planned development, that is the unique phenomenon of the 20th century. It started in the U.S.S.R. in 1917, bred contempt for planning in the market economies in the '20s and '30s became an accepted norm during the World War II, and acquired universal appeal in much of Asia, Africa and Latin America in the post-War period. The history of planned development is not only short but also riddled with crises — revolutions, depressions, wars, anti-colonial struggles, famines, floods and what not. There was neither time nor the opportunity to understand what development meant in the real sense.

Development as promoted during the past 50 years or so was the product of European economic history of the past two centuries. The meaning it acquired was, therefore, biased in favour of West European and American styles of industrialisation. More goods and more income became the major indicators of development. The theories and models which emerged from this were, therefore, partial and relevant to a given context. There is no general theory of development, as the transcendental or universal meaning of development never received the attention it ought to have.

The Real Meaning of Development

As a transcendental concept development is a human enterprise. It is a meta-disciplinary phenomenon; an ideology by itself. Since it is a human enterprise, it is culture-specific in content and manifestation. It implies organic change. Its aim is to foster a rich life as defined by a given culture. Thus, development is an *increasing attainment of one's own cultural values.* This conceptualisation emphasises the following notions. First, that development is a process, not a state. Secondly, that process ultimately refers to values, and third, that the values referred to are those of the people involved, not the values of the Western world[1] or any other world.

Among the elements of a good or rich life, the following have been stressed by various scholars in one form or the other:[2]

(a) more and better life-sustaining goods for all;
(b) respect for others and self-esteem;
(c) freedom from tyranny of any kind; and
(d) community life which gives a sense of belonging.

The above four elements are inseparable from each other. For example, if the first is achieved at the cost of the remaining three, the process could not be called development. There are two important derivative conclusions of this which should be stated here. First, the economic growth or technological progress that has been achieved during the past hundred years or so need not be considered satanic. It is its use which is satanic and anti-development. And, second, everything that is traditional should not be construed as good and development (there is a growing tendency in the developing countries to search for identity in past structures and institutions). For example, most religions in their practical forms have tended to insulate their followers from other views and have perpetrated some of the worst tyrannies on man. Instead of freeing man they put him in bondage. And all this in the name of God and religion.

Real development neither supports the tyranny of the robot nor the tyranny of the 'God'. It upholds the supremacy of man as a member of the human community and aims at promoting his welfare by way of creating conditions in which his mental, spiritual and physical potential can be realised to the best advantage of the society as a whole.

The Derived Meaning of Development

We, both individually and as a group, derive our own meaning of development usually as a conditioned response to the immediate and apparent needs and problems. These responses differ from country to country and individual to individual. Let us examine the national responses first.

Western industrialised countries started searching for a new meaning of development when they realised that (i) the task of economic emancipation of the whole of Asia, Africa and Latin America was too big in relation to their own willingness to give back to the former colonies at least part of what was received by them earlier; (ii) rapid economic development could pose a serious threat to their own economics sooner or later; (iii) development was inextricably linked with politics and should, therefore, be part of the game of international politics.

As discussed in the last section of this chapter, the economic prosperity of developed countries is largely based on poverty and helplessness of the developing countries. It stems from the dominance of one group of nations by another group and the conscious attempt to sustain and maintain this relationship. In the early stages (1945-55), there was a tremendous fund of sympathy for the developing countries in the developed parts of the world. It partly arose from a sense of guilt — for having left the colonies in utter poverty after over a century of rule. There was also a confidence in the Western concept of development and its universal applicability. The sympathy and guilt were no more there by 1955, and confidence in the model was lost by 1965.

Even food aid became a tool in the hands of the developed countries to bring the 'rebellious' developing countries to their knees. And it continues to be so until now.

Soon development became a political phenomenon in both developed and developing countries. Its meaning was distorted. Developing countries in utter desperation started seeing it "as a means-end nexus, and not as a human enterprise", it was "equated with the choice of one or another ideology of change", and was "conceived as an alternative to traditional society".[3]

This new meaning emerged from the realisation that the only way to combat backwardness was to follow the path of developed countries — a path which was well laid out and was familiar! During the pre-independence period development was used as a political tool to win freedom, and subsequently it was uses as a tool to perpetuate the leadership of a given individual or group and to strengthen the State — its power to govern an over-demanding populace. This is what came to be known as national development.

The policies and strategies to promote national development were often a reflection of what the developed countries wanted the developing countries to do. In the 1950s foreign aid and savings were the main instruments of development. Efforts were also made to activate rural communities on the initiative of some of the aid-giving countries, such as the U.S.A. But there was neither a desire to generate development from below, nor inclination to involve people in the development process. The issue of poverty ought to have been central to the development process. But the national government did not go beyond recognising it as a problem whose lasting solution (they thought) lay in a rapid increase in the Gross Domestic Product (GDP).

By the mid-1960s it became clear that high rates of growth did not guarantee the well-being of the poor and marginalised. Further, every part of the country did not benefit equally. Efforts were, therefore, made to locate industries in the backward regions. This gave rise to inclusion of regional dimensions in national development plans and respectability of the new discipline of regional science. Agricultural development was also promoted as a means to spread development more widely. The so-called Green Revolution was the outcome of this strategy.

By the late 1960s, population control became a key issue. When neither the Green Revolution nor population control could reduce poverty and pestilence, then by 1972 came the panacea of Basic Minimum Needs (BMN) which in essence sought priority for consumption over production and distribution over growth. As the 1970s rolled over we stood confused about what development really meant. It was neither growth without distribution nor distribution without growth. It included satisfaction of basic needs, but in a poverty stricken society even the satisfaction of basic needs required economic growth. If it was the welfare of man, which should be the goal of development, then *which man?* If it was the poor man, then development would have to involve a direct attack on poverty. But a direct attack on poverty did not necessarily mean a BMN approach to development. Nor did it mean a zero growth economy.

As the 1980s advanced there was a visible change in the environment for and attitude towards real development. Development was no more equated with growth in GDP. It also meant restructuring of national and international orders to release latent energy dormant in individuals, groups, and nations.

Those nations, groups, and individuals who have benefited from the old order have come to realise that their days are numbered. The violence, disorder and indiscipline that one notices in the developing countries today are the expressions of the resentment felt by the deprived majority. The police and army can postpone the consequences of these expressions but they cannot stop them. The same applies to the international scene. What happened in Iran in the recent past is an indication of what we should expect in the future.

Development, therefore, has a far deeper meaning and purpose than what the economists have been telling us so far. In fact, it is a meta-disciplinary field. It was seen as an economic phenomenon only because the economic aspects — production and consumption — were easier to comprehend. These may very well be the consequences rather than the cause of development. At best they constitute only one segment of the overall development process. Somehow we failed to pay adequate attention to the real problems of development and debated issues which were important as points of debate but trivial indeed as points of development.

Seven Issues which Caught Our Attention

In this section we propose to discuss the pros and cons of those major issues which engaged our attention during the past three decades and shaped development policies and programmes in almost all developing countries. These issues emerged as dichotomies and the debates centred on which of the two options would speed up development. The debates were often carried to the point that they became counter-productive. But each such controversy led to a new controversy — each having its own logic and rationale. It is, however, doubtful whether they guided development in the right direction.

Growth Versus Distribution

The controversy centring on economic growth measured in terms of gross national product or per capita income as against distributive justice and improvement in the quality of life of the people especially the poor is not new. The First Five-Year Plan of India (1950-54), one of the most articulate planning documents produced so far, states:

> Planning must aim both at utilising more effectively the resources, human and material, available to the community, so as to obtain from them a larger output of goods and services, and also at reducing inequalities of income, wealth and opportunity. A programme aiming only at raising output might result in most of the increased

> wealth flowing into the hands of a few, leaving the mass of the people in their present state of poverty. It would thus fail to achieve wider social objectives. On the other hand, a mere re-distribution of existing wealth would impair the well-being of certain sections of society without sensibly improving the lot of the rest. Our programme must, therefore, be two-fold, leading at once to increased productivity and reduction of inequalities.[4]

India was not the only country advocating a two-pronged development strategy. The People's Republic of China and several of the newly independent countries of Africa had similar goals. It was not, however, the course most of these countries ultimately followed. Soon, capital became the strategic variable and the Keynesian model the main instrument of development.[5] The aid-giving countries stressed savings and investment, industrialisation and urbanisation and centralised planning. The economists in the LDCs, many of them fresh from Western universities, echoed these same views. Foreign aid was legitimised on the ground that capital in a poor country was a scarce commodity. One has only to look through the development bibliographies of the 1950s and early '60s to appreciate the importance given to capital and growth measured in terms of GDP.

Growth first and distribution next suited the interests of the ruling elites of the LDCs as it suited the interests of aid-giving countries. Rostow's concept of stages of growth came in handy to both.[6] All, including the poor, were exhorted to join hands to let the economy take off the ground. Once the growth engine started moving, everyone's interests could be taken care of. What was needed was production and more production. The 'invisible hand' would take care of the distributive aspects in the long run.

Rostow not only gave a linear and deterministic view of the development process but also let loose a smoke-screen which diverted attention to rather unimportant issues. The question of social justice and the upliftment of the poor, and the issues concerning quality of life were almost lost in the wilderness. The issues for debate, were: balanced versus unbalanced growth: agriculture versus industry; diffusion of innovations; models of economic growth and so on. The celebrated Keynesian model was revised, updated, expanded and enlarged by Western (Harrod and Domar) and Eastern (Mahalanobis) economists alike.[7,8]

There were dissenting voices here and there but the growth

economists carried the day.

The disenchantment with the capital-oriented growth model started emerging rather prominently by the late '60s and became quite vocal by the mid-'70s. Country after country realised that the development course followed by them did not make any major dent in the quality of life for the majority of their people, and that it was impossible to get aid without political strings. The dependency theory explained how neo-colonialism was throttling the development process. Aid came to be treated as a means in the hands of former colonial powers and their allies to keep the developing countries under their thumb.

As the debate on these issues intensified, a new approach to development came to the surface, that is the (BMN).[9] Arguments in favour of this approach ran something like this: If development means the improved welfare of the people, especially the poor, it should be directed towards meeting the basic needs such as food, clothing, shelter, education, health and so on of the people on a priority basis. Instead of investing resources in industries which produce armaments, electric motors, tractors, we should use labour intensive technology which employs more hands. All this would also mean a change in production patterns ownership of the means of production, and access to resources and employment. The rural areas where the majority of the poor lived would, therefore, get more attention and so on.

The BMN approach started with a bang. It became the main topic of discussion in international meetings and conferences in the 1970s. The market was flooded with literature on the subject, but it could not get the currency it was expected to as a substitute to GDP-oriented development planning. The LDCs refused to toe the basic needs line. Meeting the basic needs, it was argued, was indeed important but it could not be accepted as a development model. Many critics considered it another fad created by the West to divert the attention of the developing countries from the real issues of development. It was charged that the developed countries did not want the developing countries to acquire the economic and military strength which could match their own and hence they wanted them to divert their energies exclusively to food, clothing, shelter and social services.

The idea that the welfare of the people should be the goal of development needs no defence. It is good that many governments and scholars from the developed world are concerned about growing poverty in the developing world. In fact they should be equally concerned with increasing poverty and marginalisation in their own countries because the processes which keep a section of the people poor are the same, both in developed and developing countries. What is difficult to comprehend is the overemphasis laid on the BMN. One is tempted to ask:

1. Is there a proof to demonstrate that poverty has increased in the developing countries mainly because of undue attention to capital accumulation, industrialisation and so on.
2. Does the BMN approach offer a durable solution to the poverty syndrome?
3. How can a country sustain the BMN style of development without accelerated economic growth?
4. What would the developed countries do when the developing countries exclusively concentrate on satisfying the BMN?

It is hard to prove that poverty has increased in the LDCs first because enough emphasis was not laid on the BMN. In fact if India had not developed a strong industrial base, there would have been more poverty both in absolute and relative terms. To grow food, India needed fertilisers, steel, irrigation and agricultural research. All these needed a strong industrial base. Both the Republics of Korea and Taiwan were able to remove poverty only because of industrialisation. The political and social problems, emanating largely from the large-scale penetration of capital from abroad, was the price they paid. And the countries which refused to pay this price did not grow that fast and had to live with the 'gift' of poverty which the 'Western Democracies' gave them during the colonial era!

One of the major problems that developing countries are facing today is the shaky foundation of their Statehood. International geopolitics is in full play to de-stablise these countries. The memories of the colonial days are still fresh in the minds of the elites who rule the developing countries today. The BMN could not be the main arm to protect this hard-won freedom. It is only one of the several arms. Maybe it ought to be further strengthened but there can be nothing like the BMN approach to development, BMN can be only a component of development which needs priority rating.

The facts show that the GDP of most developing countries has grown only at a snail's pace during the past three decades leading to greater poverty and pauperisation. The developing countries, therefore, need rapid economic growth as they need equally rapid social transformation. They have to create a strong industrial and technological base to protect themselves and to develop their latent resources. While doing this they have to lay adequate emphasis on equity and justice to ensure rapid improvement in the economic and social well-being of the poor. This is possible neither by pursuing a purely growth-oriented nor by a purely BMN-oriented development strategy.

The time has, therefore, come to close this fruitless debate on what should come first: GDP or basic needs. Both have to go hand-in-hand. The emphasis need not be equal. Much depends on specific circumstances and needs. Development processes in the 1980s do not offer such clear-cut choices. It is the judicious blending of the GDP and BMN that is the need of the time and each country will have to find its own blend. As rightly noted by Haq: "It is time to stand economic theory on its head, since a rising growth rate is no guarantee against worsening poverty . . . Divorce between production and distribution policies is false and dangerous: the distribution policies must be built into the very pattern and organisation of production".

Agriculture Versus Industry

The debate on what should come first — agriculture or industry — is not new. It was a major development issue in the 1950s and 1960s. The developed countries emphasised agriculture on the plea that most developing countries had shortages of food which were likely to increase with increasing population. The logic presented was something like this: The majority of the people of the developing countries are engaged in agriculture and allied activities. And hence they are better trained for agricultural pursuits. Additional investment leading to more productivity in this sector would naturally increase the earning capacities of the majority of the people. Moreover it would save and increase needed foreign exchange which could be utilised for developing other sectors. Foreign aid could provide the technical knowhow and other requirements to boost agricultural production. The past experience of the developed countries also indicated that agricultural development *must* precede industrial development.[10]

As against this, the opposite view gave primacy to industrialisation. Here again the basis was the experience of the developed countries. It was the industrial revolution that changed the face of Europe, the U.S.A. and fate of Japan. Hence the developing countries should also follow that path. There was not much concern about the style of industrial development. Everyone appeared to be convinced that the road to industrialisation could be no different from the one followed by developed countries. All that was needed were massive investments in basic industries, power, projects, machine tool industries and so on. The resources for investment could be mobilised through savings (Keynesian model) and wherever there were shortfalls, foreign aid on a massive scale (e.g., the Marshal Pan) could be resorted to.

The above controversy was closely tied to the debate concerning balanced versus unbalanced growth.[11] It was argued that growth impulses could be successfully generated only in some leading sectors of a nation's economy. The lagging sectors took time to catch up. And hence the major investment should go to those sectors which showed a higher capital output ratio. Additional resources generated from these leading sectors could be used to uplift the lagging sectors in due course.

The counter-argument was that in a developing economy only a few sectors where able to absorb modern technology. If much of the resources were diverted to them, the remaining sectors which formed the major component of the national economy would act like millstones around the necks of the leading sectors. Moreover, all sectors of the economy were so interlinked and interdependent that it would be difficult to life one sector up, neglecting the others. And hence the need for a balanced growth policy.

The controversy centring on balanced versus unbalanced growth was extended to spatial spheres also. One group advocated a spatially selective investment pattern while the other, a spatially balanced pattern. The advocates of concentrated development found the growth pole theory a handy tool to rationalise their stand.[12] The growth pole theory became the rallying point for many of the growth economists, and almost every developing country opted for the growth pole approach to industrial development during the 1960s.

The adherents of the growth pole theory and industrial fundamentalism were convinced that development was essentially spotty. It could not be started everywhere, given the limitations of resources, and hence must be promoted in selected sectors and places. In the course of time the growth impulses could move to the remaining sectors and areas leading ultimately to the development of all the sectors and regions. They depended on what is popularly known as the trickle-down process of development.

The so-called Kuznet's hypothesis suggesting that in the initial stages of development income disparities between the rich and the poor would increase but, in the long run, decrease provided the rationale for concentrated development.[13] The message was that the poor must endure the growing pains of development and accept increasing poverty in the hope that, in the ultimate analysis, their incomes were bound to rise. In the short run there was nothing that anyone could do about them!

Irrespective of the arguments advanced, experience shows that neither the so-called balanced nor the unbalanced approach could be used by any developing country as a matter of principle without further accentuating its development problems. That classical economics cannot offer solutions for non-classical development problems was realised only after the damage was already done to quite a few national economies. The developing countries needed both the approaches depending on the specificity of circumstances. None of these, either singly or jointly, could be adopted as a matter of principle because there is nothing like a single development situation in the world. The relative importance given to a particular sector, region or group must change through time. It would, therefore, be useful to debate and understand the potentialities of each sector at each stage of development rather than to base judgement on the dogmas discussed above.

Urban Versus Rural Development[14]

The controversy centring on urbanisation as against rural development as the means to achieve development objectives is not new. The debate has two main thrusts, (i) which among the rural and urban styles of life is better for mankind, and (ii) which (urbanisation or rural development) should be the strategy to develop the country.

It is now generally accepted that the old archaic rural environment is not conducive to development. It needs transformation in tune with the current needs and achievements of man. Mahatma Gandhi, the greatest proponent of rural development, did not want Indian villages to remain steeped in traditions. He wanted them to change. He did not like large cities because they did not fit in his holistic and organic scheme of human development. Gandhi wanted total transformation of villages in India not by forcing people to migrate to large cities but by developing them from within into viable units.

The Western concept of economic growth, with urbanisation and industrialisation as its main ingredients, is essentially anti-rural.

Large-scale manufacturing requires large cities which could provide skills and other infrastructures needed for mass production. Urbanisation is, therefore, taken as an indicator of development. The larger the urban component in the national population, the greater the development, so say the development experts.

Most of the developing countries were convinced that urbanisation was the answer to solve their rural problems. Mechanisation of agriculture would release a quasi-employed rural labour force which would be pulled by expanding industries in large urban centre. New industrial growth poles and centres were created to build additional capacities to absorb labour and to achieve growing demands of other sectors of the economy. The 1950s and early '60s were noted for a vigorous policy of urbanisation and industrialisation.

By the late '60s it became obvious that there were limits to industrial growth. There was neither enough local market for many industrial products, nor were the developed countries prepared to assist developing countries in creating a strong industrial base. Developed countries were prepared to accommodate the needs of the developing countries only so long as such needs did not affect their own interests. The cold war had its own impacts on the amount and direction to which aid would flow. Moreover, it soon became obvious that foreign aid without political strings was difficult to come by.

The disenchantment with past experiences is visible in all developing countries but it is more so in those countries that are predominantly rural and where rapid population growth has cancelled out any marginal increase in the income and earning capacities of the poor. Since a majority of the people of these countries lives in rural areas, there is a growing demand to reinforce rural development processes. In Asia and Africa especially, the need to tailor development strategies to rural development needs is felt more acutely in the rural areas where population growth has or is beginning to exceed the carrying capacity of land and environment; where real wages have been almost stagnant; where socio-economic structural changes have been slow; and where past development efforts have left much of the poor peasantry with diminished access to the means and ends of development.

During the '50s and '60s planners and policy-makers considered rural areas to be transitional; they thought they would disappear as the urban-industrial development process engulfed them. But experience shows that rural areas with their attendant problems are there to stay. There will be more people living in rural areas in A.D. 2000 than in

1980, the current rate of rural emigration notwithstanding. Country after country realised that the answer to the problems of development was not necessarily urbanisation and industrialisation on the pattern of Western countries. It was rather in the self-reliant development process — a process that combines the experience of others with the genius of the local people to make the optimum use of available knowledge, technology and resources.

Starting with the well-known International Labour Office (ILO) study, several other studies of the early '70s pointed to increasing poverty especially among the rural people and the need to focus development towards greater employment, satisfaction of basic needs of people, poverty eradication and so on. Urban and industrial bias in development was blamed for the increased pauperisation of people in the developing countries. It was in this context that rural development acquired added importance. Developing countries were exhorted to embark on massive programmes of rural development and basic needs. The ill-effects of the urban-industrial model of development were magnified to bring home the message of a new approach to development. They were advised to discard the old development orthodoxy in favour of a new one. The interesting part of the story was that many of those who propounded the new orthodox were the same who subscribed to the old one earlier.

This *volte-face* in approach to development raises quite a few questions. Is it possible to develop rural areas without urbanisation and urban areas without rural development? Is there any country in the world which has developed relying solely either on urban or rural development? Are poverty and underdevelopment divisible in clear-cut rural and urban components? If the answer to these is no, then the problem has to be posed differently. The issue is not which to develop first, rural or urban areas; it is rather how to develop both in order to meet various national, regional and local needs. As stated earlier, most developing countries are still in the process of consolidating their newly acquired independence: they have yet to become cohesive nation States. Many of the large urban centres become rallying points for entrepreneurs to work together to provide an economic base on which a poor country can develop. In between these, few large urban centres and a large number of rural settlements, are small and intermediate towns which offer a quality of life which is no better than that found in rural areas. These towns bridge the socio-economic gap between small villages and large urban centres. It is wrong, therefore, to say that there is urban bias in development policy. If there is any bias it is in favour of a particular pattern. It is clear that a large chunk of the rural population in developing countries will continue to live there in the foreseeable future. Urbanisation cannot absorb them because modern industries cannot employ so many people and the informal sector of the urban economy has its own limitations. The only way to raise the standard of living of the rural population is, therefore, rural development, through increased productivity of agriculture and related activities and a more organic link between rural and urban functions.

In fact the whole development process should be so articulated that urbanisation should promote rural development and rural development should back up urban development. The merging of the two processes should lead to a kind of situation in which the gap between urban and rural areas in terms of income, productivity, social services and quality of life in general is substantially narrowed. It is the task of the developing countries to promote the kind of urban-rural transformation described above and to avoid a dichotomous development of the two sectors advocated by urban and rural fundamentalists.

Capital Versus Labour Intensive Technologies

Whether the developing countries should opt for modern technology or should rely on 'appropriate' technology is another major point of debate. There are those who want developing countries to skip over technological research and development by acquiring the latest technology from developed countries. They point to the advantages of being late-comers in the race for development. These advantages, they say, should be capitalised to the maximum extent.[15]

On the other side of the spectrum are those who want technology to fit the available human skills. They want developing countries to use appropriate technology which, in the context of "unskilled, illiterate and poverty-stricken population", means simple tools—bullock-cart, improved plough, hand-pump and so on. For them small is beautiful and large is ugly.[16] Such people want to promote simple living and high thinking—village life, agriculture, cottage and small-scale industries, and so on.

A third group of people would like the developing countries to acquire advanced scientific and technical knowledge, but not the most advanced machines.[17] They want the developing countries to use this knowledge to develop machines most appropriate to the skills and needs of the people. For example, the advanced principles of physics could be used to improve bullock-carts, windmills, water-lifting devices and so on, rather than to manufacture aeroplanes, steel mills, big dams and so on. Improvement in simple machines, they say, requires advanced scientific knowledge. Why not apply this knowledge, then, to those things which benefit the people directly and immediately?

None of these appear to stand the logic of realities and emergent needs of the developing societies. To survive as nation States, the LDCs must have access to the latest technological know-how necessary for harnessing their latent resources. But in order that the poor and illiterate who form a majority participate actively in the nation-building process, they should not only tolerate but also promote and improve traditional technologies.

It is not so easy to leapfrog the technological gap as it is made out by some. To leapfrog a society needs an adequate pool of scientists, technicians and engineers. And none of these can be produced readily without a sound technological base. It almost amounts to saying that one could jump from primary school to a Ph.D. course because the intervening knowledge is already available in published form. Developing countries have to create a good foundation for science and technology through institutions of scientific research and development. Collaboration among developing countries in this respect is an urgent need in order to bridge the growing technological gap between the developed and developing countries.

To say that developing countries should concentrate and rely solely on traditional small-scale technologies is to deny them the human achievements of the past several countries. It also amounts to closing the door for innovative faculties of man to grow and flourish. Small is beautiful, but only when it is seen in the light of the so-called ugly big. Is everything 'big' ugly? Even a country such as China which developed a cult of 'traditional technology' had to abandon it in favour of a more balanced approach wherein the choice is dictated by need and not by dogma.

The dualistic, social, economic and technological structures in the developing countries keep a large section of population beyond the reach of modern technology. It is important that traditional technology is promoted for their benefit. That, however, does not mean that modern technology should be neglected. Technology is not a static phenomenon; it is something which is always evolving. The new technology, about which many have objections, is part of the achievement of man. We should not try to throw it away. We should make use of it for the benefit of man.

Some critics of modern technology quote Mao's dictum of "walking on two legs". It is true that to walk, we should have two legs. But how long should the inhabitants of developing countries continue to walk while others drive and fly. Let us not condemn them to walking forever. Let them start running and then driving and then flying. Let them benefit from the achievements of humanity. This cannot happen if the LDCs rely too heavily on traditional technologies. The question that should guide their policy in this regard is: which of the two is better for which activity and in which context? It is not the question of either this or that; it is rather the question of which one and for which purpose and situation? If our objective is to generate mass employment, we should use labour-intensive technologies. But let us not make a fetish of it and say that labour intensive technology is good for the developing countries. When we want to build a weather satellite, we should use capital-intensive technology. We should not reject it because it does not provide employment for the masses.

Allied to the controversy regarding technology is the issue of 'size'. What should be the scale of development projects? Some people think it should be large; there are others who think large projects are too expensive—they require long gestation periods and are not efficient in terms of returns on investment. They prefer small-scale projects.

Here again it appears that the controversy is based on an unrealistic assessment of the problems of developing countries. It should be realised that there is a lot to be done in these countries to harness latent resources. Large rivers have to be dammed, small rivers have to be tamed, bore wells, masonry wells, irrigation tanks, canals have to be constructed to develop water resources. To harness the irrigation potentials of a river, one needs a big dam. At the same time, to harness underground water resources, one need not have big projects. Take the case of steel manufacturing. If iron ore resources are available, a developing country should develop an iron and steel industry even if steel can be imported cheaply from developed countries. The industry cannot depend on backyard furnaces; it has to have large-scale mill. Blacksmithy can, however, be done in every village. Similarly, an electronics industry can be operated in small units. In the context of the developing countries we need both large and small-scale projects. Which project should be undertaken and where, depends on specific situations and needs.

A balanced and pragmatic approach is necessary. The question really is nct whether to opt for large-scale or for small-scale projects. It is rather where and when to have large-scale and where and when the small-scale ones. Which gives greater benefit to the people? It is the need and capacity which should determine the choice, rather than fads such as 'large is economic' and 'small is beautiful'.

Centralisation versus De-centralisation

To what extent should be the central authorities in a developing country control the economy and polity has been the subject of discussion for quite some time. The general tendency in most developing countries is to centralise the power of decision-making. The advocates of de-centralisation are, however, unconvinced of this, and would like a structure wherein the central authority has only a limited role to play.

It is often said that centralisation weakens popular participation which is an indispensable element of development. In the ultimate analysis, development means the development of people—which in effect means enhancement of their ability to make the right decision at the right time and to shape their own future in the light of their enlightened understanding of their environment. None of these could be achieved so long as decisions on matters concerning them are taken by a super agency from above. A de-centralised system which allows participatory development from below is, therefore, a must for a healthy society.

Governments in some countries contend that their people are not yet prepared to shoulder responsibilities of development. The concepts of guided democracy and limited franchise have emerged from this contention. Then there are those who would like to de-centralise everything here and now. They envisage a government which would emerge from 'active communities' at the grassroots level.

The tendency to make central authorities strong is visible all over the work—both in developed and developing countries. This is, to some extent, because national States have not yet matured. Many national States or even civilisations have withered away in the past only because the central authorities were weak. At a time when Europe was moving towards the concept of national States—in the mid-16th century—India had a mature national State under Akbar the Great. As the central authority of his empire weakened (mainly because it lost touch with the nation's socio-economic realities) a small band of traders and militiamen were ables to colonise the country. These lessons are not yet forgotten by India. Several other developing countries had similar experiences. It may take more time for the fears emanating from these experiences to wither away. Much depends on the progress that the countries make towards a new international order.

Those who advocate a de-centralised government structure based on local communities are unrealistic in many ways. In the first place they think of an ideal system of government in which the people are supreme without defining who the people are. Like Plato's Republic their village/community republics are good in concepts but beyond the realm of the present-day realities. Second the advocates of the de-centralised system often prescribe it for developing countries as if the economically developed countries do not need it. For example, Friedmann's agropolis is meant for Asian countries; it is extendable to Africa and perhaps to Latin America but not to Europe and Anglo-America. Why should Friedmann's own country not try it first? If USA cannot return to village communities, how can the developing countries return to them? The loss of community in the industrialised world should not be sought to be compensated for by the loss of polity in the Third World countries.

Centralisation in autarchic forms is bad and so is de-centralisation in anarchic forms. Neither of them is conducive to the growth of a living society. What we need is a judicious blending of the two. It is rather unimaginative to call for complete de-centralisation when national boundaries are still in the early stages of consolidation. Only developed countries are in a position to de-centralise the governance system and show the way. But they prefer to commend it to the developing countries, for developed countries have reached a stage where no structural changes are necessary!

It is equally unimaginative and native to declare that people are not yet ready to shoulder responsibilities and hence a centralised oppressive system of government is a must. Responsible people are not born, they are the product of the social system in which they are brought up. You cannot expect people to behave responsibly in an irresponsible governance system. Responsible citizenry is the product of a responsible society which cannot be created in a day. It has to be consistently nurtured and maintained. Passing on the responsibilities to people to govern themselves is one of the surest ways of creating such a society. People must commit mistakes and learn lessons. They must form the supporting pillars of national reconstruction. Each country must, therefore, try hard to seek that dynamic balance between centralisation and de-centralisation at each stage of development.

"Development from above or below" is another version of this controversy.[19] The inability of most developing countries to generate rapid enough growth, to remove mass poverty, led many a theorist to believe that it was because of the failure of central or top-down planning and development. In fact, as in the case of other theories and approaches, the tendency has been to concentrate on those apparent causes and factors which could put blame on the shoulders of the developing countries. Until very recently most Western theorists refused to go into the fundamental causes. The continuing accusation that central planning or top-down development process is the main culprit responsible for increasing poverty in the developing countries is born out of this reluctance.

Those who are opposed to development from above would like the developing countries to initiate development from below. This reversal of the development gear will help (i) meet the basic needs of the people, (ii) ensure popular participation in development and (iii) mobilise the material and human resources for development on a voluntary basis. Central planning and development from above are processes which treat human beings as statistical units and concentrate on those issues and problems which are of national importance, often ignoring or de-emphasising those which we faced by the people.

While there is some merit in what the critics of central planning and development from above have to say, their perception of the problem is unrealistic. Development is a complex process—it is a process of societal change. It is multi-directional and must work upwards, downwards and sidewards simultaneously. It is not a question of bottom-up versus top-down. Nor the question of a judicious blending of the two to meet the challenges faced by developing societies. Neither of them can be used in utter disregard of the other, without further complicating developmental problems. Development is a task which can be accomplished well only when it pervades all aspects and levels of a society. It has to initiated not only from above and below but also at all intermediate levels.

Modern versus Traditional[20]

Yet another controversy figuring in the development debate centres on modern versus traditional dualism. One stream of thought considers development as a process by which traditional thoughts and structures are replaced by the modern ones, while the other attempts to take back the developing societies to their distant past and abhors modernity. One considers traditionalism to be the main cause of underdevelopment while the other blames modernity as the root cause of all evils including poverty in the developing countries.

'Tradition' is often associated with something old and irrelevant to modern society — something which is inward-looking and which retards progress. 'Modernity' is anti-traditional, outward-looking and changing. In common parlance it is Western and conducive to development. Modernisation and Westernisation are often considered synonymous. As a consequence when a traditional mode is adopted by the West, it becomes modern. For example, breast-feeding was considered bad in the West until about 1960. Mothers in developing countries also switched over to bottle-feeding. It became a sign of backwardness. But the moment the Western women started switching back to breast-feeding, it became a modern practice in the less-developed countries too. Another interesting example. Topless dress worn by tribal women was considered traditional; but the same dress worn by Western women is modern. Nudity is traditional in the virgin forests but modern on the polluted beaches.

It is rarely realised that modernity cannot be divorced from tradition — in fact it does not exist outside it. Real modernisation is based on tradition — it means no more than the transformation of whatever is old in the light of the progress that the society has made through time. Modernisation is therefore, 'being' — it is something that is always happening. It does not come from somewhere; it emerges from within response to a changing environment. Copying something is just imitation — it does not modernisation. It is true that modernisation does involve replacement of old by new. The emerging new does not have the same meaning everywhere. Underlying the apparent physical semblance there exist different, at times even contrasting, meanings, ethos and motifs.

Until very recently the prevailing mood in the developing countries was anti-traditional. Anything old or traditional was considered bad and antiquated, something to be done away with in order that the modernisation could set in 'Western' was modern. It represented industrialisation, high income, high levels of skill and education, individual freedom and an equally high level of 'culture'. Western classics, Western music, Western art, Western mores of life and living came to be admired and anything local and traditional came to be despised. Everything was evaluated by Western standards.

The mood has, however, started to change. Realising that to acquire Western culture in its true sense was not possible without being born and brought up in that culture, and that everything Western was not necessarily good, a tendency to look into one's own culture for guidance started gaining ground. Some groups have turned obscurantist and are trying to bring back the medieval era in the 1980s. Many others are still in the process of search, and some have started thinking of a new society based on their own values and traditions fitted to the needs of the 21st century man. Such people neither accept the superiority of the West, nor the inferiority of the cultures of the rest of the world. They are looking for whatever is good and enduring in both so that the West can enrich itself with the wisdom of the East and the East can benefit from the knowledge of the West.

The time has come for the developing countries to stop admiring everything that comes from the West. They should look back to their own cultural heritage and try to strike a synthesis which helps them meet the challenges of the 20th century.To blindly copy the West is dangerous but to attempt to re-enact the medieval life is not only futile but also catastrophic. To look back to one's own culture for guidance does not mean the culture as it originated. They very term culture means some thing which has been cultivated through time. To be insensitive to time is to be insensitive to one's own future.

Socio-Economic versus Physical Planning[21]

The last of the seven major debates pertains to development planning. The planning profession suffers from a schism which continues to widen. Not too long ago, physical planners called themselves real planners. They knew something of civil engineering, architecture and infrastructure planning, a little bit of economics and government, a little less of sociology and political science and very little of the people for whom they planned. They had a set formulate for resolving various problems irrespective of locale and people. In fact their main job was to prescribe to the people how they ought to live and to see that those who broke the rules were punished, sometimes summarily.

These 'planners' formed associations such as the Institutes of Town Planners, Association of Planners, Institutes of Environmental Planners and so on One of the sole objectives, even though unwritten, of these associations was to keep the entry to the club limited to their own 'species'. In countries such as Canada and India, and may be elsewhere too, there was a move to debar anyone calling himself a planner unless he had a planning degree from a school of (physical) planning.

With the post-Second World War resurgence of economic planning, as the chief vehicle of national development, physical planning lost its original importance. It became part of a much broader system whose main task was to transform the socio-economic life of millions of deprived people through means which were far beyond the scope of physical planning. Economists, who were the leading figures in this task, did not deny the significant role physical planners could play in their own spheres, such as housing, site planning, construction and so on, but they refused to accept their leadership in policy formulation and overall planning. the Russian experience of central planning and the post-Second World War role of economists in resolving national recovery problems boosted their morale; it is now the economists who are responsible for national planning.

The physical planner was also challenged by the development administrator. Development administrators have the authority and responsibility to get national, regional and local plans implemented. They are, to be fair to them, much closer to people than the physical planner. They now head agencies in charge of urban development, slum improvement, water supply, electricity and so on which earlier used to be within the exclusive domain of physical planning. It happened because the physical planner was trained neither in policy nor in the management sciences.

The neglect of spatial dimensions in the development process by economists and physical planners alike led to the birth of Regional Science which had the precision of physical planning and analytical ability of economics. It brought revolutionary changes in almost all social and planning sciences. It tried to quantify everything and a belief that anything that was not quantifiable was also not worth studying was set in motion. It provided the tools to State problems and their solutions more clearly. At the same time it produced a plethora of literature some of which contributed almost nothing to the understanding of development problems.

Regional Science is deeply rooted in classical economics. Its mathematical solutions to regional problems were found by disaggregating the national economy. Regional Science, because of its quantitative bias, was not very sensitive to human development issues. Its emphasis that national income should also be seen in regional terms, to ensure a more equitable distribution, did focus the attention of planners to distributive issues, but it did not go far enough.

Regional Science did not take root in developing countries, the vigorous promotional efforts of Walter Isard notwithstanding. It caught the attention of a few academies who were trained in mathematical economics, geography and statistics. Others ignored it either because they did not understand it (ignorance breeds contempt) or because it fell short of the planning needs of the developing countries. Regional Science now stands cut into pieces and amalgamated with geography, economics, applied statistics and urban planning to give rise to a new discipline called regional development planning.

Until very recently, regional planning was another name for comprehensive urban planning. It meant urban (physical) planning in a regional frame-work. The impact of national economic planning and management sciences has now made it a discipline which can weave various planning and management sciences together to produce a synthesis most conducive to the evolution of a unified planning discipline.

Until we reach that stage, the fruitless controversy centring on physical versus economic planning continues. There are planners who know economics and nothing more; and there are physical planners who know architecture/civil engineering and nothing more. Both have done a lot of damage to the fields of planning and development. The type of planner, we produce today, is too much of an ethno-centric professional more concerned with his profession than with the people. In fact, he is not part of the people; he is beyond them. He understands only a segment of the development process but he blissfully thinks that he knows everything.

We do need physical planners as we do need economic, social and other types of planners, but of a different breed. Our needs have changed in quality more than in quantity in the recent past. Now we need planners who can work with the people and not for the people. Development is not something which can be given; it is to be acquired and worked for by those who are to benefit from it. A planner should understand what the people's needs are, what is the direction in which the society is moving, what the national priorities are and how the resources — physical and human — should be used to achieve the set development goals and objectives.

Viewed from this perspective there is hardly any scope for dichotomy between physical and economic planning. Both are needed and they must have well-defined tasks. In fact, planning as a field goes far beyond economic and physical planning. It is the absence of these other disciplines which made the planning profession barren and static.

Issues which Escaped Our Attention

In this section an attempt is made to identify those major issues of development which ought to receive priority attention from the very start of development planning. These issues concern all the countries — developing as well as developed — and are real determinants of quantity and quality of development. They constitute the primary issues, a satisfactory resolution of which alone can create conditions for a more humanistic development process in the world. The seven dichotomies discussed earlier are products of these primary institutional problems.

Inequitous International Order

Pattern Problems: Largely for historical reasons, the present international order is tilted in favour of developed countries. The system is so organised that it makes the rich nations richer and the poor ones poorer. The fundamental bases of the present order is the uninterrupted flow of cheap and abundant raw materials and energy resources from the Third World countries to the Western world which has "created an enormously powerful industrial machine".[23] The Third World countries, despite political independence during the past three decades, have remained economically tied to the industrial countries of the West; they are compelled to sell their raw materials and energy resources and, of late, the skills to the industrialised countries for a price determined by international marked mechanism over which they have a little or no control.

As a consequence of this, 53 per cent of the world population, living in least developed countries, shares only 5.6 per cent of the world's GNP (Table 10.1). The per capita income for S-E. Asia in 1913 was estimated to be US $ 65 as against $ 454 for North-West Europe. By 1978 it went up to US $ 7,800 for North-West Europe while for South-East Asia it was less than $ 300 (Table 10.2). During the same period the population of North-West Europe increased by 35.87 per cent as compared to 292.6 per cent of South-East Asia.

The disparities in development between the industrialised countries of the West and the Third World countries is further illustrated in

Table 10.3 which gives per capita energy consumption in different groups of countries. The pattern of distribution of income, population and energy consumption is reflected in resource consumption and sources of GDP.

The share of the manufacturing sector is fairly high in the GDP of the industrialised countries (Table 10.4). This pattern acquires far greater significance when one also sees the share of various groups of countries in foreign trade (Table 10.5) and industrial output. There is a very close relationship between the degree of industrialisation and resource use.

The Persistent Pattern: These inequalities have increased through time in favour of the developed countries. As noted earlier, the differences in the per capita income, for example, between developed and developing countries have further widened in recent years. A few small countries did make some headway but this happened largely because of their special circumstances and relationships *vis-a-vis* the developed countries. They did not set a model of international economic relations which could be adopted by other developing countries.

The developing countries entered the 1950s with a firm belief that political independence coupled with foreign assistance would help them catch up with the industrialised world by the turn of this century. But as years passed by they realised the futility of the hopes they had entertained. Their dependence on the developed countries further increased without any perceptible reduction of the fundamental inequality in economic strength.

TABLE 10.1: **Gross National Product and Population : 1980**

(as percentage)

Region	*GNP*	*Population*
Low-income countries (mixed economies)	3.03	30.47
Low-income countries (China)	2.56	22.42
Middle-income countries (mixed economies)	12.76	20.55
Middle-income countries (centrally-planned economies)*	0.28	0.73
Capital surplus oil-exporting countries**	2.34	1.41
Industrialised countries (market economies)	63.04	15.73
Industrialised countries (centrally-planned economies)	15.99	8.69
Total	100.00	100.00

Note: * Includes Dem. Rep. of Korea, Albania, Cuba and Mongolia.
** Includes Iraq, Iran, Libya, Saudi Arabia and Kuwait.

Source: Derived from Table 1 Basic Indicators. The World Bank. *World Development Report*, 1980.

TABLE 10.2: **Growing Income Disparities : Per Capita Income in Selected Regions**

Region	*1913*		*1957*		*1978*	
	Population (mil)	*Income/capita (US$)*	*Population (mil)*	*Income/capita (US$)*	*Population (mil)*	*Income/capita (US$)*
North America	105	917	188	1,868	245	9,531
N.W. Europe	184	454	211	790	250	7,825
S.E. Asia	323	5	518	67	1,268	296
China	370	50	640	61	952	230
World Population	1,463	—	2,373	—	4,247	2,012

Source: L.J. Zimmerman, *Arme en Rijke Landen* (the Hague 1959) pp. 29-31. Data for 1978 are derived from World Bank. *World Development Report*, 1980. For 1978 figures, S.E. Asia includes all Asian countries east of Afghanistan except Mongolia and Japan and N.W. Europe includes Ireland, U.K., France, the Netherlands, Belgium, Federal Republic of Germany, German Democratic Republic, Austria, Switzerland, Finland, Norway, Sweden and Denmark.

TABLE 10.3: **Per Capita Energy Consumption**

(kg of coal equivalent)

Region	*1960*	*1980*
Low-income countries	98	161
Middle-income countries	395	903
Industrialised countries	4,462	7,060
Capital-surplus oil-exporting countries	404	1,620
Centrally planned economies	1,347	2,117

Source: The World Bank, *World Development Report*, 1980, Table 7 World Development Indicators.

TABLE 10.4: **Distribution of Gross Domestic Product by Sectors, 1978**

(as percentage)

Region	*Agriculture*	*Manufacturing*	*Other Industries*	*Service*
Low-income countries	38	13	11	38
Middle-income countries	16	25	9	50
Industrialised countries	4	27	10	59
Capital-surplus oil-exporting countries	5	8	57	30
Centrally planned economies	—	—	—	—

Source: The World Bank, *World Development Report*, 1980 Table 3 Structure of Production.

TABLE 10.5: **Percentage Shares in World Exports of Goods and Non-factor Services (1977)**

Country group	*Primary commodities*	*Fuel*	*Manufacturers*	*Non-factor services*	*Total*
Developing countries	35.0	24.2	10.1	28.8	20.1
Industrialised countries	55.6	16.0	79.6	67.7	62.9
Other countries	9.4	59.8	10.8	3.5	17.0
Total	100.0	100.0	100.0	100.0	100.0

Source: The World Bank, *World Development Report*, 1980.

They have painfully realised that the so-called free market economy is free only for those who are economically, politically and militarily strong. Their economies are so small that they cannot influence the main currents of the free market system. According to some estimates, the institutional distortions inherent to the system cost the poor nations US $ 50 to US $ 100 billion a year[23] and what the Third World got as aid was more than offset by the reverse transfer of technology. According to the United Nations Conference on Trade and Development (UNCTAD) Secretariat the total aid from the U.S.A., Canada and U.K. to the developing world between 1960 and 1972 amounted to US $ 46.3 billion and the imputed capital value of the skills of technicians who migrated to these countries from developing countries amounted to US $ 50.9 billion.

The inequities in the international system are of tremendous significance. They have given rise to essentially two worlds and the disparities between them are growing. One is the world of the rich, the other the world of the poor, united by its heritage of common suffering. A poverty curtain divides the worlds materially and philosophically. One world is literate, the other largely illiterate; one industrial and urban, the other predominantly agrarian and rural; one consumption-oriented, the other striving for survival. In the rich world, there is concern about the quality of life, in the poor world about life itself which is threatened by disease, hunger and malnutrition. In the rich world there is concern about the conservation of non-renewable resources and literary books written about how the world should be kept in a stationary state. In the poor

> world there is anxiety, not about the depletion of resources, but about their exploitation and distribution for the benefit of all mankind rather than a few privileged nations. While the rich world is concerned about the impact of its pollutive activities on life-support systems, the poor world is concerned by the pollution of poverty, because its problems arise not out of an excess of development and technology but out of the lack of development and technology and inadequate control over natural phenomena.[24]

And there is no possibility of any change in this situation. The terms of trade are almost permanently set in favour of the industrialised world. The possibility of this being partly corrected by foreign aid is no longer there. The share of GNP of Western countries used for foreign aid (much of which is concessional loan) has decreased far below the one per cent level of 1951. Not many industrialised countries have reached the target of even 0.7 per cent of GNP as official development assistance.

Foreign aid has not only become more scarce than before; it is now highly politicised. Countries which question the old order do not qualify for it so easily. They are not expected to produce goods that compete with those produced by the industrialised countries. And if they do, discriminatory trade restrictions are imposed against them. These countries become intruders and enemies of the system. They are challenging the old division of labour established during the colonial ear wherein the Asian, African and Latin American countries produced the fuel and raw materials to keep the factories of the industrialised world running to optimum capacity.

The developing countries have now come tot he conclusion that:

1. The more dependent they are on the developed countries economically, politically and militarily, the lesser the chances of their survival as independent nations.
2. These developed countries are not likely to take kindly to efforts on the part of developing countries to become economically and technologically strong and hence the prospects of massive aid and technology transfers are bleak.
3. The developed countries will not give up their hold on the natural resources of the developing countries except under pressure.
4. The developing countries will always be the losers, so long as

> the rules of the game of international economics remain as they are now.

The New International Economic Order: Given the economic relations as they are, the developing countries saw a scenario of perpetual underdevelopment. They started suspecting anything that came from Western sources as diversionary and started making joint efforts to influence decisions on international, economic and political matters. In fact, the formation of the non-aligned bloc and its popularity in the 1950s was aimed at mobilising the countries for this purpose. They refused to leave decisions on vital issues affecting them to the more developed world. When the First United Nations Conference on Trade and Development (UNCTAD) was held in 1964, the developing countries formed a pressure group called Group of 77 to promote their economic interests. The group questioned the rules of General Agreement on Trade and Tariff (GATT) and asked for reforms in the system of trade, finance and technology. UNCTAD 1964 did not give much to the developing countries. Their proposals faced severe opposition from developed countries but the conference did set in motion a new thinking on international economic relations. A fairly large agenda for reform initiated buy this conference was further expanded and discussed at its subsequent meetings in 1968, 1972, 1976 and 1979. All these gave some marginal benefits to the developing countries, and the dialogue continues.

Encouraged by the achievement, even though small, of united action and also by the success of Organisation of Petroleum Exporting Countries (OPEC) in extracting favourable terms of trade by using 'commodity power', the non-aligned countries at their 1973 Summit Conference in Algiers adopted an action programme calling for a New International Economic Order. This was followed by the United Nations General Assembly in 1974[25] which adopted the Charter of Economic Rights and Duties of member States. It was further refined in the next session (1975) of the UN General Assembly and the concept of the New International Economic Order (NIEO) became a symbol of the next phase of a peaceful struggle of the former colonies to win economic freedom from the stranglehold of the developed countries. The Santiago meeting of Third World Social Scientist (April 1973) declared:

> one of the dominant features of the present day world order is the unequal relationship between the developed and the developing

> countries. The developing countries are poor and weak and, in any international bargaining, they are conveniently ignored or easily squeezed. What the Third World must ask of the international order is protection of its legitimate interests in the trade field, not trade concessions; a genuine transfer of real resources, not the present 'aid' charade; a powerful voice in the shaping of a new monetary system not formal representation in the Group of Twenty.[26]

More specific proposals for the New International Economic Order (NIEO) were made by the Third World Forum Conference held in Karachi in 1975.[27] The Club of Rome carried out a number of studies under the leadership of Tinbergen to further concretise the concept of NIEO and to bring to light the benefits which both developed and developing countries could derive from it.[28]

The issues which confront the demand for NIEO are complex and many. While the developing countries have found a new weapon — collective bargaining — to pressurise the developed countries to concede higher prices for raw materials and to transfer resources by such unconventional means as an international tax on brain-drain or sharing of the profits of seabed mining, fishing and so on, there are increasing objections from developed countries to such concession.[29] Considerable research is needed to evolve new strategies and to formulate feasible proposals. Not many social scientists in the developing world have taken interest in issues such as this. The NIEO is not an issue of confrontation; it is rather an issue of reconciliation.

Semi-feudal National Order

The struggle for freedom and the post-colonial formative years of the new States of Asia and Africa were dominated by the euphoria of socialism, and most of the newly independent countries cast their choice for socialism of one model or another. Most of them opted for a mixed model wherein the commanding heights of the economy were controlled by the government (public sector) while the rest, including agriculture, remained in the hands of private individuals. The criterion for choosing the mixed model was essentially pragmatism — in a country of paupers one cannot practise capitalism with impunity; and it is only the capitalistic drive which can produce wealth in the shortest period of time. There was no time to wait for generations. The mixed economy, however, needed a far better management (including political) system than the low-income economies could afford. Maybe what they got in the process was not the best of socialism and capitalism but rather the worst of the two but the choice they made was perhaps the best they could have under those circumstances.

In the face of serious economic, social and political problems the fundamental principles of both socialism and capitalism receded into the background and much of the energy really went in solving the day-to-day problems of managing the new state. Socialism became a slogan to win elections or to perpetuate the rule of a single individual or group. Its appeal for equality was lost in the exigencies of capitalist production which was the only hope in a hopelessly slow-moving economy.

Almost all developing countries are noted for marked inter-personal, inter-group and inter-regional disparities in income productivity and quality of life. The national economic order is so structured that it is rather hard on the poor. When the developing countries ask for NIEO, the developed countries retort: countries which do not guarantee freedom, equity and justice to their own citizens have no right to ask for an equitable international economic order. There is no denying the fact these disparities do exist. Poverty of the majority along with the affluence of the minority is the rule rather than exception in the developing countries. Many of the greatly publicised structural changes such as land reforms have not gone deep enough to make a major dent in the system.

True freedom does not mean freedom for a particular group to curb the freedom of others in the name of national development.

> There is no true freedom when all powers are concentrated in the hands of a single social class, single race, or a single group, or when the common good is merged with the interests of a single party that is identified with the State or any other group controlling the means of production directly or indirectly.[30]

The tendency in many developing countries to impose the will of the governments which represent only a miniscule constituency — the military, a single community, region or tribe, class or political party — has been on the increase. Dissent is being curbed in the name of national solidarity or an ideology which has been contrived to legitimise the national colonial structure imposed by the ruling classes. Such structures are often marked by intolerance and violence and insentivity to the needs and aspirations of the weaker sections of society. There are enough data to prove that in many countries a small group has usurped much of the available resources leaving the poor high and dry. The fruits of independence and development have gone to this small group of people.

The questions of poverty and inequity have nothing to do with socialism or capitalism. It is a simple social question which has to be faced fairly and squarely and in earnest. Not many of the developing countries, however, practise the precepts they enunciate for others. The time has come for social scientists from developing countries to offer models of new national economic orders which have built-in mechanisms to promote equality and eliminate abject poverty.

The call for a new national order is not to satisfy the moralistic attitude of developed countries towards some of the developing countries. Even though it is now fashionable among the intellectual circles of some of the developed countries, it is not infrequently that these countries have not only promoted and supported but also installed some of the most immoral regimes of the 20th century. There is utter exaggeration of what is wrong with the developing countries. The self-righteous view of the other world is diversionary and meant to sidetrack the real issues. But the developing countries do not have to live up to the expectations of others. They should first attempt to live up to the expectations of their own people and culture. It is from this perspective that we see the imperative need for a new national order which ensures dignity for man in every respect.

Alein Style of Development

A third major issue which ought to have engaged our attention is the style of development. Style of development is often confused with political ideology and branded as socialist, capitalist or mixed.[31] While ideologies do influence styles, the goals, approaches and methods of development often cut across ideologies, and it is these elements which distinguish one style from another. The style of development pursued by the less-developed countries has generated growth and change no doubt but these have been accompanied by certain unhealthy traits. These traits include:

1. Inability to offer productive and remunerative employment to an important part of the potential labour force.

> 2. Inability to distribute the fruits of growth so as to relieve mass poverty or prevent the gap between minorities enjoying 'modern' consumption patterns and the rest of the population from widening.
> 3. Inability to accord to the masses of the population either the reality or the feeling of participating in development decision-making.
> 4. Societal disruption and rising levels of violence of several kinds.
> 5. Violation of basic human rights by groups holding power.
> 6. Squandering of irreplaceable natural resources and environmental degradation.
> 7. Unmanageably rapid population growth and concentration in cities.
>
> Many of the same traits, in different combinations, have become prominent in 'advanced' countries as well and have weakened their credibility as models for the development of the rest of humanity.[32]

While there could be different explanations for each of these, and some of them could not be avoided irrespective of the style of development a country adopts, their impacts and implications could certainly be minimised. The style which is commonly adopted overemphasises economic growth as an end in itself and is often insensitive to what happens to other aspects of development under the assumption that distributive aspects would be taken care of by the market mechanism. There have also been cases of paternalistic benevolence doling out services and subsidies to less-privileged without caring for what happens to the doles. A desirable style

> means an effort to identify and understand the inter-relationships of all significant components of development system, as a requisite to the defining of strategies, instruments and action techniques through which human agents can intervene more effectively than hitherto to bring development into harmony with internationally accepted values.[33]

What should be the style of development for the Third World countries? Apparently there can be no universal style in the most general terms. Each country has to evolve its own style keeping in view its cultural heritage, its resource base, stage of development and so on. One thing that is clear, however, is that it can be none other than a self-reliant style directed mainly to ensure a strong nation State committed to protecting the legitimate economic political and social rights of its citizens, especially the poor.

It is a style which gives top priority to eradication of poverty not only by the slow process of raising the standard of living of the poorest among the poor but also by the revolutionary process of reducing the level of conspicuous consumption by the richest among the rich; and which fosters egalitarian values not in any doctrinaire sense but in a sense which encourages individual initiative without jeopardising the interests of the community as a whole.

United Nations Research Institute for Social Development, Geneva (UNRISD) has suggested seven criteria to evaluate a development style. These are:

1. The extent and nature of national *autonomy*.
2. The extent and nature of popular *participation*.
3. The emphasis given to *production* in general, to specific lines and techniques of production, incentives, and forms of control over the means of production.
4. The *distribution* of the fruits of development and mechanisms for re-distribution.
5. The encouragement or discouragement of specific forms of individual or collective *consumption* of goods and services.
6. The extent and nature of *protection of human environment.*
7. The extent of nature of *protection of human relationships* contributing to solidarity, security, self-realisation and freedom.[34]

All the above criteria are interdependent. If a country allies itself completely to one of the super-powers, it cannot evolve an independent style of development. In that event all other aspects will also follow the pattern dictated by the exigencies of the alliance. It is not to suggest that developing countries should cut their relations off with other countries. On the contrary, the idea is to have maximum autonomy with maximum interdependency. The objection is to 'dependency' and not to 'interdependency'.

Popular participation, an unusual subject-mater of seminars and conferences, presupposes equity. Beggars cannot participate with landlords except in terms that make a mockery of the very concept of popular participation. Participation means involvement in development, not only in raising hands or casting votes to legitimise what the government wishes to do. Similarly, the patterns of production and distribution will be governed by the style of development. What is produced, how much, for whom and at what cost are questions which are highly pertinent. To produce anything just to raise the GDO is not developmental in the real sense.

A desirable style of development must have the imprints of the past and must ensure a bright future for the society in question. It is not something that is available in the market place. It requires a conscious and concerted effort on the part of national leaders. It needs several things, but, above all, it needs wisdom. Unfortunately, however, wisdom is becoming scarce as knowledge doubles each decade.

REFERENCES

1. Statement by H. Merril Jackson, in *Towards a Redefinition of Development* ed. Alain Birou, Paul-Mare Henry and John P. Schlegel, Paris: Pergamon Press, (1977). p. 9.
2. Everett. E. Hagen, *The Theory of Social Change: How Economic Growth Begins* (Homewood, Ill.: Dorsey Press). (1962). Also see Denis Goulet, *The Cruel Choice: A New Concept in the Theory of Development:* (New York: Atheneum and Paulo Freire, (1972). *Pedagogy of the Oppressed* (Education series) (London: Penguin Books).
3. Statement by Syed Hasan Aksari, in *Towards a Redefinition of Development* (ed.) Birou:, Henry and Schlegel, p. 15.
4. Government of India, Planning Commission, *The First Five-Year Plan (A Summary)* New Delhi: Planning Commission, (1952). p. 2.
5. John Maynard Keynes, *The General Theory of Employment, Interest and Money*, London: Macmillan. (1936). For a concise discussion see B. Higgins and J.D. Higgins, *Economic Development of a Small Planet*, New York: W.W. Norton (1979).
6. W.W. Rostow, *The Stages of Economic Growth: A Non-Communist Manifesto* (Cambridge: Cambridge University Press 1961).
7. Roy Harrod of Oxford University and Evsey Domar of MIT developed their models independently to demonstrate the limits of Keynesian economics. They underscored the need for planning. For a concise description of their model see Michael P. Todaro, *Economic Development in the Third World*, New York: Longman, (1977). pp. 52-55.
8. Mahalanobis' model was based on the original Russian model put forward by Feldman. Priority was given to developing a capital goods sector. The model was later criticised on the grounds that it ignored the structural rigidities of the Indian economic and political system. For further details, see J.N. Bhagwati and S. Chakravarty, *Contributions to Indian Economic Analysis* Bombay: Lal-

wani Publishing House (1971), and A. Rudra: *Indian Plan Models*, Bombay: Allied Publishers (1975).

9. Literature on basic needs and related issues is now quite extensive. Those interested in going to the origin to the debate should see ILO, *The Basic Needs Approach to Development* (Geneva, 1972): *Employment, Growth and Basic Needs: A One-World Problem* (Geneva, 1976): *Meeting Basic Needs: Strategies for Eradicating Mass Poverty and Unemployment: — Conclusions of the World Employment Conference*, 1976 (Geneva, 1977). For more details see Volume 7 of this series.
10. For Agricultural fundamentalism, see John W. Mellor, *The New Economics of Growth: A Strategy for India and the Developing World*, Ithaca and London: Cornell University Press (1976). Also see T.W Schultz, *Transforming Traditional Agriculture*, (1964). New Haven: Yale University Press, Ranaan Weitz. *From Peasant to Farmer: A Revolutionary Strategy for Development*, New York: Columbia Univ. Press (1971).
11. For unbalanced growth see Albert Hirschman, *The Strategy of Economic Development*, New Haven: Yale University Press (1958). Which advocates unbalanced growth. For balanced growth, see Alfredo Navarrete, "Mexico's Growth: Prospects and problems" in *Economic Growth: Rationale, Problems*, Eastin Nelson, (ed.), Austin: Univ. of Texas), (1969). p. 127. See also Hans Singer, "The Concept of Balanced Growth and Economic Development: Theory and Facts" in the same volume, p. 80.
12. Literature on growth poles and growth centres is fairly large. Readers may like to refer to A.R. Kuklinski, ed., *Growth Poles and Growth Centres* Hague: Mouton; (1972). A.R. Kuklinski and R. Petrella. *Growth Poles and Regional Policies*, Hague: Mouton; (1972). Fu-chen Lo and Kamal Salih, *Growth Pole Strategy and Regional Development Policy* (New York: Pergamon Press) (1978). and R.P. Misra, *et al.*, *Regional Development Planning in India: A new Strategy* (New Delhi: Vikas Publishing House). (1974).
13. S. Kuznets, "Economic Growth and Income Inequality", *American Economic Review* 45: (1955). pp. 1-28. See also F. Paukert "Income Distribution at Different Levels of Development: A Survey of Evidence", *International Labour Review* (Aug-Sept.) (1973) and H.T. Oshima and B. Barros, "Trends in Growth and Distribution of Income in Selected Asian Countries", *The Philippine Economic Journal*, 15.
14. Michael Lipton, *Why Poor People Stay Poor: Urban Bias and World Development*, (Cambridge: Harvard Uni. Press) (1977). and M. Lipton and Bertrand Renaud, "National Urbanisation Policies in Developing Countries" (World Bank Staff Working Paper, No. 206, Washington) (1979).
15. See K. Norris and J. Vaisey, *The Economics of Research and Technology*, (London: George Allen & Unwin) (1973). M. Brown, *On the Theory and Measurement of Technological Change* (Cambridge: Cambridge Univ. Press) (1966). D. Dickson, *The Politics of Alternative Technology*, (New York: Universe Books) (1975).
16. E.F. Schumacher, *Small is Beautiful*, (London: Blond and Briggs) (1973).
17. A.K. Reddy, "A conceptual Frame-work for Environmentally Sound and Appropriate Technologies" Paper read in the Expert Group Meeting organised by UNEP on Dec. 1-4, 1985 at Nairobi.

18. Norman Furniss, (1974). "The Practical Significance of De-centralisation", *Journal of Politics*; John D. Montgomery, (1972). "Allocation of Authority in Land Reform Programmes: A Comparative Study of Administrative Process and Outputs", in *Administrative Science Quarterly* (March) and James W. Fesler, "Centralisation and De-centralisation" in *International Encyclopaedia of the Social Sciences*, David L. Sills, ed., New York: The Macmillan Co., (1968). p. 373.
19. See Walter Stohr and D.R.F. Taylor eds. *Development from Above or Below*, New York: John Wiley (1981).
20. C.E. Black, *The Dynamics of Modernisation: A Study in Comparative History*, New York: Harper & Row (1966). L.L. Rudolph and S.H. Rudolph, *The Modernity of Tradition: Political Development in India*, Bombay: Orient Longmans (1967).
21. United Nations, *Integration of Economic and Physical Planning* (New York: United Nations) (Sales No. E. 75, IV. 9) (ST ESA 36) (1975): M. Honjo. "Kozoji Town: Case Study for Integration of Physical Planning with Economic and Social Planning", Paper presented at the Expert Group Meeting organised by ESCAP and UNCHS, held in Bangkok on 18-24 Nov., 1980.
22. Jan Tinbergen, *Reshaping the International Order: A Report to the Club of Rome* (New York: E.P. Dutton) (1976). p. 11.
23. *Ibid.*, p. 16.
24. *Ibid.*, p. 19.
25. United Nations General Assembly Resolution A RES/3201 (S.VI). 9 May 1974. The resolution contains Charter of Economic Rights and Duties of States.
26. See *World Development* 2, (1974): pp. 52-55.
27. *Ibid.*
28. See Jan Tinbergen (co-ordinator), (1976). *Reshaping the International Order*.
29. It is a tax which would be levied by the developing countries on their citisens working in developed countries. The tax would be collected by the country where persons are working. The amount so collected would be passed on to respective developing countries through the United Nations.
30. Pope John Paul II, (1980). *Japan Times* (25 December).
31. See for example, Ralph Pieris *Asian Development Styles* (New Delhi: Abhinav Publications), (1977). p. 9. Pieris gives four styles: (i) The Post-Industrial Style, (ii) Welfare Statism Style, (iii) Mixed Development and (iv) The Socialist Style.
32. United Nations Research Institute for Social Development, *The Quest for a United approach to Development: UNRISD Report* (Geneva: UNRISD) (1980). p. 5.
33. *Ibid.*, p. 11.
34. *Ibid.*, p. 16.

11

DEVELOPMENT, RESOURCES AND CONFLICT

CHRISTOPHER C. BENNINGER

Development and Conflict: A Hypothesis

THERE IS a competition for, and exploitation of, scarce resources, encouraged by a political economy which promotes concentrated extraction and profits for a few. This takes place at the cost of sustainable development and at the price of equitable utilisation of common resources, such as water. It creates drought conditions when rainfall is low and flood conditions when rainfall is high. These imbalances are reflected in the management of political and economic institutions, as well as in the exploitation of human, water, land, animal and bio-mass resources. These imbalances create inherent conflicts between those who benefit and those who bear the costs. These imbalances are responsible for the "push" factor in migration and disfavour the poor in urban labour markets. Concerns for a halt in the destruction of the environment have taken on an international character. Nuclear testing was found to pollute the entire planet's atmosphere; inadvertent and potentially disastrous modifications in the planetary weather system over which no nation can assert sovereignty, belied pretensions of national political and economic systems to hold sway over the resolution of these environmental stresses. Concerns for our resources, our ecosystems and our environment have initiated the realisation of the oneness of mankind. As Barbara Ward so eloquently stated (Ward and Dubos, 1972).

> "It is even now possible that recognition of our environmental interdependence can do more than save us, negatively, from the final folly of war. It could, positively, give us that sense of community, of belonging and living together, without which no human society can be built up, survive and prosper. Our links of blood and history, our sense of shared culture and achievement, our traditions, our faiths are all precious and enrich and world with the variety of scale and function required for every vital eco-system. But, we have lacked a wider rationale of unity. Our prophets have sought it. Our poets have dreamed of it. But it is only in our own day that astronomers, ethnologists and archaeologists have all combined in a single witness of advanced science to tell us that, in every alphabet of our being, we do indeed belong to a single system, powered by a single energy, manifesting a fundamental unit under all its variations, depending for its survival on the balance and health of the total system" (*Only One Earth*, p. 297).

The argument which follows maintains that the exploitation of resources has been the basis of the phenomena we call "development", and has been the basis of conflicts which more and more characterise contemporary Indian society. A description of a valley in the Western Ghats is referred to for illustrative reasons.

Conflict Context

A Description: While India is a "poor country" in terms of per capita consumer expenditure, it is rich in water from precipitation, in bovine and in human resources. Its land extent is adequate for its large population but requires careful management (Centre for Science and Environment, 1987). But for such a large population, the soil and flora coverage is poor. Water, in terms of flow irrigation for cash crops, is both denying some zones of protective coverage while creating saline, or "usar lands", in other areas which are excessively irrigated.

Human settlements in the Western Ghats of Maharashtra first appeared as family and clan homesteads focused on hunting and shifting cultivation. As agricultural patterns and land ownership became more stable, with each family claiming a particular land parcel, hamlets developed. Definition of ownership spaces was demanded by commercialisation of production, imposition of taxes and tenancy systems. The first hamlets emerged in the lower "outlets" of watershed drainage systems, where good soil had been deposited and the land was relatively flat. Water was more easily attainable and stored in this area.

As population grew and there was more pressure on the land, people began to move "up" the drainage system onto higher, steeper, less fertile and less manageable land. A conflict emerged between man and access to the basic productive asset: land. This resulted in the extension of cultivable area and in the original settlements, at *sangums* of small rivers, taking on additional functions. Being the most accessible and established settlements, traders, artisans and petty administrators located their activities in these villages, as did weekly markets and seasonal festivals. Outsiders attended these markets and festivals, and the resulting interaction enriched local life by injecting new ideas and concepts. But as commerce catalysed the role of such settlements, profits accrued more to the trader and less to the producer. The mobilisation of resources into productive assets became uneconomical unless key inputs were inequitably concentrated. Unsustainable "mining" of resources was encouraged through terms of trade characterised by marginal profits to prime producers. Wealth could be accumulated only through bulk production, or through high turn over trade, and thus inequity conflicts emerged. Pockets of "profit" funded political leadership. Political institutions in turn directed their mechanisms away from conservation, equity and objective land-use planning. Institutional mechanisms focused on extraction for immediate gains. The Western Ghats' case is relevant to a large segment of India as it includes denuded high lands, eroded upper cereal and paddy lands, and fertile valley floors where flat lands are fed by water and fertile soil eroded from higher lands.

The social context is one in which inheritance of property is based on a pattern of equal division amongst male heirs and in which the social order is essentially feudal. Thus, the bridgeheaders who pioneer the less fertile lands in the upper reaches of the valleys have been, on the one hand, the sons of farmers whose shares in the inheritance have divided down to inoperable holdings. On the other hand, pioneers have been the less-privileged members of the social system who were the first to be pushed out due to increasing pressures on land in the older settlements. In both cases it was inevitable that links of kinship and commerce were maintained with the older settlements. Thus, marriages, festivals, ceremonies of birth and death, and religious observances are linked within a system of castes, clans and families in each mezo-watershed. Nodal settlements, at the confluence of natural drainage lines, also became centres of social power and determinants of social standards (Benninger, UNESCAP, 1983).

The case study area is composed of hierarchically tiered environmental systems which are physically bounded, and which are socially and culturally integrated internally through functional relations. Examples of such natural eco- and agro-systems are cultivable plots of land, watersheds and regions. The smaller systems are nested in the larger homogeneous ones (Conway, 1987). The links between components within the settlement system are primarily through the "base villages" or early settlements which are now service centres. New subsidiary centres have grown about half way up each watershed and the entire watershed has reached its saturation point in terms of "carrying capacity" to support population within the existing resource base. With increased health care, control of famine and epidemics, the population has grown rapidly. Thus, population which cannot be supported on the present resource base, at locally acceptable standards of living, is "pushed" out to higher settlement levels where sustenance can be achieved. Those pushed off the land are the least powerful, and must work in a saturated urban labour market. Their exploitation again results in the emergence of another conflict paradigm, but in a new location. For those who remain in their native settings, there is increased pressure to exploit common resources; land, water, bio-mass, animal and human resources. Common resources may be loaded and exploited on a lower tier system, say a farm, but depend on drawing a greater than proportionate share from the next tier, the watershed. Thus, a farm system may be structured around flow irrigation to nurture commercial crops. But water may have to be denied to the rest of the watershed system. Thus, in a few cases at the lower tier, systems' performance appears good, while at higher levels stresses and conflicts are created. Thus, the ancient conflict over access to productive land now emerges as a conflict over access to water (FAO, 1986).

A settlement may increase its production by grazing a portion of a watershed beyond its capability of regenerating the bio-mass. Again the performance indicators of the settlement may be good, but at the cost of stress and conflict across the higher system: the watershed. A conflict over inequitable access to the bio-mass emerges. Inversely, lack of conversation in an upper micro-watershed may yield unnatural collection of water in a storage tank down stream. Mining of water just below a downstream tank may result in wealth and political power concentrated within a boundary which is unrelated to the environmental boundaries of watersheds (Salunkhe, 1989). Such a political fraternity will create *economic incentives* to further concentrate and favour the exploitation of resources, direct *investments* to further their advantage and create *laws and regulations* of land-use and management which favour their economic mode of production. Instead of subsidising development up the drainage system which will sustain down system productivity, subsidies support exploitative commercial activities down stream! Thus, a set of natural systems under stress are related in a hierarchy and generate conflict. The hierarchy of related natural systems is basically a hierarchy from farm, village (composed of farms), watershed (composed of villages) and to region (composed of watersheds). On the other hand, decision-making political boundaries may be hierarchically ordered from village, taluka, district, State of nation. Still again, economic boundaries of sub-systems will be very different (The Working Group on Water Management and Development, 1987).

As this closed, hierarchically integrated, ecological system reaches its threshold of "load", horizontal migration takes place to areas of production where employment is generated, and where value added and profit are higher. This process is encouraged and reinforced by a formal education system emphasising reading, writing and arithmetic and by family links which create channels for future migration flows. Films and other popular media herald the glories and excitement of town and city life. National policy supports the growth of cities as a priority is given to industrialisation, import substitution, urban-based defence establishments and apex institutional development. Thus, there is also "pull" to larger settlements. It is a cultural norm in the Ghats that "larger cities are better than towns, towns better than villages and villages better than hamlets [*wadis*]". These attitudes, processes and phenomena are not bad if indeed people improve their real living conditions through daily, seasonal and permanent migration. However, unskilled migrants to cities with maturing industrial and service sectors are finding it ever more difficult to obtain employment (McGee, 1971).

People leave their native systems due to stresses related to productivity, equity and reliability of natural systems. Where mean productivity per capita falls below a certain level, at a particular systemic tier, stress will result. Where average per capita productivity is adequate, but distributed in such a manner that large segments of the population face consumption stresses, conflict will arise. Climatic fluctuations amplify the severity of mal-distribution amongst the poor. Where this happens in a sequence of small intervals, reliability is reduced, and population may leave the particular tier, farm, village, watershed or region where stress is felt. Reduction in surety is related to exploiting non-renewable resources. The carrying capacity is thus reduced. The resulting migration adds more conflict to urban labour markets where wage levels are already greatly suppressed. Ability to pay for basic services and necessities is inadequate. Thus, the conflict model is a complex one. Without moralising against urbanisation and rural-urban migration, which can be vehicles of opportunity and self-realisation, one must ask, "how can these processes be rationalised? How can more choices be crated allowing for self-fulfilment within continuity?

Out of the above emerges a systemic viewpoint of development. On the one hand is a group of natural productive systems which are externally bounded; spatially, farms, villages, watersheds and regions; economically through market mechanisms and modes of consumption demand; socially through a set of behavioural standards of who can relate with whom in which way; and culturally through patterns of behaviour which persist over time. Control and power emanate from a feudal system of obligations and rewards between castes, families and individuals within them. Control and power is directed by families who have monopolised common resources. But the political, social economic, cultural and environmental systems do not share overlapping boundaries. Thus, no trade-off logic exists that would suggest that a balanced, equitable and sustainable development should take place. There is no logic in beneficiaries of concentrated resources downstream, subsidising the regeneration and conservation of resources upstream. This is so because the boundaries of political systems are not the same as those of natural systems. Thus, the logic of one system does not invade that of the other.

Rural development has been a process of converting eco-systems into agro-systems. With new agro-technology we can do more harm with less effort than ever before to natural systems. Transport, biomass processing, major irrigation works, lethal pesticides, herbicides and polluting fertilisers can destroy an environment as fast as the pressures on resources caused by population growth. We are working in a situation where both phenomena work together. Thus, development, by its very nature, generates stresses and conflicts.

Balancing Natural Systems: Concepts

Conflict resolution is basically a problem of balancing natural resources, within systems, between hierarchical tiers of homogeneous system sets and between heterogeneous systems which act on each other. To expand on this:

An eco-system must balance land, water, animal, bio-mass and human resources. These five common resources are the *components* of all natural systems. Agro-systems concentrate these resources and introduce chemical additives which create dramatic imbalances.

A hierarchical set of homogeneous eco-system tiers must balance resource utilisation between farms, forests, grazing lands, villages, and villages within watersheds, and between watersheds within a region.

Heterogeneous systems such as political systems, natural systems and economic systems must be balanced through the common goals of equitable and sustainable growth. This is made difficult because these systems' boundaries, their constituencies and resulting objectives do not overlap. At an international scale we face the same conflicts between the first cost bearers, of atmospheric and oceanic pollution, and the casual systems, which represent a constituency of beneficiaries acting in a different system.

In order to achieve balance and reduce conflict it is important that we characterise natural systems so that we can understand how political and economic systems impinge on them. The *Character*, or nature, of a system is determined by aspects of its parts, or its components, which are very similar or the same. These aspects are called *elements*. All "natural systems" share the elements noted below and thus may be called homogeneous systems because they have the same character. These elements are (Benninger, UNESCAP, 1983):

(a) *Carrying Capacity:* The maximum human population which can be supported at local expectation levels within a natural system at given technological, investment and management levels on the existing resource base, without deteriorating the supportive capacities of resources, is the carrying capacity. The dynamic concept is that carrying capacity can increase along with enhanced techniques, management and investment. There are relative thresholds, as these three variable change, and there is an ultimate threshold beyond which the resource base cannot regenerate itself.

(b) *Population:* Here, the population means that number of people supported by a natural system. The level of migration reflects the increase in population over the carrying capacity of the system. At any given time this is assumed to be an optimisation of the independent variables (Table 11.1). Population growth is itself considered an independent variable in this frame-work.

(c) *Expectations:* This refers to the locally acceptable standards of living (consumption levels per capita per year) and quality of life (infant mortality, morbidity rate, literacy and life expectancy at birth). On a more subjective level it refers to:

(i) people's felt requirement for identity within patterns of behaviour which persist over time (culture);
(ii) people's felt requirement for mental and physical development (recreation) and,
(iii) people's felt requirement for emotional support and recognition (achievement).

(d) *Technological Level*: This refers to the production technology, the processing technology and the storage technology in natural systems. Here it is linked to the number of people which can be supported on a given unit of land of a particular type. The higher the technology the more people can be supported at a constant expectation level on a constant resource base. However, if this technology is focused on a few farms, instead of using the increased productivity to support more people, the additional productivity will generate more profit for a few elites.

(e) *Management Level:* This refers to the skills, knowledge and the awareness available to use the resource base and to use the available technology. Again, this can be monopolised by a few farms or applied to a settlement or a watershed community of users.

(f) *Investment Level:* This refers to the level of inputs which can be brought to bear on:

(i) production, both of an additive nature (permanent economic infrastructure) and of a recurring nature (seeds, fertilisers, water, labour);

(ii) social inputs which support both expectation levels and production levels (health, nutrition, education, sanitation, drinking water, training programmes and child development).

(g) *Resource Base:* This refers to the potentially productive and sustaining assets (land, water, animal-life, bio-mass, human resources, etc.). The resource base can either be enhanced, or degraded, through management. Every natural system is composed of a resource base.

(h) *Resource Mobilisation* involves directing investments and efforts towards activities which conserve, regenerate and make productive combinations of basic resources in a balanced manner. Such efforts can also be misguided toward concentration of resources at hyper-productive command areas or neglect of resources in catchment areas.

(i) *Productive Assets* are the infrastructure, management awareness and formed resources whose configuration and use result in the creation of equitable sustenance.

(j) *Productive Liabilities* are the infrastructure, management attitudes and formed resources whose configurations and use result in the degradation of the environment. Productive liabilities, such as irrigation canals flow configured for sugarcane will *reduce* the mean productivity in the watershed, *reduce reliability* and *reduce* equity of access to water.

(k) *Resource Utilisation and Exploitation* refer to the level at which resources are used as productive inputs. Where the level regenerates capability, which producing, such practices can be called resource utilisation. But where use has a negative impact and resource capacity is continuously reduced, or is so concentrated as to de-nigh use by all the population, then resource exploitation is taking place.

Migration is a good indicator of inequity and unreliable sustenance. This is particularly so in India where urban labour markets are oversaturated, environmental conditions in urban slums are very poor and where wage differentials of the rural and unskilled urban poor would not "pull" population to cities. Migration for the mass of landless and marginal farmers represents a last desperate step towards survival. Migration transposes stress and conflict from one system to another, from a conflict source to a system where stress is more symptomatic of conflicts elsewhere.

The working assumption here is that no migration will take place when population growth, expectations, technology, management, investment and resource base remain in equilibrium. This can be achieved through resource mobilisation which conserves resources and directs them to be accessible, sustained and productive assets. If technology, investment and management are monopolised, resource exploitation by a few will take place. If micro-level, participatory, political institutions are created to control them, then issues of equity and of reliable sustenance will emerge.

Historically when population grew it moved up the watershed onto an equivalent resource base. An equivalent resource base, "up" a watershed, would consume a larger land area as (a) soil is of poorer quality; (b) slope and, therefore, soil erosion and water run-off is more; and, (c) water management requires more effort. When the available land is saturated, that option no longer exists. Resource mobilisation focused on flow irrigation, in pockets, has turned catchment areas into productive liabilities, which silt tanks, rivers, flood basins and produce only commercial crops for export. Protective irrigation and community watershed management, as demonstrated by Pani *Panchayat* at Naigaon in Maharashtra, create productive assets by afforesting and "grassing" uplands, planning appropriate crop patterns in the catchment beds of storage tanks and limiting commercial crops in the command areas below (CDSA, 1983).

Framework for Analysis

The conceptual framework has been defined as a set of natural systems which are each composed of components which are externally bounded and internally integrated. Functional relations in these networks have developed, which persist over time, giving a structure to these farm, settlement, watershed and regional systems. Certain elements have been abstracted and defined which characterise natural systems, but whose patterns also change and become basic variables. In the first section they were defined as:

1. Carrying capacity.
2. Population.
3. Expectation level.

4. Technology level.
5. Management level.
6. Investment level.
7. Resource base.
8. Resource mobilisation.
9. Productive assets and productive liabilities.
10. Resource utilisation and exploitation.

In this framework, carrying capacity and migration are seen as dependent variables. The levels of population growth, expectation, technology, management and investment are seen as independent variable *vis-a-vis* this conceptual frame. Intermediate variables link independent variables to dependent ones. They also describe practices and the situation of a system.

Externalities, or demands from other natural systems, also put stresses on a given natural system. Water, for example, can be denied to a farm in a lower watershed area because of exploitation in farms higher up the watershed. Higher watersheds along and drainage system of a region likewise can exploit the lower watersheds in the region.

TABLE 11.1: **Elements of Natural Systems and their Systemic Processes**

Independent Variables (elements)*		*Intermediate Variable (character)*	*Dependent Variables (systems stress)*
Management Level	Resource		
Technology Level	Mobilisation		Carrying
Expectation Level		Resource	Capacity
Investment Level	Productive	Base	
Population Growth	—assets		
	—liabilities		Migration
CONDITIONS	PRACTICES	SITUATION	PHENOMENON

* Listed in order of their assumed range of variability from management (most variable) to population growth (least variable).
Source: Benninger, UN-ESCAP, 1983.

All the variables work within relative societal and ultimate ecological limit. The independent variables are tempered by each other and again by externalities. The way management, technology, expectations and investments are applied to resources can have either a positive or negative impact on the carrying capacity. This capacity is being put under continuous stress by population growth.

Operationally this means:

(a) We are concerned with the dynamics of population, its present standard of living, quality of life, skill levels, expectations, growth and movement;

(b) We are concerned with the constraints and potentials of the resource base, and opportunities to develop and diversify it;

(c) We are concerned with enhancing the carrying capacity by:

   (i) introducing appropriate economic activities and processes, which would increase resources utilisation;

   (ii) introducing appropriate technology, relevant management and effective and efficient investment which conserve and regenerate resources;

   (iii) evolving a participatory system of decision-making which helps the community regulate its expectations and resource mobilisation to equitable and sustainable levels;

   (iv) linking social and economic activities to environmental upgradation; and

   (v) more optimally structuring rural-urban linkages so they are not exploitative.

(d) We are studying the needs and potentials for new skills, organising capabilities and enhanced awareness in local people about their own environmental context and the processes which control that context. Human resources mobilisation is seen as increasing the capacity of the local population to manage and participate in the utilisation of their own resources and to protect these resources from exploitation.

(e) We are searching for institutional mechanisms to link the concerns and goals of eco-systems, of agro-systems with those of political and economic systems. We are trying to reduce stresses and revolve conflicts through environmental planning and management which includes economic and institutional management, not just the management of environmental resources in isolation.

The above has an *exploration* attempting to map interactive phenomena, and inherent decisions and goals, rather than a quantitative description of known parts. The methodological problem here has been to obtain a working description of the systems. While this may seem complex, both analysis and action can be greatly simplified by reducing the larger development systems (regions) into their smaller tiers (watersheds, settlements, farms and farm plots) and abstracting them by simple performance indicators such as productivity, equity and reliability.

Conceptual Models

Through institutional mechanisms *we can change* the levels of reliability, the levels of equitable access, the levels of mean productivity of these natural systems. Institutional mechanisms can increase and reduce stresses which impinge on the population. Some of the chosen change models are noted below:

(a) *Population Growth Model:* Population grows, all other factors remain constant, and population in excess of the existing carrying capacity leaves;

(b) *Exploitation Model:* The resource base deteriorates, cash crop incomes increase dramatically for a few, all other factors remain constant, and population leaves. This occurs when resources are exploited, or "mind", beyond their replacement capability over a period of time.

(c) *Information Revolution Model:* Expectations increase, productive liabilities are created, all other factors remain the same, and population leaves; or,

(d) *Resource Equilibrium Model:* Population grows moderately, the resource base is enhanced, other factors remain the same, and no population leaves.

Obviously, these models overlap each other in the real world. But, by isolating elements and using them as change factors, one can create abstract conceptual frame-works to study options. Thus, population, expectations, technology, investment, management, resource mobilisation and resource base are hypothesised as the factors which determine a system's stability, equity and long-term productivity.

These conceptual models are used to demonstrate a framework of relationships within natural systems in developing contexts and between natural systems themselves. A study of the whole multi-tier system structure and contextual stresses may obscure causes at lower tiers in the systemic hierarchy, and thus obscure conflict resolution potentials. Analysis must be holistic in that disaggregated parts are abstracted and defined, which, when re-aggregated, sum up the whole.

Such a conceptual frame can explain daily commuting between settlements, seasonal migration and permanent migration. It explains conflict between those who control resources and those who do not. It explains conflict between one spatial system and another and between political groups who make decisions about resources for others. It suggests that the equilibrium described is dynamic in the relationship between characteristics of each system, between tiers of homogeneous natural systems and interacting types of heterogeneous systems; and, in terms of seasons, drought cycles and long-term climatic changes.

These models have dynamic and cybernetic characteristics. Migration acts as a balancing or control function where productive, equity and surety stresses emerge. But the relief on the system is temporary, as long-term damage to the environment continues. Patterns of change in models may also be selected as performance indicators in an instrumentalist framework where purposive programmes are being designed to reduce conflict. Alternatives in development can be evaluated through these indicators and strategies accordingly assessed. Options exist which could balance systems without displacing population or degrading resources. These are explored in more detail below:

Alternatives to Development Conflict

In the preceding sections a systemic view of development and resulting conflicts of equity, ecological balance, production and reliability are presented. General components and characteristics of natural development units are explored. The inter-relations are explored between homogeneous, tiered systems, nested in a hierarchy, and heterogeneous, external systems, which do not share either boundaries or constituencies. These systems interact through process which exploit resources, promote productive liabilities, produce for urban consumer markets and concentrate profits amongst a few families who relate to the others through feudal links. With manageable water effectively controlled by a small elite and cash crops promoted amongst the remaining marginal farmers, surety depends on the vagarities of rainfall and urban price mechanisms. These processes must be "turned around" and rationalised. More options must be created for individuals to fulfil their expectations within their own contexts or through objective choices between external contexts.

Historically, three fundamental strategy sets have competed — each with its own constituency, goals and objectives. None of these classic strategy sets prioritises "environment", simply because each set has its own elite constituency and these constituencies do not directly depend on a balanced resource base. But it is important to review these.

The rural elite and traders who control decision-making institutions favour conservative strategies. The bureaucracy who work for these institutions is easily swayed to support such strategies.

Urban leaders of landless and marginal peasants, urban intellectuals and many enlightened peasants themselves promote a radical strategy. But "activists" from this elite are suppressed through conservative institutions. Thus, the focus of radicals, of either an ideological or a fundamentalist nature, is concentrated on political power.

The bureaucracy, enlightened capitalists, the middle class service sector, most voluntary agencies and international funding agencies support an ameliorative strategy.

None of these constituencies are dependent on balanced natural systems, we are discussing, for direct sustenance. However, they are all concerned with stress and conflict! It is, therefore, essential to advocate this approach within ameliorist and radical political groups, as well as with activists who directly create awareness amongst the people. "Progressive" leaders amongst conservatives may also be targets of advocacy. Scholars and academics, teachers and students, must also go directly to the people, as only mass awareness and complete community involvement can bring resources into balance.

Ameliorative Strategies

Ameliorist strategies accept the political, social and economic systems as given and work within this structure. Historically conflict resolution has been attempted by elites who benefit from the *status quo*, fear violence and the counter productive chaos of a revolution, but see the present state of affairs as far from acceptable. They believe in the structural and institutional merit of the State but desire more directed and effective implementation. They are the indirect beneficiaries of productive liabilities, monopoly control and exploitation. But they are intellectually sensitive to inequalities. They understand that there will have to be an ultimate reckoning of ecological accounts and that either they or their children will have to bear the costs. They feel that through advocacy they can make political systems, which do not share boundaries with environmental systems, understand the need for a balanced distribution of costs and benefits between systemic parts. They support the view that enhanced planning and management can bring equity. Historically they have favoured new economic opportunities for the poor, greater access to education, the expansion of social services, integrated development, representative democracy and a soft, "open", State.

The ameliorist option and inherent strategies focus on the improvement of performance. The strategy assumes that stress and conflict are manageable. But they do not see them as embedded in the structure of institutional systems. Strategies which focus on the protection and regeneration of the environment have not played an important role. Neither has there been a focus on natural systems, such as watersheds, nor their component common resources. Ameliorist strategies basically react to symptoms and do not focus on causes. Ameliorist strategies work through political, administrative and economies systems whose boundaries do not align with natural systems. Thus, their decision-making system do not share the concerns, constituencies and goals that are required in environmental systems where stress originates. Such an anomaly will create more conflict.

Conservative Strategies

These strategies assume that present inequity is unavoidable and that growth should be accelerated to accommodate more population. These strategies are based on the hypothesis that the system is very appropriate. Conservative strategies presuppose that by widening and structurally deepening the economy into more sectors, poverty will be gradually obliterated. Some examples of conservative strategies are:

The Economic Growth model is the most popular conservative concept. Increases in commercial production is sought through: (a) flow irrigation schemes, based on large dam projects and processing plants (b) concentration of productive resources with more efficient, larger, corporate productive units, and (c) promotion of chemical fertilisers, pesticides and hybrid seeds to increase production. This strategy has resulted in the neglect of catchment areas, forests, grass-lands, water bodies, wastelands and of the poor.

Enhanced Management Control through centralisation of decision-making is a major conservative strategy. This is sought by: (a) de-concentrating, where efficiency demands, to local offices of central agencies and (b) devolving central authority to public corporations and monopolies, who are given powers of technocratic decision-making. These mechanisms are given the misnomer of "de-centralisation". Conservative strategies also see people's behaviour as deviant from modern goal settings and objective development procedures. Regulation and policing are thus considered important aspects of conservative development management. This strategy has alienated people and their communities from resources which only they can protect, manage and maintain.

Enhanced Capability: Another favourite conservative strategy is to promote *enhanced capability*, prioritising high technology and competitive commercial practices. Such approaches are seen to prepare the economy to compete internationally and to substitute imports. These strategies have done a great deal of harm to the environment.

Exploiting human, animal, bio-mass, land and water resources is promoted through incentives to increase the standard of living and to promote conspicuous consumer expenditure. Credit systems encourage borrowing for consumption and encourage repayment through commercial production and marketing. Implicitly, quality of life investments are de-prioritised, with the intention to make the economy more efficient. Benefits are expected to "filter down" to the poor.

The conservative strategies are aggressively stress generating. They see police power as the mechanism for the resolution of conflict. While present forms of environmental management are passively oppressive, suppression of "activists" is integral to conservative development policy. Rural development, through conservative strategies, results in resource mobilisation to create productive liabilities. Urbanisation is a key component of such strategies as it presents the only receptical for displaced persons. Many ameliorative strategies are totally unacceptable to feudal, conservative elites who control the institutions which are expected to implement them.

Radical Strategies

These maintain that the present structure is untenable and must be dismantled, re-designed and a new systemic relation emplaced. This approach has been favoured by academics in the post-Warld War II era. It was especially popular prior to a number of revolutionary societies going beserk and information on the classical revolutions emerging to belie earlier in the mid-1980s. Issues of sustained growth, utilisation of common resources and conservation of the environment appear to be no better managed, or of any greater concern, in these societies than in other ones. In fact the resource bases in modern "radical societies" such as Iran, Ethiopia and Cambodia have been decimated by extremist policies, heightening conflict. But this does not lessen the intellectual attraction to the notion of a complete re-design of the institutional mechanisms which relate the utilisation of resources to each other. But such concerns are not likely to be shared by the constituencies who actually implement revolutionary change. Most are focused on the consolidation of power.

What emerges here is a development dilemma where ideological, political and participatory struggles are around meaning systems embedded in sets of concerns detached from basic causes of stress and conflict. Radical thought has focused on the exploitation of human resources and resultant stresses, but operationally has argued against general participation in decision-making for fear of democratic processes being used to undermine revolutionary processes. As such the real users and managers of resources are again silenced.

Ameliorist, conservative and radical development strategies are not inherently "environment friendly". All of these strategies emanate from political and economic stresses which operate within structures whose functions are not directly perceived to depend on natural systems. the linkages between these heterogeneous systems, types and natural systems must be studied and documented. Through institutional mechanisms, practices, attitudes, approaches and strategies must be built into either radical or ameliorists frameworks. Advocacy must present the case that just as political and economic systems can destabilise natural eco- and agro- ones, the reverse is also true. Here lies the crux of conflict resolution! Such links must also be tied to practices and to institutional mechanisms which promote reliable, equitable and productive natural systems.

A Proposition: Practices and Strategies for Optimal Use of Common Resources

In the previous section i.e., *Development and Conflict: A Hypothesis*, the concepts of common resources, systems load and carrying capacity were introduced. Common resources were identified as land, water, man, vegetation and animal life. These were described as the components of natural systems. A clear distinction was made between their utilisation and their exploitation and the thresholds beyond which these common resources cannot be utilised. In practice these thresholds are points where, in simple terms, one is taking out more than one is putting back into the common resources system. Concepts, such as water harvesting can be extended to soil harvesting, human resources harvesting and the optimal use of other resources within their regenerating limits. As Brown and Chandler stated:

> "With so many natural systems becoming unstable within such a short period of time, discontinuous, surprising and rapid changes may become common place. Resulting economic and political pressures could overwhelm the capacity of governments and individuals to adjust adequately. Societies faced with multiplying, self-generated stresses have two options: Initiate the needed reforms in population, energy, agricultural and economic policies, or risk deterioration and decline" (*State of the World*, 1987).

The exploitation of one resource beyond limits will degrade other resources. The break down of the total ecological system is often, simply, called "drought", or as a result when people and animals starve it is called "famine". Indicators like productivity, equity and reliability may also be described, using simple patterns, to describe systems performance within each system; farm, watershed, resource region, nation and multi-national resource zones.

Universities, colleges and research institutions have a role to play in analysing critical functional relations and in evaluating pertinent management decisions at each systemic tier in development contexts. But in order to do this they will have to *work in the field* and must use the field as a laboratory for learning and experimenting. Stress causing relationships and the types of conflict which emerge, have been analysed to some extent in the hypothesis of this chapter. Universities must play an active role through field surveys, field experiments, extension work and finally *development experiments*. Development experiments would involve key actors within a system and the application of changes in relationships through the implementation of management decisions. Field experiments may be done on a demonstration-cum-training farm, for example, tapping outcomes of "on campus" laboratory experiments. Field surveys would document existing patterns such as system-wide equity levels, mean productivity, target group productivity and performance reliability. The academic community must design simple patterns which display systems performance. Practices which "touch" resources, changing patterns, should be studied and their impacts documented.

In this section a set of practices and strategies, around which relationships must be organised and pertinent planning and management decisions made, are presented. The relationships, resulting stresses, constraints and potentials, issues, problems and actions would be different depending on which system in a hierarchy of natural systems we are looking at. They would be different in a particular farm plot, a farm, a settlement, a watershed and a region! Very similar patterns, functional relations and management decisions are required at each level of homogeneous natural systems. As one moves to higher systemic levels the "fit" between political and economic decision-making and natural systems becomes closer, but at lower levels, practices within the boundaries of smaller systems have no alignment with decision-making practices at higher levels. As one moves up in scale, the social costs of development and their locations become less visible than do the explicit benefits of an investment.

In our conceptual framework farms, settlements, watersheds and regions are not merely units of planning based on an eco-system, but also represent systematic groups with integrated sets of strategies for conflict resolution. Each of these natural system is build out of components. These components are land, water, bio-mass, animals and human being. Each strategy focuses on a systemic component and is supported by a number of possible practices which become the basis of a conflict resolution approach. These are priority activities in their contexts. Key strategies include the following (Table 11.2):

Regeneration of the Bio-mass, through the practices which follow, is a key strategy. This strategy includes the creation of enhancement of:

(a) forest horticulture coverage on slopes and along bunds, roads and canals,
(b) grass and grazing lands on dry lands, steeper slopes and common plots,
(c) nurseries to support the upgradation to the bio-mass,
(d) crops which produce the maximum calorific and protein content with the minimum water. For example, 30 hectares of *Bajari* can be grown using the same volume of water to produce one hectare of sugarcane. Either 12 hectares of groundnut, 15 of jowar or 22 of gram can be grown with the same water resources, (Dandekar, 1984),
(e) inter-cropping which increases enhances surety of crops. For example, mono-cropping of pigeonpea and of sorghum fail, respectively, every five and eight years, while pigeonpea-sorghum inter-cropping fails only once in 36 years (ICRISAT, 1986). Inter-cropping must also include forestry and horticulture. This will stabilise soil at different levels, enhance natural mulching and provide wind protection to standing crops,
(f) regenerated waste and denuded forest lands for common development of fuel, fibre and fodder. These could be leased to individual plot managers, or co-operatives, by the government,
(g) community compost pits and bio-gas harvesting to enrich soil and reduce dependence on chemical fertilisers,
(h) land-use plans to assure a few pockets of water hungry commercial crops do not consume all of the water.

Utilising Water Optimally, through the practices below, is an important strategy. This strategy includes the creation and enhancement of:

(a) Rational management practices for irrigation, applying concepts of equity, protective watering and storage through the construction of small *bandharas* and contour canals.
(b) water harvesting practices, such as collecting run-off and increasing percolation. Conservation of surface water is another major initiative which can increase yields of rain-fed crops. Run-off can be managed by mulching, contour ploughing, farm ponds and small *bandharas* (dams) and contour canals). Supplemental irrigation of rain-fed crops can increase yields significantly.

(c) *Ground-water Resources*: Regeneration acts as a reserve against droughts. Ground-water resources account for only 15 per cent of India's rain water distribution, but act as a reservoir for drought years. At a more micro-level, ground-water is being exploited to such an extent that rivers and *nallas* are draining into the sub-terrainian aquifer. Normally such aquifer systems would feed the drainage system creating perennial rivers! About 42 per cent of the rainfall is stored as soil moisture and another 30 per cent drains into the ocean as surface water run-off. But ground-water accounts for 34 per cent of the total water utilised and surface water for the rest (Nag and Kathpalia, 1975). Measures such as percolation tanks, *nalla* and contour bunding can restore ground-water. Afforestation can retard evapotranspiration through which soil moisture and subsequently ground-water can be lost. Restriction of tube-well sinking will also protect ground-water.

(d) *Equitable distribution* of ground-water which enables communities, instead of individuals, to participate in development.

Balancing Animal Life through the practices is another essential strategy. This includes:

(a) upgradation of the production of existing animal stock;
(b) diversifying animal husbandry to include poultry, bee, worm and fish husbandry;
(c) providing veterinary services;
(d) balancing the "load" of these creatures on land, water, and biomass so that grazing areas are maintained and animal products are adequate; and,
(e) intergrating natural predators to control "pests".

Upgrading the Land Capability by implementing the practices listed hereunder is key strategy:

(a) regenerating denuded soil and other eroded surfaces. This can be done by terracing to collect soil run-off and improving pH values through such steps as hemp plantation and its ploughing under, i.e., green manuring. Of the 5,334 million tonnes of soil eroded every year, 29 per cent goes into the sea, 61 per cent is relocated, most of it in river beds widening them and worsening flood conditions, and 10 per cent settles in dams reducing storage capacity by one to two per cent every year (Dhruva and Baba, 1983). Again afforestation plays a significant role in checking erosion and water run-off.

(b) improving the organic cover of soil through mulching and organic manuring

(c) use of pesticides, hybrids and irrigation to reduce toxicity, infertility and saliniation.

Improving Human Resources through the practices is an essential strategy. Such practices include:

TABLE 11.2: **Practices to Reach the Goal of Utilising Common Optimally**

Regeneration of Bio-mass by: I	*Utilising Water Optimally by:* II	*Balancing Animal Life with the Ecology by:* III	*Upgrading Land Capability by:* IV	*Improving Human Resources by:* V	*Amplifying Impact by:* VI
(a) Development of forestry and horticulture on slopes, along bunds, roads and canals. (b) Development of grass and grazing lands on steeper and common plots (c) Create nurseries to support watershed development (d) Promotion of crops which are not water gluttens (e) Promotion of inter-cropping (f) Lease government waste and required forest lands for common development of fuel and fodder (g) Promote community compost pits	(a) Promote equitable distribution by: 1. lifting water from wells under tanks and from drainage lines 2. building small *bandharas* and contour canals 3. using more water protective irrigation (b) Water harvesting by collecting run-off in village ponds, community wells and tanks (c) Regeneration of groundwater resources by: 1. building percolation tanks 2. terrace bunding 3. nalla bunding.	(a) Increasing yields of milch animals by: 1. AI 2. better feeding practices 3. upgrading bovine stock. (b) promote fish ponds (c) promote deshi/backyard poultry; co-operative co-ops (d) provide veterinary services (e) honey-bee culture (f) Balancing the load of animals on land and water	(a) Regenerating denuded soil 1. terracing 2. planting grass 3. afforestation promoting contour ploughing (b) Improving Organic Cover and soil moisture by 1. mulching 2. organic manuring 3. strategy I (c) Reducing salinity, toxicity and infertility by: 1. judicious use of irrigation 2. gypsum treatment 3. use of natural fertilisers 4. moderate use of pesticides, funguidices. (d) Water management as in strategy II	(a) Increasing skill levels related to resource management (b) Increasing knowledge of ecological balance, thresholds of loads on resources, terms of trade, inter-cropping, health, hygiene and nutrition, (c) Creating awareness of 1. equity 2. political systems 3. institutions 4. civic duties 5. ecological systems	(a) Creating micro-level institutions 1. co-operatives 2. marketing federations 3. multi-purpose *mondals* (b) Promoting land-use planning/management at the watershed/village level through: 1. expert advice 2. community gaming 3. participatory planning (c) Building community awareness of common resources and their balanced utilisation through: 1. films 2. training 3. demonstrations 4. dialogue schools 5. through schools 6. application of appropriate technology 7. (a) and; (b) above

Source: Benninger, Christopher in "Recommendations for Watershed Development, Planning and Management", (Benninger, Aneeta, Editor, C.D.S.A. 1988).

(a) Increasing *skills* related to resources management. These are skills which enhance traditional ones in the areas of water, land, animal, bio-mass and crop management. Civic skills in holding meetings, carrying out elections, taking and repaying loans are also important. Training to improve skills is essential.

(b) Increasing *knowledge* of ecological balance; the nature of common resources and their interdependence; the difference between utilisation and exploitation; and, the relationship between environment, bio-mass, animal husbandry, nutrition, hygiene and health. Functional education which promotes such awareness is an essential element of the common resources approach.

(c) Creating *awareness* of concepts like equity; enterprise; private and public investment; eco-systems; rent and interest; political systems and public institutions; civic duties and responsibilities. This can be achieved through training, dialogues, films and development support communications in general.

Amplifying action by Integrating practices is an essential strategy which be done by:

(a) Promoting community co-operation in the development of common resources, ensuring their *equitable use*. Self-organised and self-managed micro-level development institutions, therefore, must be promoted.

(b) Promoting *land-use planning* which utilises land most appropriately to its slope, soil and water absorption.

(c) Building community sensitivity about common resources, their management and conservation so that traditional knowledge is supplemented with new skills and appropriate technology. This should lead to the conservation, renewal and harvesting of resources.

Approaches

Governments, indeed most NGOs in rural development, have three basic approaches which temper their work with environment and equity practices. For simplicity these can be labelled as charity, modernisation and development. It is important that we assess each proposed plan of action in terms of its approach to development prior to making a substantial commitment.

Charity

This is the "giving" goal. Most missionary work, many Gandhian activities, indeed the social work tradition itself, began from this direction. It builds a relation of giver and receiver, it sponsors a paternalistic relationship between the donor and the receiver. This approach is to be highly criticised. It impoverishes the recipient in terms of his self-image, his sense of power over the future and his sense of relationship with others. But in many contexts even essentials like drinking water and day-to-day food requirements are absent. To promote "environment", equity or concentisation in such a context, in isolation of these realities, would be a cruel rule of intellectual purity over critical immediate need. Many activists are faced with this dilemma. Should they choose to opt for a "watershed approach" to gain the approval of a funder, or select a "liberation" approach to appease an intellectual constituency? Then one must question the basic values of an activist who dared not go against the tide.

If charity is truly required it must be provided; but we live in a culture of patronage and dependency. The temptation to "give" and be "thanked" must be overcome. Schemes like feeding programmes; free sapplings, free drinking water-pumps and even free clothes and blankets are typical schemes. Often the beneficiaries could afford to pay for these themselves. NGOs, of the charity type, tend to focus on individuals and households, not on natural systems. They would not be prime candidates as partners in the common resources approach. But they should use their schools and contacts to propagate common resources regeneration. They may even take up a small watershed as a pilot project.

Charity may artificially reduce stress amongst a few families, but the detrimental processes, which created the target group in the first place, go unattended. In the long run such an approach aggrevates stresses and conflicts.

Modernisation

Another approach followed by government and NGO development agencies alike is modernisation. This approach focuses on bringing new technology or "progress" into contexts. The "green revolution" package (flow irrigation, hybrid seeds pesticides and fertilisers) often symbolises this. But it prioritises the concept of *growth* as the goal and seeks to link activities into an urban dominated market system. In the name of growth resources may be exploited beyond their thresholds! A number of development agencies have taken this direction. Projects like irrigation, well digging, land levelling and house construction are typical of this approach. Buildings and infrastructure are popular. Projects generally function through elite controlled co-operatives or federations. Sometimes micro-level institutions are initiated for finance and marketing. Increased production, better terms of trade, improved equipment and supplementary income generating activities are typical schemes reflecting the approach. Agencies following this path are often technically and attitudinally prepared to apply common resource strategies. In fact, a number of components of the strategy may already be used in an *ad hoc* manner. Percolation tanks, check dams, terrace bunding, forestry, grass-lands upgradation are all development schemes these agencies are familiar with. With training and technical advice they can make a real impact in the area of natural systems development. But they will have to expand their social awareness, change their priorities from "things" to processes, re-consider their attitudes about participation and take difficult sides on economic, political and environmental issues.

Development

Finally, a limited number of agencies have accepted a definition of development as activities which support processes of transference of power to institutions controlled by the participants whose futures are determined by these institutions. Self-organisation, self-management and democratic decisions about resources supporting equitable access and balanced utilisation are typical goals. Schemes tend to be ones which enhance common resources, enhance natural systems and promote democratic micro-level institutions. They tend to be sensitive to ecological balance. They tend to work within the carrying capacity of resources and to prepare people for public participation in planning and managing their own futures. Within the NGO community there are a number of such agencies. They are already active in facilitating groups of resource users who are encouraged in their efforts to create community based co-operatives, *mandals* and even federations of such micro-level development institutions.

Participation

There are three attitudes amongst development agencies and activist workers regarding participation. By using the word "participation" they appear to be like-minded, but they are not. Participation can be to:

(a) *Facilitate* the NGO, or development agency, in reaching its desired targets, outputs and coverage, instead of the agency facilitating community decisions. These agencies often use "self-help" to achieve their own objectives. They hold "community meetings" to gain support for inputs they have already decided to make;
(b) *mediate* between the agency's interest, government interests, local power group interests and community interest; and,
(c) *Support community control* over decision-making, and local level institutions. This has been noted above. Such agencies are acting as technical, management and planning advisers *to* institutions *of* the community. They facilitate the community rather than the other way around! Their efforts are likely to be most long lasting.

Liberation

A number of the target communities supported by NGOs are economically, socially and culturally oppressed. They do not have access to the means of production which would make them self-sufficient in terms of basic consumption. They live at about the subsistency level. Their role in production systems excludes them from an income by which they can live a dignified life. Their common resources are controlled by a small number of dominant families. These resources are being exploited, actually "mined", far beyond their re-charge thresholds. Terms of trade, modes of production, access to productive assets are key issues. Many NGOs are successfully supporting community institutions to overcome these critical constraints, even with strong opposition from feudal interests.

The vast majority of people has some kind of bonded relationship with those who control the common resources. Social oppression is mainly in the form of denying communities access to functional learning, basic education and knowledge of common resources. Without knowledge they cannot even mediate their own interests. They become socially dependent on persons whose "human resources" are more developed. Without skills they cannot carry out tasks and functions to enhance and utilise their own common resources. Without awareness they cannot control and genuinely participate in local level development institutions. The planning, management and use of common resources depend on this.

Strategies

Strategies will have to focus on a specific group of environment nurturing practices; they will have to reflect a liberal attitude toward participation; they will have to use incentives to regenerate and conserve resources; they will have to apply regulation to ensure equitable access to and use of water, land and productive inputs to assure resources are not exploited for personal gain; and they will have to direct investment toward resource mobilisation which creates common resources and productive assets.

Environmental strategies cannot be applied independently in situations where oppression is characteristic of the relations between elites and the poor, between decision-making and those who depend on the environment. Cultural oppression is commonly practised by purposive development agencies also. It is an instrument of the political economy we live in. Local dress habits, congregating norms, festivals and folk systems are demeaned and projected as inferior. Instead of strengthening traditions, many development agents glorify patterns of behaviour alien to the contexts within which they work.

Development agents who do not recognise even the existence of economic, social and cultural oppression could become unwilling participants in *suppressing* the poor. Many NGOs believe their "beneficiaries", as they call them, live in homogeneous environment. They have not identified a power structure amongst the system users. They argue their case stating such facts as "95 per cent of the people in our area are tribals". Such "activists", even with years of experience in the field, require skills in social science analysis. They require exposure to the literature, which is vast, and which documents oppression in the areas where they work, or in contexts similar to their own. A common resources development approach and the necessary underpinning strategies depend first and foremost on the development of human resources and this cannot be done by agencies who have no concept of the nature of oppression in the very context where they work.

On the other hand there are agencies which actively promote participant-controlled co-operatives, enterprises, collectives, marketing federations and, yes, utilisation and appropriate management of common resources. These catalysts are the most potential for the promotion of a common resources' approach and are possible partners who seek an active role in conflict resolution.

Ultimately, strategies are a public, political and government concern. It is important that we advocate international, national and State strategies which translate into concrete awareness and action. Concern over water issues and resource regions has already led to the creation of administrative and organisational mechanisms which cut across political systems' boundaries to encompass key natural boundaries. The Tennessee Valley Authority is an example in a developed setting. The Delaware River Compact is a case where watershed management is based on natural rather than political boundaries. The Western Ghats Development Programme and the Ganges River Basin Development Authority have similar potentials, but have fallen far short of promises. Japan has used institutional mechanisms to distribute the costs and benefits associated with watershed management, including incentives, to encourage environmentally sound land-use patterns in natural systems (Kumazaki, 1982). Inter-State and inter-district commissions are needed to assure the equitable allocation of water resources amongst participants. New models, like the *Pani Panchayat* experiment, must be built upon to cover entire watersheds and community level, *taluka* level and district level agreements reached on the use of water. Such strategies require statutory backing and can help prevent disputes during droughts, not to mention the prevention of droughts all together!

Human Resources Mobilisation

Sections I and II put forward a hypothesis, and a possible set of practices through which stresses could be reduced and conflicts resolved. These sections suggest a link between laboratory, field and development experiments. They suggest that field surveys and extension work would be integral to such strategies. Colleges, research institutions and universities must play an active role in such a process. But presently our universities are highly isolated from their development contexts and thus are ill-equipped to participate in the practices and strategies noted in section II. As Robert Chambers has stated:

> "Putting the last first means reversals in learning. The litanies of rural developers include: 'We must educate the farmers' and 'We must uplift the rural poor'. These can be stood on their heads. Outsiders have first to learn from farmers and from the rural poor. But many outsiders are hindered from such learning in reverse by their educational attainment, urban status and roles as bearers and dispensers of modern knowledge. Staff working in rural areas distance themselves from rural people, showing their separate style and standing through clothing, shoes, vehicles, office briefcase, documents and manner and speech. Hierarchy, authority and superiority prevent learning 'from below'. Knowledge of one sort perpetuates ignorance of another. Learning has to start at the other end. The farmer must educate outsiders; the poor must bring outsiders down to earth" (*Rural Development: Putting the Last First*, 1983).

Universities will have to support nodes of action-research, holism, field-based learning and doing, as opposed to multi-disciplinary seminars and classroom discussions. Development planning and development management courses will have to be designed which prepare a new kind of professional for a new kind of function. Such courses will have to *use field contexts* as learning laboratories. They will have to *link diverse types of research together*: (a) highly specialised laboratory-based research with field experiments and (b) both of these with development experiments. Field experiments are generally carried out on demonstration farms, while development experiments work with communities in contexts.

This infers a different kind of *relationship* between academics and: (a) the bureaucracy, (b) field-based development workers, and (c) communities in contexts.

In order for this to work, *teachers* will also have to become *part of learning teams* in which their role is more than one of facilitators to active, curious students. Teachers will also have to *advocate* concepts and practices.

We must initiate new learning tools and experiences to create a new kind of professional and to play a role in conflict resolution at the same time. In addition to traditional lectures from the physical and social sciences, such courses could use the following mechanisms to involve faculty and students in "live projects" and field contexts which focus on environmental upgradation, stress reduction and conflict resolution.

Learning Laboratories

Natural, economic and political systems can be studied through laboratory activities. The laboratory uses a *team* approach and an *actual context* for study and planning. The context in a laboratory may be a farm, a village or a watershed depending on the level of the students. It could be a single farm plot, a settlement or a resource region. About three weeks in each semester should be spent in the systemic contexts carrying out field surveys, collecting secondary data, holding group discussions and making observations to document patterns of indicators which describe situations. Laboratories should apply common resources concepts and practices to natural systems like watersheds.

Laboratories should focus on natural systems, meet daily for several hours of applied work, must go through a process of analysing natural systems and designing strategies for action. This process would include the following steps:

1. *Contextual Factors* such as socio-economic history, geo-climatic patterns, socio-economic structure and demographic patterns must be documented. The physical quality of life and standard of living should be analysed. The present state of water, land, animal, bio-mass and human resources should be studied and stated in terms of indicators. The political bodies and the types of decisions about natural systems, they make, should be described. Constraints and potentials will emerge from these studies and must be stated.
2. *Sectoral factors*, such as existing services, facilities, productivity, markets, economic activities, terms of trade and modes of production, should be analysed. Practices and processes which have either a positive or negative impact on the environment should be analysed. Lacunae and opportunities emerge from these studies.
3. *Stress analysis* is then carried out to determine which practices, which lacunae and which constraints are putting stresses on the system. These are illustrated in terms of patterns related to performance indicators. Reliability, equity and productivity, with regard to target groups and natural eco- and agro-systems, are

stated. Goals, or broad aims to be achieved, can then be stated.

4. *Plan-options* are then stated along with implied supporting practices. The costs, benefits and impacts of actions are stated.
5. *Issues should then be stated* in terms of choices between different plan-opts. The social, economic, political and environmental costs and benefits should be compared and weighed. Evaluations between them result in a framework and an appropriate set of strategies.
6. *Objectives* are stated in terms of desired: (a) *Outcomes*: including spatial coverage, target populations, time frames and changes in states of resources, or relations between them; and (b) *Schemes* are designed to create these changes and are defined in terms of required inputs, expected outputs and selected practices.
7. *A Programme* is then designed with a schedule, targets, investment plan, source-wise, cash flow, performance indicators and monitoring tools.
8. Finally, a framework, including required institutional mechanisms, an organisational structure and personnel functions, is designed for implementation.

Ideally, over a four-semester course, students should be exposed, through the laboratory, to four different tiers of natural systems: a farm, a village, a watershed and a natural region of watersheds.

The Watershed Project

This should be an eight-week independent project wherein the student works with a community group or an NGO in a context and carries out a programmed analysis of a watershed and designs an action plan for stress reduction and conflict resolution. Both are integrated into a formal report which would highlight concepts, practices, strategies and priorities. Ideally, this would take place between the second and third semesters of a four-semester postgraduate course.

Special Paper

Each student should carry out an individual project designed by him/her in consultation with a guide and resource persons. This project should result in a formal study, presented in the form of a paper at a seminar at the end of the course. Generally, the special paper will focus on the programmatic impact of practices on a watershed. The study may highlight economic and political systems and their impact on natural systems. It may look at a single natural system as a case study. It may look at links between common resources or between homogeneous systems. The resulting paper should relate to the evaluation of an on-going programme, the test of a hypothesis in the field, or a descriptive study of a development process. Such studies should be divided into:

a. a review of the literature, in which the context typology, concerned sectors of development, and/or systemic approach to development, is presented by other scholars and field-based activists;
b. the design of an analytical methodology, including the design of survey tools. Students should be encouraged to use case studies, group discussions, process and procedure "informants", as well as traditional "respondents" to surveys;
c. field experiences should be used both to carry out the analytical methodology and as a participant observer in a changing context. Students should be encouraged to identify actors and their functional links and roles; and ,
d. Analysis of information, data and observations should be carried out. Process documentation of resources acting on each other and on an environment is the focus of the special paper. This should be formally presented at a seminar, and then presented as a formal academic paper. Such papers would then become advocacy tools to promote "environment friendly" strategies and policies.

Seminars

Seminars focused on issues of resources, inequality and public policy should be organised in a structured series to encourage students to: (a) think on their feet, (b) speak out, and (c) write succinct reports. Advocacy of strategies, approaches, practices and policies should be encouraged. The seminars could cover topics such as: (a) water, land, animal husbandry, bio-mass, cropping, nutrition and health; (b) education, employment and human resources development, and (c) eco- and agro-systems, resource bases, carrying capacities, migration and urbanisation. During the seminars students should present an inception report, a preliminary seminar and their final presentation.

Activism/Practice

After completing their academic requirements, graduates should be placed with NGOs or government development agencies to work in the field on "live projects". The length of this experience should be open-ended. It could result in a career opening, or merely be a first professional exposure.

The Centre for Development Studies and Activities at Poona, is experimenting with such an approach through its postgraduate professional diploma course in development planning and management under the University of Poona. This programme of inquiry and experience is focused on the creation of a new profession of catalysts whose values, efforts, skills, knowledge and awareness are directed toward and derived from change processes which put people first and, amongst people, put the vulnerable foremost. This programme uses natural systems, such as farms, watersheds and regions, as units of analysis and analyses common resource patterns in these units. The approach is holistic, field based and learning from people through joint analysis and understanding. This new profession works in uncontrolled, real conditions where variable new arrangements are the outcomes as opposed to sets of pre-determined solutions. Emphasis is placed on developing subjective and qualitative sensitivities, gaining knowledge from contexts and building skills which bring professionals into contact with processes, relationships, localised awareness and primary sources of information.

The Role of the University

The prime role of the University is to create graduates with sensitivity to development processes and issues; knowledge of contexts and sectors; and skills analysis, planning and management of strategy options. *Relevant education* is the first role.

The second role is to research of the *study of natural development systems*, their components, the functional relations between their parts, their elemental characteristics and the key management decisions which reduce stress and resolve conflict. We spend far too much time focused on "disciplines" imported from foreign contexts, reading irrelevant texts from alien societies and in isolating ourselves from contemporary, real world problems and objective reality. We spend far too much time in classrooms away from landless labourers, farmers, villages, watersheds and community leaders.

Finally, universities must use their vast resources to *catalyse other agencies* to become activists in a constructive spirit. Rather than isolating themselves in ivory towers, universities must reach out to their contextual communities and involve themselves in real issues. Both as individuals, as colleges and departments, we tend to isolate ourselves from social work, democratic processes, community work and action. We see our scholarly pursuits as different from the processes around us. A new style of functioning will have to emerge where teachers also become students, where collegiate teams solve problems jointly and where the field replaces the text as a laboratory for learning. We must find stresses, isolate their causal factors and adopt measures to reduce them.

We must see development as our prime concern and realise that reform and conflict resolutions require research and educated young development professionals and that our society looks toward us for solutions!

REFERENCES

Aneeta, Benninger, et al., "Recommendations for Watershed Development, Planning and Management", Poona: Centre for Development Studies and Activities (1988).

Christopher, Benninger, *Migration, Spatial Planning and Human Resources Development*, Kuala Lumpur, UN-APDC/ESCAP (1983).

Lester R., Brown, et al., *State of the World*: New York: Norton (1987).

Centre for Development Studies and Activities, *Pani Panchayat*: *Conservation and Equitable Distribution of Water*, Poona, India: CDSA (1983).

Centre for Science and Environment, *The State of India's Environment*: New Delhi: Centre for Science and Technology (1982).

Centre for Science and Environment, *The Wrath of Nature*, New Delhi: Centre for Science and Technology (1987).

Chambers, Robert, *Rural Development: Putting the Last First*, New York: Longman (1983).

Conway, Gordon, *Rapid Appraisal for Agro-system Analysis*, London: Centre of Environmental Technology, Imperial College of Science and Technology (1985).

Dhruva, Narayana and Babu Ram, "Estimation of Soil Erosion in India", *Journal of Irrigation and Drainage Engineering*, 109, 4, December (1983).

Food and Agricultural Organisation (FAO), "Watershed Management in Asia and the Pacific: Needs and Opportunities for Action", Rome: Technical Report FO: RAS/85/017, (1986).

International Crops Research Institute for Semi-Arid Tropics (ICRISAT), "Medium and Low Rainfall Areas: Hydrology and Possible Research Trusts in Water Management", Hyderabad: Mimeo (1986).

Kumazaki, M., "Sharing Financial Responsibility with Water Users for Improvement of Forest Watersheds: A Historical Review of the Japanese Experience". *The Current State of Japanese Forestry*, II, R. Hand, Editor, Tokyo (1982).

McGee, T.G., *The Urbanisation Process in the Third World*, London, G. Bell and Sons. (1971).

Nag, B.S., and Kathpalia, "Water resource in India", in *Water and Human Needs*: Proceedings of the Second World Congress on Water Resources, 2, New Delhi: Central Board of Irrigation and Power (1975).

Salunkhe, Vilasrao, Naigaon: discussions with the author regarding various water management approaches at Naigaon Village, March, 1989.

Ward, Barbara, and Dubos, Rene, *Only One Earth* London: Andre Deutch. (1972).

The Working Group on Watershed Management and Development, "Sustainable Growth and Development: The Role of Watershed Management", University of Minnesota, Ad-hoc Working Paper (1987).

12

CONFLICT IN TRIBAL AREAS AND PERSPECTIVE OF PEACEFUL RESOLUTION

B.K. ROY BURMAN

MAX WEBER characterises a social relation as conflict insofar as action within it is oriented intentionally to carry out the actor's own will against the resistance of the other party or parties. He uses the term peaceful conflict to cases in which actual physical violence is not used.[1]

In this formulation peace has been conceptualised in an amorphous manner. Even when physical violence is pushed under the carpet under the threat of more severe, more ruthless violence it can be projected as peace. As pointed out by Fanon, in colonial countries, the policeman and the soldier, by their immediate presence, can enforce silence.[2] This is tranquillity of the grave and it is difficult to say that colonial legacy has disappeared from all parts of the world. There is, however, tranquillising violence of a different order. In the words of Fanon:

> "The colonialist bourgeoisie, expounded by the members of the universities, had in fact deeply implanted in the minds of the colonised intellectual that the essential qualities remain eternal in spite of all the blunders man may make: the essential qualities of the West of course. The native intellectual accepted the cogency of these ideas, and deep down in his brain you could always find a vigilant sentinel ready to defend the Greco-Latin pedestal." This tranquillising violence without bloodshed is nothing more than

'negative peace', it, however, is not eternal"[3] the moment the native intellectual comes into touch again with his people, this artificial sentinel is turned into dust."[4]

Gandhi recognised very clearly that the human family may perhaps never reach a state where there will be no conflict, or where conflict will no longer have to be resolved by "direct action". So he tried to find a substitute which would not leave man debased, as he now is, after a conflict. It was in the pursuit of this that he invented the technique of *Satyagraha*, by which conflicts could be conducted at a civilised moral level. *Satyagraha* literally means "insistence upon truth". The basic assumption underlying it is that no man sees truth, in its entirety, and he, therefore, has no moral right to impose a particular view of truth upon others. However, it is his right and duty to live according to his own lights, and to oppose whatever seems to him wrong in the views of others. The *Satyagrahi*, the man who practises *Satyagraha*, refuses to co-operate with a social system based upon immorality. At the same time, he tries to built up a different way of life in terms of what he considers to be moral. *Satyagraha* has thus two aspects: one which is constructive and the other which leads to militant, but civil, opposition to wrongs. In the course of such resistance, the *Satyagrahi*, patiently and courageously bears all the violence which his 'opponent' may shower upon him, yet refuses to regard the opponent as an enemy and aims at his conversion. For him, the human family can never be divided into those who are friends and those who are enemies.[5]

According to this perspective, questions of positive values and strategies of liberation from domination and imposition are involved in the pursuit of peace. 'Peace', Gandhi advocated, 'is integrally related to justice'. "Peace must be just." Peace is not mere cessation of hostilities. Peace for him connotated a positive state of affairs, the precondition being freedom from exploitation.[6] Gandhi was not a pacifist in the sense that he was against all wars whether just or unjust. He was of the view that fellow war resisters in the West were participants in war even in peace time inasmuch as they paid for the preparations that were made for it and otherwise sustained governments whose main occupation was such preparations.[7] Gandhi considered righteous and wished success to the Spanish Republicans fighting Franco, the Chinese struggling against Japan and the Poles resisting Germany, though in each case he wished that they had offered non-violent resistance. Speaking about Nazi German's oppression of the Jews, he said "if ever there could be a justifiable war in the name of, and for, humanity, a war against Germany to prevent the wanton persecution of whole race would be completely justified. But I do not believe in any war." Further, he observed:

> "I believe all wars to be wholly wrong. But if we scrutinise the motives of the two warring parties, we may find one to be in the right and the other in the wrong."

An escapist, self-righteous, neutralism was incompatible with the tenets of, Gandhi's pursuit of peace. But though his sympathies were wholly with the allies, he was aware that Hitler and Mussolini could defy the world opinion because none of the so-called great powers could come to them with clean hands and they had a rankling sense of injustice done by themselves to their people.[8] Thus, Gandhi's conditional support to the allies even to the extent of hoping for their victory in the violent war against fascism was an extension of his relentless struggle against the systems of internal domination and suppression of human freedom, though, in less odious forms, imposed over large section of humanity by those very powers.

It is against this backdrop of conceptualisation of the issues of war and peace, embedded in mainstream of India's freedom struggle under the leadership of Gandhi, that the conflicts in tribal areas and the traditions and prospects of their peaceful resolution are to be considered.

Four types of conflict can be envisaged in tribal areas:

(a) Diffused conflict at the ideational level.
(b) Conflicts within the tribal communities.
(c) Conflicts in tribal areas involving different communities.
(d) Conflicts in tribal areas involving tribal communities and the State.

These four types of conflict are not wholly mutually exclusive. However, for analytical purpose each of these will be examined separately and some broad indications will be given of how they impinge on one another.

Diffused Conflict at the Ideational Level

For Godelier[9] the social formation, tribe is identified in two ways: first, as a stage in the history of evolution of societies, second, as a type of society organised on the basis of kinship which enables it to be a multi-functional grouping.

This duality in the conceptualisation of tribe has an important implication. Analytically, and historically, it is possible to envisage the world view of communion and reciprocity between man and man and between man and nature (rather than that of competition and coercion) can be dissociated from the imagery of primitiveness associated with it.[10]

In the contemporary world, tribe is more frequently looked upon from the first vantage point of evolutionary scheme and this is a source of much conflict. This perspective is implicit in the Convention on Indigenous Peoples adopted by ILO in 1957 and later ratified by India. It envisages 'integration' of the indigenous peoples into the dominant society and 'development' in the Western sense over a length of time. But in recent years the indigenous peoples in different parts of the world are objecting to the convention's paternalism. In 1975 a World Council of Indigenous People (WCIP) was formed and was later conferred NGO status by the U.N. In 1987 a Council of Indigenous and Tribal Peoples was constituted in India and was granted the status of an affiliate of WCIP. The official point of view is to deny the existence of any distinct indigenous population in India; but this seems to be informed by historical nominalism; it is very different from critical realism. Irrespective of the place and time of their origin or their occupation of the present habitats in India, there are certain communities which, until recently maintained practically autogenous sources of legitimation of cultural and social processes, are actuated by the ideology of self-regulated economy and have only marginal articulation with external political structures. Their indigenous identity cannot be brushed away by juxtaposition of non-meaningful occurrences in space and time in systemic terms. Identity is a question of consciousness of the persistence of the imagery of historical meaning-related events in the lives of individuals and collectivities. While non-recognition of at least some ethnic entities in India as indigenous population will accentuate the conflict, even formal recognition, will not clinch the issue.[11] In a statement to the working group on indigenous people, set up by the U.N., Samar Brahma Choudhury, a tribal MP of India, observed:

> "The concept of self-determination is in-built in our relationship with nature and with one another, both as individuals and as

groups. It is fundamental, related and consequential. Just as we find a relationship with the sun, the moon, the universe, the change of season and its reflections in nature and in relationship with fellow human beings, so also the concept of self-determination has in itself a rhythm, a balance, an excellence and conscience. It means to achieve harmony, cohesion with other groups in the country so that in a peaceful atmosphere even the ethnic minorities and weaker sections of the population can preserve their geographical boundary or territory and maintain their distributive ethnic identity and that way help attaining dignity and self-respect, attaining highest standard of civilisation. Self-determination is a principle to live and let live."[12]

But the indigenous peoples all over the world have become sceptical about their prospect to live and let live. In a statement, issued by WCIP, it has been asserted that "Government officials, executives of transnational corporations and officers of development banks have often only a limited knowledge of indigenous societies. Yet the projects of these officials — authorise dams, roads, re-locations of population — affect irrevocably the peoples who lie in their paths. It is not just a case of ignorance; a basic change of attitude is required.[13]

What is significant is that the indigenous and tribal population is on a course of vigorous self-assertion and is taking strident postures. At the same time they are forming horizontal linkages on a global plane to espouse their cause in international forums and carry out a joint struggle.

Conflict within Tribal Communities

Ethnographic accounts are replete with intra-tribal conflicts and feuds centering access to land and resources. These accounts also describe the traditional arrangement for keeping these conflicts within manageable limits. Here conflict of a particular order, namely those related to the State processes and intervention of State apparatuses, will only be discussed.

Traditionally, in most tribal areas, individual rights of enjoyment of land and land-based resources are embedded in communal systems of access to and management of resources. While in the middle ages in some of the tribal areas feudal control was imposed by colonial system, during the later part of the colonial rule, attempts were made to convert the political rights of the military overlords into proprietary rights of feudal nature. But, due to lack of administrative infrastructure, such attempts mostly remained on paper. In the post-independence period, rather than correcting these attempts towards feudal distortion, these were accepted as crucial elements in the legal framework for implementation of policies and programmes in the tribal areas. Paper laws of the coloniai dispensation were given the place of pride over the laws on the ground by which the people lived, and, by and large, still live.[14] This has accentuated internal contradictions within the tribal communities. In some cases, as in the Kuki areas of Manipur, the tribal chiefs, who were promoted by the colonial rule and the subsidiary agencies of the same almost as landlords, were removed from their position by popular upsurge more than two decades ago. But recently when attempts were made to extend the so-called land reform law to the tribal areas, it was found that the law was framed in such a manner that unless the chiefs were recognised as the holders of the lands at the disposal of the tribal communities, the communities as such had no *locus standi* to lay claim on the lands enjoyed by them. Thus, there was a danger of non-feudalism being fasted on the tribal communities. Some of the tribal communities tried to meet the challenge by reinterpreting and strengthening the social control over the chiefs through the instrumentality of culture mechanism. But it may not be far off the mark to think that much of ongoing upsurge, violent and nonviolent in the tribal areas of North-East India, is related to the question of control and management of land.[15] Problem of the same order has been found in the tribal areas of Chota Nagpur and recent studies show that here also a neo-deudalisation process has been promoted during the recent land survey and settlement operation.[16] In some areas, the tribals, however, have offered stiff resistance resulting in the suspension of survey and settlement operation due to the non-cooperation of the concerned people.

Inter-community Conflict in Tribal Areas

During the colonial rule large-scale in-migration of non-tribal population had taken place in tribal areas like Chota Nagpur, borders of Assam and North Bengal and so on. Apart from generating acute strain for control of resources, there was also strain of coping with exploitation by money-lenders and traders, backed by State power. There was also the strain of cultural invasion. The tribal upsurges of the 19th and early 20th centuries, which mostly took violent form, are related to this phenomenon.[17] One of the interesting features of some of these upsurges is that non-tribal artisans and other village functionaries, who were equally subjected to many inequities, associated themselves with their tribal neighbours. Another feature is that when the violent upsurges failed immediately the tribal communities took to cult movements.[18] These cult movements were of two types. The cult movement of Birsa Munda was associated with the strategy of social mobilisation for political action in violent form. The cult movement of Jatra Oraon was also associated with political action, but this was of non-violent type and tended to merge with the national movement under Gandhi's leadership. There were also cult movements of violent type, as the one led by Gadonang and Gaidinliu which swore by Gandhi and sought for peace by removing foreign domination. There was another type of cult movement which mainly confined to the religious field with occasional forages into politics. Among them mention may be made of the Kherwari movement of the Santhals in the late 19th century; various Bhagat movements of the Bhils also belong to this category. Adoption of Christianity by the tribes of North-East India on large scale, and by sections of the tribal communities in the central belt as well as adoption of a Hindu puritanism by sections of plains tribals of Assam also deserve mention in this connection. All these can be described as social mobility movements through ritual rank path, rather than as mobilisation strategies with political goals or structural change.[19]

In the post-independence period, however, pursuit of ritual rank-path seems to have lost much of its momentum. As it has been found that it does not solve the basic problem of retention of control over resources; on the other hand it tends not only to aggravate economic dependence but also to attract, sometimes the stamp of social inferiority.

Conflict in Tribal Areas Involving Tribal Communities and the State

The basic source of conflict is the State process itself. Max Weber has described tribal social formation as "regulated anarchy."[20] It is the moral binding rather than the coercive power, of agony ridden State apparatus, which is the basis of solidarity of tribal communities. Thus, there is inherent contradiction in tribal and State systems. This contradiction is accentuated in welfare state, which, according to both Gandhi and Mao, in the long run favours the elite.[21]

Many of the tribal communities respond to the presence of the State through minimal articulation with the State apparatus, on the one hand, and, on the other hand, through the functioning and traditional mechanising of social control as "shadow State" — neither in confrontation nor in dialogue with the State. These are not alternative centres of power, but non-power *sanctum sanctorum* of community life.

There are again cases where articulation with the State takes place through a transformation of the original meaning of articulation. As illustration will bring out the point. In the border of West Bengal and Bhutan lives a small tribe, the Totos. They are found in only one village Totopara. Till the middle of the last century Totopara was under Bhutia rule; then it came under the control of the British in the aftermath of Anglo-Bhutan was in which the Totos did not play any role. The Totos were conditioned to the legitimisation of power and actual exercise of power by the functionaries of Bhutan kingdom. As in the formulation of Fernand Broad[22] history is not mere sequence of events, but a process of adaptation of conditioned facts, change in the actual exercise of power did not automatically change the source of legitimisation of power. Earlier to the extension of British rule to the area, the Totos used to pay tax to the functionaries of the Bhutan king: In the new situation they began to pay tax to the revenue officials of the British; but they did not discontinue payment to the Bhutan King. Only the secular tax was converted to sacred homage and till the early part of the '50s they made the payment. On the death bed of the secular, the sacred had emerged.[23]

But the sacred was not born, it was all the time these in sub surface psyche. One requires to delve in the basic world view of the tribal communities to understand this. In the words of the Vice-President of International Working Group for Indigenous Affairs (IWGIA): "For indigenous peoples, life and earth are synonymous."[24] Again in the words of the Co-Chairman of International Commission of Indigenous People. "Indigenous peoples have custodial attitudes toward land and life."[25] Related to this world view is the legal philosophy of historical-axiology as against that of legal positivism. The former lends support to the legal concept of *lex loci ri-sitae* (law of the place where the thing is situated), the latter upholds the legal concept of *res nullius* (rights to property accrues to individuals from the property of nobody, thus the State is having superior right over all lands). As pointed out by Justice

Hidayatullah,[26] the concept of *res nullius* is a colonial legacy. Many of the problems in 'political, economic and social' areas in tribal India hinge on to this legacy.

On the other hand, a closer look at the custodial attitudes of the tribals to·land and life immediately reveals the fact that these bear close similarity to Gandhi's concept of trusteeship in its revised version of 1945.[27] This aspect of the matter has not received the attention that it deserves from the academics. A systematic study of tribal world-view and polity in the light of Gandhi's approach to war and peace and his formulation regarding trusteeship he will do immense good to the country.

NOTES

1. Max Weber, *Theory of Social and Economic Organisation*, Glencoe, Free Press (1947).
2. Franz Fanon, *The Wretched of the Earth*, Penguin Books (1963), p.36.
3. Johan Galtung, Quoted by Robin Clark in *The Science of War and Peace*, McGraw-Hill Book Co., New York (1971). p.302.
4. Franz Fanon, (1965). *op. cit.*
5. N.K. Bose, *Gandhi, Humanist and Socialist*, (ed. Erich Fromm, Socialist Humanism; Anchor Books, Dubleday & Co., Garden City, New York (1965).
6. Buddhadeb Bhattacharya, *Evolution of the Political Philosophy of Gandhi*, Calcutta: Calcutta Book House (1968), p.457.
7. J.B. Kripalani, *Gandhian Thought*, Bombay, Oriental Longman (1961), p.141.
8. Buddhadeb Bhattacharya, *op. cit.* (1968), pp.443-46.
9. Maurice Godelier, *Perspective in Marxist Anthropology* Cambridge, Cambridge University Press (1977).
10. B.K. Roy Burman, Transformation of Tribes and Analogous Social Formation, *EPW* 18 (27), July (1983).
11. B.K. Roy Burman, Indigenous Peoples and Their Quest for Justice, *Social Action*, 39, Jan-March (1989).
12. Workings of the All India Consultation on Indigenous and Tribal Peoples, Deptt. of Tribal and Regional Languages, Ranchi University, 1986.
13. *International Work Group for Indigenous Affairs (IWGIA) Year Book for 1986*; Copenhagen, Denmark.
14. Report of the Committee on Land Holding system of the Tribal Planning Commission, Govt. of India (1987).
15. B.K. Roy Burman, Issues in Land Reforms in N-E Tribal Areas; *Mainstream*, August 1 and 8 (1987).
16. B.K. Roy Burman, Historical Process in Respect of Communal Land System and Poverty Alleviation among Tribals; *Social Action* 37, Oct.-Dec (1987).
17. D.G. Mandelbaum, *Society in India* 11 (1970), pp.572-86.
18. K.S. Singh, *Tribal Society in India*, Bombay, Manohar Publications (1985).

19. B.K. Roy Burman *Challenges and Response in Tribal India* in M.S. Rao, *Social Movements in India* (ed.), 11 (1978).
20. Max Weber, *Wirts chaft and Gesellschaft* (1922).
21. Rafiq Khan A comparative study of Gandhi and Mao Peace Research For Peace Action; Gandhian Institute of Studies, Varanasi (1972).
22. Braudal Fernand, *On history*, Widen feld and Nicoloson, London (1980).
23. B.K. Roy Burman Hundred Years in a Tribal Village Nihar Ranjan Roy, (ed.), *Trends of socio-economic change in India*. (1969).
24. IWGIA *op. cit.*
25. *Indigenous Peoples a Global Quest for Justice*, London and New Jersey, Zed Books (1987).
26. M. Hidayatullah, *Rights to property and Indian Constitution*, New Delhi: Arnold Heinmann publishers (India) Pvt. Ltd (1983).
27. M.L. Dantwala, "Trusteeship Its Value Implications" *Gandhi Marg* Nov.-Dec (1985).

13

RESOLUTION OF CONFLICT BETWEEN MOTHER-IN-LAW AND DAUGHTER-IN-LAW: A Social Work Approach

K.D. GANGRADE

THE PURPOSE of this chapter is to emphasise that enough recognition has not been given to the family of the client who is in need of help. The case record presented here intends to stress that the family should be taken into account in a major way in the Indian context in "study", "diagnosis" and "treatment" of the client. The emphasis in the record is that it is not the individual but the family that should be considered as the unit of work. The whole burden of the record is to shift the emphasis from one-to-one relationship of a client and a case worker to that of a family in the Indian situation. The emphasis of the workers should be family centred rather than individual-centred for the clients who are in need of help.

Family-centred approach, if it is to deserve this name, is not only concerned with the client and his family but also helps us to understand in which manner the client fits into his family of which he is a product and member. We have to know about the way the family lives, the way the members of the family interact and about the way the roles are assigned to members of the family. We have to know whether the family of the client is different from any other family. Is the family with a problem member (client) also a problem family? Do we deal with the problem by treating symptoms? These are some of the questions to be asked in order to understand the client and his problems fully.

Description of the Village

Village Shantipur is a multi-caste village. Twelve castes live in the village with the following distribution: eighty Jat (peasant), 20 Brahmin (priest), 15 *Chamar* (cobbler), eight *bhangi* (sweeper), seven *Kumhar* (potter), five *Jhinvar* (water carrier), four *dhobi* (washerman), four *Khati* (carpanter), three *Nai* (barber), two *Shilpi* (calico-printer or tailor), one *Lohar* (blacksmith) and one *Bania* (merchant) families.

The village has a population of 1080 people. There is a total of 648 Jats, 110 Brahmins, 107 *Chamars*, 52 *Bhangis* and 163 members of the other remaining castes' households. The Jat households are by far the largest. The average family sise for Jat's is 8.3, for Brahmin's 7.3, for *chamar's* 5, for *Bania's* 5.2 and for the remaining castes 6.8.

Types of Family Constellation

An analysis of kinship composition of each household in the village shows that there are three or four major family constellations. The first type consists of simple biological family of father and mother with unmarried children; the second of father, mother with or without unmarried children plus one, two, three or even more married sons and their wives and children; the third represents a stage further of brothers and their spouses and children with only the husband's father or mother; and the fourth is of widows and widowers living alone.

Seventy-seven per cent of all house-sites with extended families of type two and three in village are Jats and almost 70 per cent of Jat households are of the extended family type. The Brahmin family constellation follows the Jat pattern but among the lower castes, the nuclear family predominates. This shows that majority of Jats and Brahmins have been influenced by the model of the joint family system and its social structure.

Social History of the Client

The client Kamla is a married woman of about 23 years of age. She is the eldest child in the family and has four siblings — two brothers and two sisters. Both the brothers are in college and sisters in the school. Her parents are well-educated. The father is a law graduate and the mother is a matriculate. The family is richest amongst the Jat families in the village. Her father has two residences — one in the village and the other in the town. He visits the village once a week and on holidays to supervise and help in the agricultural operations. He runs the farm on modern lines. His father and brothers are primarily responsible for agricultural operations in the village.

Kamla's mother after five years of marriage came to live in the town. The change in residence was necessitated because her father found it very difficult to commute from the village frequently to the town to attend to his flourishing practice. The other reason was that the city provided better educational facilities to the growing children than the village. The mother of the client also resumed her studies in the town as she had plenty of leisure time. Both the mother and daughter matriculated together in the same year. The mother found it difficult to pursue her studies in college due to her age and distance. The client, however, continued her studies and took a B.Sc. degree in Home Science. After graduation she was married to the eldest son of a retired army major of Shantipur village, who was a lecturer. This match was arranged by her grandfather.

She came to live with her in-laws soon after marriage. Her father-in-law is considered very rich in the village. He is the elected *Pradhan* (Chairman) of the village *Panchayat* (council), is a good worker and has completed a large number of self-help projects int he village. He has also introduced new innovations in the village, has very good relations with his caste-brethern in other villages and is also the Chairman of the caste *Panchayat* of a few adjoining Jat villages. The client finds her father-in-law an enlightened, understanding and affectionate person towards her.

The client's mother-in-law is an orthodox and dominating person. She has no education, wants her daughter-in-law to observe *pardah* (veil) and not to talk to any man in the village. She also does not approve of her going to the woman's Centre regularly.

Her husband commutes to the college in the town every day. He has one younger brother and one younger sister. The brother-in-law is very respectful to the client as she is much more educated and is also older than him. He himself is not much educated and looks after agriculture. The sister-in-law has recently been married to a captain in the Army. She is educated only up to the middle level in the village school. The client and the sister-in-law get along very well with each other.

The Client Refers her Problem

The client is a regular visitor to the Centre. She finds in the social worker a very good company. She helps the worker by taking an active interest in the activities of the Centre. Despite these good relations, the client did not come out with her problem at once and tried to postpone telling the worker thinking that she would be able to sort out her problem with her mother-in-law.

She was feeling ashamed to talk to the worker directly about her own problem. She, therefore, talked to her in an indirect manner in the beginning. She told the worker that there was a girl in the village who was being treated very badly by her mother-in-law does not even allow her to talk to her husband and also forbids her son to talk or meet his wife whenever he wishes. One day seeing both husband and wife taking milk together she scolded both of them bitterly. The son left the house to allow the matter to settle down and to avoid further provocation. The daughter-in-law became the target and was severely reprimanded. Her parents were also dragged in. This being intolerable, the girl asked her mother-in-law to spare her parents from the tirade. This further enraged the mother-in-law who reprimanded the girl for answering back to elders. The client could hardly finish the story when she broke down, thus exposing who the real client was. The worker consoled the client and extended her assistance in getting over her difficulties.

First Interview

The client in her next visit to the centre wanted to narrate to the worker her plight but she was hesitant because there were other women of the village present. The worker sensed the embarrassment of the client and thought it better to discuss the issue of daughter-in-law and mother-in-law relationship with village women who were present at the time.

Most of the women present were daughters but a few of them were daughters-in-law as well. The client was the most educated among them. One of the daughters-in-law opined that in modern days the educated girls resent the authority and control of mothers-in-law. On the other hand, the mother-in-law also wants her daughter-in-law to be submissive in every respect. A few of the daughters-in-law expressed the feeling that their mother-in-law were not treating them nicely. They wanted to be with their husband, to talk and go out with them as the women of the city do. But this was considered very much shameful by the mothers-in-law and contrary to the local custom and norms.

The client who had been a silent participant in the discussion was asked about her point of view on the relationship between daughter-in-law and mother-in-law. She said that it should be of mutual respect. The daughter-in-law should be given a rightful place in the home and should not be treated as somebody inferior and subordinate. Most of the women present agreed with her point of view.

The client looked relaxed and more comfortable. She felt happy that her ideas were shared by most women and that others were also facing similar difficulties in their relationships. When the other women left the Centre, she shared this with the worker:

Worker:

"I am extremely happy to know that the discussion had given you an opportunity of sharing your problem. If you wish to tell me any of your difficulties, I shall postpone my home visit".

Client:

"Yes, sister, I want to tell you about my difficulties. As you know, my husband is a lecturer in the University. He wants me to dress well and smartly and go out with him to restaurants, etc. We also visit my parents when we go to the city. All this is not liked by my mother-in-law. She taunts by saying that I have done something to her son who dances to my tunes. She becomes very angry when my husband takes me out or looks after my little comforts. She spreads all types of stories about me among neighbours. I want to respect her like my own mother but she does not even like my calling her *mataji* (mother) but insists that I call her *sasji* (mother-in-law). My husband on the other hand says that I should not care about the social formalities and listen to him only. I feel very much confused and depressed because of all these things. My mother-in-law wants me to remain traditional while my husband desires that I should adopt modern ways of living".

Worker:

"I am sorry to learn about the attitude of your mother-in-law towards you but I am happy to know that your husband cares a lot about you. You should ask your husband not to neglect and ignore his mother and give her the social importance that she deserves."

Client:

"Yes, I am very lucky in having a loving husband. My mother-in-law feels that I have snatched away her son from her. I shall act on your advice and persuade my husband to recognise the superiority of his mother in the household and in matters concerning me".

Second Interview

Client:

"I have persuaded my husband to give all respect to his mother. But she does not tolerate even the smallest freedom on our part. I shall tell you an incident that occurred the other day. My mother-in-law's brother is hospitalised in the town. My mother-in-law asked my husband and me to go and visit him. We were a little late in coming back since we visited my parents on way back. This annoyed her very much because we had not taken her permission to visit my parents. She accused my husband of having changed and not caring about his parents and said I was mainly responsible for all this change in the attitude of her son. My husband tried to pacify her by saying that he had not changed at all and that it was not a sin to visit one's in-laws. My mother-in-law went to the kitchen after saying that one loses one's respect if one goes to the in-law's house without being invited. I went to help her in the kitchen but she completely ignored me and would neither talk to me nor take notice of my presence. I, then, went to my room. My husband was taking milk and forced me also to take some. My mother-in-law came to our room and was very angry and asked what was the happy occasion which was prompting them to take glass after glass of milk. My husband said that it was on his insistence that I was taking milk. This enraged her further and she asked him whether he was going to make me a wrestler by forcing me to take so much milk. She called me a *Rani Sahiba* (Queen of the house) sarcastically who could not eat *dal* (pulses) without four or five spoons of *ghee* (clarified butter). Remarks like this disturb me very much and I do not know what I shall do."

Worker:

"What was your husband's reaction to all this?"

Client:

"He says that I should be prepared to set up a separate house in the city which will also save him the trouble of going to town every day for college. But I do not want the joint family to break up and moreover this will confirm my mother-in-law's belief that I have taken her son away from her and I am the cause of breaking the family."

Worker:

"I am glad that you have not taken a hasty step of setting up a separate house."

Client:

"But, sister, how can I go on tolerating all this?"

Worker:

"What is your father-in-law's attitude towards you?"

Client:

"He is a very nice person. He often talks to my mother-in-law to treat me like a daughter. He often says that it is not easy to get an educated but simple girl like me."

Worker:

"I am so glad to hear this. Has your sister-in-law come to the village?"

Client:

Yes, brother-in-law was sent to fetch her from her in-laws' house for the festival of Diwali."

Worker:

"I should like to meet her. She was an active member of the centre before she was married."

Client:

"I have found her very sympathetic towards me. We both like each other. She may not be able to come to the centre as she has a small baby."

Worker:

"Then I shall come to your house to meet her. I shall also have the chance to meeting your mother-in-law and see how your problem can be solved."

Client:

"You will be welcomed any day you choose to come."

Third Interview

The worker, on the next visit to her village, went to the house of the client. She along with her mother-in-law and sister-in-law was sitting inside the house. Her sister-in-law felt so happy on seeing the worker that she hugged and embraced her and then took her inside the house where she was offered a seat. She greeted the old lady who smiled back and said that the worker had come to their house after many days. The worker told her that she had been very busy and hence was not able to visit the households. The worker enquired from the daughter about her in-laws and the following discussion ensued:

Sister-in-law:

"All of them are very nice and my mother-in-law is very

understanding."

Worker:

"That is very good, I am happy to hear it."

Mother-in-law:

"This is not true at all. I know my daughter is saying all this so that we may not feel worried about her but otherwise her mother-in-law treats her very harshly. Once I went to visit her and imagine what she was doing. She had a whole pile of clothes before her to do all the washing of the household. I can understand that she should wash her own clothes and that of her husband but why should she do the washing for every member of the family? Her mother-in-law was sitting comfortably and was not helping this poor child (pointing to her daughter) at all. I felt so bad that I wanted to bring her with me for some days but her mother-in-law said that she should be sent back in the evening or at the most the following day. Oh, my daughter was given so much love and affection in our house but she is being tortured in her husband's house."

Sister-in-law:

"No, mother, this is not so. I am really very happy there. You are getting worried unnecessarily."

Worker:

"It is only natural for you to get worried because you are missing your daughter. I am sure you will get over it."

To divert the mother-in-law from that topic, the worker started playing and fondling her grandson. This made the old lady very happy. The worker's eyes fell on a bundle of clothes, nearby. She enquired whether or not the bundle contained sarees?

Mother-in-law:

"I have bought these 'sarees' for my daughter-in-law. One of these is for my daughter."

Worker:

"I am surprised to see that you have purchased such expensive sarees for the daily wear of your daughter-in-law".

Mother-in-law:

"Yes, I believe that a newly-wed woman should put on nice clothes. Besides, this is the age for her to enjoy and clothe and eat well."

Worker:

"I am so happy that you are considerate about your daughter-in-law."

Two women entered at this point. They were addressed as *Chachi* (paternal uncle's wife) and *Bua* (father's sister), respectively. They were also shown the sarees after they took their seats.

Chachi and Bua:

"We are happy that you are treating your daughter-in-law so nicely. This was expected of you."

Mother-in-law:

"I do not know. I have got so much attached to her that even if she goes out of the house for a while, it looks so empty."

The *Bua*, also knew the way the daughter-in-law was treated, turned to the worker.

Bua:

"When is the Diwali programme in the Centre?"

Worker:

"It would be on Wednesday. We have also arranged a baby-show this time (to mother-in-law). You must come there with your daughter, daughter-in-law and the baby.'

Mother-in-law:

"Yes we will come. My daughter-in-law may not be able to come as she will have to attend to the household work if I am to come."

The daughter-in-law was listening to all the lies till now but she could not contain herself any longer and silently began to cry. Her sister-in-law tried to console her. The worker found herself in a difficult situation and counting on the help of the sister-in-law asked her to come to the Centre.

Worker:

"Will you come to the centre Today?"

Sister-in-law:

"I will not come without my *bhabhi* (brother's wife)."

Worker:

(To mother-in-law) "Both your daughter and daughter-in-law are active members of the centre. I really want their help for Wednesday's function and preparation. Please send them to the Centre."

The worker asked *Chachi* and *Bua* also to send daughter and daughter-in-law to help her in the work.

Chachi and Bua:

"Yes, they will all come in the afternoon and help you."

The mother-in-law at this point told her daughter and daughter-in law that they could go to the Centre.

The Diwali programme was a great success. The grandson of the old lady got the prize for the best baby. The old lady was very happy and invited the worker to have tea with them the next afternoon. The worker accepted the invitation. She understood now that the mother-in-law was applying double standards one for her daughter and another for her daughter-in-law. She was expecting different treatment for her daughter in their husband's house while the same was denied by her to her own daughter-in-law.

The worker went to the client's house the next day and was greeted by all the members of the family.

Father-in-law:

"What are the new developments at the centre."

Worker:

"You will be glad to know that a lady doctor from the town will be coming now regularly."

Father-in-law:

"That is very good. We really need the services of a doctor in our village. I wanted to send at least one of my children to the profession of medicine but my desire could not be fulfilled. However, we are lucky to get an educated and cultured girl as our daughter-in-law."

Mother-in-law:

"Now, do not talk too much and allow her (worker) to eat something — (to her daughter-in-law) — why do you not eat this (pointing to a particular dish)?"

Client:

"I do not feel like eating."

Mother-in-law:

"I am fed up with this woman. She is very fussy about her food. I do not know how to put up with her. Do you know that she cannot eat '*dal*' unless it is splashed with *ghee*?"

The client felt very embarrassed, the husband also did not say anything lest it offended his mother further.

Sister-in-law:

"Mother, this is not the way to speak of my *bhabhi*? How will you feel it I also do not eat *dal* without *ghee*?"

Mother-in-law:

"Your case is different. You are a daughter of the house and you should have whatever you desire. But if she is so choosy about food, her parents should have kept her with them and not married her off."

Worker:

"Please excuse my saying this but how will you feel if your daughter is given this type of treatment by her in-laws?"

Mother-in-law:

(Shocked but not willing to give in) "Oh, well, a daughter-in-law is a daughter-in-law."

The father-in-law got very angry at the behaviour of his wife and could not control himself any longer.

Father-in-law:

"In future, if you speak in this manner I shall take out your tongue. My daughter-in-law will have everything she wants. I have told you this earlier also, now I will see that this is done. How do you expect your daughter's mother-in-law to be nice if you behave so meanly towards your own daughter-in-law?"

Sister-in-law:

"Please treat my *Bhabhi* nicely if you wish the same for me. I never dreamt that you were so cruel to her."

These showers from all sides had some effect on the mother-in-law.

Mother-in-law:

> "I am sorry to be angry with her. I shall try to be nice to her in future (then to her embarrassment) — you see, I am getting old now but my daughter-in-law will excuse me."

The client was happy that her mother-in-law will mend her ways. She did not want her mother-in-law to apologise for her past behaviour. Therefore, the client herself touched her mother-in-law's feet as the custom demanded to keep the respect and ego of the mother-in-law.

A follow up of the case showed that the attitude and behaviour of the mother-in-law was certainly undergoing change. The client felt relieved and happy although there were still occasional outbursts on the part of the mother-in-law but they were not often. The client felt that she would be able to change her mother-in-law's attitude completely because now she had started listening to her (daughter-in-law).

Analysis

The analysis of the case brings out the fact that the worker has not followed the conventional method of "the individual centred" approach. The worker has mostly used the family as the unit of her work. She has not insisted on meeting the client separately. On the other hand, she has successfully "capitalised" on the social relationships in the family and helped the persons concerned to see the situation and correct their behaviour towards the member who was the subject of torture.,

The case shows that the mother-in-law failed recognise the self-identity of the daughter-in-law. She was not allowed to exist as a person in her own right but had to carry the role designed for her. In such cases, the parents are in a constant struggle to preserve their own precarious integration by rigidly adhering to a pre-conceived pattern. The emotional needs of a member of the family which run counter to this pattern are a threat to their status and must be disregarded.

In the North American culture, the problem faced by the client in the case, would have been solved by setting up a separate establishment. But in Indian culture — especially in villages — the joint family is still considered as an ideal unit of living. The client, therefore, did not agree to set up a separate house. The worker also tried to integrate the family.

The case also shows that there was some conflict in the value orientation of the mother-in-law, the father-in-law, the son and the client. It was very difficult for the old lady to treat her daughter-in-law as a person and not to boss her.

The importance of the case lies not in the successful solution of the problem but the type of approach followed by the worker. In order to get a clearer view of the family relationships, the worker saw the client in the family and did not follow the conventional approach of taking social history separately form the client or her relatives. Instead of collecting facts or their subjective interpretation, one can almost relieve the past history with the family. One sees clearly how the client and her family react to each other. If we see the family as a problem rather than the client, then such interviews are meaningful apart from being economical in terms of time and effort. Such family interviews, apart from their diagnostic value, can be therapeutic as well, both for the client and the family.

In fact, it is difficult to point out the client in this case. Is it the daughter-in-law or the mother-in-law? It is only be taking the whole family as a unit of work that necessary adjustments were made in the family for a happy living.

In our country, there seems to be a strong case for the exploration and treatment of individual social problems in terms of its meanings within the family. A type of community care, which ignores the existence of the family in this context and which unwillingly accepts and perpetuates the *status quo*, may not get to the root of the trouble and may, therefore, often be unable to prevent individuals form break down.

Conclusion

We should make up our minds whether we look upon individual's social problems in the same light as his physical complaints or we see it, at least to some extent, in terms of social relationships. Some of us may feel that the family has the moral duty to care for "casualities" while others may think that the family should be relieved of them. If, however, we feel that the client carries the family illness, we cannot make arbitrary divisions any longer and those engaged in the treatment of the deviants will have to learn new skills.

It is heartening to note that in North America, workers have begun to feel the importance of the family as a unit of work but enough is not being done on these lines and the worker often relapses into the old rut of treating the individual.

The emphasis in this chapter has been that every human being is not only a biological entity but he is also a husband, a father, a son and so on. It should be noted that each of these descriptions refers to a social relationship and to a place in the social structure. It is, therefore, suggested that the family should be regarded as a unit for social work and the "family-centred" approach should be adopted for diagnostic and treatment purposes.

14

PEACE EDUCATION IN THE UNIVERSITY

S.L. MALHOTRA

THE PROBLEM of war or violence today is more pressing than before since humanity is dangerously perched on a precipice of annihilation as a result of race for nuclear weapons among nations. The extinction of world has now become a possibility. An observer in a preface to Quincy Wright's contribution to the study of war rightly says : "In the age of nuclear weapons if we do not abolish war, war is likely to abolish most of us".[1]

It is true that mankind has been confronted with the problem of peace for more than two thousand years. But it had been the theme adumbrated in the words and works of theologians, philosophers, poets, preachers are sometime statesmen and politicians. Their appeal had been mostly to the good sense of the individuals for eschewing violence in the course of settling their disputes with their fellow human beings. This approach, though having greater emotive value for creating an atmosphere favourable for the establishment of peace, has not been found adequate for this purpose. For, it has been argued that since war and violence are complex phenomena resulting from various social, economic or political conditions, mere moral injunctions against violence and exhartations in favour of love and non-violence cannot be very effective in ending war. This means that lasting peace is not possible unless all such conditions are identified and effective peaceful measures discovered for their removal and new peaceful means developed for the settlement of disputes. This realisation has led to the emergence of organised peace research and peace studies in present century mostly as a result of the efforts of the leaders of the organised peace movements in Europe and the United States which had its modest beginning in the 19th century. So, at the turn of 20th century, De, Bloc and Fried advocated a scientific approach to peace. The work of the former translated into English as the 'Future of War' makes for the first time an empirical investigation into the nature of modern warfare. His main effort was to educate and enlighten both policy-makers and general public on the nature of war. He was a tireless peace activist and scientific peace researcher. His was an important influence behind the decision of the Russian Czar to call a peace conference at the Hague in 1899 and he conceived and paid for a remarkable institution, the International Museum of War and Peace in Lucrne.[2] Similarly, Austrian journalist and peace activist Alfred H. Fried propagated De Bloc's thesis and made strenuous efforts to make pacifism scientific by arguing against war on rational grounds. As against romantic pacifism of Tolstoy, Fried argued that it was only when "pacifism undertook to demonstrate peace as material interest, that it was able to win the hearts of the masses and the minds of political leaders".[3] Between the two World Wars, a Dutch peace activist, Bar de Ligt, made a monumental study of the Direct Action against war in his works *Peace As Deed* and *Conquest of Violence* in an effort to seek effective methods as alternative to war for the settlement of disputes. He traces the history of peace and examines the things needed for peace.[4]

In fact, development of effective peaceful methods for the settlement of disputes between individuals, groups and nations are the right steps for the abolition of violence from human society. The acceptance of arbitration for the settlement of disputes between States leading to the creation of permanent court of arbitration at the Hague, the development of international law for regulating the conduct of States and the establishment of international court of justice are the right steps in this direction. However, such measures can work only when parties to the disputes are ready to adopt them. In case a powerful party to the dispute does not accept it, what is the remedy ? In this regard Gandhiji's discovery and development of *Satyagraha* is the answer. It reveals the power of non-violence as an active force for creating a just society and for settling the disputes without resort to violence. According to Martin Luther King.

"Gandhi was the first person in history to lift the love ethic of Jesus above mere interaction between individuals to a powerful and effective social force on a large scale."

Another scholar observes: "Gandhi was to the science of non-violence what his great admirer Einstein was to modern physics". In fact, Gandhi's experiments with non-violence disprove the charge that non-violence is hand and glove with *status quo*. For, Gandhi's *Satyagraha* leads to *Sarvodaya*, a programme involving comprehensive changes at individual, social, economic and political levels. In other words, 'Total Revolution' as Jaiprakash Narain termed it. For, Gandhi extended the meaning of non-violence to cover both negative and positive concepts of peace. His view of non-violence is an anti-thesis of both direct and structural violence. That accounts for Galtung's observation that Gandhi was the major peace theoretcian and practitioner in human history. He "was amasingly eclectic, fighting both direct and structural violence, with both dissociative and associative methods. . . ."[5]

Besides Galtung, several social scientists heavily rely upon Gandhi's experiments in their efforts to make non-violence and peace studies as a scientific subject for study and practice. Gene Sharp in his three-volume work, *The Politics of Non-Violence*, draws heavily on Gandhi's *Satyagraha* in meeting tyranny, aggression, injustice and oppression without resort to violence on the conviction that both moral injunctions against violence and exhortations in favour of love and non-violence have made little or no contribution in ending war and major political violence. Earlier, Quincy Wright's *A Study of War*, published in 1942 in two volumes, had covered another milestone on the road to the study of peace as a subject demanding scientific investigation. For, in his view "war to be abolished must be understood, to be understood it must be studied".

Consequently, the study of peace and non-violence has developed into a distinct discipline involving systematic and scientific study. Lentz in his valuable work *Towards a Science of Peace* argues that lasting peace can be established if our search is scientific and systematically carried on with the utmost use of human intelligence. It is only when all aspects of human behaviour — political, religious, economic, artistic, emotional and intellectual — are scrutinised with utmost objectivity, we will be able to find out effective methods for removing war and violence.[6] For, quite often human conflicts cannot be resolve peacefully because of the lack of peace know-how or training in methods of resolving disputes peacefully.

As a result, a number of institutions have come up all over the world for the study of peace. In some of the countries such institutions are totally or partially supported by the Government. Peace study began to develop in mid-1950s on a modest scale. But by early 1970s, it made long strides as a result of the threat of nuclear war. Thus, most of the peace study institutes have appeared during the past three decades. Some of them are engaged in scholarly research in the areas of conflict management, disarmament and arms control — topics relating to the conditions necessary for peaceful relations between nations, groups and individuals — while others have taken up both research and teaching in peace studies. Among them Peace Research Institutes in the Nordic countries (Finland, Iceland, Norway, Sweden, Denmark) have acquired a place of great repute. The International Peace Research at Oslo (Norway) was established in 1959 as a section of the Institute of Social Research and in 1966 it became an autonomous institute. Similarly, in Sweden, the Stockholm International Peace Research Institute (SIPRI) was established by its Parliament in 1966. In the United Kingdom several universities have special centres concerning areas of peace research such as Armament and Disarmament Information Unit (ADIU) of the University of Sussex, Centre for the Analysis of Conflict, Rutherfold College, University of Kent, Centre for the Study of Arms Control and International Security, University of Lancaster, etc.

In the United States there are 15 such institutes. In Canada, Peace Research Institute (Dundas) was sept up in 1962 to carry on research in the areas of conflict management and disarmament technique. The Club of Rome, an informal association of 100 members, founded in 1968, takes up the study of the conditions of a non-violent society, analysis of the basic causes of violence, consequences of world population, etc. In Germany, France and Italy there are a number of peace research institutes. Among them Peace Research Institute at Frankfurt (PRIF) founded in 1970 and AFB in Bonn established in 1984 are important.

In Asia, Peace Studies Association in Japan in 1973 (Tokyo), Centre for Reconstruction of Human Society in 1976 and Consortium of South-East Asian Institute for Peace and Development in Philippines in 1983 were established.

In Australia, Peace Research Centre was set up in 1984 as a result of the initiative of the Government to carry out high quality research on topics relating to peace.

In our own country, the Gandhian Institute of Studies, Rajghat, Varanasi, the Gujarat Vidyapith, the Department of Gandhian Studies of the Panjab University, the Gandhi Bhavan of the Allahabad University and the Department of Gandhian Studies of the Madurai University have made serious efforts in this direction. An effort was also made in the early 1970s on the initiative of Sugatadas Gupta of the Gandhian Institute, Ramlal Parikh, Vice-Chancellor of Gujarat Vidyapith, Radhakrishna of Gandhi Peace Foundation and the Education Secretary, Shri Prem Kripal, to set up an All India Association of Peace Studies. Panjab University became one of its members and the centre was inaugurated by Shri Prem Kripal. Somehow it did not acquire strong roots. We have now a separate department of Gandhian and Peace Studies which receives supports from the University Grants Commission under Special Assistance Programme.

Peace research alone cannot liberate individuals from destructive and aggressive tendencies. That requires peace education, which demands a fundamental change in human behaviour or revolution in mental outlook. For, though we have made tremendous progress in the field of science and technology, our thinking level remains at the level of primitive or uncivilised people. As Albert Einstein observed :

> "The splitting of atom has changed everything save our mode of thinking and thus we drift towards unparalleled catastrophe".[7]

The solution lies with education. According to R.G. Wells "human history becomes more and more a race between education and catastrophe".[8] Consequently serious efforts are being made by peace activists and peace scholars to identify issues and contents for the study of peace. In September 1974, the first World Council for Curriculum and Instruction was held at the University of Keele in the United Kingdom, the proceedings of which were published under the title Education for Peace — Reflection Action.

Similarly, in view of the importance for establishing peace, most of the peace movements in Europe and the United States have been laying great emphasis on it for several decades. For instance, the International Fellowship of Reconciliation and War Resistance International include in their activities and programmes peace education. Similarly, the Peace Pledge Union (PPU) in United Kingdom has in its programme peace education project that encourages new, creative and less dogmatic approaches to the study of peace and war and the related issues in schools and colleges. Teachers in the United States have founded an organisation for imparting peace education under the name Educators for Social Responsibility. In the Nordic countries the school teachers' peace groups are known for promoting peace education.

As a result, several colleges and the universities have recently taken up peace studies as a separate discipline. At Costa Rica, a University for Peace has been set up recently for seeking peace through education with humanistic purposes. It is based on the principle of disarmament of the mind for building of peace. The University was approved by the General Assembly of the United Nations on 5 December, 1980. It began its first Master's programme of communications for peace in January 1985. Its President who was also once the President of the States of Costa Rica, with whom I had the privilege of discussing various aspects of peace studies at his institute, has great appreciation of Gandhiji's contribution to the promotion of peace and was keen to introduce a course on Gandhi's non-violence and *Satyagraha*.

Two scholars and peace activists, Wehr and Washburn, have listed no less than 86 graduate or undergraduate programmes in peace studies in their survey of peace activities in the United States. In the United Kingdom a conspicuous development was the setting up of peace studies programme at the relatively new University of Bradford. There were also press reports of peace study advisers being employed by local education authorities in order to co-ordinate introduction of peace studies in the secondary school curriculum.

The International Peace Academy in New York has been established to teach the skills of peace keeping and peace-making and peace-building to mid-career diplomats and military officers. The International Association of Educators for World Peace (IAEWP) associated with United Nations Educational Scientific and Cultural Organisation (UNESCO) has development of colleges and universities for peace research as one of its aims. The principle underlying this approach is 'World peace through wisdom'.

In our own country, Madurai University has post-graduate course in Peace-keeping. The Panjab University has been running M.A. in Gandhian and Peace studies as a regular course for more than four years and from the next year we hope to make it available through correspondence.

Several journals have also been started by various institutions and peace associations for promoting peace research and for co-ordinating the activities of peace activists all over the world. Among them are *Journal of Peace Research,* the *Journal of Conflict Resolution. Peace News — Weekly* first as the official weekly newspaper of Peace Pledge Union (PPU) and, after 1961, independent publication, the Pacifist-monthly of PPU, *Studies in Non-violence.*

Recently Aldous Huxley, Galtung, de Ligt and Jene Sharp have made extensive studies in the field of peace. So there is no dearth of scholarly material on the subject.

The aforesaid discussion reveals that peace study is a distinct branch of knowledge. It is a multi-disciplinary and inter-disciplinary subject since the problem of peace has to be studied from various angles as the causes of peacelessness in our society are multifarious touching economics, politics, sociology, etc. For, there is a close link between violence and maldevelopment, poverty, relations of production, social structure, power politics, etc. It may be argued that 'what is the necessity of treating it as a separate subject of study if its areas fall in other disciplines'. In other words the subject of peace can be discussed in other disciplines such as history, politics, economics, etc. But the difficulty is that no other discipline is adequately fit to investigate peace problems. Peace study is designed explicitly to deal with the matter of peace in rather a more straightforward, direct and different perspective with peace as the central focus. In other words peace study is but another perspective of human behaviour drawing upon many disciplines with express intention of studying peace. Moreover, peace is the immediate need of humanity since it is facing the most serious threat to its existence. We cannot avoid conflicts. But violence as a method of resolving them has to be abandoned if humanity has to exist. We, therefore, need today experts equipped with the know-how of seeking peaceful solution to all our problems. If we have schools for engineers, book-keeping, medicine, tailoring and for subjects such as management, administration, where is the objection of having schools and departments in the universities for understanding the problem of peace and training personnels for keeping peace.

In our own country, there is now a greater need for such trained persons, as violence is rocking every section of our society endangering the unity and development of the country.

Another objection that can be raised against peace studies, as a separate subject, is that our approach may become biased in view of our commitment to peace. But this is based on misunderstanding. The objective of peace studies is to educate which means to put the various issues fairly and squarely in order that, having done a course, a student is better informed, more sensitive to the issue and perhaps motivated to do something about them. Scientists and doctors do not lose objectivity if they are kept solely engaged in finding the cause and remedy of a disease.

Another problem especially in our country that makes our educationists and administrators sceptical about the wisdom of introducing peace studies as a separate subject is that it lacks opening for careers. It is a genuine difficulty which I faced in Panjab University while developing Gandhian studies as a separate subject and recently of peace studies. Initially, I tried to overcome this difficulty at the research level and I was successful to some extent. For Ph.D. and, later on, M. Phil., a subject was allotted to a candidate which fell in his or her discipline in M.A., and a supervisor was appointed from the university who held expertise in that field. So a person who did Ph.D. or M. Phil. in Peace Studies had equal chances for jobs with those who held a research degree from their respective departments. Consequently all the persons who have done Ph.D. in Peace Studies have been absorbed in different services. There is some difficulty at present for those who are doing M.A. in Gandhian and Peace Studies. If they have interest in research, they can be absorbed in research. Some of them who are interested and preparing for competition have found this subject quite helpful. I am sure if more universities offer this subject and we make sincere efforts, M.A. in Peace Studies will be recognised by the Public Service Commission in our country and then this subject will be one of the subjects of social sciences with added advantage of training the youth for a specialised type of work the importance of which is being felt all over the world because of the spread of violence in every walk of life. In our country we are immediately facing the menace of violence even on the campuses of the universities and colleges, besides bigger political issues.

If we keep in view our immediate problems while framing our syllabi for peace studies and impart know-how to the students for settling disputes in different fields, the value of this subject will be soon realised by the educationists and framers of the policies of the country. It is the society that has to decide what type of jobs are required and as soon as its importance is realised, our students will not be handicapped.

Nevertheless, I may be permitted to draw your attention to the fact that the sole purpose of education is not to prepare students for jobs. I remember that this question was raised by one of the senior staff members of our university when committee of the U.G.C. visited Panjab University to consider our request for special assistance in Gandhian and Peace Studies. The reply by one of the members of the U.G.C. team was the purpose of education is also to produce good citizen, to cultivate values which we cherish. No one can deny that peace study is in accord with the values of democracy, equality and secularism which our society stands for. At a time when national integration is viewed as the fundamental problem of our country, peace studies can be very useful.

However, in spite of the importance of this subject for our country as well as for the humanity, we cannot afford to go the whole hog in the introduction of this subject in our educational institutions because of the lack of trained staff, infrastructure, books, etc. But steps should be taken in this direction immediately. The suggestions made in this connection are as follows:

1. The addition of peace education can be introduced in two ways, that is, through exfusion and infusion. Exfusion means the addition of specific courses in peace education by expanding curricular or by substituting the existing curricula. Infusion means the introduction of peace education into existing curricula.

   It means that all the institutions, which are running peace study courses successfully, should strengthen it and carry it on an all India pattern. It means that they should have uniform syllabi. The courses be framed with a view to serve the immediate need of the society so that better results can be shown. For instance, they should have courses to train the students for overcoming violence between different communities and groups whether in the area around them or on the campuses.
2. Where there are strong departments of social sciences, those who are interested in these areas of study be identified, encouraged and organised to take up subjects of peace research and be kept in touch with the centres of peace research in the country as well as in the world through participation in seminars, conferences and supply of material on peace research.
3. The University Grants Commission be approached to write to the universities to encourage peace research.
4. Important subjects of peace and non-violence be identified and

departments of social sciences be approached to introduce such courses in their existing syllabi.

5. The centres, which are running the courses, may also start short courses for peace activists as well as all the teachers who are interested in this field.
6. The Union Public Service be approached to recognise this subject for any competitive examination.
7. The courses be so designed that the candidates are equipped to serve in specified fields, such as social service, rural development, labour-capital relations or fields where disputes can lead to violence.
8. An all India body be organised to co-ordinate the activities of peace centres as well as to provide a forum for organising the peace researchers, peace activists and peace students.

NOTES

1. Pauling Linus (Editor), *World Encyclopaedia of Peace*, Oxford : Pergamon Press, I, (1986), p. xxxviii.
2. *Ibid.*, p. xxiv.
3. *Ibid.*
4. *Ibid.*, p. xxiii.
5. *Ibid.*, II, p. 259.
6. Lentz, *Towards a Science of Peace.*
7. Pauling Linus (Editor), *op.cit.*, II.
8. *Ibid.*

INDEX